THE COMPLETE BĪJAK *of* KABĪR

GURU KABĪR'S MYSTICAL TEACHINGS ON GOD-REALIZATION

THE COMPLETE BĪJAK *of* KABĪR

GURU KABĪR'S MYSTICAL TEACHINGS ON GOD-REALIZATION

JAGESSAR DAS, M.D.
President of the Kabīr Association of Canada

MOTILAL BANARSIDASS PUBLISHING HOUSE • SINCE 1903

MOTILAL BANARSIDASS
PUBLISHING HOUSE • DELHI
Email: mlbd@mlbd.in • Website: www.mlbd.in

2nd Reprint : Delhi, **2021**
First Edition : Delhi, 2015

ISBN: 978-93-90713-39-4 (Hardcover)
ISBN: 978-93-90713-10-3 (Paperback)

Printed & Published by
RP Jain for
Motilal Banarsidass Publishing House
A-44, Naraina Industrial Area, Phase I,
New Delhi–110 028 (INDIA)
Email: mlbd@mlbd.in
Website: www.mlbd.in

I dedicate this book to my late parents Sādhu Rambali Das and Māharāni Das. It is through their inspiration that I developed a keen interest in the spirituality and mysticism of Kabīr.

CONTENTS

Preface

The Bījak of Kabīr consists of the main teachings imparted to the world by the 15th century mystic saint of India, Kabīr. Many writers and research scholars have written on the Bījak in English, but most of their texts are not complete works and consist of selections. In Hindi I have the complete Bījak by Shri Jairamdeoji Maharaj of Vrindavan, and the complete Bījak by Shri Hazur Prakashmaninām Sāheb of Lahartara, Varanasi. Prakashmaninām Sāheb was a foremost Kabīr scholar and head of the Dharamdas branch of the Kabīr Panth (Kabīr Path) at Lahartārā. His book has been translated into English with a Roman transliteration of the Hindi by Dr. M. T. Buch who was professor of Sanskrit at Municipal Arts and Commerce College in Jamnagar, Gujarat. The translated version was published by the Shri Kabīr Ashram of Jamnagar, Gujarat, in 1987. I also have a volume by Shri Manohardasji Shastri of Lahartara, Varanasi, published in 1987. In addition, I have a volume published in Delhi by Dehāti Pustak Bhandār in 1936. I have used these Hindi books to help render my translation.

In English I have the complete Bījak by Ahmad Shah. The book was first published in Hindi in 1911 while the English translation was published in 1977. Ahmad Shah tried to retain the terseness of Kabīr's style, but his text rendered into English lost much of the beauty and depth of Kabīr's compositions. I have two volumes by Charlotte Vaudeville who is a foremost researcher and writer on Kabīr. The first volume is titled *Kabir,* and the second, *A Weaver Named Kabir*. These were published in 1974 and 1993, respectively. Both books consist of selections of the Bījak, but they have extensive research material contained in the introductions. *The Bījak of Kabir*, written by Linda Hess in collaboration with Dr. Shukdeo Singh of Banaras Hindu University, was published in 1983 and consists of selections of the Bījak.

After studying the preceding volumes, I found that there was a need for a complete Bījak in English supplemented by an extensive commentary to make the teachings of Kabīr understandable to the Western reader. Because of this, I have added an extensive commentary to each of the compositions of the Bījak. The reason for this is that Kabīr's style was terse and his language mixed with Persian, Sanskrit, Urdu and a few other medieval dialects. In addition, Kabīr's teaching is essentially mystical and devotional in nature. The mysticism of Kabīr is not easily understood by many writers and readers. It was my good fortune to have been brought up in the Kabīr Panth tradition as my parents were devotees of Kabīr from India. They took this teaching with them to Guyana (British Guiana) where I was born, prior to my moving to Canada to study medicine. Because of my deep interest in Kabīr, and especially in his mysticism, I have long felt that a complete version of the Bījak with commentaries in English would be a valuable contribution to mystic and devotional literature in general, and to understanding the mystical teachings of Kabīr in particular.

In rendering this book into English, I was assisted initially by Pandit Gianchand Shastri of Vishva Hindu Parishad of B.C., Canada. The translation was then reviewed and modified by Mahant Jagdish Das Shastri of Kabīr Ashram, Jamnagar, India, an accomplished scholar in the teachings of Kabīr.

The commentaries in this book are entirely my own as this was the primary motivation in rendering the Bījak into English and making the teachings of Kabīr understandable to the Western reader. It must be borne in mind that Kabīr taught in the 15th century and that his compositions are often epigrammatic and enigmatic. Although the symbologies used are essentially Indian, Kabīr used a great deal of allegorical, mythological, and paradoxical language. In the commentaries I have attempted to make the various meanings as clear as possible.

In translating the Bījak I have tried to maintain the spirit of the original teaching. Each composition was treated individually and, as a result, the commentaries will sometimes display repetitions of certain teachings and references. The commentaries were written from my own study and experience as a devotee of Kabīr. I have not used footnotes but have opted to make references in the commentaries and in certain areas within the translations to further make the meanings clear. Overall, I felt that this would make the reading of the text easier.

It is my hope that readers of this book will have a better understanding of the teachings of Kabīr, and of his contribution to the spiritual and mystical life of all people who are interested in their own spiritual development. Spiritual life is the quintessence of our existence as humans, and brings us transcendental joy manifesting as peace, love, harmony, and bliss. It is indeed the fulfillment of life.

I gratefully acknowledge the assistance of the late Pandit Gianchand Shastri in translating the Bījak from Hindi into English and the assistance of the late Mahant Jagdish Das Shastri for reviewing the translation and making valuable suggestions so the book conforms to Kabīr's mysticism. I also acknowledge the assistance of Sorojini Ramprashad for typing, and my wife Urmila Das, for proofreading and typing. Without the valuable assistance of these persons, it would not have been possible for me to produce this book.

INTRODUCTION

Kabīr the Mystic Saint

Kabīr (1398–1518 CE) is one of the most famous mystic saints India has produced. His teachings are important for people of all religions equally because he spoke impartially. In one of his famous couplets (*sākhīs*), he says: *kabir khade bazār men, sab kī chāche khair; na kāhū se dostī, na kāhū se bair* (*Kabīr stands in the open market place and seeks the welfare of all. He is neither friend nor enemy to anyone*). His goal was to teach people a true religion of the heart. He wanted to turn people away from the empty ritualism of religion, and to show them the inner path that leads to union with the Divine. In other words, he was teaching Self-realization and loving devotion to the formless Divine Power that dwells within all.

Although Self-realization had been taught in the Advaita Vedānta or non-dualistic school of philosophy in India, Kabīr re-emphasized this teaching focusing on the need for loving devotion of great intensity and fervour. Kabīr therefore taught and lived a combination of Gyān yoga (yoga of spiritual knowledge), Bhakti yoga (yoga of loving devotion), and Karma yoga (yoga of action). He did all of these as an expression of his own inner realization and identification with the Divine. He said: "*lālī merī lāl kī, jit dekhūn ti lāl; lālī dekhan mein gayī, mein bhī ho gayī lāl.*" (*I went searching for the beautiful colour of my Beloved, and I saw that colour manifesting everywhere. As I searched for it, I found that I too was coloured by the same beautiful colour.*) He also said: "*tū tū kartā tū bhaiyā, mujh men rahī na hūn; bārī pherī bali gayī, jit dekhun tit tū.*" (*Uttering Your name, I have become You. I have no individuality or ego left in me. My coming and going has vanished, as everywhere I see only You.*) Further, he stated: "*hindū kahūn toh hūn nahīn, musulmān bhī nāhīn; pānch tattva kī pūtalā, giabī khele māhīn.*" (*I am neither a Hindu nor a Muslim, but a five-element puppet in which the Mysterious Being dwells.*)

Kabīr's influence on the religious life of the people of India has been quite substantial. He has been recognized as noteworthy in many spheres of spiritual activity:

i. Kabīr is hailed as the father of Hindi poetry. Prior to Kabīr scriptural teachings were generally in Sanskrit, a language that was not understood by people at large, but was confined to priests and scholars. He conveyed the highest spiritual teachings in the spoken language of the people so everyone could understand them. For this reason, his songs and couplets are still sung by people in India and abroad.

ii. Kabīr was the initiator of Sant Mat, or the practice of keeping the company of saintly people. He said: "*sant milan ko jāyiye, taji mamtā abhimān; jo jo pag āge dhare, kotin yagya samān.*" (*Give up ego and humbly seek the company of saintly people. Each step you take towards them will be equal to countless ceremonies.*)

iii. Kabīr was the founder of the *Nirgun* school of Bhakti. This is the practice of loving devotion to the formless Divine. Prior to Kabīr, the *bhakti* movement was called *Sagun* Bhakti, or devotion to the Divine Being who incarnates in physical forms.

iv. Kabīr also introduced Sahaj yoga or the yoga of easy and natural union with God. This yoga leads to *sahaj samādhī* or the realization of one's unity with God. Kabīr therefore sang: "*santo! sahaj samādhī bhalī.*" (*O my brothers! Easy, natural union with God is best.*)

v. Kabīr strongly emphasized vegetarianism so one does not need to take the lives of other living creatures, since as he saw it, their lives are as dear to them as ours are to us. He stated: "*jīw mat māro bāpurā, sab men ekai prān; hatyā kabahūn na chhūti hai, kotin suno purān.*" (*Do not take life for the same life force pervades all. The sin of such actions will never leave you, even if you listened to millions of scriptures.*) Again, "*jaise pīr āpan anga jānā, taise sab jīw men mānā.*" (*Just as you feel pain, realize other living beings feel pain the same way.*)

vi. Kabīr laid great emphasis on the realization of the Self or Soul and saw it as the manifestation of the Divine in all of us and in all beings. This realization produces enlightenment and release from the clutches of Māyā (the illusory power within material creation). This theme occurs frequently in Kabīr's poems.

Kabīr's Early Life

Kabīr's parents are unknown. Tradition says he was found as an infant by a young Muslim couple named Niru and Nima at a small lake called Lahartara outside the city of Varanasi. They were weavers and taught Kabīr weaving. There are many legends about his actual birth, but none is known to be authentic. One such popular legend is that the great saint, Swami Ramananda, blessed a Brāhmin widow saying she will be blessed with a son. Because of his spiritual accomplishments, the blessing came true, but since the lady was a widow, she abandoned the child.

The Kabīr Panth does not generally accept these legends. They quote the words of Kabīr himself: "*ab ham avigat se chali āye, koī bhed marm nahīn pāye; nā ham janme garbh baserā, bālak hoi dikhlāe.*" (*Now that I have come from the Unconditioned, people do not know my secret. I did not dwell in the womb, but manifested as a baby.*) Another famous couplet by a contemporary saint from Kabīr's era, Garib Dass, states: "*gagan mandal se utare satguru sat kabir; jalaj māhīn powdhan kiye, doū dīnan ke pīr.*" (*Satguru Kabīr descended from the heavens. He came amidst the blooming lotuses as the spiritual guide of both religions* (Hindu and Muslim).)

There is some justification in accepting this view of Kabīr's birth origins. He asserted that the body is very subtle but that people have defiled it. In another place, pointing towards his departure he said, "*jyon kī tyon dhar dīnī chadariyā*." (*I have returned the body in the condition that I received it.*) Tradition says that just as he was found among lotus flowers, Kabīr departed from his life in a place called Magahar, leaving not a corpse, but a heap of lotus flowers. Although there were many disciples present and two notable kings Vir Singh Baghail and Bijli Khan Pathan among them, no one was able to find his body. All they found upon lifting the shroud, was a heap of lotus flowers. Muslims buried half, and Hindus cremated the other half. Two mausoleums representing this event stand side by side at Magahar. Until now, research has failed to find evidence of Kabīr's body.

Although Kabīr grew up in a Muslim home, he did not accept the Muslim way of life and did not observe the rituals of circumcision and sacrifice of animals. As he grew up, his mind was concentrated on God. Among playmates he would keep uttering the name of God as Rāma, which is a Hindu name for God. His Muslim playmates objected to this and complained to their parents. When he put on the sandalwood mark on his forehead, his Hindu playmates objected, saying he was a Muslim and could not do so. His Hindu playmates also objected to Kabīr using the Muslim name for God and to him speaking the Hindu name for God. They teased him that he did not have a guru and therefore whatever he uttered was unacceptable. Kabīr then decided to choose Swami Ramananda as his guru.

Being brought in a Muslim home, it appears quite unusual that Kabīr sought out a Hindu guru. I feel that even at a young age, Kabīr had a clear vision of his mission in life and that it was above religious confinement. He taught that the soul is Divine and knows no religious boundaries. Since Swami Ramananda did not accept non-Hindus as disciples, Kabīr resorted to a stratagem. He lay on the steps that led to the Ganges where Swami Ramananda went in the early morning, while it was still dark, to have his bath. Swami Ramananda accidentally stepped on Kabīr and on realizing it, uttered the Hindi name for God, crying Rāma, Rāma. Kabīr then took this name of God as his Guru mantra. Later, when some of Swami Ramananda's disciples objected to their guru accepting a low caste Muslim as a disciple, Swami Ramananda summoned Kabīr to find out if this was true. Kabīr then related the incident of their meeting, and Swami Ramananda openly accepted Kabīr as his disciple since he could not go back on his word of uttering the name of God to Kabīr. It is said that it was through Kabīr's influence that Swami Ramananda began accepting disciples of other religions. Because of this practice, he was excommunicated from his religious order.

Kabīr's Literary Style

As Kabīr grew up he continued weaving, and while doing so he composed many *bhajans* (hymns), *shabda* (poems) and *sākhīs* (testimonies). Since he had no formal education, he composed everything in his mind and did not write. He sang as he wove, and also traveled to the market and other places where he sang his beautiful compositions. People would gather around him to listen to his singing and preaching.

Kabīr spoke fearlessly concerning pure spiritual doctrine. Whether he spoke to religious or temporal authorities, it did not matter to him. He insisted on teaching people the truth about spirituality, and the uselessness of empty formal rituals and practices. He was against all types of hypocrisy and caste distinctions. In the book *Kabir the Great Mystic*, the author Isaac Ezekiel writes, "Kabir's songs seek nobody's approbation. They seek no sanction, ask for no approval, search for no popularity, invite no commendation, crave no compliment. They stand independent of these considerations, and they constitute the most uninhibited literature, the freest of free writing ever produced by a saint." Ezekiel also writes, "Banter, ridicule, sarcasm, wit and humour – these are the weapons he wields! Nor does he hesitate to hit straight-from-the-shoulder, hitting hard, ceaselessly and without stop, till the face of false piety and hypocrisy is battered out of shape and exposed to the view of the general public for general laughter." (Ezekiel. Radha Soami Satsang: Beas, India: 1978, p64; p62).

The reason for Kabīr's forceful and fearless language is easily understood when we realize that priestcraft held sway during his time. Religion was reduced to commercial activity for priests to earn a living. Priests did not instruct people in the true religious way of life. They also scorned people of the lower castes whom they forbade from entering temples and reading the holy books. The priests themselves committed evil actions and animal slaughter. They formulated elaborate rituals that did not mean anything to the average person. Kabīr observed these practices in both of the major religions of Hinduism and Islam. He felt that there was no place in spiritual life for such behaviour, and thus spoke out, often in confrontational and challenging language, to try to awaken people to the realization of their errors. He was well-known for his *ultā bānī* or paradoxical sayings, and challenged the priests to see if they had the spiritual wisdom to supply the right answers to them.

Kabīr's teachings are now part of the social fabric of India and are taught in many schools and universities. Many theses are written by university scholars on the life and works of Kabīr from a research standpoint while other writers write about him and his teachings out of spiritual interest. Many other people, including those not belonging to the Kabīr Panth, are able to quote him freely. Many of Kabīr's *sākhīs* (couplets) are quoted as popular wisdom in all parts of India as well as abroad. This is probably because Kabīr had a piercing wit and clarity of thought that people still find compelling.

Kabīr's Objectives

Kabīr was not preaching against religion, but against the hypocrisy committed by people in the name of religion. Even now we are all aware of the wrong things religious people commit, even by individuals belonging to the highest religious circles. Kabīr's objectives can briefly be stated as follows:

i. To detach people from Māyā (worldly bondage), and passions born out of desires, and to restore them to God through the attainment of absolute freedom.

ii. He wished for all people to attain the realization of unity with the Divine. He used no scripture but taught from his own inner realization of union with God. He stated, "*kāmī krodhī lālchī, inse bhakti na hoi; bhakti kare koī sūrmā, jāti baran kul khoi.*" (*Only the brave who can give up lust, anger, greed, and the pride of caste and clan can do devotion.*)

iii. He espoused fearlessness in spiritual life. He said, "*chhodo apne tan kī āshā, nirbhai ho gun gāwo.*" (*Give up dependence on the physical body and be fearless and sing the glories of* God.)

iv. He emphasized the need for purity in thought, word, and deed in order to attain God-realization. He said, "*darshan karnā chāhiye, toh darpan malte rahiye; darpan men lag gai kāī, toh daras kahān se pāī.*" (*If you wish to see yourself, you must clean the mirror again and again; if the mirror* is *covered with dust how can you see yourself?*) That is, if your heart is not pure like a clean mirror, how can you see your real Self reflected in your own being?

v. He wanted people to merge with God, and to lose the individual identity of ego, just as a drop of water merges with the ocean. He said, "*būnd samānā samund men, jānat hai sab koī; samund samānā būnd men, jāne birlā koī.*" (*When the drop of water merges with the ocean, all understand this; but when the ocean merges with the drop, people do not understand.*) God and the soul are ever merged, one in the other.

vi. He stood for truth in thought, word, and deed. He stated, "*sānch barābar tap nahīn, jhūth barābar pāp; jāko hridai sānch hai, tāke hridai āp.*" (*There is no austerity greater than truth, and there is no sin greater than falsehood. In whose heart truth dwells, in that heart God dwells.*)

vii. He taught universal and unconditional love for all people and all of God's creation. He said, "*prem prem sab koī kahe, prem na chīnhe koī; āth prahar bhījā rahe, prem kahāwai soī.*" (*Everybody speaks of love, but scarcely do they understand it. If they were immersed in love twenty-four hours a day, then it can be said to be love.*)

Kabīr instructed people that they came from the Eternal abode and that it is to the Eternal that they must return. In order for us to return to the Eternal abode, Kabīr taught that we have to be free from the clutches of Māyā and the bondage imposed on us by our absorption in a wholly worldly existence. Our lives must be made truly spiritual so we can achieve the highest spiritual goal destined for us.

PART ONE

RAMAINĪ

RAMAINĪ

A ramainī is a freely uttered poetic composition by Kabīr that was written down by his disciples. Kabīr himself said he did not touch ink nor paper and did not hold a pen, but that he was presenting the teaching of all ages orally. He used language to conform to his needs of teaching spiritual truth. The ramainīs do not follow any strict rules of prosody such as syllable counts or grammar, but represent Kabīr's words and ideas as they presented themselves to him. In the original Hindi there is alliteration and rhyme in each half line, with four half lines forming a *chaupai* or quatrain of two lines; but the lines do not rhyme. The word *ramainī* may have derived from *ramaiyā* referring to Rāma or God. Kabīr used the word Rāma to mean God that is formless (*nirākār*) and beyond all attributes (*gunateet*) and is present in all beings (*sarvvyāpak*).

Ramainī 1

In the beginning there was God and he was the Inner Light and Sound. He was with his creative power Māyā who brought forth Hari, Brahmā and Shiva. These three then created the countless women and men. None of them knew their beginning nor end.

Brahmā created a house (universe) that was divided into fourteen parts. The names of Hari (Vishnu), Har (Shiva), Brahmā are great. They established three settlements or Lokas – Earth, Heaven, and Hell. They created many parts in the universe and their followers created six schools of philosophy and ninety-six hypocrisies (false religions).

No Hindu came out of the womb with knowledge of the Vedas, and no Muslim came out of the womb circumcised. All people are born from the womb of the mother; it is after birth that they accept many pretentious forms and actions.

We are of the same blood, and the same breath sustains us. One mother (Māyā) created the world. Then with what kind of knowledge do you become different from one another as Hindu or Muslim? As a baby you came out through the mother's genital organ; after you grew up, you enjoyed the genital organ and was called a man.

No one knows the state of the indescribable God. With one tongue how can I explain it? If someone has one million tongues, then he may speak of the greatness of God.

Sākhī: Kabīr proclaims loudly – all affairs in the world are not real. They are all illusory and perishable. Without knowing God's name this world drowns and dies.

Commentary: In this ramainī Kabīr speaks of the mythological concept of creation as prevalent in India. The three 'gods,' Brahmā, Vishnu and Shiva represent the three functions of God as creator (Brahmā), sustainer (Vishnu), and destroyer (Shiva). These creative aspects are thought to be responsible for the universe with all beings in it. Brahmā created this universe and divided it into fourteen parts – seven heavens and seven hells. The seven heavens are Bhur Lok, Bhuvar Lok, Svar Lok, Tap Lok, Jan Lok, Mahar Lok, and Sat Lok. The seven hells are Atal Lok, Vital Lok, Sutal Lok, Rasātal Lok, Talātal Lok, Mahātal

Lok, and Patāl Lok. The six schools of philosophy alluded to are Sānkhya, Yoga, Nyāya, Mimānsa, Vaisheshika, and Vedānta. The ninety-six hypocrisies are the ninety-six forms of religious sects prevalent in India at that time.

Because of the caste system in India, it was held that one is born into a caste, no matter if he lived up to caste prescribed rules or not. Kabīr pointed out the fallacy of this system by saying that no Brāhmin was born with knowledge of the Vedas (scriptures); that he was born as anyone else was, so how could he be said to be a Brāhmin by birth? Similarly, for Muslims who circumcise males, Kabīr points out that Muslims are not born circumcised. Was God not able to have him be born circumcised if it were necessary?

The gist of this ramainī is that all people are manifestations of God, are born the same way, with the same organs and tissues, so with what kind of intellect do people create all the differences and divisions that lead to disharmony, intolerance, bigotry, and foolishness? All people are equal at birth, but as they grow up they are taught and quickly learn to create differences in ideology, morals, value systems, class divisions, religious beliefs, and so forth. They adhere to these distinctions as if they were ordained by God. These are all 'pretend' forms since, basically, all people are equal and the same to God.

People continue to fool themselves and each other. All forms are traps of Māyā (illusion) and prevent us from obtaining salvation. Kabīr tells us that God's greatness is indescribable. We should give up all the mythological and false teachings and practices that are prevalent in the world, and try to know God. Without the knowledge of God the whole world will drown in ignorance and cannot obtain the sought-after goal of enlightenment.

Ramainī 2

One Soul is living in the heart of all living beings, and that Soul manifests Consciousness (Inner Light).

A female (desire) came from the Soul, and her name was Gayatri. She produced three sons – Brahmā, Vishnu and Mahesh. Then Brahmā asked his mother, 'Who is your husband, and whose wife are you?' She replied, 'There is only you and I, and no one else. You are my husband and I am your wife.'

Sākhī: Father (God) and son (soul) have one wife (Māyā). One Māyā produced them both. I have not seen such a worthy son, who hastens to recognize his own father (God).

Commentary: It is important to realize that there is only one Soul in the universe and that Soul is God. That Soul manifests in all living beings. But for the Soul to be manifested as living beings 'It' produced Consciousness from 'Itself'. The Soul and Consciousness are thus intimately interconnected. However, before any creation could take place, there had to be desire to create in the Primal Soul. That desire manifested as Gayatri, another name for Māyā. Māyā in turn produced Brahmā, Vishnu and Mahesh (Shiva) as explained in ramainī one. Brahmā, not seeing any father figure (as God the Father was in-dwelling as the Soul), asked his mother who her husband was and whose wife she was. She told him, quite logically and correctly, that he was her husband and she was his wife. This relationship existed because God, the Father, who was the male principle of creation, resided within Brahmā, and so he was the husband of the female principle of creation called Gayatri.

In the sākhī Kabīr points out that God and the soul have one wife whose name is Māyā. From a human standpoint this is incest and quite unacceptable. But as stated above, the soul is God and the same Soul resides in all beings. Kabīr points out that the son is the soul and the Father is God, and that they are both the product of Māyā. If Māyā did not exist, living beings would not exist, and it would naturally follow that God would not exist.

Referring to the human situation, Kabīr points out that he has not seen a worthy son who hastens to recognize his own father. In this world not many people make a real effort to know God. They are satisfied with reading the scriptures, attending church, singing prayers and hymns, and doing other ceremonial and ritual types of worship. These activities do not give God-realization, unless the heart is purified by giving up all passions, greed, ego, violence in thought, word and deed, and practicing love for all of God's creation. Kabīr's teachings point out that as long as people are preoccupied with a materialistic life, and do not realize that God is dwelling in all beings, they will not obtain salvation.

Ramainī 3

Who existed in the very beginning at the time of creation? Who was the next who existed?

God existed in the beginning, then Brahmā, Vishnu, Shiva and Shaktī came into being. All of them did devotion to God.

Then wind, water, and fire appeared, and Māyā appeared and manifested as many forms of life. Then egg-laying and viviparous (live bearing) animals appeared in the universe. The earth appeared and was divided into nine parts. Then siddhas (adepts) sadhaks (devotees) and sanyasis (renunciates) appeared and they all did devotion to the Eternal. Then gods, men and munis (philosophers) appeared, and they all searched for God but were unsuccessful.

Sākhī: All the jivas (humans) and shivas (gods) appeared.

The gods became the masters and the humans their servants.

Kabīr says: I do not recognize any of this. I put trust only in the name of God.

Commentary: In this ramainī Kabīr expands on the mythological concept of creation. He first asks the question: Who existed in the beginning and who existed next? He becomes more specific and lists, in no particular order, the various gods, other beings and elements in the universe. From God and his creative power, Māyā, came the three 'god sons,' Brahmā, Vishnu and Shiva. Shaktī means energy and is also used interchangeably for Māyā or the female principle of creation.

Creation is the process that starts from the subtle and progresses to the gross aspect of manifestation. Ether is the most refined natural element in creation and it progressively manifests as air (wind), fire, water, and earth. After this all the various forms of life appear. All these various physical forms of manifestation are due to the power of Māyā, including the various species of egg-laying and viviparous (live born) animals as well as microscopic beings that divide by cell division and budding.

Once humans arrived in the world they took on various forms such as ordinary people, adepts (those who perfected themselves with austerity), devotees, renunciates, and philosophers. Humans then created the various gods and goddess such as Indra, Varuna, Surya, Durga. Kabīr says that all these various categories of humans and gods did devotion to the supreme God, but they all failed to achieve salvation because they were full of human frailties like anger, ego, passion, and so forth.

Kabīr speaks essentially of creation on one hand, and the various class systems or divisions in society on the other. At the end he summarizes his own position by saying he does not recognize any of the mythology or class distinctions created in the world. Just as he emphasized the importance of God at the end of the first two ramainīs, he again states that there is only one hope for liberation, and that it lies in the name of God (the realization of God as the Indwelling Self).

Ramainī 4

In the beginning Brahmā began to think that he should sing the glory of God, the Creator.

To obtain God he created many actions (rituals) motivated by desires, and because of them the people became confused. Due to their devotion to desire, Māyā placed them in bondage.

Brahmā created languages in wondrous form and variety. When love came up in him, he created ramainīs (prayers). Scholars and non-scholars alike could not understand them, and many could not realize their value. Whoever could understand them became purified, and those who could not understand became insects (subject to birth and death).

Sākhī: O foolish people! You think that you know the language, but not knowing its inner meaning, what are you saying? Language itself explains that there is beginning and end, creation and destruction.

Commentary: In this ramainī *Kabīr* deals with scriptures that resulted from language and with religious actions that are motivated by the desire to obtain certain benefits. Brahmā is supposed to be the originator of the Vedas, the holy scriptures of India. Brahmā, however, was not almighty God and felt the need for devotion to the almighty. He created the various scriptures and religious duties, rites, and ceremonies towards this end. People of the world started to follow these scriptures and to carry out the prescribed rituals, but always having in their mind certain hopes of reward, thus making their devotion selfish. Meaningful devotion must have no selfish desire attached to it, and must be done purely for the glorification of God. Kabīr points out that following the prescribed practices, people have become foolish and bound up by Māyā. They are confused in the sense that they are not progressing spiritually to an experiential knowledge of the soul, and knowledge of God dwelling within.

Those who could understand the secret of devotion became enlightened, but those who could not, failed to obtain salvation. They were attracted to the illusion of Māyā, just as a moth is attracted to a flame and sacrifices its life for it.

In the sākhī Kabīr is trying to rouse people by asking what they are saying. They say the words most certainly, but does it create the dawning of Self-knowledge in their heart? He tells them that the same language they are using has explained to them that there is a beginning, an end, and creation and destruction, but that they will not know the secret of any of it by merely following the scriptures and practicing rites and rituals.

Ramainī 5

How long can I talk of the yugas (ages or eons)? Brahmā himself got lost and could not understand the right path.

Vishnu, Shiva, and Brahmā thought of a method for man to get salvation. They made a plan by using two letters (Hindi *ra* and *ma*).

They made a bond of these letters. He who practiced them would hear the anāhad shabd (divine melody) and see the Light.

The scholars study the scriptures and established a path. Sanak and Sanandan (sons of Brahmā) liked the path.

The Vedas and Koran explained the way of salvation in detail, but the people's mind formed countless numbers of creeds from them.

In the four yugas devotees formed many creeds, but they could not see that their bundle of creeds was defective.
Being in fear, people run all over the world seeking salvation but, being unsteady in mind, they do not take the proper medicine (God).
He, whose mind does not waver, can obtain heaven. Leaving God, he can only go to hell.
When one follows the eastern direction for realization, one becomes a haṇsā (liberated soul). Liberation is near at hand if one realizes union with God.
Devotees decorate their devotion with rituals, but they all drown in the middle of the stream of this material life.
Sākhī: Without knowledge given by the Guru, man is subject to repeated births and deaths. People say that they have connected with God, but that is wishful thinking.
Satguru Kabīr taught in every yuga that people must connect with God but nobody obeys his word.

Commentary: Here Kabīr is explaining the plight of the people who are preoccupied with religious scriptures but do not find the real path to salvation. This has been the condition of people for age after age and Kabīr asks himself the question: "How long can I talk of the yugas?" People seem to not understand what a true spiritual life is, and become entangled with rituals and external forms of worship and pilgrimages, etc. They are seeking salvation by going from one place to another, either to temples, or to various gurus, holy places, places of austerity, monasteries, retreats and many other places. They, however, do not find the path to salvation by doing so.

Kabīr states that Vishnu, Shiva and Brahmā formed a method for God-realization using two letters 'ra' and 'ma' which together spelled the name of God – Rāma. This method of obtaining liberation has been explained in the Vedas and the Koran as the attaching of oneself to God, but what do people do? They instead form various creeds and sects and become lost in them. If one follows the practice of uniting one's self with God through meditation, then he will hear the Divine Melody and see the Light of spiritual enlightenment. If however, he remains occupied with creeds, rituals, and dogmas, and does not follow the instructions of a true spiritual teacher, instead of obtaining liberation, he will be subject to birth and death in repeated cycles, that is, be in 'hell'.

Kabīr states that following the eastern direction (symbolizing dawning Light or the instruction of a Guru) people would realize that God is quite near at hand, but if their minds remain unsteady and they keep running from here to there, then they will drown in the middle of the stream of the material world. In the sākhī Kabīr laments that although he has been giving this true instruction to people age after age, people still do not obey his words and thus do not obtain liberation.

Ramainī 6

Who can explain the form and outline of God? Who was there who saw Him? Neither Onkār nor the Vedas were there.

Who can explain His clan and secret? In that state there are neither groups of stars, nor sun, nor moon. There are none born of a father's semen. There is neither water, nor land, nor air.

Who can name that state? There is no one there to give orders. In that state there is neither day nor night. Tell me then, what clan and caste has He?

Sākhī: If one meditates with an empty and relaxed mind, a light manifests in him. That light is the great *Purush* who is without support. I adore Him.

Commentary: In this ramainī Kabīr is explaining the experience a devotee obtains when he meditates earnestly and obtains God-realization. God has no form and is not limited by space and time. He has neither clan nor caste, nor relations. God is a Universal Being and thus cannot be reduced to any physical form, nor limited by delineations of clan, caste, or religious denomination. There are no Vedas, no stars, sun or moon, and there is no birth of anyone. There is no water, land or air; there is no day or night, and no division of people into various castes and clans.

This ramainī points out a very important feature of spiritual life, that when one attains God-realization through meditation, one becomes free of the various divisions of class, religion, sects, and so forth. When one realizes God, it is knowledge beyond the existence of Onkār, who is responsible for the creation of the world through Brahmā, his son. Being in tune with the Divine, there is no question of material manifestation, because consciousness has risen above the material manifestations of the world, or of the universe, and is centered in God alone.

In the sākhī Kabīr states that in meditation there manifests a Light. That Light is Sat Purush, or the Supreme Lord, who is Self-existent and is not dependent on anyone or anything for existence. That Supreme Lord manifests in all of us and deserves our adoration.

Ramainī 7

A state that has no air nor water, and no creation nor creator.
No bud nor flower, and no fetus nor semen.
No education nor Vedas, and no word nor senses.
There is no body nor settlement, and no earth, air, nor space.
There is no guru nor disciple, and no easy or difficult path.

Sākhī: That state is very strange. I cannot explain it. It has no village or resting place. It is a state that has no attributes; what name can one give it?

Commentary: In this ramainī Kabīr speaks of the state of God-realization, or the state of consciousness in which the individual Self or soul realizes its unity with the Universal Self or God. Since this is a state of consciousness, it is beyond all physical conditions, and so Kabīr lists various attributes that the state is not conditioned by. This state of consciousness is often called the super-conscious state, to distinguish it from our ordinary everyday consciousness. To attain the super-conscious state, one has to withdraw the mind from all external physical manifestations, and concentrate on the soul within, and through meditation, arrive at a realization that the soul within and God are the same in Spirit.

This state of consciousness lies beyond the functioning of the mind, body, emotions, and above all types of cognition. It is an intuitive experience that cannot be explained to anyone else. This is why Kabīr lists what it is not, and says that he cannot explain it to others. One has to purify oneself in thought, word and deed, and practice meditation in order to attain the state of realized consciousness.

Ramainī 8

'That thou art' is the instruction of the non-dualists. This is the message of the Upanishads.

This is the great faith of the non-dualist. Scholars explain the same thing.

The Supreme Truth is its own proof. This was accepted by the sons of Brahmā, Nārad and Suka.

Dialogues of Yajnāvalik and Janak explained the same Truth. Dattatreya also tasted the same essence of

Truth.

The subject was sung by Rāma and Vashisht. The same subject was explained by Krishna to Udhow.

When Janak strengthened this philosophy in his life, he, though in body, rose above body consciousness.

Sākhī: Nobody will attain salvation in life without leaving the ego of clan and tradition behind.

Whatever we cannot see even with effort, we say it is unseen (the state of Self-realization).

Commentary: *'tat tvam asi'* (that thou art) is one of the four *Mahavakyas* (supreme statements) contained in the Vedas. This one is found in the *Chhandogya Upanishad* of the Sāma Veda. The phrase states unequivocally that Thou (the soul) art that (Brahman). That is, the Divine Soul within you is the same as the formless God. This is why it can be stated that the soul is divine, that God dwells in us, and that we are created in the 'image' of God. It means that God consciousness and our consciousness are inseparable, and that we can realize this unity of consciousness through purity of life and control of desires, and through practicing meditation. God consciousness is then realized inwardly.

This is the basic philosophy of non-dualism or the Advaita Vedānta school of philosophy. Kabīr lists a number of great personalities mentioned in various scriptures who realized the supreme identity between the soul and God. The same can be realized today in what is called Self-realization or God-realization. But there is a precondition mentioned in Kabīr's sākhī. The precondition is that one must give up the ego of clan and tradition, which means giving up identification with any clan or tradition, or religious order or philosophical system. By accepting any of these systems one would be confining the soul that is by nature eternal and free. Any such confinement into a system of dogmas, creeds, and beliefs is due to one's own spiritual shortsightedness. The mind must be ever free before it can realize that which is eternally free from all encumbrances. The state of Self-realization ever remains unseen, but can be experienced internally.

Ramainī 9

Māyā has bound the soul with eight sufferings and nine threads. She has bound Yama and her own sons (humans).

Māyā has bound the bearers of Yama (animals of conveyance) and all of creation. How many can one count?

Māyā has bound three hundred and thirty million devas (gods), but by worship of God iron shackles are broken.

By worshipping God, the Raja yogi attains the super-conscious state.

The traveller worships God on his journey; the lady also worships God, but they do it without knowing the meaning. People all over the world also worship God, yet without knowing the meaning.

Sākhī: One who desires the fruit of actions becomes the victim of bondage.

Kabīr says, he who utters the name of God night and day will obtain liberation.

Commentary: In this ramainī Kabīr speaks of the power of Māyā over all beings, including humans, gods, goddesses, angels, Yama (the God of death), and animals – all of creation. Māyā is the 'grand illusion' or 'veil' that prevents us from seeing God manifest in the world. If we can remove Māyā from our consciousness, we will be able to realize God.

The eight sufferings are: ignorance, ego, attachment, aversion, fear of death, and the three gunas (attributes – sattva, rajas, tamas) that are inherent in all of us. The nine threads are the five sense organs, plus the mind, intellect, consciousness, and ego. All of these manifest in us because of the power of Māyā that has operated from the beginning of creation, in order to facilitate differentiation into various forms of living beings, or for God to be projected into the various forms of His own creation. Kabīr states that by remembering and worshipping God, the iron shackles of Māyā can be removed. The Raja yogi, by control of his mind and meditation, reached the super-conscious state. He states that people all over the world are engaged in reciting God's name and worshipping Him, but often do not realize God because of the veil of Māyā clouding their spiritual consciousness.

In the sākhī Kabīr explains that the desire for the fruits of one's actions is the cause of bondage. Such desire is born out of Māyā and keeps us trapped in the wheel of birth and death. Kabīr tells us though, that the way of overcoming Māyā is by uttering the name of God at all times, that is, by living in the consciousness of God.

Ramainī 10

The traveller sheltering under the banyan tree (world) was washed away. No one told him of the coming flood (Māyā).
When the flood came, the world was deceived. Life after life Yama (God of death) bears the power of death.
Bearing this power Yama enters the three worlds.
He ensnared Brahmā, Vishnu, Shiva, gods, men, ascetics, and Ganesha.
He has bound air, fire, water and the brave sun and moon.
People, thinking the mantras to be true, bind themselves in their recitation. Such ignorant people do not know the Eternal Soul (God).

Sākhī: The world is absorbed in worldly pleasures; no one understands Immortal God. Kabīr says, he who is free of desires will not be subject to death and rebirth.

Commentary: Kabīr keeps hammering into us the temporary and illusory nature of the material world that cannot give us eternal peace, joy and happiness. He tells us that coming into this world, we are preoccupied with material pursuits believing that these are the main purpose of life, but, in the end, we find that they are not the means of liberation. He likens the soul to a traveller coming into the world, and the banyan tree as all the material pursuits in this life. While people are thus engaged in their material life, they become fascinated by it and, in the end, are cheated, because death inevitably comes to all.

Without devotion to, and knowledge of God, people fail to attain salvation. The whole material manifestation is an illusion perpetrated by Māyā. We must look behind Māyā, or the material manifestations, to find God, the Divine Being, who is ever-present everywhere. Kabīr states that various gods, men, and holy people were caught in this noose of Māyā. Even the natural elements, the sun, the moon and other planets and stars are all bound by Māyā because it is by her power that they became differentiated into their various forms. People are often ignorant of the reality of God as the basis of all material manifestations. Even if they, theoretically, know this, it does not form a basis for transcendental knowledge. People are thus preoccupied with reciting various mantras and with various rites and rituals, but they do not obtain the secret knowledge of God.

In the sākhī Kabīr summarizes that people are absorbed in worldly pleasures and do not know God. He outlines the method of obtaining liberation. We have to free ourselves from all material desires that keep us bound to worldly existence. Freedom from desires gives freedom to the soul. One who has been able to conquer his desires, and have knowledge of the Reality manifesting in life, will be free from birth and death, because he will be free from the effects of karma.

Ramainī 11

Like a meeting of blind people, this world has gone mad.
Māyā has cheated the three worlds.
Brahmā, himself, is cheated. How can Naga escape? Shiva, along with the gods, is cheated.
Māyā has cheated Vishnu, the leader of the three worlds.
She has cheated the leaders of the fourteen worlds.
Why do you fear what you do not even know and what is merely the reflection of the beginning and the end?
Why do you kill yourself like a moth in the flame of desires, and keep company with Yama, the god of death?
Just as the neem worm relishes the bitter neem juice, just so the foolish people accept poison as nectar.
What benefit can one get with the poison of passions? For a small gain he loses his capital.
If poison and nectar are mixed together, the wise person knows that the mixture remains poisonous.
If man has no intelligence, what is the use of his manhood?
Being foolish he unwittingly drowns in this world.
Those devoid of intellect, what quality can we say they have? They are caught up in false greed and hopes.
Sākhī: Many have died. You also will die. The drum of death is being beaten.
The world has fallen in love with a dream. Only sayings of the wise will remain.

Commentary: Kabīr uses this ramainī to instruct us of the great power of Māyā which has ensnared all beings in the world. Māyā is the 'grand illusion' that makes us see only differences between us and all other beings, and veils from our view the

Divinity that is the same in all beings. He says that even the gods, Brahmā, Vishnu, and Shiva, have been deceived by Māyā, as are the demi-gods who rule over the various astral and sub-astral worlds. These beings are well known by reading their stories in the *Purānas*. Kabīr instructs us that we must not be like the moth that flies to its death in the flames. The flames here are the passions and desires that seem to hold such a great sway on us. The more we become subjected to passions, the more we are courting death, thus he says we are keeping company with Yama (god of death). He compares us to the neem worm that relishes the bitter neem juice. Just so, we appear to relish the various desires and passions, not realizing that they are 'bitter' for us. He tells us that if passions and pleasures are mixed together we must have the discriminating intellect to realize that the mixture remains poisonous for us, because it will continue to create karmas for us that we have to repay sooner or later. He warns us not to be devoid of intellect and attached to the false greeds and hopes of this world, or else we will relinquish our status as humans with an intellect, created by God. He tells us that we really do not know Māyā and therefore should not fear her. We should fearlessly follow the teachings of the saints that lead to salvation, and not remain in love with the dream that is the power of Māyā manifesting in the material world.

Ramainī 12

This body is a fort of clay secured with a lock (mind) of stone.
The fort is in the jungle of doubts, and doubt is its keeper.
Seeing the doubts, the soul is sorely afraid. The Brahmins and Vaishnavas are trapped in the same doubts.
Just as the farmer tends his fields, just so, the farm of doubts exist, but it flourishes without seed.

O man, give up the pulling and pushing (arguments indicating doubt). Because of doubt, both the guru and disciple drown.
The third to drown is the hunter who sets fire to the jungle to drive out the animals.
The dog has died of barking, and the jackal could not accomplish his task.
Sākhī: When the rat and the cat are placed together, tell me, how can they remain together?
O saints! I see such a marvel – the elephant is eating up the lion.

Commentary: In this ramainī Kabīr tells us that we become victims of doubt if we do not have a clear perception of the spiritual path to God-realization. We have this body, which can function only by the dictates of the mind. The mind, however, is full of ignorance when it comes to the subject of a true spiritual life. Doubts are fed to us from all around, by people who, themselves, have not realized God, and are thus not able to give us the true teachings. Thus Kabīr says doubts spring up, just as the carefully tended field of the farmer springs up in abundance.

None is actually spared these doubts, whether he is a Brāhmin, a Vaishnāva, or any other caste. Kabīr advises us to give up argumentations and seek to know God who dwells within. There are many false gurus who, along with their disciples, drown in this world of materialism and bondage. Kabīr likens the leader of the false gurus to the hunter who sets fire to the jungle in order to drive out the animals to be captured. Just so, false gurus put the fire of doubts in the minds of the people.

The dog represents the ignorant person who gives endless talks, but dies without God-realization. Similarly, the jackal represents the cunning person, who in his cunningness thinks he knows God yet has only fooled himself. In the sākhī, Kabīr points to the rat as the ignorant person and the cat as Māyā. Just as the rat and the cat cannot stay together, just so, Māyā destroys the ignorant person. The marvel that he describes concerning the elephant eating the lion refers to the mind full of doubts, figuratively destroying the soul. In essence, Kabīr teaches us to get rid of doubts by seeking the truth so we may not be fooled by Māyā, but rise to spiritual illumination and salvation.

Ramainī 13

The world does not believe my word because their pride has severely crippled them.
Because of pride people lost everything. They did not believe in the troubles caused by pride.
They all left this world losing their capital (soul); they could not escape Yama's flood of troubles.
Today, (in the human life) you can fulfill your destiny, but not tomorrow.
One who is king today could leave the world loaded with karma.
The foolish person, thinking of more wealth, loses his capital (soul). Instead of gain he suffers loss.
Because of evil thinking man loses the moon (intellect). The master resides at the *trikuti* (third eye).
Vishnu advises the conquering of desire for the eight kinds of sexual gratification.
The Sankādik (sons of Brahmā) thought upon that philosophy and were happy, just as a poor man who finds great wealth on a path.
The rishis (sages) followed the discipline of brahmcharya (continence) and became immensely happy, and all their doubts vanished.
One sees birth and death, thinks upon them, yet fails to follow the proper way.
None of the dead return to tell their story. This world is

attached to a false hope.

Sākhī: You can be saved from the fire of the mother's womb. Why don't you call out to God?

You eat the poison of worldly desires and day and night you burn in the fire.

Commentary: Kabīr always points out to us the shortcomings that prevent us from leading a pure spiritual life. In this ramainī he speaks of pride that has inflicted a severe wound on us. Pride depends on egoism which, in turn, creates a sense of self that is separate from God. Since God is not separate from anyone, and is, in the final analysis, the animating and motive force in all beings, we cannot be on a true spiritual path as long as we live with a separate sense of ego. Ego is one of the greatest stumbling blocks in spiritual life.

By not being on a true spiritual path because of pride, we are creating bondage for the soul. In this materialistic life full of pride, we are, figuratively, losing our soul. The end result is that we face Yama, the god of death, with the soul still in bondage. The soul, not having obtained liberation, is subjected to rebirth so that it may reap its rewards and punishments. The soul needs liberation not bondage. Kabīr states that it is only in this life that we can live righteously in thought, word, and deed in order to obtain salvation. We cannot do it in death. Even a king living a life of pride will have to return to this world because of his karma.

Kabīr states that evil thinking results in the loss of our intellect. The moon is mythologically thought of as the god of wisdom; the soul is inherently wise, but evil thinking results in the loss of this innate wisdom. One who wishes spiritual progress must control his various passions. Here Kabīr mentions lust for sex that is enjoyed in different ways using the various organs of sense and action. When the rishis (sages) followed Lord Vishnu's advice and controlled sense gratifications, they became very happy because the happiness they got from their inner being surpassed any happiness they could obtain from satisfying the senses. Kabīr states that although we see birth and death and think upon their significance, that does not spur us to live the spiritual life in order to obtain liberation. And if we do not obtain liberation, we have to be reborn. We are born again and eat the poison of worldly desires, and thereby continue to repeat the cycle over and over. If we truly called to God, we could obtain salvation.

Ramainī 14

Pride is the great sinner and hypocrite that has cheated mankind.
Lord Vishnu, becoming a dwarf, cheated King Bali.
To whom do Brahmins do any good? The Brahmins have deceived people, and they are to be blamed.
Brahmins interpreted the Vedas and Purānas so that people would bestow honour on them.
Brahmā started a path of rituals, and Vishnu sang of the path of devotion.
Shiva started the path of yoga, and another started the worship of ghosts and spirits.
The Jains started one type of worship, and the Muslims started another form of prayer called namāz (bowing and praying towards Mecca).
No one accepted the instructions of the others. Foolish people accept false masters as genuine ones.
O devotees! With body and mind sing Kabīr is truth and the speaker of truth.
God is, Himself, God and Offering. He is, Himself, the clan and the caste.
God resides in all beings in the world. He is the Master and Abode of Bliss.

I have been saying this for four yugas. To whom should I now proclaim this message?

Sākhī: No one accepts the truth; all follow the liars.

The liar gets together with the liar and the foolish people bite the dust.

Commentary: Although Kabīr appears to be critical of the Brahmins, he is in fact highlighting the lack of religious unity among the people of the world. When God is one and is in fact all manifestations, what need was there for people to start various religions? If the founders of religions knew the Real Truth – the Absolute – then they would not have created various religions and sects. Because of pride, however, each felt that he had the answer to the Absolute and thus started a religion, yet no one accepted the instructions of the others.

Referring specifically to India, it is necessary to understand that priestcraft held sway over the religious life of the people during Kabīr's time. The priests who were Brahmins laid great stress on the studying of the Vedas, Purānas and other scriptures, but did not search within themselves to find the Reality of which Kabīr is speaking. They were thus not enlightened, nor could they enlighten others. They began to follow the exoteric form of the religion, satisfied with reading the scriptures, praying, going to temple, offering alms, making pilgrimages, and so forth. People thus became preoccupied with these external observances of religion to the end of their days and could not obtain salvation.

Kabīr is saying that if people followed the esoteric teaching, they would realize that God is the Universal, Omnipotent, and Omniscient Being. They would realize that He is the devotee and the offering, and is the clan and caste of all. God is the manifestation of all beings in the whole universe, and dwells within them all. With this realization, people could have been truly enlightened. Kabīr continually stresses the necessity of seeking and knowing Truth, knowing God, and not settling for less. He says, almost in resignation, "To whom should I now proclaim this message?"

In the sākhī he summarizes that people do not accept truth but are more enchanted by the 'liars' who keep on deceiving them. The foolish people remain unrealized and die without knowing God.

Ramainī 15

New clouds gathered and it became evening. The guide lost his way in the jungle.
The husband is one place and the wife somewhere else. She places the folded blanket on her head.
Sākhī: When her friends decorated her with flowers, she cried out to them she could not bear the weight. Now as the blanket gets wet, it has become heavier and heavier on her head.

Commentary: This is a short ramainī that Kabīr has packed with metaphysical meaning. The ramainī is based on a story in which a king was under threat by an opposing army. He secretly sent his son and daughter-in-law through a hidden passage to obtain help from the prince's father-in-law. He arranged for a guide to show them the way through the forest. After arriving in the forest the princess became thirsty and asked her husband for water. He sent the guide for water and he got lost. The prince himself then went in search for water and also lost his way.

Meanwhile it started to rain. The princess took the blanket she had folded in four and had been sitting on, and placed it on her head to keep herself dry. As it became dark and the rain continued to fall, the blanket got wet and became heavier and heavier. In the palace the princess had complained of the weight of the flowers with which her friends had decorated her, but now she had to bear the weight of the wet blanket.

Kabīr, with his usual vivid imagination, used this story to illustrate the condition of the world. The clouds represent doubts and the night is ignorance. The four-folded blanket are our actions while the rain symbolizes desires. The wife is the soul and the husband is God. The guide is Brahmā and the jungle is Māyā (illusion).

In this life we are under the influence of the clouds of doubts and the night of ignorance. The guides, who are the priests, are themselves lost in the jungle of Māyā in this world. They have not attained God-realization, the goal that they are seeking. People, goaded on by desires, are occupied by various activities that, like the heavy wet blanket, keep weighing them down in this material world. Meanwhile the soul, separate from God, longs for union with Him, just as the wife in the jungle longs for her husband to return.

Ramainī 16

Walking and walking in search of a false destination, the feet become very tired and, on not reaching the goal, the walker becomes very angry.

Ganas (servants of Shiva), Gandharv (celestial musicians), and munis (philosophers) were unable to fathom the mystery of God.

God remains hidden in the world while the world keeps busy in its works.

The binder (their actions) is also the bondage but is not visible.

They all become tired and cannot realize anything.

Night comes like a blind well in which the jivas fall with great fear.

Māyā (illusion) and attachment are in full force. Frogs (hope), lightning (greed), and wind (desires) are also in

full force.
Desires rain like an unbroken stream.
Their night (ignorance) is very fearful, but there is no help for them in that delusion.
Sākhī: All the people are deceived and are lost in darkness. None obeys my instructions; all have been caught in the trap of Māyā.

Commentary: People are searching for God in many ways. Some search for Him in distant pilgrimages. Others search for Him in various austerities and fasting, while others search for Him by bathing in the holy rivers. Others search for Him by the arduous study of scriptures. In the end, though, their 'feet' literally become tired, they exhaust their search but still do not find God. Even those favoured of the gods such as the servants of Shiva, the celestial musicians, and the philosophers were not able to fathom the mystery of God.

The mystery of God is that God is with them in their search and God is the very thing for which they are searching. In other words, God in them becomes the searcher. God, in the holy objects, becomes the object of their search, and the energy expended by them is also the energy of God. These people, however, do not understand this depth of philosophy and mystery of God, so they go on searching and become tired and frustrated, and thus angry. They do not realize that it is their own actions and desires that are the real bondage that prevents them from seeing God.

Not having found God, they face the night of ignorance and become fearful. Figuratively, they fall into the well of ignorance. The night of ignorance does not abate without the sun of knowledge. In this well Māyā, the great illusion, along with attachment, hope, greed, and desire hold full sway and play havoc with the lives of those caught in their net. In this state of existence desires reign supreme and keep the mind occupied in all types of pursuits, none of which bring peace and illumination to the mind.

In the sākhī, Kabīr laments the state in which people find themselves. The state of affairs described above appears to be the average state of the majority of mankind. They all want freedom but are seeking in the wrong places. They are caught in the trap of Māyā.

Ramainī 17

If I meet a person as pure-minded as you, Dharam Dass, I will be extremely happy.
When I speak about God residing in the heart, others do not like it.
One who discerns the condition of the world everywhere and detaches his mind from it is a wise person. He will be able to get rid of the shackles of passions and attachment.
Ignorant people will see Kal (the butcher) within themselves, ready to slay them wherever they go.
The butcher stands waiting with knife in hand. As soon as anyone approaches he is ready to sever their head.
Humans came as the greatest of all forms, but fell into the trap of rituals. One pandit (Brahmā) taught them these rituals.
Study your lesson of Self-knowledge and do not hide it from others, otherwise you too will be lost.
Sākhī: Sing the glories of God and give up the desire for worldly enjoyments. If not, Māyā will crush you with fifty million millstones on your head.

Commentary: In this ramainī Kabīr is speaking to Dharam Dass who was his foremost disciple. He states when people of similar interests get together they have happiness. Kabīr however, recognizes that when a devotee speaks of God, people often do not like him. This is because people are too attached to the material world and are busy pursuing various types of sense pleasures. They seek immediate pleasure, often without thought of what will be beneficial for their life later on. The pleasures, however, are transient. Kabīr advises that one should be wise and see that the condition of material bondage prevails in the whole world, and to detach oneself from it by using spiritual discrimination. If he does so, he will remove the bondage of passions and desires that keep him bound in his daily life. If not, Kal – the negative power, will figuratively be ready to cut off his head. Such a person will be subjected to the rounds of rebirths in order to satisfy his desires, along with all their accompanying sorrows.

Kabīr states that humans are the highest form of life that has evolved, manifesting a high degree of consciousness. But what happens to this highly evolved creature? He becomes entangled with the trappings of rituals of various kinds. Brahmā was the first pandit or Brāhmin to teach rituals, but these do not give Self-knowledge. Kabīr advises us and Dharam Dass to master the lesson of Self-knowledge that will remove all doubts and give liberation. In the sākhī he states that the devotee must give up worldly desires and sing the glories of God. Those who remain entangled with Māyā will be crushed, as if by fifty million millstones crushing down on them.

Ramainī 18

There are many strange religions, and it is difficult to describe them.
Beguiled by Māyā, people have forgotten God who dwells in every heart.
O my brother! If you wish to awaken, then wake up, or else Yama will take your life.
Yama has given a refuge to a person who does not know

the Word yet discusses words of wisdom.
Doubts, like wild animals, are residing in the body and eating up the precious, flawless diamond.
Sākhī: Doubts, like wild animals, are dwelling in the body and gambling with the soul. They are sorely wounding the poor soul and destroying it.

Commentary: The world has many religions that are divided into many sects and sub-sects. Kabīr calls them strange because they all profess to worship God, the one Truth. Each interprets scriptures according to its own understanding and devises various ways of worshipping God and practising religious life according to those interpretations. The followers of each sect have the same spirit dwelling in them. God resides in all equally, and yet they have caused confusion among themselves because of the proliferation of various beliefs. As a result, they have missed the point, and have lost sight of God in the process. In other words, they have failed to realize the Truth. They remain fooled by Māyā (illusion) because they continue to be driven by the various passions of ego, lust, anger, greed, and attachments to the world of materialism.

The Soul resides within all beings and it manifests the consciousness of God. People cannot find God anywhere else in the world except in their own selves. Of what use then are the various belief systems and practices that people follow. They only cause misunderstanding and intolerance, and God 'falls through the cracks' between them. Without realizing the Truth, they try to discuss words of wisdom with great conviction.

Kabīr exhorts people to wake up. If they do not, they will not find the salvation they are seeking, but will find death awaiting them. Because they have not realized the Truth, doubts are having a grand time 'gambling' with the soul. The soul is divine, eternal and flawless, but the mind of man cannot grasp its reality because it is caught up with doubts perpetrated by all the various religions and their fragmentary branches.

Kabīr has used the symbolism of destroying the soul figuratively, since the soul cannot be destroyed. The depiction means that doubts are keeping the soul in bondage due to spiritual ignorance. When doubts are removed, only then can Self-realization occur.

Ramainī 19

If one hopes to experience the limitless (*Anāhad*) without a Guru, that is both foolish and funny.
O my brother consider this comical scene! Where there is emptiness, that is where people rush to.
They want the void so they enter the void. But giving up what they had in hand, they become empty-handed.
The whole world is full of doubts that are like wild animals, and death the hunter, awaits to stalk the soul from morning to night.
Sākhī: O man! Recite God's name; death is holding you by the hair. You do not know when he will slay you, whether at home or on foreign land.

Commentary: People want to obtain liberation or salvation, but this is not possible until one realizes God within. The word 'Anāhad' means limitless, therefore, it refers to God who is the Infinite Being. It is spiritual tradition that a disciple should be initiated by his guru and be guided on his spiritual path towards liberation. People who try to follow the path without guidance often fall into various traps and doubts. God-realization thus becomes difficult. There are many people who say they do not need a spiritual guide. Kabīr states that such claims would appear hilarious to a knowledgeable observer. It is similar to a first grade student who says he will graduate from university without a teacher.

In meditation, people generally try to achieve a state of emptiness or voidness, that is, a complete stillness of the mind, with no thought on any object or idea. But meditation which ends in the void does not give one God-realization. God is already dwelling in the meditator, and is closer even than the breath. God is the very source of life and being. One should realize this in meditation. Without this realization one falls into the traps of many doubts and thus becomes prey to the hunter who is Kal (death).

Kabīr advises us to recite the name of God, that is, to always keep God foremost in the mind in every undertaking. Death is lurking around the corner and can strike one at any time. One does not know if death will occur at home, or in some other place, or whether it will occur in the next moment, or some long time in the future. Liberation depends on constantly remembering God as the source of being, and personally realizing that the soul is really God dwelling within.

Ramainī 20

Now, O soul! Recite God's Eternal name. Do not give up and run somewhere else.
Wherever you go you will suffer, just like the moth to flame. Understand what is poison and don't burn in it.
Fix your love strongly on God's name. Understand the nature of the wasp and fix your mind on Him.
This world is weighed down with severe miseries. O soul, realize this and try to overcome it.
The mind is full of worldly desires as the sea is full of waves, and none is able to see their beginning nor end.
Sākhī: In a world full of desires as the ocean is full of waves, the refuge of God is like a ship on the ocean.
Kabīr urges you to accept the refuge of God and the worldly expanse will become as small as a calf's hoof.

Commentary: In this ramainī Kabīr contrasts the pursuit of God on the one hand, and pursuit of worldly things on the other. He entreats the devotee not to give up God and pursue the worldly things, because the things of the world are like poison that superficially appears to be attractive. People have not obtained bliss by pursuing material gain, fame, and pleasures. In the modern world, although there is greater leisure time, and many more opportunities for recreation and other accomplishments, people are generally not happier. More and more people are suffering from mental and physical ailments, and the various stresses of life that make people anxious, depressed, apathetic, and lonely. Even people who enjoy themselves in various social and cultural activities undergo such turmoil. However, if a person places trust in God and makes God the motivating principle of life, then it follows, naturally, that their life will become stable, and they will enjoy inner peace and bliss.

Kabīr used the example of the moth burning in the flame to which it is attracted. Just so, people are attracted to worldly things and end up paying for it, often painfully, by suffering in one way or another. He advises us not to burn in the flames of this world, nor to die from the poison of this material world. He advises to control the material desires that occupy the mind and make it restless, just as the waves of the ocean keep the water restless. When a person attains a spiritual life, his desires become less and less as he progresses higher and higher. He finally reaches a state of indifference to the so-called worldly attractions because he has tasted the joy of inner bliss. With this experience he sees the expanse of the world, with its accompanying problems, reduced to insignificance when compared to the Infinity of God.

Ramainī 21

There are many sufferings. The world is a mine of sufferings. You will be saved only when you know God.
Knowing God, if you follow the Satguru's teachings, you will not fall into other traps.
But people flit about from one method to another. Although I have spoken with emphasis, no one has heeded my words.
People became involved with money, women, horses, and clothes. There is much wealth but life is short for enjoying them.
People's folly is that they get intoxicated with a small amount of wealth and pay no attention to Yama (death). Upon seeing the suffering inflicted by Yama their faces wilt.
They swallow the poison of the world mistaking it for nectar.
Sākhī: I create, I destroy, I burn, and I devour. I pervade the water and the earth and my name is Niranjan.

Commentary: Religions of the world have followers because there is suffering in the world. Religions endeavour to teach people a path of life that alleviates suffering, and give them an understanding of God. People, however, do not pay attention to the spiritual injunctions given by their spiritual teachers, or by the scriptures. They lack commitment and flit about from one method to another in an effort to find solace for their troubled soul.

God has spoken with emphasis through his saints, but people generally do not follow the way of the saints. Instead, they are attracted to worldly things such as wealth, women, horses, clothing and other things that indulge their senses. Life, however, is very short, and they have to leave all their material possessions behind. Being attracted by the things of the world, people rarely pay attention to approaching death. When death is close at hand, their faces wilt with fear and with the thought that they will not be any more. In life they did not accept the nectar of God's words, but instead swallowed the poison of material attractions.

In the sākhī Kabīr speaks as Niranjan. In order to understand this sākhī it is necessary to understand that God is omnipresent and dwells everywhere in the universe at the same time. He is, thus, the Power that does everything in the universe. It is not the emanation of God (Niranjan) who does anything, but God who does everything through him. Niranjan is only the agent, and God is the motive power that enables him to do anything.

Ramainī 22

Niranjan is invisible but his power has bound everyone.
Whoever is bound by this illusory bondage is ignorant. He has accepted false words to be true.
All the people are bound by their karmic work but those who remained free of karma lived free from bondage.
Although people established six ashrams (stages of life) and six philosophies, and accepted the six tastes, all these kept them in bondage.
They talk of the four trees (Vedas) and six branches (philosophies) and of countless other forms of knowledge.
They also study the various Purānas, but are not able to fathom the ocean of birth and death.
They observe recitations, pilgrimages, fasting and various forms of worship and give alms and do noble deeds.
Sākhī: This is the temple of love. Do not rush to enter it.
Whoever rushes in will first have to surrender his head.

Commentary: In this ramainī Kabīr talks of the necessity of developing a discriminating spiritual intellect in order to decide what is truly spiritual and what is not. People are caught up in various types of activities, whether they are for supporting livelihood, or for worshipping with the aim of obtaining salvation. They are, nevertheless, on the wrong path until they can realize what is real spiritual life and what is not.

Figuratively, Niranjan is the demigod who keeps all people in bondage and vets their progress towards almighty God. People do not see Niranjan but, nevertheless, they are caught in the traps he has set. These traps are types of karma (work or occupation), the adorning of various forms of clothing to denote different ranks and castes, or religious affiliations. There are also various preoccupation with scriptures and philosophies, and also the six stages of life called *brahmacharya, ghrihast, vānaprast, sanyās, hans,* and *paramhans.*

People are also preoccupied with the various tastes of the world, but these only serve to further keep them in bondage, because they are not able to free themselves from all these paraphernalia of life, and to realize the Eternal God that dwells within them. People are naturally drawn towards performing various kinds of religious observances, reading scriptures, adorning themselves in their particular identifiers, but these do not free them from karmic effects.

The person who, through spiritual discrimination, is aware of the bondage and what constitutes Truth, frees himself from bondage, and enjoys union with God. Kabīr summarizes that God dwells in the temple of love, and no one can rush into it carrying his head, figuratively full of the paraphernalia of worldly bondage with him. Whoever wants to enter that temple must sacrifice his head, that is, give up his worldly bondage, ego, and attachments, and become pure in heart. Only then can he enter the temple of love and unite with God.

Ramainī 23

From beginning to end there is little happiness but much suffering in the world.
The mind, full of ego, is deluded just as an intoxicated elephant.
How can one obtain liberation while giving up the supremely blissful Self? One gives up truth and runs after falsehood.
People burn in the fires of three types of suffering, just as the moth, with love in its eyes for the flame, burns in it.
If someone considers this and gives up friendship with falsehood, then all his sufferings will cease.
Because of greed people waste their lives, while old age and death are fast approaching.
Sākhī: This world is entangled by doubts, and yet people constantly come and go. O friend! Having obtained human birth, why do you go astray?

Commentary: In this ramainī Kabīr reminds us that there is a great deal of suffering in the world. Birth is a suffering, and so is old age and death. During the lifetime there are innumerable sources of suffering. True happiness is rare. This is so, because people do not tap into the source of eternal happiness that lies within them. Instead, they run after the temporary and vanishing pleasures of the world. These pleasures give momentary happiness that is followed by distress again.

There are three types of suffering: (i) Those arising within the body, such as mental illness, cancers, and degenerative diseases. (ii) Those arising from other beings, such as those inflicted by animals and other human beings. (iii) Those caused by elements of nature, such as floods, hurricanes, earthquakes, droughts, fires, and so forth.

Kabīr compares people to the moth that is attracted to the

flame and gets burned by it. Just so, people are attracted to various sense pleasures, and according to their karma, have to be born over and over and endure all types of sufferings. If they considered the Reality which lies within, and obtained salvation, they would enjoy only eternal happiness and no suffering. But people remain intoxicated with greed for the pleasures of the world, and pay no heed to the fact that death is fast approaching. In the end, it becomes too late for them to rectify their ways.

In the sākhī Kabīr says the world is entangled in doubts, and that people are also entangled. He urges us to use the opportunity of human birth well and not go astray again.

Ramainī 24

The truth of the soul and God is explained as the love of the chakor for the moon; but the intellect of humans has turned things around.
The four stages of consciousness are but a dream to them. They understand falsehood to be the truth. No one knows what is false. In this way all have lost their way.
They have lost everything in false hopes of the future. With this kind of thinking, people cannot obtain God, not even in a dream.
He who rises above the thirty-four letters (scriptures) will be able to understand what is sin and what is virtue.
Sākhī: As you speak, so you become. Why don't you escape from the traps of illusion?
Kabīr says: Come to me! I am standing here calling you. Why do you lose your life to falsehood?

Commentary: The chakor is a mythological bird that gazes longingly at the moon as if transfixed with great love. The soul, similarly has a great yearning for union with God, but human beings, in their "sophisticated" wisdom have produced all kinds of philosophies, dogmas, creeds, religions and rituals, and thus confounding themselves, straying far from the path of simple Truth.

There are four stages of consciousness: waking, dreaming, dreamless sleep, and super-consciousness. People generally do not pay attention to any of these, but are preoccupied with their material existence. They do not seem to realize that life is meant for salvation, which is in effect, the realization of the fourth stage of consciousness. Although they have hopes of a better future, they continue in the same old merry-go-round, losing sight of the fact that they will reap what they are sowing, according to the law of karma.

Unless people improve themselves day by day in thought, word, and deed, there will be no chance for them to ever realize God, or obtain liberation. In order to attain to God-realization, people have to rise above the alphabets, that is, all the scriptures. The scriptures do not give God-realization. God resides in the hearts of all people, and that is where He will be found. In the sākhī Kabīr is beckoning all devotees to him so they may free themselves from the traps of falsehood and illusion.Unless people follow the path of Truth, they will again lose the opportunity given to them in this precious lifetime, to obtain God-realization.

Ramainī 25

The speciality of the thirty-four letters is that thousands of names can be composed from them.

Being lost in these thirty-four letters (scriptures) people are constantly being reborn. They remain spiritually ignorant and lose the All.

Brahmā, Vishnu, Shiva and Shaktī searched for Him. Countless people, following countless ways of devotion, searched for Him.

Groups of gandharvas, munis and devas searched for Him.
Countless people in many forms searched for Him.
Sākhī: The jati and sati searched for Him and do not think that they were defeated.
Kabīr says, shouting, even the greatest people cannot be saved from the trap of Māyā in this way.

Commentary: The thirty-four letters are letters that compose the Hindi alphabet. The letters refer to the alphabet of any language really, for they are what all scriptures and languages are composed of. People spend a great deal of time studying various scriptures, thinking that they are actually on the proper path to knowing God. However, scriptures do not give people God-realization. People can become very knowledgeable in the scriptures, and still not have purified their minds, nor given up various passions such as anger, greed and egoism.

People can follow certain scriptural injunctions, and practice various forms of worship according to their various denominations, but unless they realize God within themselves, their learning will be purely academic. The gods, Brahmā, Vishnu, Shiva, and the goddess Shaktī, along with the celestial musicians, philosophers and countless other people of various sects, have been searching for the omnipotent and eternal infinite God, but have failed to find Him. All of them have remained caught in the trap of Māyā.

Scriptures and philosophies cannot be made ends in themselves. They are only stepping stones that should be used in conjunction with internal and external purity, simplicity, humility, nobility and other divine qualities, in order for us to reach the goal of God-realization.

Ramainī 26

Just as a potter makes different types of pottery using various means, just so, Brahmā acted as a potter in creation.

He placed all beings in one world, and with much effort he named them variously.

He fired them in the fire of the womb and protected them in that process.

The bodies that he formed with much effort and made manifest are variously named Shiva or Shaktī (male or female).

If a son in the home is foolish, the others who are wise do not follow him.

I am telling you the truth that I have realized, but you listen to the words of others and become confused.

Those who are unknown and those who are known belong to the same caste, who then is to be called Brāhmin or Shudra?

No one should be fooled by false pride. The clans of both Hindu and Turk are false.

Sākhī: He who made this picture (universe) is the true puppeteer. Kabīr says people who realize this are fortunate.

Commentary: In this ramainī Kabīr talks about the one Creator who created all living beings and is thus the Father of all. In Hindu mythology Brahmā is accepted as the God of creation. Here Kabīr talks of the Creator making various forms of bodies, just as a potter makes various forms of pottery. The potter fires his pottery in a kiln, and takes care that they are all done properly. Just so, God takes care of the developing body within the womb when that body is helpless. After birth, however, people are given various names and they are said to be male and female.

Having come from the same parent (God) we are all therefore, brothers and sisters. Kabīr advises us that we must not be lost in false ego and pride. He has explained the Truth to us, but we often listen to the words of others who preach of various types of castes and segregations and we become confused by their teachings, and deviate from the path of Truth. If we all belong to the same 'caste' (human), who then can be spoken of as being of a high caste, as the Brāhmin, or of low caste, as the Shudras. Similarly, who can be called a Hindu and who a Turk (Muslim) when the same God is the Father of both, and they are therefore, brothers embodying the same spirit?

In the sākhī Kabīr refers to God, the Absolute, as the puppeteer who holds the strings and controls everything. He is the controller of Brahmā who is mythologically thought to be the creator. He says people who know the Creator of the universe are really fortunate. When we know the Absolute Creator who remains the same for all of us, then how can we be misled by the false pride of various religious distinctions?

Ramainī 27

God gave Brahmā this universe to create, and he created the 'seven islands' and 'nine parts' of the earth.
Vishnu, being truthful to his mother, was given the power to protect the three worlds.
Then Shiva came, in the form of linga (male genital organ), pierced the earth and reached the nether world.
God then created a young maiden (Adhya) with eight parts (Māyā) and the three worlds became fascinated with her. Her other name was Parvati. She married Shiva who was doing austerity.
There is one Purush named Niranjan, and one woman named Māyā. The four kinds of life and the Brahmins, Kshatrīyas, Vaishyas, and Shudras came from them. The three gunas (attributes) – rajas, tamas, and sattva – also came from them and these were spread from earth to heaven.

Sākhī: Onkār is like an egg and the whole world manifested from it.
Kabīr says: All are the wives of Rāma; He is the husband and Imperishable Lord.

Commentary: In this ramainī Kabīr talks about God and the mythological concept of creation according to Hindu scriptures. God first created Niranjan and Adhya, and from them proceeded Brahmā, Vishnu, and Shiva who each have different functions. Brahmā creates the universe, Vishnu protects it, while Shiva dissolves it, or is responsible for decay and death. The four forms of life are four classifications of manifested life: (i) Those that are live born (placental); (ii) those that are egg born (oviparous); (iii) those that are self-propagating such as bacteria; and (iv) plants. Various castes of people displaying different qualities of goodness, activity, and inertia then pervaded the whole universe.

This is a simplistic view of the creation of all things. However, the mystical point of view that Kabīr intends to convey is that God is the 'husband' and that creation, that is, the material universe, with all its various aspects, is the 'wife'. Thus he states that Rāma is the husband and all else are the wives. The eight parts of nature that are contained in all life forms are earth, water, fire, air, ether, mind, intellect and ego. All of these have resulted from Māyā who is considered to be female. Kabīr points to all of these as the wives, and to God as the husband. Māyā is responsible for the impermanent and illusory world, but people are beguiled by her and forget God.

Ramainī 28

No one can understand the secret of this weaver.
Coming into existence, he spread the world as the warp.
He fixed the earth and sky as the pillars, and used the sun

and moon as two shuttles.
He took thousands of stars and perfected the fabric.
Even today he weaves, and the end is difficult to fathom.
Kabīr says: Whether with good or bad yarn coloured with karmas, the weaver weaves beautifully.

Commentary: Kabīr was a weaver and was quite familiar with the process of making a piece of cloth using yarns of cotton. Sometimes the yarn was good and sometimes bad, but he was still able to weave his fabric. He was in the habit of using homely metaphors for explaining God, creation, and spiritual matters.

In this ramainī Kabīr speaks of God as a weaver. He likens the earth and the sky to the supports of the loom, and the creation in the world as the warp and the woof for weaving the fabric of creation. Similarly, he likens the sun and moon to two shuttles used in the weaving. Metaphysically, the sun and the moon represent the positive and negative energies (in yoga the right and left nostrils, or nerve currents) that are necessary for the manifestation of conscious life.

The thousands of stars represent the various forms of life including their karmas or actions. Using all of these, God created this world, but God's work is not done because he keeps creating. Everything is in a state of evolution, or in dynamic motion. Nothing in the world is static. The end of this evolution is difficult to fathom, so Kabīr says no one can understand the secret of this weaver.

People are born according to their samskārs (subconscious imprints) whether good or bad, and are also subject to good and bad karmas (actions). Kabīr points out that although the yarn may be good or bad and the finished cloth (living being) good or bad, God's work of creation will always result in something beautiful.

Ramainī 29

In a moment the mind becomes hard like a club and in another soft as a straw.
The desires of the mind flow incessantly like a waterfall.
Knowing this, the sadhus control the mind, but a man in pursuit of desires performs many actions and becomes bound by karma.
Because of weakness of mind, people give up noble actions, intellect, and wisdom, and accept the false name as the true name.
When *rajogun* (bad qualities) became active, they manifested in the three worlds and destroyed righteousness, noble actions, and intellect.
When the sun rises all the stars grow dim, and the sunlight shines in place of the movable and immovable things.
One does not cure poison by eating poison. The garur bird gives life by removing poison from the dying person.
Sākhī: The snake bites in that moment when one blinks and does not see. The snake does not obey the orders of the garur. What then can the garur do?

Commentary: In this ramainī Kabīr speaks about the condition of the mind. The mind is never steady. At times it becomes hard and at other times soft and polite. The mind is full of desires that flow continuously like a waterfall, and keep people bound up by making them perform all types of actions. The sādhu (wise person) knows this and controls his mind, but the average person, because of the weakness of his mind, becomes entangled by the activities of the world. He gives up noble actions, intellect, and wisdom because of the false lure of the material world.

Rajogun is that quality of activity and passion that keeps the mind of man bound up in karmas. But just as the rising sun causes the stars to grow dim and 'disappear' just so, when knowledge of the Self appears, the person sees God everywhere, in both the things that are movable and immovable. The ego and passions grow weak and disappear.

The garur is a bird that kills the poisonous snake. In this ramainī Kabīr is referring to the guru as the garur. Just as the garur destroys the poisonous snake, just so the guru destroys the poison of desires and attachments, ignorance, ego, passions, and evil from a sincere devotee. The devotee has to be ever watchful because if he slips up even for a moment, desires and passions will crowd his mind and lead him down the road of bondage. But if the devotee does not obey the guru and follow instructions, then the guru becomes helpless, despite his love and goodwill towards the devotee. To achieve spiritual progress the devotee must remain vigilant and conquer the mind.

Ramainī 30

O brother! You follow the six philosophies and have lost your way. You are entangled in their hypocrisies.
These hypocrisies destroy life's welfare, yet the four Vedas and their four categories of instructions are silent about them.
The Jains do not know the secret of dharma. They bring plucked leaves to the temple.
They pluck the flowers of *dawnā, maruā* and *champā* which is like the killing of ten million lives.
They pluck the hairs from their bodies and knowingly lose their life.
Some speak against losing a drop of semen, and practice cruelty by withholding it while enjoying sex.
Because of these practices the Jains face a terrible fate. The six philosophies fault the Jains.
Sākhī: The Immortal state is above worldly knowledge. It

is near yet people think it is far. But for him who understands the Everlasting, it is very near, because it pervades all beings.

Commentary: Kabīr taught a rational and logical path to God-realization and liberation. He did not adhere to the teachings contained in the various scriptures and philosophies that were plentiful around him. He stated in many places that they could not give one the knowledge of the soul and of God, for they were mere words. One has to develop an inner realization of what he taught in order to obtain liberation. He thus criticized all followers of religion who veered to extremes, and away from a rational and a logical path.

It is in this vein that Kabīr speaks of the Jains who are supposed to be very non-violent. Although strict adherents (mainly monks) will cover their nostrils and mouths with masks to avoid inhaling insects, and carry a broom to sweep the path so as not to tread on insects, they nevertheless pluck the hairs from their bodies which in itself is painful, cruel, and unnatural. They believe in self-mortification, which again is unnatural and not conducive to God-realization. Although they are non-violent, some still pluck leaves and flowers, which also contain life, and take them to the temple to offer as worship. Similarly, they enjoy sex but practice withholding the semen that should naturally be ejaculated (a practice called *amrowlī*). Jain monks (Digambar sect) believe that one has to practice nudity to show total non-attachment so as to obtain liberation. Since women cannot practice nudity in this group, they are not likely to obtain liberation until they are reborn as a monk.

All people who stray from a logical and rational spiritual path face the same fate, of being deluded into thinking they are saved or will obtain liberation, when in fact, they are wasting their lives following various religious hypocrisies. Kabīr points out that a spiritual path must be natural, moderate, logical, and rational in its approach to God-realization. He teaches against going off on tangents with scraps of truth as many religious people tend to do. He teaches us to realize the presence of God within. Thus, in the sākhī, he states that he who understands, realizes that God pervades all beings, but to one who does not understand, God, though near, appears very far from him. Kabīr advises not get hung up on religious books and philosophies and instead focus on developing the means of the awareness of God dwelling within.

Ramainī 31

Smritis speak about God's attributes and lay down the path of sin and virtue.
Some people always study the Smritis and the Vedas, but become hypocritical and egotistical.
They read the Vedas then boast. The knot of doubts, even now, does not disappear from their hearts.
They read the Shastras but kill living beings. They cut the head and offer it to the deities and images.
Sākhī: Kabīr says because of hypocrisy, people destroy many lives. Because they lack realization, they do not know that God lives in all beings as the Soul.

Commentary: It always pains a saint to see people not using their God-given intellect and spiritual discriminative ability to live a truly virtuous and spiritual life. He has to speak out against the unrighteous practices in which people engage. In this ramainī Kabīr does exactly that.

People all over the world read their various scriptures and become very versed in them. They display their knowledge in eloquent speeches, and display their egoism and pedantry. However, in their hearts and personal lives, they practice various forms of hypocrisies. They do not personally realize God who is dwelling in their hearts, and in the hearts of all living creatures. God is omnipresent and is therefore present in all living beings.

Scriptures also teach people not to kill. But what we see all around us is the killing that is taking place on a massive scale, of both humans and animals. If people could see how young animals are taken from their mothers, confined in feed lots, fattened and then slaughtered in the abattoirs, with blood flowing, most would soon turn against killing. Every animal that is slaughtered, wishes to live every bit as much as its slayer.

To confound this folly, humans even sacrifice animals and offer them to statutes of various gods and goddesses. The whole universe, including all of us, belongs to God. What need does God have for a few sacrificed animals from errant human beings? Kabīr, ever compassionate towards all living beings, taught non-violence. People professing to have love but who practice violence in thought, word, and deed, are being hypocritical. They ignore that God dwells in all beings, and continue to perpetrate such sinful actions.

Ramainī 32

To the ignorant person, the Vedas and Purānas are like a mirror to a blind person. What does the spoon know of the flavour of the food?

Just as a donkey loaded with sandalwood does not know its fragrance, just so the ignorant person does not know the essence of the Vedas and the Purānas.

Kabīr says: Ignorant people try to find God in the heavens but, lacking Self-realization, their egos remain and do not vanish.

Commentary: Such an apt metaphor expressed in this ramainī – people read the scriptures but do not get the essence! Just as the blind person cannot see himself in the mirror, just so many people read the scriptures but, not obtaining their essence, are not able to mould their own lives into truly spiritual ones. Just as the spoon, though it is repeatedly dipped into the flavourful food, does not know its taste, nor a donkey loaded with fragrant sandalwood realize the import of the fragrance. Just so, many people read the scriptures but do not grasp the essence which flows from them. They continue in their old patterns of life and behaviours. They think that God dwells somewhere in heaven, not realizing that God is present in their own being. They manifest the consciousness of God, and yet remain separated from Him. As long as people lack Self-realization they will continue to blunder on in life's path. It would be wonderful if people could dispel their ignorance and egos, and awaken to a spiritual life.

Ramainī 33

O brother! The Smritis are the daughter of the Vedas but she comes with a rope in her hand. The man accepts her and ties the noose around his own neck.
The false attachment to worldly things is the bondage of kal (time). Once bound, it is difficult to obtain freedom; the world remains tangled in sensual forms.
Before my very eyes the whole world is being plundered, but the servant Kabīr won salvation by Rāma's name.
Sākhī: People's tongues have become callused by merely repeating the name of Rāma. They do not drink the pure water that is available, but yearn to dig a well to obtain it.

Commentary: The Smritis are non-Vedic texts and consist of the Purānas and various writings of sages such as Manu and Parashar. They deal with codes of conduct, customs, rituals, and stories of the various gods. They often contradict or misrepresent the Vedic teachings. People accept them as scriptures and live by them. However the texts represent bondage as they tie people up by their teachings and rituals, and people then have difficulty freeing their mind to accept the uncluttered spiritual life as outlined in the Vedas, and especially so, in the Upanishads.

Kabīr says that once a person becomes ensnared by all the worldly entanglements that were created by Kal, it becomes very difficult to obtain freedom. Even before his very eyes, as he was teaching people the true spiritual life, Kabīr observed people being plundered by false teachings and being driven by their desires and attachments to sense objects, which only served to entangle them further into the materialistic web. He states that people keep repeating the name of Rāma, but their tongues have, figuratively, become callused. Even so, by not perfecting their hearts they were not able to obtain salvation.

God is easy to find and available at all times, as He is the innermost part of every being. God is omnipresent and dwells as the Soul in all. People often refuse to accept His omnipresence and instead, opt to search everywhere to find Him or to obtain salvation. They are not drinking the water that is readily available, but are digging a well in order to find water to quench their spiritual thirst. Rāma here refers to God. Whenever Kabīr used the name Rāma he meant the Almighty, All-Pervading, Omnipotent and Omniscient Lord - Satpurush.

People should awaken to realize that spiritual life is simple and uncluttered, and should be free from dogmas, speculations, rituals, and complexities.

Ramainī 34

O pandit! By reading and reading you have shown your cleverness. Tell me about your own liberation!

Do you know the Supreme Lord and the village where He dwells? O pandit, tell me His name!

Brahmā himself created the four Vedas, but he did not know the secret of salvation.

He explained a great deal about alms giving and noble deeds, but he did not know of his own death.

There is one name that is unfathomable. There the servant Kabīr has found tranquility.

Sākhī: Where the ant cannot climb, and where the mustard seed cannot get a resting place; where birth and death have no power, let the whole world go there!

Commentary: Priests of all religions become versed in their scriptures and display their learning in their various sermons, arguments, debates, and discussions. These, however, are all displays of external learning based on their scriptures and not based on inner spiritual awakening. The priests (Brahmins) of India were no exception. Priestcraft flourished in India, and ordinary people were made to pay obeisances to the priests who thought of themselves as high caste. They possessed the requisite spiritual knowledge to perform various ceremonies, read horoscopes and practice astrology, but they preyed on the simplicity and gullibility of other people. Their conduct was not in keeping with that of a spiritually developed person.

It is for this reason that Kabīr challenges the pandit (Vedic scholar) to talk about his own liberation, and whether he knows the Supreme Lord, where He dwells, and what His name is? Priests do not generally have answers to these questions, but they would like to have others presume they possess this knowledge. Kabīr knew their shortcomings and, as he was always in sympathy with the average person, he often challenged the learned priests in this manner.

Brahmā is part of the trinity that is supposed to have created the universe. He is thought to have produced the four Vedas from his four mouths. The Vedas are the most ancient scriptures in the world. The Brāhmin caste traces its origins to

Brahmā. Despite Brahmā's exalted position, Kabīr states that he did not know of his own death. His weaknesses are outlined in the Purānas. In the Vedas there is a great deal of instruction about noble deeds, the conduct of life, almsgiving and various ceremonials. But these did not help the priest to obtain liberation.

The Vedic scholar or pandit has six duties: (i) To study the Vedas; (ii) to teach the Vedas to others; (iii) to do yajnas (ceremonies); (iv) to have others do yajnas; (v) to receive alms; (vi) to give alms. An examination of these will show that these activities do not produce liberation. Liberation results only from an inner spiritual awakening and purification.

Kabīr states that he has found tranquility in the profound and unfathomable name of God. In the sākhī he states that the whole world should be guided to attain to that state because it is a 'state' of pure Consciousness beyond space, and not a 'place' where an ant can climb or a mustard seed can rest. It is also a state beyond birth and death as these occur only in a material life.

Ramainī 35

The pandits have gone astray in their study and practice of the teachings of the Vedas because they do not know the secret of their own Self.
They perform the evening and morning prayers, and offer water to their ancestors, and perform their six karmas. In these many ways they perform their religious duties.
They have taught the Gayatri mantra in the four yugas, but go ask them who obtained liberation?
If an untouchable person touches you, you sprinkle water on yourself. Tell me then, who is lower than you?
You indulge in this kind of behaviour and yet you still boast. There is no benefit from so much pride.

He whose name is killer of pride, how could he tolerate your pride?
Sākhī: Give up the pride of clan and tradition. Try to find the true place of immortality.
By destroying the seed and sprout of pride, people become liberated in this very life.

Commentary: The pandits are Brahmins who study the Vedas, the most ancient scriptures of India. The Vedas contain a great deal of instruction on various aspects of life, philosophy and religious practice. The pandits become very versed in the Vedas and perform various ceremonies and their six religious duties as outlined in the preceding commentary. They initiate disciples and teach them the Gayatri mantra. If a person they consider 'low caste' touches them, they feel polluted and have to ceremonially sprinkle water on themselves to become purified.

Kabīr is pointing out here that the pandits have really gone astray because they have developed pride in their clan, caste and religious education, but have not really experienced the Reality of their own souls. The same holds true for most religious priests everywhere. They are preoccupied with their doctrines, dogmas, and rituals, but do not delve deeply within to know the Reality of God who is within. All religious practices are of no avail unless one gives up pride and the other passions, purifies the heart, and humbly approaches the indwelling, ever-present and eternal Master.

Ramainī 36

O wise and clever men of sharp intellect!
The non-dualists are not wise because non-dualism depends on dualism.
Dualists do not know the secret of God, and fall into the cycle of creation and destruction, light and darkness.

They have made a business of religion with rules, regulations and duties to obtain God.

O soul! Do not give up the Master dwelling in you as your own Self. Many people childishly believe God dwells in heaven, and with childish intellect they sing songs of such a heaven.

Sākhī: Where are those people to whom the false gurus gave false knowledge? They have become lost.

Kabīr says: Give up false teachings and realize that God dwells in your own Self.

Commentary: The world is full of many smart and clever people who argue and split hairs about various points of philosophy and religion. There is the philosophy of non-dualism and dualism. The former accepts that only God exists, and all else are only reflections or projections of the Being of God. This is possible because of the great elusive power of Māyā that overshadows our true perception of what Reality is. The latter postulates that God and his creation are separate, and that people need to worship an omnipotent and omnipresent Being. There are also branches with various shades of meaning and interpretation based on these philosophies. In the end, such postulations do not give liberation until one becomes enlightened to the divine Being dwelling within, as Kabīr states.

Various clever people have started various forms of religion with many rules of conduct, codes to follow, rituals to be performed, in order to obtain God. Kabīr says you should not be fooled by such paraphernalia because God dwells within you as your own Self. It is commonly accepted by people that the dwelling place of God is heaven. But one can ask the question: "Where is heaven?" If God is in heaven, and that heaven is not the Earth and all the beings in it, then God is not on Earth nor in all the beings on Earth. Therefore, God cannot be omnipresent.

People sing of God in heaven, or of the glories of heaven, as if they have only a childish intellect. People have played with images and idols as children play with their dolls. People have killed innocent lives in the name of God who lives somewhere in "heaven" and remains unseen to them. Kabīr rightly asks where all the people who were so instructed are now. He points out that these are not the practices of a truly religious person. He advises us to give up the false teachings, and to know that God dwells within as the real and ever-present Self.

Ramainī 37

The first clever non-dualist person is not clever because non-dualism and dualism have a relative existence to each other.
The second clever person is preoccupied with the theory of Māyā (Māyāvādi) and is lost in Māyā.
The third clever person has been eaten by his own cleverness (ignorance that obscures the soul).
The fourth clever person took the people with him (people who believe in different gods and wander in many heavens and hells of their own beliefs).
Who knows the fifth clever person? He is one who enjoys the pleasures of the senses and gets lost.
All become puzzled about the sixth clever person who got lost in imagining the mind to be the soul.
O brother! If you know the seventh cleverness show it to me in the Vedas or in the behaviour of the people.
Sākhī: Just as a coded document shows the way to a hidden treasure, just so this bījak shows the way to realize the soul. It teaches instructive words to the soul, but there is seldom anyone who considers them.

Commentary: This ramainī is a condensed but critical examination of the theories of the various schools of thought. These schools of philosophy and other belief systems are present in India and, in varying forms, in other countries. There are dualists and non-dualists described in the previous ramainī. There is the Māyāvadi school of thought that seeks to criticize Advaita, but does not properly understand the Ultimate Reality itself. Kabīr does not mention the names of each school, but he has highlighted the key belief systems to which people adhere, and accordingly teach their followers.

These various systems of belief comprise only external, philosophical knowledge. They contain beliefs in various doctrines and dogmas, rituals, and ceremonies, theories about heaven and hell, belief in the mind and the soul being the same, belief that pleasure is the highest goal in life, and so forth. None of these belief systems gives knowledge of an inner, intuitive realization of God as the Supreme Consciousness and only Reality that exists without a cause. This Reality dwells within.

Saints and satgurus do not pay attention to the wrangling and hair splitting of philosophical thoughts, whether practical or theoretical. They dive directly into the source and experience God for themselves. Thus, whatever they say becomes scripture. They do not teach philosophy, doctrine or dogma, but teach the Reality of God as the ever-present Master dwelling within. They have no confusion about whether the mind is the soul, or whether the body is the soul, or whether pleasure is the highest good in life. They have no confusion about heaven and hell. They have no confusion about Māyā and Reality. As long as people are preoccupied with such thought systems, they will not obtain Self-realization.

Bījak means a coded document that leads to a hidden treasure. The Bījak of Kabīr explains the path to that hidden treasure that is within, and is not visible to the objective senses. It is a map of discovery to God dwelling within.

Ramainī 38

I instructed the people in this way, but they did not heed my words. Instead, on their path in this world, they spread the loom of rites and rituals.

Day and night they continually join the threads of their karmas, and continue to weave their karmic cloth. They cannot get rid of their doubts.

Doubts are pervading the whole world and by not giving up doubts, people do not make spiritual progress.

Day by day their knowledge grows weaker and they fail to reach perfection. Wherever they go they lose part of themselves (loss of spiritual knowledge).

I am explaining to you the essence of religion that was from the beginning, and will be to the end.

Sākhī: Accept this message as true and place it on your head. O friends! Contentment is real happiness. With it the heart remains satisfied.

Commentary: In this ramainī Kabīr speaks of the bondage that people create for themselves by not clearly comprehending what spiritual life is. Without understanding the nature of the Self, and without developing contentment in all aspects of life, people cannot obtain the supreme bliss that is the ultimate goal of life. Instead, people are preoccupied with weaving the fabric of karmas (actions), without paying attention to the ultimate results of such actions.

People practice all kinds of rites and rituals in the name of religion, yet they are no further along spiritually day after day. Actually, people appear to lose true spiritual knowledge as they go through this earthly life. Kabīr says he has been explaining the real essence of a religion that is eternal. He says it should be placed on the head, that is, accepted with a great deal of humility and reverence. The goal of life is to obtain liberation through knowledge of the Self but, unfortunately, doubts create a great obstacle for humanity.

Ramainī 39

Even the Prophet Mohammed who taught the Kalmā in this Kaliyug (iron age) could not fathom the meaning of Māyā.
It is karma when both Hindus and Muslims perform religious rites, but they have rendered the Vedas and Koran fruitless for themselves.
It was because of karma that the soul is born into the world, and through karma the naming ceremony is performed.
It is karma when the Muslim performs circumcision and the Hindu accepts the sacred thread. Both Hindu and Muslim do not understand their inner meaning.
Sākhī: It is by the combination of water and air that all life was made. If one meditates on the 'void,' he realizes all are made from the same water and vital force. Of whom then should he ask what their caste is?

Commentary: This ramainī deals with karmas which in this case carry two meanings. One meaning is the law of karma or cause and effect that determines the circumstances of one's rebirth into the world. The second refers to the various rites and rituals (sacraments) which people perform, such as the naming ceremony, circumcision, baptism, investment with the sacred thread, funeral rites, and so forth. Kabīr is saying that all the people are preoccupied with the externals made possible by their religious beliefs, but they have not understood the real karma or the law of cause and effect that operates in everyone's life.

The word *kudrat* means nature as a physical manifestation made possible by the power of Māyā. People who follow orthodox religions do not know, nor do they try to know, what Māyā is, and how it operates in their lives. Kabīr states that even Mohammed, who was the messenger of God, and who revealed the Koran to the people, did not truly understand the power of Māyā. When people become preoccupied with all the sacramental duties, they lose the true essence of a spiritual life, and thus make their scriptures ineffective in promoting their spiritual path to salvation.

The word water in the sākhī also carries the meaning of semen, and pawan (air) also refers to prāna or vital energy. Both of these are necessary in order to manifest life. When one meditates deeply, he understands how God has made life manifest in the physical form by the use of the power of Māyā. When he realizes that all people are created in the same way, are of the same elements and energies, he has no need to ask what the caste of anyone is. Everybody belongs to that same "human caste."

Ramainī 40

Adam, who was supposed to be the first born, did not know the beginning of creation, nor did he know where Eve came from.

In the beginning there was no Muslim and no Hindu. There was no blood of the mother nor semen of the father.

There was no cow nor butcher. So who at that time ordered the recitation of the bismillāh?

There was no clan nor caste. Who then created hell and heaven?

People do not know the philosophy of the mind, and so speak of religion with confused intellects.

Sākhī: A man improves his good qualities with self-control, without it he loses them. But to satisfy the pleasure of the tongue, people indulge in all sorts of activities.

Commentary: In this ramainī Kabīr discusses the condition that existed before creation and asks questions concerning religious claims about that beginning. These are legitimate questions when one considers that God exists as Consciousness in all beings. God manifests in all of us as Consciousness that is an attribute of the soul. The soul possesses an innate knowledge of its connection or identity with God, but because of its entanglement through the body and senses, it loses its knowledge of that connection.

Because people do not realize their connection with God as the very soul and consciousness of their beings, they remain confused and created religions. In such confusion they also created heaven and hell, and the distinctions of clan and caste. Kabīr wishes to point out that all of these are creations of the mind that did not know the essence of its own existence, and did not realize the soul and God are eternally united. There is no need for the various distinctions and divisions created by the mind of man.

In the sākhī Kabīr further points out that we need mental self-control in order to improve our good qualities. If we allow the mind to be controlled by all the senses and passions, we lose our virtues or good qualities. In order to satisfy the tongue, people have learned to kill animals and often offer the dead animals or their blood, to God. They really wish to satisfy their taste for meat. If they truly understood their connection with God, what need is there to slaughter animals to offer to Him? All living animals belong to God and are more precious to Him alive than dead. How then can God be made happy with animal sacrifice? People do this in ignorance of God's laws and to satisfy their own cravings.

Ramainī 41

The universe is like a huge ocean full of the water of desires. The sun, moon, and three hundred and thirty million gods are immersed in it.
The soul took its seat in the whirlpool of this ocean. It wishes happiness but does not give up its association with suffering.
No one understands the secret of this suffering so people become victims of doubts.
Sometimes people act foolishly other times wisely, yet still they do not know God who lives in their own hearts.
Sākhī: Ignorant people do not know that the same Rāma they call to is God, and the Lord, and also the servant of God.
When the devotee knows Himself neither Yama (god of death) nor Yamini (ignorance, darkness) can cause him fear. The woman (Māyā) departs from him disappointed.

Commentary: In this ramainī Kabīr speaks of the darkness of ignorance that often overshadows the knowledge of our relationship with God. There is an intimate connection between the soul and God, and, in fact, there can be no separation. But people do not realize this connection, so they are living in doubt and spiritual ignorance. All people in the world live in an ocean of desires and are driven here and there pursuing them. The soul has found itself adrift in this whirlpool, preoccupied with desires. Just as the whirlpool goes round and round, just so desires go round and round in the mind. Driven by desires the individual suffers, but does not realize the cause of his suffering. As long as he is driven by desires, he cannot fathom that God is dwelling in his own heart.

In the sākhī Kabīr outlines the true mystical relationship between the soul and God, or between the Lord and the servant of the Lord. In effect, they are one and the same and not separate because God is omnipresent and dwells in every heart. The same soul that is the servant or devotee of God, manifests God within. When a person realizes this, he obtains salvation and the gods of death and ignorance depart from him. Māyā who is the prime cause of this world of illusion and doubts departs in disappointment because the illusion has dissolved and spiritual enlightenment has taken place.

Ramainī 42

When I existed in the beginning no one else existed. All existed in me.
Tell me, O Rāma! Who served you then? Explain this to me.
If I explain the truth everyone wants to beat me. Liars enjoy the company of other liars.
If the blind person says he sees everything, the person with sight looks at him in surprise.
I preach as one with sight, if people would listen to me. It is proper that people's words and actions should agree.
Kabīr smilingly says to the devotee: O brother! You will obtain liberation if you follow my teaching.

Commentary: The purpose of this ramainī is to explain two very important concepts in spiritual life. The first is that before creation only God existed, and all beings and things existed in God. The second is that liberation can come about only by understanding the nature of the soul. Kabīr states that it is necessary to understand that the soul is eternal and existed in the being of God at the very "beginning." No one else existed then. All beings emanated from, or were projected from, the being of God. Since no other living being existed, Kabīr is asking the question of God: Tell me who served you then?"

When Kabīr tells the truth and asks troubling questions like these, people do not understand; they oppose him or try to beat him. People seem to be contented to follow the company of those who propagate spiritual falsehood and hypocrisy. It is like following a blind (ignorant) person who says he sees everything. Someone with true vision would look at him in surprise. That is, the person with spiritual wisdom looks with bewilderment at the spiritually ignorant person who is still deluded by his ignorance, yet proclaims he has spiritual enlightenment.

Kabīr explains, quite correctly, that people's words should match their actions. Yet people say things that are false and do not talk about the divine soul with any understanding. Kabīr endeavored to teach the truth about the divine soul, and spoke to them with a benevolent smile to follow his teachings and obtain liberation. Liberation comes from the knowledge of the soul, or the absolute Atman that is always in union with God, the omniscient and omnipotent Lord.

Ramainī 43

The people who believed they were Brahmins, and acted according to worldly desires, went to hell and remained there.

Coming and going from this world takes no time. Kal hunts for the soul morning and evening.

The people who think themselves to be Brahmins, teach others the fourteen vidyas (14 branches of knowledge), but they do not know of their own death.

These clever persons also have doubts and fear of Māyā, but without realization, give their false message to others.

They give up the company of true seekers and indulge in quarrels. They are themselves the victim of hell, yet they say they are liberating others.

Sākhī: Those who are enemies of the guru and act according to their own impulses, whether man or woman, will wander the 8.4 million species of life, as long as the sun and the moon exist.

Commentary: There are many learned people in the world in various branches of knowledge. There are people that are very learned in the philosophies of the nature of the soul and God as a formless being. For instance, the Advaita Vedānta school of philosophy asserts that only God exists. Since the soul is a projection of God and is co-eternal with God, and cannot exist apart from God, they assert that the soul and God are one. This is similar to the analogy of saying the water in the drop and in the ocean is the same. The problem, however, is that although these people have this knowledge, they are still driven by worldly desires. Thus they are not free from the clutches of Māyā, and death stalks them as it stalks anyone else.

Kabīr points to learned people who teach others the fourteen types of knowledge – six parts of the Vedas, six philosophies, archery and ayurvedic medicine. They feel themselves to be very clever and avoid the company of humble but true seekers of God. They remain victims of hell, yet they boast that they are liberating others. They have fear of Māyā and are bound by doubts. Thus, the message they teach to others is likewise false, and will not liberate others from the clutches of Māyā and this worldly, materialistic existence.

Clever people such as this are often enemies of the true guru who teaches the path of Self-realization and liberation. Instead of being *gurmukh* (those who live by the teachings of the guru), they are *manmukh* (those who live by the dictates of their own minds). The result is they do not obtain liberation, but wander in the endless cycles of births and deaths.

Ramainī 44

A person destroys his noble life for nothing, choosing not to keep company with noble and saintly people.

You will not get such an opportunity again, and do not realize the value of saintly company.

In the end you will get a dwelling place in hell, just as you have done day and night by keeping the company of false people.

Sākhī: Kabīr says shouting to all: I see people dying and leaving empty-handed. If you wish to awaken to realization, do it now, for the day will come when death will strike you.

Commentary: Not many people in this world try to keep the company of noble and saintly people. They are more attracted to the alluring worldly life of sense gratification. Even if they go to the temples or holy places, and sing the glories of God, they still drift back into the mainstream of worldly life, beset with the passions of anger and hate, greed and ego. Their minds are full with worries and anxieties that keep their hearts unresponsive to the Divine presence that is within.

Many people falsely believe they are 'saved' and are assured of heaven. But they are still entangled by the life of passions. The majority of such people are therefore not fit to enter the kingdom of God, but are fit to enter the kingdom of Kal (death). Kabīr ceaselessly exhorted people to awaken to the Reality within them. He exhorted them to keep the company of noble and saintly people, and to give up the teachings of false teachers, and the traps of the glittering worldly life. He exhorted them to realize the Truth that will give them liberation.

Ramainī 45

Hirnakush, Rāvan, Kansa, Krishna, the gods, many humans, and clans of the sages, all left this world.

Brahmā left without knowing the secret. All those who were great and wise also left the world. No one truly understands the story of Rāma. Is it because of drinking non-nutritious milk or tasteless water?

People's breaths were exhausted but their paths remained. They departed, but left ten directions in a void.

This world is like a net and all the souls are like fishes. Ignorance is like a boat of iron carrying a burden of karmas as stones.

The false gurus reassure their disciples that they know the secret of rowing the boat that is sinking fast, yet they say they are reaching the other shore.

Sākhī: Just as the worm is in the mouth of the fish, the chameleon in the mouth of the rodent, and the muskrat in the mouth of the snake, just so I see the lives of people being devoured.

Commentary: This ramainī deals with the transitory nature of this world and the spiritual ignorance in which people live. Hirnakush (or Hiranyakashipu), Rāvan, and Kansa were great and pompous ancient kings. Despite their power, they had to leave this world. Krishna, the incarnation of God, also left the world, as did the various gods and demi-gods, the sages and ordinary people. The god Brahmā, who is said to be the creator aspect of God, also departed his life.

Kabīr states that all the great beings of the past departed from this world without really knowing the "Truth" about the eternal, self-existent and infinite Rāma that dwells within us as the Ultimate Reality. He humorously asks the question whether this was due to their use of non-nutritious milk or just plain water. Whatever the answer, it is certainly due to a weakness of human nature that prevents people from realizing God. Many people have followed religious paths, but they departed from the world leaving those paths behind them.

Kabīr is saying that this world is like a net that traps the soul just as the net traps the fish. The soul, embodied in the physical from, is beset with ignorance and carries a load of karmas, just like a boat of iron carrying a heavy load of stones and is likely to sink. Just so the embodied soul is sinking in this world under the weight of its own karmas. There are many false teachers who reassure their disciples that they know the secret of 'rowing' the boat to the other shore, when in fact, the boat is actually sinking.

In the sākhī Kabīr compares the human being to animals that are being eaten by other animals or reptiles. He relates this to people dying and departing from this world in the same way, devoured by their own spiritual ignorance and various passions and attachments to the transitory objects of the world. The truth is, in order to obtain liberation, one has to use spiritual discernment and purify one's life in all aspects, before one can safely reach the 'other shore' of this life.

Ramainī 46

Both Sheshnag and Garud died.
Those who are cheaters and betrayers will also die.
Those who do evil deeds or do virtuous deeds also die.
Those who believe in God without attributes or believe in God with attributes, will also die.
Fire, air, and water are perishable, they are all part of creation. How much more can I relate?
Even Vishnu Lok is destroyed in a moment. Everything is destroyed under the influence of maha pralai (great dissolution).

Sākhī: Māyā is like a fish that is always preoccupied with hunting for food. Vishnu, Shiva, and Brahmā could not attain freedom from Māyā. What then can one say of gods, men, and sages?

Commentary: In this ramainī Kabīr speaks of the perishability of all physical bodies or things, whether living or non-living. Sheshnag is the great mythological serpent that floats on an ocean of milk and on which Lord Vishnu rests. Similarly, the Garud is a great mythological bird similar to an eagle, and on which Lord Vishnu rides. Kabīr says these are no more. All people are destructible whether they are cheaters or evildoers, or even if they are virtuous. Even religious people who say God has attributes (*sagun*) and those who say God has no attributes (*nirgun*) are perishable. Even inanimate things such as fire, air and water are perishable just as is all of creation. Vishnu Lok is the heaven where Lord Vishnu resides. Even that is perishable when the great dissolution called pralai takes place. The gods, men and sages have all perished under the influence of Māyā.

In order to understand this ramainī, one has to understand what Māyā is. This is something discussed in the philosophy of Vedānta. All things in the universe, both animate and inanimate, became differentiated into their various manifestations from the undifferentiated nature of God because of the power of Māyā. There are two levels of understanding in this ramainī. One is that we should see all things around us as destructible. According to Indian cosmology, a time will come when there will be a great dissolution of all things on Earth, and all things will then be recreated or differentiated again from the primal Being. The second level of meaning is that when one obtains Self-realization, one immediately sees that all things have dissolved into the being of God, as all already are as part and parcel of God.

What then is the point of this ramainī? Kabīr intends to

point out that we must not lose sight of our true being which is the indestructible eternal Soul. Too often we are pre-occupied with the destructible material things of life, and become victims of Māyā who keeps us from realizing the true Self.

Ramainī 47

Jarasandh and Sishupal were slain. Sahasrarjun was killed deceitfully.
The great deceiver Rāvan, who lived in walls of gold in Lanka, was also slaughtered.
Duryodhan got killed because of his pride. No one even knows the final whereabouts of the Pandavas.
All the kings who were sons of Māyā, who played their best or mediocre music also died.
The six emperors died and mingled with the earth. Yet none of them believed in their mortality.
How much more can I say? Everyone of these went without attaining realization. Still, the clever and the ignorant are busy with their arguments.
Sākhī: Just how fascinating can Māyā be, that she has allured the whole world.
Harischandra, so concerned for the sake of this truth, sold himself in sorrow as a slave from house to house.

Commentary: The themes of this ramainī are the power of Māyā and the perishability of the world. Kabīr refers to several ancient kings and emperors who met their death because of their own ego, greed, and deceitfulness. They felt invincible, yet Māyā, with her great power of delusion, defeated them all. The rulers mentioned are prominent characters in the two great epics of India, the Mahābhārata and the Ramāyana. It is beyond the scope of this commentary to go into details about these characters. Modern equivalents can be found in some of the recent dictators such as Ferdinand Marcos of the Philippines, Mao Tsetung of China, Adolf Hitler, Baby Doc Duvalier of Haiti and several others, who despite their assumed power and apparent invincibility, were defeated by revolts against them and by death. They were all perishable.

Kabīr is saying that we should uphold truth at all costs, and obtain liberation from this world. We should not become victims of Māyā nor be fooled by her allurements. She arouses the passions, cravings, and desires, and these keep us in bondage. We become slaves to them. We should see the reality of the Divine Being manifested everywhere, and live this truth in thought, word, deed, and purity. Kabīr points to Harischandra who was a king, but who, in order to uphold the truth, lost his kingdom and even sold his family and himself to fulfill his word.

But what do we see in the world? People perpetually engaged in quarrels. They quarrel on the basis of religious beliefs, races, and artificial classes. They are all motivated by their own ego and vanity. They do not think that all of their wrangling is entirely useless, as it will not help them to obtain Self-realization and liberation from this world. They will all die and leave everything behind. Our daily activities should be motivated by the eternal issues that ultimately govern our lives.

Ramainī 48

When Kabīr lived in Manikpur, he heard of the fame of Shaikh Taqqi.

In Jaunpur he heard the name Ujjai, and in Jhusi he heard the names of the pīrs (Muslim saints). They read discourses in the name of the prophet.

There he also found the inscribed names of twenty-one pīrs and saw how people got deluded upon seeing the tombs of these pīrs.

Hearing all of this, I could not hold myself back.

The pīrs used the names Habi and Nabi but look at their actions. In practice they would be considered harām (impure).

Sākhī: O Shaikh Akardi and Shaikh Sakardi! Listen to my words: From the beginning to the end of time, and in every age, see things with your own eyes.

Commentary: It must be remembered that Kabīr was opposed to false piety and external shows of religious fervour, when true religious or spiritual feeling was not embedded in the heart. He spoke out against these whether the practitioners were of the Islamic or the Hindu faith. In this ramainī he is pointing out some of the deficiencies practiced by the Muslim saints and the lay-people who paid homage to them. He met these holy Muslim preachers in various places where he travelled. He heard them giving discourses and reading scriptures in the name of the Prophet. Some of the saints were called Nabi meaning prophet, and others Habi meaning friend of God. Despite being religious leaders, their practices were not always pure and would be considered harām. Muslims use the word *harām* to mean that which is not pure, or is bad, or not sanctified.

Kabīr also saw the names of famous pīrs or religious leaders inscribed on tombstones. People went and prayed to these tombstones and made requests for their wellbeing, somehow feeling they would obtain some blessing or favour by praying to the tombstones in the names of the people listed there. Kabīr points out that the people doing so were deluded because they could not get anything by praying to the dead. The people were not aware of the law of cause and effect that operated in their lives.

In the sākhī, Kabīr speaks to two famous pīrs named Shaikh Akardi and Shaikh Sakardi. He admonishes them to pay attention to his words and to always use their spiritual intellect to see things in the proper light.

Kabīr was a down-to-earth saint who was very concerned with the spiritual welfare of common people. It hurt him a great deal to see people falling victim to hypocrisy, and being deluded into believing they were on the right spiritual path. He tried to open their spiritual eyes wherever he went and preached. That is why he states that he could not hold himself back when he saw wrong things being committed in the name of religion, and people remaining gullible.

Ramainī 49

O dervish! Tell me God's address and the type of clothes He wears?
Where does He travel and where does He live? O Musalmān! I am asking you.
You talk of red and yellow colours in heaven. To what sort of meditation did you pay respect?
O Kāzi! What sort of work do you perform? You help the people by moving from house to house to kill the buffalo.
Who ordered you to kill the goat and the hen? Who advised you to use the knife on the animals?
You are called a saint, yet you do not understand the pain of others. You deceive the people by pretending you comprehend the verses.
Kabīr knows of the sect called Sayyad that threatens the world to agree with it.
Sākhī: During the day you observe the rozā, and at night you kill the cow. On one hand you spill blood, and on the other you do devotion. How can you please God?

Commentary: In this ramainī Kabīr is asking some pointed questions of the Muslims, urging them to examine their conduct, and see if God will be pleased with what they are doing.

He has also done the same thing with the Hindus, as Hindus and Muslims were the two major religious groups in India. A dervish is a Muslim ascetic who dresses in white and dances in a whirling fashion. They do this in order to obtain attunement with God, thus the term whirling dervishes.

Musalmān is a general term used for Muslims. Muslims pray to God (Allah) facing Mecca five times a day, and must affirm that there is no God but Allah, and that Mohammed is His prophet. Kabīr is asking them who their God is, where He lives, and what clothes He wears. Muslims believe that when they go to paradise there will be beautiful colours and maidens to wait on them, and they will enjoy life immensely. Kabīr is asking from what sort of meditation, or spiritual discernment, did they arrive at such knowledge.

Kabīr also addresses the Kāzi (or Qādi), the Muslim adjudicator who maintains law and order for the religion, and asks him about his work. The Kāzi is instrumental in helping Muslims kill animals by offering prayers, thus making it *halāl* or pure as opposed to *harām* or bad. Kabīr asks who has ordered the Kāzi to kill the goat, the hen or any other animal? All scriptures and holy people, and saints, have taught not to kill. Thus Kabīr states that even though he may be called a *pīr*, or holy man, he does not understand the pain (*pīr*) that others feel. Kabīr also points to one sect of Muslims called Sayyad or Wahabi who force other people to agree with them and become Muslims. Holy people do not behave in this way. In the sākhī Kabīr asks how God can be pleased with Muslims who observed the rozā (fasting) during the day and then at night kill the cow. They show devotion on the one hand and then on the other spill blood and practice violence.

It is our duty in life to love God. If we love God we must also love all the creatures that God created. All scriptures teach us to be non-violent. If we practice violence against God's innocent creatures, how can we please God? Kabīr was a mystic saint and, as such, he could not fail to point out to people of any religion their deficiencies and wrong practices in the name of their religion. A religious person needs to be compassionate towards all living beings.

Ramainī 50

Four yugas have gone by, and I am still advising the people. Because of their attachment to sons and wives, they do not understand my teaching.
The bamboo rubbing on bamboo sets fire to the bamboo grove. Man, lost in doubts, becomes entangled in worldly affairs.
The male elephant is trapped by the female, and the male deer is trapped by the female.
The wise person cuts iron with iron, and a woman recognizes the duplicity of another woman.
Sākhī: A woman is attracted to a man, and a man to a woman. In this world it is rare to find a man in love with the Man.

Commentary: Kabīr is explaining the strong hold that passions, such as infatuation and love, can have on people. Because of passions people do not set their priorities correctly, and suffer as a consequence. Our foremost goal in life is to know the real Self, which is God dwelling within us. However, people become entangled with family relationships, such as wives and sons, or husbands and daughters for that matter, and live their lives in pursuit of material and emotional satisfactions to the exclusion of the spiritual ideal.

Kabīr cites the example of a bamboo rubbing on another bamboo that results in fire that burns down the bamboo grove. Just so, people entangled with their materialistic pursuits burn with all the passions that such a life arouses. Kabīr also cites the example of a male elephant being trapped by the female elephant, or the male deer being trapped by the female deer (the females being seen as lures for the males). He advises that we must not be similarly allured by passions and become trapped in the material world. He uses the example of the wise person who cuts iron with iron. This means that people should be wise and know how to be in the midst of worldly activities and still be able to use those worldly activities to steer them towards a spiritual life. Just as a woman understands the mystique of another woman, just so, a person should understand the duplicity of the world and not be trapped by it.

In the sākhī Kabīr points out what is obvious to all, that women love men and men love women. He contrasts this with the idea of a man loving the Man, which he considers rare. This is not a reference to homosexuality but rather a reference to the Self, or the Soul, which is Purush and is considered of male gender. Thus a man who loves the Man (Purush or Soul) is truly the wise person who frees himself from the material world traps of Māyā and obtains freedom.

Ramainī 51

O my brother! How can one sing glories to one whose name is indescribable?
Consider how to describe a traveller who boards a boat and sits in it. This is a matter for your discernment.
People are inclined to say the traveller is seated but, in fact, he is proceeding on a journey in the boat.
The traveller (knowledgeable person) does not show false pretense on his face. His mind is steadfast; he does not speak much to others.
Sākhī: Ignorant people have the body in one place while the mind is wandering elsewhere and vice versa.
When the mind and body are steadfast and working in

harmony, then the soul is called *hansā,* so says Kabīr.

Commentary: God is Infinite and is not bound by time, space or causation. Our minds and intellects are finite, and the finite cannot grasp the immensity of what is Infinite. Therefore, it is impossible to describe God. We give names to God but how can words be used to describe the indescribable? What glories can we sing of God, when we do not really comprehend His immensity, infinity, omnipresence, omnipotence and omniscience? Kabīr states that trying to describe or to sing the glories of God is similar to a person on a riverbank, looking at a traveller sitting in a boat. To all intents and purposes, the position of the traveller appears to be seated, but in fact, he is going along with the boat, so the description of being seated is incorrect.

Just so, any description of the indescribable is also incorrect, and only reflects our limited understanding or the qualities that we care to give to the infinite divine Being. In reality, God and His glories are really indescribable. They can be experienced only at an intuitive level. That is the reason why Self-realized people do not say very much about their inner experiences. This is partly because language does not exist to express that which is not part of the ordinary experience of humanity. Historically, when saints have tried to express their inward realized states, they have been castigated, ridiculed, burned, crucified, stoned to death, and so forth.

A realized person has a steadfast mind. Whatever is in his mind is reflected in his life and work. He does not show pretence, or false facial expressions which are not consistent with his inner experience. There are many false teachers who may have an external appearance of being holy or Self-realized, but who inwardly remain as ignorant as those who have not realized God. A realized person does not have much need to speak. But those whose minds are restless, and who have not tasted the nectar of divine realization, speak a great deal.

Generally, people are quite restless. They can be physically present in one place, but their minds are roaming around restlessly. If their mind appears to be steady for a moment, their bodies are restless and they are incessantly doing one thing or another, or going from one place to another in an agitated way. Kabīr says that when the mind is steadfast and the body controlled, and both are working in harmony, then such a person can be called a *hansā* or realized person. It is the mark of a Self-realized person to radiate peace, love, and harmony. His words are few, but enriching and consoling to anyone who hears them.

What Kabīr teaches in this ramainī is that we have no need to try and describe the indescribable. We should instead try to develop ourselves spiritually, and to inwardly realize the divine presence. When we have done this, we will automatically be at peace and harmony. It is only then that we will be fit for liberation, and to consciously be in God's divine presence.

Ramainī 52

For what reason did Shiva suffer the pain of separation, smear his body with ashes, and become a yogi?
Even Sheshnag with its thousand mouths could not fathom the secret of God.
The all-powerful Lord himself teaches me.
Whoever meditates on me, will see me in his purified heart. In some way, I will show myself to him. Though hidden, I will accept his sincere devotion.
Sākhī: Kabīr speaks loudly about the condition of people.
If they do not listen to my words, how can they get rid of their doubts?

Commentary: The theme of this ramainī is the realization of God by a purified heart. The disciple must meditate by controlling all of his senses, and turning his mind within, so he can realize the divine consciousness within. Many great personalities meditate to find God within, or to realize the eternal Brahman, but fail to do so. God remains hidden from view, but the pure disciple realizes Him and sees Him through his spiritual vision. God is pleased with truthful devotion.

Shiva is part of the trinity in Hinduism. His wife is Parvati, but he is always shown as a yogi separated from his wife. He smears his body with ashes and does meditation on the supreme Lord. Sheshnag is the mythological serpent with a thousand mouths (heads) that floats on an ocean of milk. Lord Vishnu himself rests on Sheshnag. Kabīr says that even Sheshnag, worshiping the supreme Lord with a thousand mouths cannot fathom the secret of God. Kabīr uses these two examples to show that realization of God does not depend on the external show of sacrifices, isolation, smearing the body with ashes or putting on certain garments, or even literally praising God with a thousand mouths. These practices are the teachings of the false gurus.

Kabīr teaches Surat Shabd yoga, or yoga of meditation on the divine sound. By this, one obtains an easy union (sahaj samādhī) with God. This is entirely an inner process that has no external show to it. People, however, insist on following certain traditional and ritualistic practices, often without logic or spiritual discernment. Kabīr teaches the mystical way of union with God that is quite natural. He observes that if people do not follow the proper way he has shown them, but persist in practicing and propagating the wrong teachings and methods, then how can they be free of doubts and obtain spiritual enlightenment?

Ramainī 53

The ascetic Mahadev could not fathom the mysteries of the mind. Together with Uma, he spent his life trying to fathom them. Who can definitely say that there were greater adepts than Mahadev and Uma?

While life is still in the body, people do not try to be awakened. When life is about to depart they will awaken. They will be proved foolish and will repent.

Hearing this, some people came to me, but they could not give up the defects of their mind.

Sākhī: The three worlds making crow-like noises perished. No one could give up their desires. Darkness ate up the world, and all were destroyed.

Commentary: Mahadev (Shiva) was a great ascetic, and is generally depicted as sitting in deep meditation. He is a divine personality that is one of the three aspects of God. Uma (Parvati) was his wife. Prior to her becoming his wife, she was impressed with his ascetic devotion, and wanted to serve him. In order to accomplish her aim, she danced before the meditating Shiva. He eventually broke his meditation and both of them lived an ascetic life. There is hardly any person who could be said to be a greater ascetic than they were in the world. Kabīr is saying that even these two great ascetics could not fathom the mysteries of the mind.

People, generally, do not appear to be concerned about the need to awaken from spiritual ignorance to spiritual enlightenment. They are more preoccupied with sense gratification and the material pleasures of the world. When there is suffering and illness, and life is about to depart, then people start to think about the reality of life. They then truly turn to God, but often it is too late. What has not been cultivated in them all along cannot be attained at the end of life. There is a saying, 'What the rain cannot fill the dew will not fill.' The end is the time of life when people remember their past, and often have regrets that they have done many wrong things, or that they did not pay attention to religion or a spiritual life. But then it is too late. This is why Kabīr so often exhorts people to wake up from spiritual ignorance and attain enlightenment. Hearing what Kabīr had to say, many people came to him for instruction, but they were not able to give up their defective ways of thinking.

In the sākhī Kabīr states that the three worlds (heaven, hell, earth) perished. They made noises, like the crows, but could not give up their desires. Crow-like noises refer to the readings of scriptures, preaching, and philosophizing that go on in the world. These do not help people to truly awaken to the divine presence within them. The darkness of ignorance continues to devour the world, and all are destroyed. Kabīr means that people do not achieve liberation and, bound by their karmas, are subject to the cycle of rebirths.

Ramainī 54

Brahmā, claiming to be indestructible, died, so did Shiva who was an inhabitant of Kāshi.
Krishna, the cowherd of Mathurā, died, so did all the ten incarnations of God.
Disciples who practiced devotion also died. Those who pursued God with qualities, or God without qualities, also died.
Sākhī: Machchandar Nāth could not be saved from death, nor could Gorakh, Dattatreya, and Vyās.
Kabīr teaches emphatically, that all of these were subject to the trap of death.

Commentary: Every living being is subject to physical death. Death, however, does not mean the destruction of the Reality that exists in living beings. Death represents a transition of that Reality, of the soul which is everlasting. It does not matter how exalted a being is, he or she will be subject to the natural laws of physical death.

In the ramainī Kabīr lists a few of the great beings of India who suffered death. Brahmā, who is the creator aspect of

God as one member of the trinity, became subject to death, even though he was thought to be imperishable. Shiva, the destroyer aspect of the trinity, was also thought to be imperishable. It is said he lived in the holy city of Kāshi, which is also called the City of Shiva. He also met his death. Krishna, who was a cowherd and one of the famous incarnations of God for the removal of evil from the world, also died. The ten famous incarnations of Vishnu, the preserver aspect of the trinity, also met with death. All the people who were thought to be devotees of God, and accepted devotion as their religious practice, also died. It did not matter whether they realized God as a being with qualities, or a being without qualities.

Other famous personalities also died – Machchandar Nāth, Gorakhnath, Dattatreya and Vyās. Vyās was the compiler of the Vedas and the Mahabharata.

Kabīr is emphasizing to all people that even these great personalities were subject to death. No matter who we think we are, we will all still face death as long as we have this physical body. That is why in many places, Kabīr emphasizes the removal of attachment to the perishable body. The context in which he gives this type of teaching is that the only thing that will go with you is your spiritual development, your character, and your realization of unity with God.

If we are fascinated with this temporary body and adorn it in many ways, it will still leave us and mingle with the earth. We must therefore pay more attention to what will go with us. That is what will determine what type of fruits we will reap in another life. Since the soul is eternal, it must continue to exist. But it will not be able to function in any way unless it assumes a body again. This is the basis upon which the law of karma operates in the lives of all people, and it makes a great deal of sense if you understand the functioning of this law, as it will help you practice a righteous and dharmic life now. We must not be fooled by the physical beauties of the bodies, but be illuminated by the eternal Spirit that dwells within.

Ramainī 55

Both Rāma and Lakshman departed from this world; the peerless Sita could not follow them.
The Kouravas died quickly. King Bhoja who glorified the city of Dhara also departed.
The Pandavas and the great queen Kunti also departed. Sahadeo who was very wise also departed.
Rāvan built the city of Lanka of gold, but at his departure nothing followed him.
King Harischandra, whose fame reached the sky, cannot be seen any more.
The foolish man gathers many things around him. He also will die. He cries at the death of others but does not think about his own death. Instead, he tries to increase his possessions.
Sākhī: Everyone comes and performs their actions, but wealth follows none of them. Both Rāvan and Dasrath performed their actions in this world and departed.

Commentary: The theme of this ramainī is the impermanence of mundane existence. All people must depart from this world no matter how famous or how humble they are. Kabīr has stated that whoever has come into the world must leave whether he is a king, pauper, or ascetic.

The story of Rāma and Sita is in the Ramayana. The summary is that Rāma and his brother Lakshman departed from this world and Rāma could not take his faithful wife Sita with him. Similarly, the Kouravas who were warriors in the Mahabharata epic also died taking nothing with them. King Bhoja whose capital city was Dhara, also died and took nothing. The Pandavas also from the Mahabharata and queen Kunti went empty handed. Sahadeo, one of the Pandavas, and noted for his intellectual genius, also died and went empty-handed. The great Rāvan who was proud of his invincibility and is portrayed in the Ramayana as a demon king, and who abducted the faithful Sita, left his golden kingdom and departed empty-handed. King Harischandra, who was noteworthy for his truthfulness and great fame, also left. Kabīr enumerates these great personalities of ancient times who are glorified even today, and some worshipped by the devout. All of them left without taking anything with them.

People gather many things in their lifetime, not paying attention to the fact that they will die and leave everything behind. They clutter their lives with things and relationships, and are preoccupied with fame, honour, pride, and ego, all to no use in the end. They see others dying around them, and yet remain preoccupied with their material way of life. Each person comes and goes. Thus it is said the world is like a stage on which the actor comes and plays his part, and then leaves the stage. But during life people do not reflect upon that impermanence. Kabīr teaches the lesson that we should realize the impermanence of this earthly life, and try to devote ourselves to the search for the Essence of existence. This Essence is the Reality that pervades all existence, and what we need to become aware of, much more so than gathering things and entangling ourselves in material bondage.

Ramainī 56

Ignorant people follow the footsteps of false gurus and continue burning with three types of sufferings day after day. None is able to come out from the abyss of ignorance.

The false gurus do not support their disciples by giving true teachings, but instead make jokes. Tell me then, how can disciples of such gurus obtain liberation?

These gurus perform ignoble actions and chase after rituals. They read the Vedas or listen to them, then explain them to others.
Followers of this type of guru waste their lives without having knowledge.
Kabīr advises: O brother! Be careful now.

Commentary: The world is full of false spiritual teachers who are primarily motivated by ego, pride, and vanity. They like to gather disciples around them and earn a very good living. But they do not have spiritual depth. Ignorant disciples, without examining the merits and spiritual depths of such a person, usually accept such as a guru. Unfortunately, the disciples thus remain ignorant of true knowledge.

The three types of sufferings Kabīr mentions are due to three types of agents: (i) Suffering inflicted by other people and other living beings; (ii) suffering inflicted by nature, such as earthquakes, volcanoes, and floods and (iii) suffering from within, such as from mental disease, heart disease, pneumonia, stroke, cancer, etc. People would like to free themselves from such suffering, but because of their karmas they cannot escape. When they follow a dishonest guru, their suffering persists compounded by the falsehoods fed to them by their so-called teacher.

Many false gurus are quite good at telling stories and sounding very plausible, but they lack spiritual depth. Kabīr asks how followers of such deceptive teachers could obtain liberation. These false teachers often perform many ignoble actions as we have seen and heard many, many times on television and newspapers. They often perform elaborate rituals, all to no spiritual benefit of disciples. They read the scriptures, such as the Vedas, and explain them to others, but they do not have any conviction in the teachings of the scriptures themselves, so their teachings are in vain. They cannot show by example what a true spiritual teacher should be. Kabīr, always concerned about the welfare of ordinary people, advises: O brother! Be careful now.

Ramainī 57

According to the sutra of rituals, there is a world where a man's life is thought to be 5 million years.
Some people versed in the knowledge of the Vedas explain it as if they have seen it with their own eyes.
They delve into the scriptures, read some stories, and then explain them by exaggerating. Listeners believe their stories and become the victims of great doubts.
Sākhī: O brothers! You are searching the sky of imagination for the bird that is the mind, but you are leaving the limitless and unfathomable God behind. Without understanding, how can you know Him? Kabīr says all pride is false.

Commentary: In this ramainī Kabīr recounts some of the falsehoods and exaggerations that false and shallow teachers expound to their unwitting victim disciples. No one has actually been to heaven and personally knows of its attributes, yet they speak to the lay people as if they have personal, authoritative knowledge of it. They exaggerate what they conceive to be heaven and what they perceive the lifespan of the inhabitants of heaven to be. They exaggerate the luxuries of paradise, and the life of ease and contentment it affords. Often it is depicted as a place flowing with milk and honey.

After having listened to these types of sermons, people become no wiser and, in fact, they get farther away from the divinity that resides within their own hearts. They seek after a mirage instead of the real thirst-quenching lake that is right at hand. Kabīr uses a very apt example of people searching in the sky of imagination for a bird that does not actually exist. The bird is the mind that soars to heights of fancy. But in doing so, it leaves the unfathomable and limitless God behind residing right within them.

Kabīr states that without having proper understanding, and proper spiritual discrimination, one remains ignorant, and is liable to follow people full of pride. He emphasizes that pride is false. Be wise and examine a spiritual teacher, just as you would objectively examine an article you wish to purchase. The article will likely cost you some money, but the false spiritual teacher can cost you your life of liberation.

Ramainī 58

O son! Render service to me. I will give you the kingdom of the gods.
I will release you from the strong and inaccessible fortress of the world. Come to me and listen to my teachings.
I will show you the creation and the destruction of the world. You will enjoy pleasures and bliss in the Kingdom of God.
No one will be able to harm a single hair on you, and you will not be born again in this world.
Evils will vanish and you will reach supreme bliss. Follow the infallible words of Kabīr.
Sākhī: Those who have obeyed my teachings are the real sadhus and saints. Casting their vision, they can see both the beginning and the end, creation and destruction.

Commentary: A guru will often consider his disciple to be a son (or daughter) and so would speak to him, or her, addressing the disciple as a son or daughter. This is the same concept as that of God being the Father and we being the sons or daughters. Kabīr, being a true guru, speaks to us addressing us as sons (or daughters). Rendering service to the guru is the supreme duty of the disciple, because it is through the guru's teaching, blessing, and grace that he obtains spiritual wisdom and emancipation. Kabīr taught that worship of the guru contains all other worship, just as when you water the root of a tree the branches, leaves, flowers, and fruits become watered.

Kabīr explains some of the benefits to be derived from following his teachings. These include a release from the strong bonds of this material world that keep people on the merry-go-around of the wheel of karma. The disciple will be able to perceive the creation and destruction of the world, and will be able rise above these and enjoy the bliss available in the Kingdom of God.

Creation and destruction are going on all the time, as new life emerges and old and diseased life decays and dies. When a disciple becomes attuned to God, his spiritual vision allows him to see and understand the creative and destructive energies in the world, as both are equally the function of God. When one is attuned to God none will be able to harm him in any way. Even what appears to be harm will, to such a disciple, be accepted as good because he has risen above the dualities of good and bad, pain and pleasure. For such a disciple there is never any evil, but only the bliss of divine consciousness that is present everywhere. It is with this kind of authority that Kabīr instructs us to follow his teachings because they will lead to liberation.

Ramainī 59

The vessel is broken by the passions that rise up one after another.
The mind does not know who has robbed it.
There is one thief who robs the whole world. It is a rare person who understands this.
From heaven, to hell, to earth, there is only one Rāma who protects all.
Sākhī: All those people who seemed as strong stones have vanished. They were as drawings without a wall.

The wealth that they tried to befriend did not become a friend after all.

Commentary: Life is full of problems that are often innocently brought on by people on themselves. Some of these problems are caused by various passions, and by wrong thinking caused by the mind. In this ramainī Kabīr speaks of the passions as thieves that rise up one after another, such as anger at one time and lust at another, or hate at one time and greed at another. He refers to life as a vessel. Just as an earthen vessel can be broken by a force applied to it, just so, life can be broken by the force of the various passions that arise time after time.

One is often helpless once the passions have their way. In the end, only suffering occurs when the mind cannot control the passions. The mind is the most powerful tool at the disposal of humanity. However, the mind itself is the great thief that Kabīr says robs the whole world. People all over the world are subject to the same treacherous workings of the mind. The mind robs us of proper knowledge and understanding, and often causes us to do foolish things while we continue to innocently think we are doing what is right.

There is only one God, as all things in the universe are projected from the being of the 'only' God. Thus, God is present in heaven, hell, and earth, and the same God is the protector of all. But we foolishly place God in heaven and outside of hell when we know fully well and even confess that God is present everywhere. Very few people in the world think clearly enough about these matters to be able to discern them.

People come and go from this world, and Kabīr states that they had become like stones. People become very hard-hearted and rigid in their belief systems, and figuratively, become as insentient as stones. Just as a stone drowns very quickly in water, just so people drown in their passions and spiritual ignorance. In the end, they become like drawings without walls, that is, they simply vanish. Even though they valiantly try to befriend wealth, such friendship betrays them in the end because all have to leave the world, unable to take anything with them, except their own spiritual growth.

The lesson taught in this ramainī is that we must examine ourselves through introspection and be aware of what we are doing. We must use spiritual discrimination at all times to examine our behaviour, attitudes, and belief systems, and try to steer our lives in such a way that they become uncluttered and out of reach of the various passions and tricks of the mind.

Ramainī 60

Give up ego and falsehood. Only then will the pride of your mind be broken.
If you eat by stealing and begging, then you are causing a tree of bad karmas to flourish.
If you run after wealth and honour, the tree of bad karmas will bring you back into the world.
Sākhī: O false person! Give up your falsehood. This world is false. It is for this reason that I am advising you, so you may obtain liberation.

Commentary: Egotism, falsehood, and pride are quite widespread. It is only by giving these up that the mind can be purified. Conversely, it is by behaviours such as stealing, begging, running after wealth, fame, and honour, that the mind is made impure. These negative actions literally plant a tree that will flourish as long as the bad actions are continued. These bad actions are responsible for our rebirth into the world to reap the rewards or punishments that ensue from their commitment. People have to realize that they cannot escape the law of karma. As long as they do not realize the harm done by their evil karma, they will not think it necessary or important to purify their behaviour.

Kabīr urges us not to be false to ourselves. In reality, the whole world is false in the sense that nothing endures. Anything that does not endure eternally, is metaphysically false. Only the reality of God and the spirit of God dwelling within are real because they are eternal and can never be made false or non-existent. Kabīr wished to emphasize the fact that as long as people are engaged in falsehoods of one type or another, or are after fame and honour, or committing evil actions, they will not be able to obtain liberation. Kabīr instructed people to wake up and become aware of their activities in thought, word, and deed, and rectify anything in them that is wrong. Unless people do this they will not be able to obtain liberation because the law of karma ensures that they remain in the bondage of their own desires.

Ramainī 61

Those who keep on giving religious discourses persistently get up in the morning and start telling lies.

They tell lies in the morning and in the evening. Only one thing remains transfixed in their hearts, falsehood.

They do not know the secret of God, but they give discourses on the Vedas and the Purānas.

They do not even obey the teachings of the Vedas. They keep on burning, yet their zeal for lying does not subside.

Sākhī: Though they sing the glories of God, people still become lost. The body of clay mingles with the clay and the breath with the air.

Commentary: People belonging to various religions, keep on giving religious discourses to their congregations. Somehow their messages do not get through to their audience because people ever remain the same. The main reason for not effecting a change in people's hearts is that the preachers are not saintly. They are involved in various passions of the mind, and are driven by sense gratifications. They have personal biases and pet theories and are swayed by certain traditions to which they belong, and close their minds to other traditions, even to sources of truth.

A religion can be popular and have a large following, but not touch the fountain of Truth. The reason is that it is humans that have propagated all religions. As Mahatma Gandhi pointed out: "Man is himself imperfect. Any spiritual truth that has to go through an imperfect medium itself becomes imperfect." Preachers do not preach universal scripture, but sectarian scriptures, and so cannot achieve a universal appeal.

It is because of such conditions existing in the world that Kabīr points out that people giving religious discourses are just telling lies. They do not truly understand the mystical or metaphysical teaching of their religion, and yet they speak as if they have authority. People with intelligence and open minds cannot accept the false teachings propagated by such preachers. It is for such a reason that there are many people who grow disillusioned with religion. Often religion remains a hollow shell without a spiritual heart.

If a religious teacher does not know the secret of God that dwells as the spirit within himself, how can he make it apparent to his congregation? God is that ever-present, eternal Power dwelling within and that manifests as life and consciousness. One does not have to go anywhere to find God, but within. And when one finds God within, he does not have to teach as preachers do all over the world. He imparts his teaching humbly to true seekers, as any Satguru will do. A self-realized spiritual teacher does not deliver fist-pounding, guilt-evoking, haranguing, passionate and magnified gestural lectures. He simply and humbly imparts spiritual teaching to his disciples. Such theatrical performers are aflame in their own ego and passions. How can they convey Truth to others? In the end, they mingle with the clay, not having realized the secret of God in their own lives.

Ramainī 62

O Brahmins! If you are proud of your caste, why were you not born holding the three staffs?
You are born as a Shudra and you die as a shudra, yet you put on the artificial janeo (sacred thread) so you can do business in the world.
If you are a Brāhmin born of a Brāhmin woman, why were you not born in a different way? (Shudras are born the same way.)
If you are a Turk born of a Muslim woman, why were you not born circumcised in the womb?
When you milk two cows, one black and one yellow, are you able to distinguish between their milk?
You think you are clever! Give up your cunning ways. Kabīr advises all to worship the holder of the bow (Rāma).

Commentary: India has four major castes – Brāhmin, Kshatrīya, Vaishya, and Shudra. The Brahmins are generally the scholars and are held to be of high caste. But Brahmins have held themselves superior to all other castes, not because of learning but because of birth. So even if a Brāhmin is of bad character, he is still regarded as one high birth. The Shudras are considered of low caste and are not even supposed to read the scriptures. They are relegated to doing menial jobs. Kabīr taught people to give up the caste system, and it is on that basis that he speaks in this ramainī.

Kabīr says if the Brāhmin considers himself of high caste, why was he not born with the three staffs, that is, why was he not born a *tridandī* Brāhmin or of the highest order of Brahmins. The three staffs represent control over thoughts, control over speech, and control over the senses. In actual fact, every Brāhmin is born from his mother, just as a Shudra is. The Brahmins say a woman is unclean when she gives birth. This makes the Brāhmin woman a Shudra and the baby also a Shudra. When the Brāhmin dies his body is also considered unclean, just as the corpse of the Shudras. After visiting the dead, a Brāhmin will cleanse by sprinkling water over himself. Brahmins put on the sacred thread as a way of propagating the caste system and maintaining their own status.

Kabīr attests that if a person is a Brāhmin, he should probably not be born the same way as Shudras are. Similarly, Kabīr addresses the Muslim. Since a Muslim thinks he is a true Muslim only after being circumcised, Kabīr says if circumcision makes one a Muslim, then why is he not born already circumcised. Kabīr gives another example of milk from cows of different colours. One cannot tell their milk apart. Just so, one cannot tell people apart when one observes them from within. They all embody the spirit of God. Kabīr advises the proud Brahmins to give up their cunning ways and to worship Rāma. Kabīr generally uses the word Rāma to refer to God, the Ultimate Reality. In this case Kabīr uses the expression 'holder of the bow' referring to Rāma the incarnation of God as depicted in the Ramayana.

The caste system, under different guises, is prevalent in all societies. People of different classes or social strata mingle with one another of their own kind, often at the exclusion of others. Kabīr's teaching applies to everyone and to all such systems.

Ramainī 63

God created people in various external forms but without
castes. Why did He not create them in four castes?
People destroy themselves without knowing their Creator,
and by occupying their minds with irrelevant subjects.
Those who read and expound the Vedas without really

know the secret they teach are also destroyed.

They try to clean the eyes of others when their own eyes cannot see. They become ignorant and are not able to understand anything.

Sākhī: O Shaikh Taqqi, listen to my words! God, the Imperishable, pervades every heart. Because of His various forms he dances and makes them all dance.

Commentary: God, in His wisdom created people in various external forms differing in colour and certain racial characteristics, but He created them all in one human race. Kabīr asks, if God wanted people to belong to different castes, why did He not create the various castes from the beginning, so that the castes were distinguishable merely by their physical characteristics? Nobody in the world can be placed into any caste according to the way he looks, and not simply on the outward appearance denoted by certain clothing and external marks.

People, out of their own ignorance, created the four major castes in India and in various types of occupational and social strata in other parts of the world. In some of the more developed countries where there are numerous people of different races, racism has become a social problem. This is common in Canada, the United States, and Europe, especially as these countries increasingly have minority racial groups.

Religious leaders, and often well-meaning people, though they read and expound the Vedas and various other scriptures belonging to their own religion, destroy themselves without attaining spiritual enlightenment. They read their scriptures but do not grasp the secret of spiritual life. Thus, their minds become preoccupied with various irrelevant types of ideas and practices which keep them straying from the true spiritual path. Many of these well-meaning people, priests and spiritual educators, try to open the spiritual eyes of others but they, themselves, have not been able to grasp the secret of God. Their minds are full of various philosophies, creeds and rituals, but they are not truly spiritual.

Kabīr was explaining these things to Shaikh Taqqi who was a Muslim saint, and with whom he had many debates. Kabīr explains that God, the Imperishable, dwells in every heart no matter how they appear in external form. It is because of His indwelling presence that all of humanity 'dances' in its various forms. In fact it is not the people but God Himself dancing, for He is the conscious motive force present in all beings.

Kabīr wishes to teach us that we should not pay attention to castes, or social classes that people form and to which they adhere, often over-zealously. He teaches that the same God dwells in the hearts of all. We must try to understand the true secret of God and rise above the various classifications that we create, and to which we often give spiritual sanction. We must not destroy ourselves spiritually, through our own creations, when the Imperishable is within us.

Ramainī 64

A man struggles hard to take care of his body and his gold.
In many ways, his mind becomes perverted.
Even if I were to instruct him a hundred times, he would not give up what he has accepted.
The man who follows the advice of a saintly person will gain the nine *niddhi* (treasures) and *siddhi* (perfections).
God always tests the person in whose heart righteousness and spirituality reside.
If he, after such examination, strays from his path, then he is indeed foolish, even insane.
Sākhī: Without your realization, the noose of death is hanging around your neck. Will you not think of your own salvation?
Saints go where other saints are, while exploiters go where

there are other exploiters.

Commentary: People are strongly motivated towards taking care of their physical bodies and possessions, sometimes at the expense of inner development and spiritual growth. Thus, we find that although people are constantly occupied in improving their material and physical welfare, they still suffer from various stresses and anxieties, depression, and unhappiness. Kabīr states that their minds are perverted because they do not understand where to place the proper emphasis in terms of achieving peace, happiness, and contentment.

It is common knowledge that when people have accepted certain values, practices and traditions, they will guard these to the utmost. They often become bigoted and fundamentalist, without caring to examine things in the light of reason, and to make the proper changes for spiritual growth. Kabīr points out that the person who is wise enough to follow the instructions of a saint, will gain nine niddhis and siddhis, respectively nine treasures and nine perfections that adepts attain. In fact, he will gain more than these, in that he will gain knowledge of the limitless treasure that resides within him.

A person who is following a spiritual path will always be tested. There will always be temptations to lure him away from his path. Pleasures, sense gratifications, and material possessions are all around him. He has to be very strong to rise above them and stay on his spiritual path. All the attractions of the world are like a flame that burns the insects that are attracted to it. But when a person has gained a certain spiritual height, and then gives in to perishable material things around him, then he is indeed foolish, or we can even say insane. Kabīr instructs us that we must seek the real treasure that is everlasting and resides within us.

What is life really worth when we cannot take anything from here? Death can strike us at any time. Are we not going to become wise and go after the 'grain' of salvation rather the 'chaff' of worldly life? Kabīr points out that saintly people go where other saints reside. If we become spiritual beings, we will also gather where other spiritual beings are, and this will help us grow spiritually. Exploiters and cheaters will also seek out similar company and become further entangled in the materialistic web of life. The mind is both the source of liberation and of bondage. Let us use our minds wisely and obtain the eternal treasure.

Ramainī 65

O worshippers! You have forgotten your pure original nature and are desecrating it. It is your misfortune for not having carefully considered it using discriminative knowledge.
You have endured many sufferings; how can a fish find happiness without water?
You have assumed many forms in order to find salvation from this world. But, like the chatrick bird, there is water all around yet you will not use it.
Though there is water all around it, the chatrick will not use it; if it does not rain, it remains thirsty, disappointed.
God's Name is the essence of salvation. Everything else in the world is transitory and false.
If you think Hari is great then you are like a moth; consider that he also will go with you to the house of Yama.
If you have a small treasure, even in a dream, you hardly know where you can hide it.
You cannot keep it in your mind, nor do you understand its end. You have failed to consider that greed is false.
You taught the smritis (traditions) but did not follow them. You have been deceived like the hunter who mistakes a shade for a goat.

Not understanding the way of transcending it, those with evil thinking continue to dwell in the world.

Sākhī: Those who live in this world blindly do not think of the way of liberation. Since they will not accept what I teach them, how can they be freed from doubts?

Commentary: The greatest qualities we can have are divine qualities. They come from within because they are the qualities of the Soul. We often forget this fact and become wrapped up in worldly affairs and suffer as a result. Just as the fish cannot exist without water, just so, we cannot truly exist without God. Religious teachers assumed various approaches according to their denominations trying to obtain liberation, but they have failed to seek the true path that is within. They are like the mythological chatrick bird waiting for a raindrop, and will not drink of the plentiful water that is available all around it.

It is customary to say that God is great and that we are like moths, but we must remember that God dwells within so, figuratively, God also goes to the house of death with us.

In this world, we are often caught in the trap of pride and vanity so that even if we have the smallest bit of merit, figuratively like a small treasure in a dream, we are not able to let it go. We fail to realize that what is motivated by greed, pride, or vanity is of no use to us. We become like the hunter who sees a shade under a tree and thinks that it is a goat and wants to shoot it. Just so, if we read the scriptures, and do not understand their secret, we are likewise deceived. We become like lost wanderers in the world because of our own evil thinking and behaviour. The law of karma applies, and we keep on wandering without truly understanding the path of liberation.

Kabīr observes that many people in the world behave as if they are blind because they do not understand the divine Being that dwells within. People scarcely give a thought to such matters, as they are too busy with their material lives. He observes that if they do not listen to his impartial instructions, then how can they be free of doubts? This ramainī instructs us that we should become knowledgeable about our spiritual purpose in life, and follow the path that will remove us from bondage and give us liberation.

Ramainī 66

I like the relative who prevents me from going into evil ways, and guides me into the righteous path.
He who remains on the righteous path is wise. He makes others search, and never forgets the path himself.
A teacher who does not show the real path to his disciple is a false guru.
If the disciple gets the grace of the Satguru then he will worship God.
A small amount of success is enough to misguide a man. Seeing wealth and family, he easily becomes a victim of pride.
Sākhī: The soul departed and the lamp of life went out. The body turned to dust. Those who died are already dead. Let those who are living save themselves.

Commentary: In this ramainī, Kabīr talks about living in the righteous path. This path is shown to a disciple by a true guru. But there are false gurus who do not truly guide their disciples in the spiritual path. If the disciple is fortunate to have the grace of the true guru, then he will be shown the way to worship God. True worship of God resides in the heart, and is not an external practice as many people display in the world. A true guru will remain on the path, and will encourage others to follow in the same path, so he may also gain freedom from the bondage of the world.

Just as a person develops pride by obtaining some material

wealth, just so, a person can develop pride by having a small amount of spiritual wealth. Such a person fails to obtain liberation from this world. There are many false teachers in the world who pride themselves with their learning. But their learning is shallow when it comes to knowledge of God. They are full of words but not of realization. Such a teacher cannot guide a disciple into a righteous path and help him obtain liberation.

Kabīr emphasizes the point that we should not be concerned about those who have already died. They are gone and cannot be of any help to us who are living. Each of us has to travel on the path of righteousness, and try to obtain liberation for ourselves. We should try to find a living spiritual teacher who has the light of spiritual wisdom shining in him. We should be able to receive illumination from him and become enlightened ourselves.

Ramainī 67

Movements of the body, such as dancing and jumping, are not an indication of devotion, even if one assumes many pretentious roles doing them.

Forced action and devotion is not proper. It is better to realize me in the heart.

People whose words and thoughts are at variance cannot know me, not even inside a dream. They will suffer in this world, while those who will awaken to truth will find liberation.

He who speaks ill of his spiritual guru, even in the slightest tones, will suffer the fate of being born as a pig or a dog.

Sākhī: The soul has wandered and suffered in 8.4 million forms of life.

Kabīr says: He who knows God in his heart is dear to me.

Commentary: It is well known that people practice their religion and devotion in many ways. Prominent among these practices are rituals, dancing, jumping, and chanting to musical rhythms. Some followers put on various types of garb and adornments to signify the order they belong to. Some shave their heads and some wear coloured sandalwood marks on their forehead, or they wear beads, caps, rosaries, flowing gowns and so forth. All of these are external and may lull the person into believing they represent the depth of his devotion, or he may consciously or unconsciously try to impress others with what he is doing.

True devotion is silent and is in the heart. A true follower conducts his whole life righteously, free from ego and pride. He does not seek to impress anyone. His heart remains pure and he treats all with love. Many of the people that assume the external formalities of religion have evils and passions in their hearts. Because of this, Kabīr states that the external movements of bodies, and various external forms and practices do not necessarily indicate devotion. He says that such people whose external and internal states are at variance will suffer in the world because they are pretending to do one thing while internally saying something else. In other words, they are hypocritical. Such people are not pure in their hearts and cannot know God.

Kabīr states that if someone is speaking ill of his spiritual guru then he will suffer being reborn as a pig or a dog. This of course is symbolic language. It really means that such a person will suffer by incurring bad karmas. If a disciple has a pure heart, he will cease to be negative towards his guru. The guru will reap whatever he sows. The true disciple will not be passing judgement on him.

Kabīr has often stated that human life is the highest in spiritual evolution. All other forms of life are manifesting souls at a lower stage of spiritual evolution. In order to make this life worthwhile, people should know God in their own hearts. Kabīr says that such people are dear to Him, because they are genuine in their efforts. Their words and thoughts harmonize. They do not put on an outward show of religion. Liberation comes only to those who are inwardly awakened spiritually.

Ramainī 68

The soul was orphaned due to separation from God, and could not find its way through the forest of the world.

Those who know say that the Vedas are only imitations of knowledge. Those with Self-realization do not like the imitations.

An actor performing tricks knows they are false, but the master appreciates and enjoys the trickery.

God who plays in all beings is the real juggler. There is no one to equal Him.

Whatever opportunity a person gets, whether good or bad, he should by all means, make the best use of it.

Sākhī: He who is pierced by the arrow of God's love knows the pangs of separation. Kabīr says, if he does not run away when pierced, he will realize the ocean of bliss.

Commentary: God is said to be our father or our mother, so we become the children. When a child loses his parents he becomes an orphan. Similarly, when we become separated from God we become spiritual orphans. The reason for our separation from God is that we become fascinated by the attractions of the world, and try very hard to enjoy pleasures. In doing so, we forget that all the things we are enjoying bring only temporary pleasure, and then cause an increase of desire for further enjoyment. In this process people tend to forget God and become orphans.

The Vedas are ancient scriptures of India and are considered authoritative. But, like any scripture, the Vedas are not experiential knowledge. They contain words that convey ideas which can only become knowledge when realized. Without realization of the contents, the Vedas remain books. In this sense they are only imitations of knowledge. This is why Kabīr says that people who have understanding and knowledge do not content themselves with the imitation. Instead, they pursue the realization of the infinity and eternity of God. It is because of this that people who are God-realized do not depend on any scripture.

When a juggler is on stage performing tricks, the tricks appear to be real, but he knows they are tricks. Nevertheless, the master who employs the juggler enjoys the trickery. In life, we must try to realize what things are false and what are real. The material things that occupy our attention are all temporary and therefore false. The only reality is the divine Being within. Kabīr states that God, who plays in all beings, is the real juggler. No one else can occupy that position. Kabīr instructs us to use every opportunity we have to know God who is the real source of our lives.

Just as a lover suffers pangs of pain when separated from the beloved, just so, a God-loving person suffers the pain of separation from God. When that deep love abides in the loving person's heart, he will make every effort to realize God. If he can adhere to the spiritual path and not run away because of the challenges, he will realize the ocean of bliss within himself.

Ramainī 69

O brother! I have not seen a yogi such as this really united with God – a yogi who wanders around lost in errors.
He started the Siva Panth (Shaivism) and came to be called a great mahant.
He demonstrates his meditation prowess in the market place. He loves Māyā and is an imperfect adept.
When did Dattatreya defeat the fort? When did Sukhdev

fire the cannon?
When did Nārad fire a rifle? When did Vyasadev explode a bomb?
Foolish people like to fight. Are these people above worldly affairs, or are they soldiers?
They appear unattached, but their minds are full of greed. They wear gold and put to shame their dress of asceticism.
They gather horses and mares in large numbers, and own villages and travel around like millionaires.
Sākhī: It does not look proper for a beautiful woman to be in the company of Sanak, Sanatan, Sanandan, and Sanatkumar.
A blackened pot, at any time, can stain the hand.

Commentary: When a person adopts the path of yoga, he must give up violence, pretence, passions, and materialism. Kabīr points out that there are many people who profess to be on the path of yoga, but are not sincere in their hearts, and do not really have union with God. Instead, they put on a show, and are attached to materialism and accumulate wealth and many disciples. It is well known in India, that holy people will often sit in meditation in public places in order to draw attention to themselves, and to win devotees. They make a living by putting on a show, but in the process they are themselves spiritually lost, and fool others in the process.

In this ramainī, Kabīr speaks of certain Shaivas, or yogis, who perform these types of activities. There is a group of ascetics called Nāgas who are affiliated with both the followers of Shiva (Shaivism) and Vishnu (Vaishnavism). One group of such Shaivas (Nāga warrior ascetics) accepts the sage Dattatreya as their tutelary deity. This is why Kabīr asks when did Dattatreya defeat a fort, that is, when did he ever fight to do so? He similarly asks when did Shukdev, who was God-realized, and Nārad, a great divine personality in the scriptures, and Vyāsdev, who wrote the ancient scriptures of India, partake in any violence. These personalities are held in the greatest esteem, and they were non-violent.

If yogis and spiritual people, believing in these great personalities, partake in violence, then they are betraying their own spiritual path in life. If they fight then they are devoid of proper intellect to realize that their path is different. Kabīr would ask, "Are these people above worldly affairs, or are they soldiers?" It is not proper for ascetics to gather wealth and wear gold, and to acquire villages, and still pretend to be detached, when their minds are full of greed which they flaunt.

In the sākhī Kabīr speaks of the sons of Brahmā who were great ascetics. It does not look proper for them to be in the company of a beautiful woman. This is not acceptable when a person has accepted the path of asceticism or monkhood. Just so, it is not proper for spiritual people to partake of, or associate with, the world of passion, greed, pretence, and materialism. Once one is linked to them, one is bound to be coloured by them, just as holding a blackened pot will stain the hand.

It must not be understood here that a woman is being labelled as bad, but she can arouse the passions of men who have not fully mastered their emotions. So from the point of view of people who want to follow the disciplines of yoga, asceticism, or monkhood, a woman is looked upon as inimical to that path. Kabīr does not mean to teach that women are to be likened to the black pot he alludes to. Kabīr states elsewhere that a woman and a man form one body when they are husband and wife. Both sexes have female and male characteristics; a man's body is male and female, and a woman's body is female and male.

Ramainī 70

O brother! With whom should I speak? By speaking one

can lose one's essential good nature? By continuing to speak and speak quarrel often ensues; one should speak only what is essential.

If you meet a saintly person say a few essential words. If you meet a base person then remain silent.

It is beneficial to speak to a learned person (pandit), but restrain yourself when you are with a foolish person.

Kabīr says water in a half-filled pot still splashes. He who is perfect speaks thoughtfully.

Commentary: We are all familiar with people who seem to speak just for the sake of speaking, when they have nothing valuable to talk about. Unless there is something useful to talk about, speaking can often cause trouble. Useless and harmful talk involves talking about other people, such as gossiping, criticizing, defaming. Many people get together and talk, endlessly, about other people, their modes of life, their clothes, their travels, their sports interests, their likes and dislikes, and about many other things that form part of life experiences. We all know that quarrels and enmities can develop from such useless and ill-considered talk. Kabīr said, "Speech is priceless if you know how to use words wisely. First weigh the words on the scale of your heart before you let them proceed from your mouth." (See Sakhi 276)

Kabīr instructs us to speak very little, and only that which is essential. If we meet a saintly person then we can speak with that person about things that are important for our development. But, if you meet an evil person, talking with him will not improve our welfare. Doing so may even cause a great deal of harm. It is beneficial to talk to a learned person, such as a priest, or a professional in a certain field, but it is useless to engage in talk with a foolish person. Most people are familiar with the saying 'Empty barrels make the most noise.' Kabīr uses the analogy of a half filled pitcher in which the water can splash about and make a noise. If the pitcher is full, the water cannot splash about. Just so, people who have little knowledge often speak too much, and listeners who are gullible, often get deceived. The person who has wisdom and knowledge speaks very little because he knows the true value of words. As is often said, 'Silence is golden.'

Ramainī 71

Not even Indra could fathom the depth of the God-realized person who accepts sorrow and pleasure alike.
There are many false yogis without realization who shave their matted locks and wear caps. They are doubly proud because of their yoga and their practice.
They boast about being able to levitate from their seats, but the crow and the kite fly naturally in the air.
They say that they accept a wall and a woman to be the same, and that property and wealth to them are equal to ruins.
They say dirt and sandalwood are equal to them, and yet still say they are wise people while acting as if they are insane.
They say sweet pudding and cloves are the same to them, and forsake sugar and eat ashes.
Sākhī: By thinking and over-thinking all these things, these people have lost their wisdom, strength, and realization. Both knowledge and ignorance mingle in them.
To whom then should ordinary people turn for direction?

Commentary: This ramainī points out the difference between a truly realized person, and one who pretends to be realized. The average person has difficulty in telling them apart because, outwardly, they appear to be similar in terms of practices, clothing, and so forth. It takes skillful and analytical observation to evaluate the one who is genuine, and the one who is a fake. The truly God-realized person looks upon the pairs of opposites with equal vision because be remains neutral, just as God would remain neutral. He understands the law of cause and effect, and how it operates in life to cause sorrow or happiness.

There are many people who pose as genuinely realized people, and perform certain external things such as keeping matted hair, or shaving the head, or wearing certain types of caps or outfits, or practicing yoga, or showing their powers of levitation. But these practices do not make them genuinely God-realized people.

Some of these people say they are so detached that they see no difference between a wall and a woman. This means they are claiming to have perfect control over their desires. This is why they would also say wealth and ruin are alike, as are dirt and beautifully scented sandalwood. Pudding that is sweet and the clove that is bitter become equal to them. And to show that they are truly detached from the desire of taste, they will set aside sugar and put ashes in their mouths. All of these routines are only for external show; the heart has not been purified, and they have not reached God-realization. Ordinary people get fooled and pay a great deal of respect to these antics, while in turn the deceivers get to make a living from the admiration.

Kabīr is saying that people who practice these deceptions are so involved in their deceptions that their wisdom, strength, and true goal of realization are lost to them. They are spiritually bankrupt. How can an ordinary person discern what is what?

Ramainī 72

A very strange woman has come into the world, and she has neither mother nor father.
She has neither legs nor head, nor life, yet she beguiles the whole world.

Her charm lasts only a few days, but both the prudent and foolish find her fascinating.
All people, the wise and the unwise , worship her, and that is a great surprise.
Sākhī: The mouse and the cat are together. Tell me, how will this turn out?
O saints! Behold this marvel. The elephant is eating the lion.

Commentary: In this ramainī, Kabīr speaks about the power which Māyā has over people. Māyā consists of all the material and transitory things of the world that people are eternally fascinated with. But Māyā is also the power that creates illusions in the world. It is through Māyā that God has projected Himself into all beings in the universe. Māyā allows differentiation into various species and forms of life, and also all non-living things. This is discussed in the Vedānta philosophy.

Because of Māyā, we look at all the things and feel that they are real. But, in fact, everything is temporary and illusory from the point of view of eternity. So what is the reality of the world? The reality consists of the original Power, the original Intelligence and original Being, which is God. It is therefore proper to say that God manifests everywhere in all things. The attractions of the world last only for a few days, for all things eventually pass away. It is in this context that Kabīr says it is a great wonder that both the wise and unwise are enraptured by the illusory world. All people are in awe of the wonderful display of Māyā around us.

In the sākhī Kabīr uses the mouse to symbolize the soul and the cat to symbolize Māyā, and asks how they can be together. It is our purpose in life to obtain knowledge of the soul, which is the real Self. Once this knowledge is obtained, Māyā (the cat) ceases to exist. That is, the soul finally perceives the Reality behind all the fascinations of the world. In the next line Kabīr uses the elephant to symbolize the mind with its passions, and the lion as the soul. The soul exists in this material world and becomes prey to the mind, the ego, and all the passions. In order to obtain realization of the real Self, the mind, ego, and passions have to be controlled. But what is happening in most peoples' lives is that the mind, ego, and passions are figuratively destroying the soul. Kabīr teaches that even though Māyā has a great power over all people, one has to overcome the power of Māyā and obtain the knowledge of Self-realization.

Ramainī 73

I see a woman going on her journey. She is a water woman, but she is actually on top of her water pot.
She keeps going on the path, crossing the steps one by one, while the bed is on top of the sleeper.
Though she is covered with a white quilt, she is dying of cold. She does not know her husband and behaves like a foolish woman.
Evening and morning she lights her lamps, but she leaves her husband and wanders, loving others.
Night and day she is in love with others but does not tell the truth to her husband.
She thinks her husband is asleep, and she steals out seeking enjoyment. How can one openly speak of such suffering?
Sākhī: It is difficult to speak of one's secrets. It is just like exposing one's thighs. Either her own mind knows her trouble, or someone who has experienced it.

Commentary: This ramainī represents one of the *ultā bānī* or contrary sayings of Kabīr. Kabīr is well known for saying these types of contrary things, which superficially do not make sense but mystically convey deep wisdom. He said such things, because there were many learned people who boasted of their learning, yet did not know the heart of spiritual truth. He often challenged people to explain these riddles.

In this ramainī Kabīr is talking about meditation, the mind, and the body. The water woman is meditation, or consciousness, which rises higher and higher, as the meditator advances in his practice. The water pot is the body. The mind is the person who is sleeping and who is attracted to various things in the outside world. As meditation progresses, the consciousness rises through the various stages, or chakras, until it reaches the highest chakra in the brain. This is called the thousand-petalled lotus. The physical body, which is the water pot, remains below as the consciousness progresses higher and higher. The mind has to be kept under control, so it is said that the mind is asleep, and that the bed (consciousness) is on top of it. In another place Kabīr states that the mind must be like a deerskin on which the meditator sits, meaning that the mind must be under control.

The mind lives in this body, which is likened to a white quilt, yet the mind is dying of cold because it is attracted to all the fascinating things of the material world. It has become crazy and does not recognize its own husband, the soul. The mind lights lamps morning and night which means that it takes part in various kinds of ceremonies and rituals, yet it forgets its own husband and becomes pre-occupied in loving many material things in the world. The mind, day and night, is in love with external things just as an unchaste woman is in love with various lovers. Such a woman will not tell the truth to her husband. Just so, the mind makes excuses and tries to justify its behaviour, trying to make itself acceptable to the husband. The mind often thinks the soul is asleep and justifies skipping out to find enjoyment. How can one talk about the suffering that the mind endures in perpetrating its foolish games.

In the sākhī, Kabīr says that it is difficult for the mind to expose itself, just as it would be difficult for a decent woman to expose her thighs. He observes that the mind, which is involved in these activities, already knows the indecency of its behaviour. Likewise, people who have experienced such behaviour also know of it.

In this ramainī Kabīr is teaching us that the mind often acts foolishly and will not be completely truthful to the ever-pure soul. The consciousness passes through the various stages to attain the highest in meditation, and the body remains a body, that is, it remains physical. The wise person will not play mind-games, and will honestly pursue his spiritual and meditative practice.

Ramainī 74

In the beginning everything was unmanifest. There was no gross physical body and no sorrow, but there was Māyā.

The lotus leaf and the wave remain together, but the leaf does not become wet with the water.

Because of desires the soul wanders the universe, and no one can measure the extent of the universe.

In the unsupported universe, the soul takes the support of Rāma Nām and is then able to speak the language of realization.

Religions teach that water is important for purification in rituals, but due to caste influence that water becomes polluted by touch.

Cattle, insects, and reptiles rot in the water, but with that water you perform cleansing rituals.

Whoever escapes from this trap (of superstition) will never again follow the same path of ignorance.

Sākhī: This world is bound up with superstitions but no one considers it. Without knowing true devotion to God, the world is drowning and dying.

Commentary: In this ramainī, Kabīr is talking about Māyā and the way she entraps people. In the beginning Māyā existed with God, because it is the projecting power of God. So God used His power of Māyā in order to make manifest all physical things, including the physical universe. But the same Māyā has the power to conceal the truth about things. That is why Māyā is said to be a deluding power. Because of the deluding influence of Māyā we live in ignorance of the true Reality that exists all around us. This does not mean reality as we see things, but what lies behind all manifestation, namely, God.

Because of the power of Māyā, people become bound to the material things of the world. They become bound by various desires and impulses. This bondage makes it difficult for people to obtain liberation. Kabīr gives the example of the lotus leaf which is in the water but does not become wet. The water simply runs off from its surface. This example is often used to teach us to live in this world, but to not become 'wet' with all the desires and bondage of the world.

Kabīr gives another example of bondage due to superstition. People, generally, use water for purification either for bathing, washing, or ritual performances. Yet some people, because of caste influences, feel that this water becomes polluted from the touch of an 'untouchable' person. But when the same water is polluted by dead animals, people do not pay attention to this fact.

Kabīr is saying that those who are fortunate to escape from the traps of Māyā and various superstitions, will not again become victims of ignorance. They have realized the truth. But for the majority of the world, Māyā and superstitions have great control. If people truly knew how to do devotion to God, with purity in their hearts, thoughts, words, and deeds, they would obtain liberation. If not, people will continue to drown in superstitions and Māyā, and continue to die without obtaining liberation.

Ramainī 75

Be attached to Rāma and you will remove your two sufferings (birth and death) and be with the Master.
My Rāma did not come in the clan of Dasrath, and did not kill Rāvan of Lanka.
He did not come into the womb of Devaki, and Yasoda did not play with him on her lap.
He did not come as the boar to rescue the Earth from the waters. He did not go to Patāl to cheat King Bali.
He did not fight with King Bali, and did not defeat Hiranyakashipu by killing him.
He did not, as a boar, lift up the Earth, and did not kill the Kshattriyas and free the world of them.
He did not support the Govardhan Mountain with his hand, and did not wander in the jungles with the cowboys.
Saligram found in the river Gandika are not my Rāma. My Rāma did not take the form of a fish and tortoise and wander the waters.
He did not give up his body in Dwarka, and was not buried in Jagannath.
Sākhī: Kabīr says shouting: Do not be misled by the various religions. According to your imagination, you think the Omnipresent Rāma has a gross or subtle form, but He has neither.

Commentary: In this ramainī, Kabīr is making a distinction between Formless, Eternal, and Omnipresent God, and the god of the Purānas that, according to Hindu mythology, incarnated in ten forms. He is saying he is devoted to, and attached to the Formless God that he also calls Rāma. But the Rāma that Kabīr speaks about is not the same as Lord Rāma of Ayodhya, whose story is written in the Ramayana epic. That Rāma was born a prince in the clan of King Dasrath, and his main objective was to destroy Rāvan, the King of Lanka.

Another incarnation of God (Vishnu) is supposed to be Krishna, born of Devaki and brought up by Yasoda. Krishna played with the cowboys and cowgirls in Vrindavan. Vishnu is said to have taken the form of a fish to save King Manu when a great deluge covered the Earth. As a tortoise he supported the pivot of Mount Mandara on his back, as the demons and the gods churned the ocean of milk. As a wild boar he supported the Earth on his tusks, when the Earth was submerged under water. As a half man and half lion, he destroyed the demon king Hiranyakashipu. As Parsuram, he used an axe to destroy the warrior caste. As Rāma he destroyed the demon king Ravana, and as Krishna he destroyed the demon king Kansa. Vishnu, as a dwarf, cheated King Bali in the nether worlds, and took over his kingdom. People also used saligram (aniconic stones) found in the Gandak river to represent God and worship them. Lord Buddha is also thought to be an incarnation of Vishnu. The tenth incarnation, Kalkī, is supposed to be due later in this Iron Age.

All these various forms are of Vishnu who is the preserver aspect of the trinity consisting of Brahmā, Vishnu, and Shiva. He is supposed to incarnate whenever there is a great deal of trouble and suffering for humanity. He tries to re-establish the natural order of things.

Kabīr did not accept these incarnations as being those of the Formless, Immanent, Eternal, and Omnipresent God. For a mystic and a saint with divine knowledge, God does not take any form. God cannot be limited to time and place and forms. God is not born through the womb, nor does he die. For the mystic, God is ever present everywhere, and dwells in the hearts of all beings.

Kabīr is saying to everybody that they should not be misled by the teachings of the various religions. According to their imaginations people think beings are either gross or subtle, but all these are tricks of Māyā. Once the illusive power of Māyā is destroyed through spiritual knowledge, the reality of God is realized within one's own self.

Ramainī 76

The world is full of illusion and attachment, but no one appears to be concerned.
The trap of Māyā and of attachment is very strong. Only the seeker who has discriminative power can cut himself free.
Take the name of God as the boat to cross this worldly ocean. Only then can you reach the other shore of this world.
Sākhī: The attainment of God's name is very difficult, yet I have no need for other names. From beginning to end, and from age to age, I am connected to God.

Commentary: In this ramainī Kabīr speaks of the powerful trap of Māyā and attachment in the world. Māyā is the great illusive power that makes us feel the material things that we see around us, including human beings, are the Reality. But, in fact, according to discriminative thinking, all things in the world are transitory, and the only Reality is God. It is because of this 'divine ground' that all things have their existence. The transitory material things keep on changing, dying, and being reborn or recreated. That which has no eternal existence cannot be the Reality. According to Vedānta philosophy, attachment to the world is therefore like attachment to a shadow that vanishes. The only Reality is God.

People of the world scarcely think about Māyā and attachment from this angle. Those few people who have developed their discriminative thinking, are able to perceive the trap of

Māyā and attachment, and to step beyond them to a realization of the Reality that exists behind all the transitory manifestations.

Kabīr says that we should make God's name the boat that will take us across this worldly ocean. Yet, the name of God is difficult for most people to attain. The difficulty arises because merely saying the name of God, in whatever form people have of that name, is not enough. It must be done with understanding and feeling. It must lead to a realization of what the name really means. In other words, it must awaken the spiritual consciousness that ultimately must realize its own union with God. Unless this occurs, the mere repetition of God's name, and the reading of all scriptures, becomes useless. Kabīr is saying that from the beginning to the end of life, from age to age, or from the beginning and end of creation, one must struggle to know God. All religions teach, in their own way, a path to God, but because people are so fascinated by the attachments to the worldly things, they find it difficult to progress spiritually to a realization of God.

Ramainī 77

Just as there is one death in the whole world, just so there is one name loved by all in the world.

That name (God) is neither male nor female, but it pervades the entire universe.

It cannot be said to be with form, or without form and, if weighed, it is neither light nor heavy.

It is beyond hunger and thirst, and beyond sunshine and shade. It is beyond suffering and happiness, and it dwells within you as the soul.

Sākhī: The form of God is unfathomable and the path to Him is knowledge. God is really beyond form or formlessness. Searching for Him through prolonged meditation, one realizes that He is beyond number.

Commentary: Death is pervasive in the whole world; no one can escape it. But there is also the name of God, or His presence, that is also in the whole universe. God is really without gender and form, and dwells subtly in all forms. God cannot be measured, nor can He be weighed. He cannot be said to suffer from hunger or thirst, nor affected by sunshine or shade. He is beyond suffering and pleasure, yet is the supreme Power that dwells within all beings. If one tries to fathom the mystery of God, he finds it very difficult, for God is unfathomable through any type of logical reasoning. But those who meditate on Him find that He is neither one nor two, for He cannot be reduced to any number. God is the indwelling spirit that gives consciousness and life to all beings, and is beyond all limitations. God dwells within as the soul, and there is only one path to realize Him. That path is to develop discriminative spiritual knowledge, aided by meditation and purity of the body and mind.

Ramainī 78

O sinner! You have obtained human birth and are wasting it. There are many claimants to your body.
Your father and mother say you are their son. They reared you for their own selfish motives.
The mistress says you are her beloved and, like a tigress, she wishes to devour you.
The son and wife remain attached for their selfish motives, and they want you just as much as the god of death wants you.
The crow and the vulture also contemplate your death, and the dog and the jackal also await it.
The fire says, "I will burn this body," and the water says, "I will extinguish the flame and claim the body."

The earth says, "This body will mingle with me," and the air says, "I will fly his ashes with me."
That house which you foolishly call yours is really a noose around your neck.
Even though you say the body is actually yours, you are ignorantly losing it to passions.
Sākhī: There are so many claimants awaiting your body, yet you suffer your whole life striving to maintaining it.
O foolish man! You keep uttering, "It's mine. It's mine." You are not becoming wise.

Commentary: As human beings we become very attached to the body, and identify ourselves with it. Saints teach that the body is not really who we are, but is only a vehicle for the soul. At death the soul departs from the body and, since the soul does not die, it takes on another body. The soul is the real Self. When a person says, "I am this body," it is similar to the clothes on the body saying, "I am this body." The body discards the clothes, just as the soul will discard the body.

In order to explain how the body does not really belong to the person, Kabīr used many examples of agents that make a claim on the body. First are parents of the man, then the mistress who is in love with him. Similarly, his son and wife feel they have a deserving claim on him. The crow and the vulture who are always waiting for other animals to die, contemplate his death as well. So do the dog and the jackal, waiting for pieces of flesh. After death the body is often cremated and the ashes thrown in the water. The water can also claim the body by drowning it. The earth accepts the buried body, and the wind can fly its ashes around.

The lesson of the ramainī is that the body is not really yours in the end, for you cannot retain it. People who think that the body is theirs are misled, and have a false understanding. The body has to be maintained at great expense and effort and can, in effect, become a noose around the neck limiting our freedom. Kabīr summarizes that it is indeed foolish to keep claiming the body is yours when in the end you cannot keep it.

The instruction here is that we must try to rise above our own body consciousness and realize that we are spiritual beings. Our goal in life is not merely to maintain this physical and temporary body, but to take care of the soul that is the permanent Being.

Ramainī 79

If you wish, you may increase or decrease something.
You may realize something that is true, but have difficulty proving it to others.
I have said much already. How much more can I say? If people believe what I am saying, then I can say more.
But I cannot refrain from saying that the dog is eating up the separated being.
Sākhī: You have been enjoying your desires for ages, and have not tried to obtain realization.
Kabīr says, emphatically: Without realization, your life is wasted.

Commentary: In this ramainī Kabīr is explaining that each of us has the ability to either increase or decrease our own attainments, according to our dedication and sincerity. We are truly masters of our own destiny. One may realize something to be true, such as an inner experience, but may not be able to convince others who may not necessarily have the same experience and knowledge. Spiritual attainment is a very personal and intuitive experience that amounts to an inner awakening or realization of the divinity that resides within.

Kabīr states that he has been teaching this type of philosophy, but how much more can he teach the people? If people do not apply themselves and obtain the inner realization, they will not care to listen and learn anything further. Those who believe are able to develop themselves by applying their learning in order to realize their own true Self.

Even with this considered, Kabīr says he cannot refrain from teaching people after seeing the condition of the world. The condition of the world is that the soul becomes entangled in the world of Māyā, and the dog (passions and doubts), starts eating up the separated being (soul). In the sākhī Kabīr explains that people are pre-occupied, age after age, in satisfying their senses and cravings. As long as they remain separated from God, the dog will keep eating up the soul. They do not try to obtain realization and liberation. He says, emphatically, that life is wasted unless one seeks and obtains realization.

Spiritual life should be geared towards obtaining realization of your own inner nature. The well-known ancient axiom states, 'Know thyself.' To know yourself means to know that you are a spiritual being with the consciousness of God dwelling within you. Attaining this type of realization sets you free from all the doubts and illusions, and all the passions that keep you entangled in the web of worldly life. Realization of the true Self gives immense peace and bliss, and fills the heart with abiding love for all.

Ramainī 80

O mind! Even though you show great courage in your life,
 you will not meet the Lord, not even inside a dream.
He who does not examine what is good or bad, though
 wishing profit, loses his capital.
He does not understand the knot of Māyā, whether it is
 small or big, is so subtle that all are deceived by it.
Kabīr says: Who will you blame when you leave this world,
 and all your small desires are unfulfilled?

Commentary: Many religious people show great courage and discipline in the practice of their religion, but many do not examine the reality of God that dwells within. Their motives are good and they wish to benefit by obtaining salvation, or by bringing peace and harmony in their lives, but because they have not understood, through spiritual discrimination, how to separate the kernel from the chaff, they are not going to obtain the desired result. Māyā is the great illusive power that keeps people from realizing their true nature, and from seeing God manifesting in the universe. People, in their zeal for religious practices, do not examine the power of Māyā that works its subtle mischief by deluding well-meaning religious people. Kabīr says that there is no one to blame, but yourself, if you have not applied yourself sincerely, and followed the proper spiritual path and instruction. Though you have worthy zeal for knowing God and obtaining salvation, your desires will remain unfulfilled.

Ramainī 81

O brother! Listen to the character of the deities:
Brahmā seduced his own daughter.
And what can one say of Mandodari and Tara, when their husbands' elder brothers lived with them as lovers.
Indra, king of the gods, cheated the devotee Ahilya, and the moon abducted the wife of Brihaspati.
Kabīr says: Sing the glories of God. Remember that Kunti gave birth to Karn when she was still a virgin.

Commentary: These gods and goddesses mentioned in this ramainī are similar to the gods and goddesses of Greek and Roman mythology. They take on human characteristics and are subject to the same passions as humans. Yet, people pray to them, as if they are truly God who can offer them any benefit, or salvation. These are the gods of Hindu mythology and Brahmā, who is supposed to be the Creator, after producing a daughter, Saraswati, seduced her. Mandodari was the wife of the demon king Rāvan and after Rāma killed him, his brother Bhibhishan took Mandodari as his wife.

Without going into the details of the mythology, Kabīr wants to point out that one must not be deceived by mythological beings. Though great stories are written about them and about their powers, they are not God who transcends Māyā and all the human passions and weaknesses. One who truly wants to know God, must leave the various mythological gods and goddesses aside, and go directly to the ever-present, pure and blissful Being that resides within the heart.

Ramainī 82

Māyā created this world like a tree of happiness. The game of Māyā is difficult to understand.
The tree of Māyā has six branches (philosophies), four leaves (Vedas) and four yugas (ages). It yields two fruits (sin and virtue) for the people.
The number of tastes of the fruit is countless, and cannot be described.
Māyā created this world and pervaded it.
Just as a puppeteer arranges his game, just so, Māyā arranged her game. Those who play this game see that they become trapped in it. But because of its attraction, they cannot find a way out. Even Shiva, Shaktī, and Brahmā did not find the way.
Sākhī: Māyā moves onwards secretly and people do not understand her language. Those who do understand the language are saved. The others suffer loss.

Commentary: Māyā created this world and the universe, and is the creative power of God. Māyā has the power of projection, that is, the power to make all things manifest in the universe. She also has the power to conceal illusion, to make all things appear as real to our senses, when, in fact, they are unreal. All things will disintegrate and be gone in time, therefore, they have no reality in the spiritual sense. The only reality that will be left is the creative power in the being of God. As Kabīr says, the game of Māyā is very difficult to understand.

It is through Māyā that the world has created many philosophies and scriptures through the ages, and they all are concerned with sin and virtue. In India the main scriptures are the four Vedas, and the six philosophies that stem from them. The countless number of tastes of the fruit are the results of actions that are innumerable. Every action brings forth a reaction, thus, in anyone's lifetime, the innumerable actions of thought, words, and deeds create many effects.

Māyā indeed pervades the whole world. Kabīr uses the example of a puppeteer who arranges his show very carefully so spectators are fascinated and captivated by the show. They cease to see the puppeteer. Just so, Māyā has arranged everything in this world so people see the material world, but they do not see Māyā as the power behind all the manifestations. All the material things and pleasures of the world fascinate people. They cannot find a way of escape from them. Māyā trapped even the great beings Shiva, Shaktī, and Brahmā.

It is a rare person who is able to understand and know the power of Māyā by comprehending her language. Those who understand Māyā can liberate themselves from her fascinating illusory traps. Those who do not understand will continue in bondage to the desires and sense gratifications of the material world.

The lesson here is to understand the illusive power of Māyā and the greater reality of God, and to not be fooled by the attractions of the temporary, vanishing material world.

Ramainī 83

It is said the Kshatri should perform his duty, but in doing so, he increases his karmas.
The teacher who gave this instruction, is also misled by his mind and will gain the same result.
The true Kshatri is he who fights the family of passions, destroying all five passions and realizing the true One.
Subduing the mind, he nurtures the soul. While living in the body he surrenders himself to God.
He attacks and wounds his target. He attacks the passions and wounds the king of lust.
Sākhī: If the king of lust dies and is not reborn, then the soul becomes free from birth and death.
Without awakening the deep love for God, the soul departs, remaining lost.

Commentary: According to the scriptures, the Kshatrīyas are the warrior caste whose duty is to protect the king, his subjects, and territories. But since the law of karma operates, as the warrior commits violent actions, his karmas keep on increasing and eventually he has to face retribution. Strangely, the gurus who have instructed the Kshatrīyas to act this way are also in the same predicament.

Kabīr says the true Kshatri is not one who battles with human enemies, but one who battles with the enemies of the mind, namely, the passions of lust, anger, attachment, greed, and egoism. Once he conquers these, he will have a serene mind which will be able to realize the one true Soul that is manifesting within him. The Kshatri must conquer his negative thoughts, and nurture the good qualities that help the soul realize God. He will then be able to surrender himself to God in this lifetime.

The true Kshatri attacks all negative emotions and passions, and destroys them. This also includes the very strong passion of lust. Kabīr says that if the true Kshatri destroys the god of lust, then his soul will be liberated and will not be subjected to birth and death. But for this to occur, the soul must have a deep love for God, otherwise the Kshatri will not be able to muster the discipline required to conquer the enemies. Without such love for God, he will remain entangled in the material web of this mundane life, and will figuratively lose himself and not obtain liberation.

In this ramainī, Kabīr is teaching us that we need to fight our inner enemies so we can obtain self-control and be able to obtain liberation through the realization of our own true Self. If we are battling external enemies, we will only increase our karmas and sink deeper into the world of bondage and rebirths.

Ramainī 84

O soul! Get rid of your suffering – the suffering that afflicts the whole world.
All are bound by illusion and attachments. For a small gain they lose their capital.
Being entangled with claims of 'mine' and 'yours,' they again sleep in the womb of the mother (are reborn).
They play games of various kinds and, just like the flittering bumble bee, many have gone from the world.
They are born, then die, and again are reborn. They do not enjoy a trace of real happiness, not even in the dream.
They endure many sorrows, hardships, and sufferings, but do not discover what could relieve their burning.
The whole world burns with 'mine' and 'yours.' Doom awaits such selfishness and false egotism.
The whole world is attached to false hope. Those who think to run from them burn in the same fire.
Even those who considered themselves wise, and thought of what was beneficial for all, were not able to save them-

selves.

Sākhī: People do not come to realization of the Truth by themselves, but if told, they become angry.

Kabīr says those who awaken from the dream of Māyā finally see the idea of being and non-being disappear.

Commentary: This is the last of the ramainīs in the Bījak, and Kabīr here issues a warning to all of us to save ourselves from suffering caused by ignorance and passions. He means that we must overcome the bondage of worldly existence which keeps us on a merry-go-around that is hard to escape from. Escape occurs only when we realize the illusory nature of material existence that, in time, decays and vanishes. The only reality is the soul that is a part of God. We are not really the body nor the sense organs, nor are we the mind or even the intellect. These are only attributes of our true Self. With this realization people free themselves from attachments arising from ego, such as the ideas of 'mine' and 'yours.'

People with attachments and desires of all kinds are bound by the law of karma and must take birth again. Each birth can be thought of as going from one level to another, with one having the opportunity to advance to another level. But in this world people are occupied with all kinds of games that only continue to create bondage for them. Just as the bee goes from flower to flower, just so, people go from birth to birth. But until they have attained knowledge of the Reality within, they will not enjoy real happiness.

What is it that removes suffering? Kabīr has often stated that the guru who has freed himself from the bondage of the world, is the only person to guide one to the precious jewel of Self-realization. It is only the Self or God-realization that removes all types of sorrows from life. Selfishness and ego need to be shunned. Ego does not merely mean self-identification, it also means the sense of separate existence from God where one identifies with the body. This ego-identification is an obstacle to God-realization. Without removing all these obstacles, the law of karma ensures that people keep getting re-born. Many people who have considered themselves wise, and thought of what was materially good have come into the world and gone from it, yet they did not obtain the precious jewel of liberation.

In the sākhī, Kabīr says that people do not realize what is good for them, namely, the true spiritual path that leads to liberation. When people are told of the true path, they often become resentful, angry, or argumentative. Kabīr says that people are generally living inside a dream, but if they awaken and realize the soul united with God, then the question of being and non-being ceases to have relevance.

PART TWO

*

SHABDA

SHABDA

Shabda ordinarily refers to word, but mystically it refers to sound, as is seen in the yoga of meditation on the Divine Sound (Surat Shabda yoga) as taught by Kabīr. Shabda also refers to the Eternal Word of God (nirakshar shabda).

In the shabda, as in the ramainī, Kabīr did not follow strict rules of prosody; he used alliteration and rhyme but no poetic metre. The lines have varying numbers of syllables and have a beauty of their own. The shabda can also be sung to musical accompaniment. In the shabda, Kabīr expounded his spiritual teachings, often challenging people and the teachers of religion to assess humanity's spiritual condition if we are to seek enlightenment.

Shabda 1

O saints! Satguru has brought devotion to the world!
There is one woman who produced two males. O learned pandits, explain this to me!
Upon breaking the stone (mind), a river (meditation) came forth, and there was only water (God consciousness) – water all around.
Two mountains (ego and ignorance) drowned in that water. Its waves (souls) then merged into the ocean (God).
A fly (Māyā) flew and sat on the tree (world), and spoke

only one word (delusion).
That fly had no mate, but she became pregnant without semen.
She ate up all the males (people) and only God escaped.
Kabīr says whoever can explain this will be my guru and I will be the disciple.

Commentary: This shabda is very allegorical and paradoxical, and therefore can be subjected to varying interpretations. Saints often use this technique to get people to think in some depth about spiritual life. In this shabda Kabīr says that Satguru brought devotion to the world. Satguru here means God. It also means any saint who has realized God in his or her own life. The woman referred to is Māyā who is the creative aspect of God and emanates from Him. Without Māyā no creation can take place, because creation means differentiation from the unitary being of God. It is Māyā that has this ability to enable God to manifest creation. The two males Māyā produced are Jiva and Īshwar. Jiva is the soul that takes on gunas or qualities in order to manifest life. Īshwar is God with attributes that can be thought of as the creative aspect of God. In combination with Māyā, Īshwar produces the multiform universe. Kabīr is asking the learned pandits to explain this parable.

The stone that is broken is the mind, and the river that flows from it is meditation. The mind has to be broken, or subdued, in order for meditation to flow, in an unbroken stream, to God. The soul, in meditation, then finds itself surrounded by God consciousness, or as Kabīr puts it, water everywhere. The two mountains that drown in this water are ego and ignorance, both of which must be overcome in order to reach the meditative state. During meditation, the wave (soul) becomes merged in the ocean (God).

The fly in the shabda also refers to Māyā that has flown onto the tree, or the world. Māyā only has one utterance, and that is to create delusion. In other words, Māyā manifests itself in the whole world as illusion which keeps people away from direct knowledge of God. Māyā has two powers: first, the power to project into being, and second, the power to veil Reality from sensory perception. People see the material world but fail to see the divine power manifesting behind creation.

Māyā needs no male counterpart in order to procreate the world. Māyā, being the creative energy of God, has brought forth everything in the universe. But Māyā figuratively eats up all the 'males,' a figurative reference to humanity being held captive in delusion. In order to avoid being eaten by Māyā, or delusion, it is necessary to escape from her and merge into God through meditation. God-realization occurs only after Māyā has been overcome.

Because this shabda has such lofty teachings, and is given in allegorical form, Kabīr states that whoever can explain this shabda satisfactorily will be considered by him to be his guru and he will become the disciple.

This shabda is meant for us to give deep thought to spirituality – the meaning of God, Māyā, soul, creation, and meditation. This is the only way we can obtain divine knowledge and attain liberation.

Shabda 2

O saints, be awake! Do not fall asleep!
Death does not destroy you, nor does age affect you. The body is not weakened with old age.
The river (meditation) turns and dries up the ocean. It controls both the moon and the sun.
The sick mind blocks the nine gates (of the body), and sees its reflection in the water (of the heart).
Without feet, the mind can run in all ten directions, and without eyes, it sees the whole world.

The rabbit (doubts), in turn, devours the lion (knowledge).
Some rare person may understand this wonder.
The overturned pitcher cannot be drowned in water but, if upright, it can be drowned.
The cause that has kept man separated from God, can be removed by the grace of the Guru.
The devotee sitting in the cave of his mind, sees the whole world and remains unconcerned about external things.
The arrow turns back and hits the hunter (mind). Only the brave can understand this.
The singer (self-realized) says he will never sing, yet without words he continuously sings.
When the puppet (human being) sees God manifested in all, he increases his love for the anāhad shabda (divine melody).
Giving up speaking and explaining, he realizes himself. These are all difficult things to explain.
In meditation the earth (microcosm) turns around and pierces the sky (macrocosm). This is explained by the realized souls.
The soul then drinks nectar without a cup, and keeps the mind full of the water of love for God.
Kabīr says he who tastes the nectar of the name of God lives age after age.

Commentary: This shabda is a very mystical one. Kabīr is using concrete examples to represent abstract ideas and achievements. For example, river means meditation, and ocean refers to all the passions that can drown us in this world. Meditation can control the sun and the moon. The sun and the moon are the right and left nostrils, as explained in yoga philosophy. The breath must be controlled in order for meditation to be achieved.

Kabīr is telling the saints to realize their own connection with God and to not be asleep. This means that they should not become subject to ignorance and to the trap of Māyā. In meditation, the mind must be controlled, but the mind that is sick and affected by passions and negative thoughts, actually blocks the nine gates (bodily apertures), and prevents the body from progressing towards God-realization. When the mind is obstructed by doubts (the rabbit), it can destroy the lion (knowledge). The water is the heart. The mind sees the reflection of its own achievements in the water of the heart. But when the mind attains realization and unity with God, it escapes the limitations of time and space. It can then travel in all directions without feet, and without eyes can see everything in the world.

When the pitcher is held up side down, it cannot be drowned. The down-turned pitcher represents the empty mind free of passions and doubts. It cannot be affected. But when the mind is right side up and becomes full of desires and passions, and it can easily be drowned. Because of attachment to desires and worldly things, people remain separated from God, but if they obtain the grace of Satguru, then they can overcome all obstacles.

In meditation the mind figuratively enters a cave from which it can see the whole world with its spiritual eyes, while remaining unattached to it. The arrow that turns back and hits the hunter, or the mind, is meditation. In meditation the mind must be overcome just as a hunter overcomes an animal with his arrow. Similarly, the person who is self-realized does not need words to sing, because silently he is always singing with the bliss of God in his own heart. Such a person is like a puppet in God's hands, he sees God manifested everywhere. His love for God becomes intensified. When a person obtains such realization he, figuratively, drinks the nectar of God without having a cup, for this is all done intuitively within. In meditation the soul realizes its union with God, and so realizes its own eternity. Kabīr observes that these things are difficult for people to understand.

In this very mystical shabda, Kabīr says we must be ever alert and remain awake, so we may not be overtaken by the material passions and worldly desires. We must use meditation to control the mind, and allow the soul to realize its union with God. On obtaining such a realization, we free ourselves from the clutches of Māyā and the cycle of birth and death.

Shabda 3

O saints, there is a great quarrel in that house.
Night and day the five young men (senses) get up and start quarrelling with one woman (intellect).
Each desires his separate type of food and each is exceedingly fond of his own tastes.
None of them listens to the others, and each wishes to fulfill his own desires.
One who can control the young men and the evil thinking is a real devotee.
Kabīr says only the truly devoted can abolish the quarrel in that house.

Commentary: In this allegorical shabda Kabīr compares the body to a house. People of different temperaments and desires may live in a house, and can constantly bicker and quarrel with each other because they have differing needs and do not care about the needs of the others. Similarly, the five senses of the body are like five young men, and each has its own separate type of 'food' that satisfies it. Broadly speaking, the eyes need colour and form, the ears need sound, the nose needs smell, the skin needs touch, and the tongue needs taste. The eyes cannot deal with sound, nor can the ears with smell, et cetera. Each is a connoisseur of the type of food it wants.

The one woman in the midst of this chaos is the intellect that needs to exercise control over the senses. We can also say the woman is the mind. If the five senses are not controlled, then the person is dragged hither and yon trying to satisfy the cravings of the senses. This creates a great deal of suffering and disharmony in the mind. The intellect, therefore, needs to exercise control because it can use its power of discrimination to decide what is right and what is wrong, and which needs to be cultivated, and which not. The soul is a witness to this quarrel that goes on day and night in the individual. Kabīr states that the five senses must be brought under control for a person to be a devotee. Desires for the satisfaction of the various senses need to be controlled by constant vigilance, discipline, and devotion. Only then can we progress on the spiritual path.

Shabda 4

O saints, I see the world going mad!
When I tell the truth they rush to beat me, yet they believe in falsehood.
I have seen people practicing religious disciplines and bathing early in the morning. Then they turn around and kill living beings and worship stones. They appear not to have any wisdom.
I have seen Muslim priests and holy men reading their Koran and holy books. Then they seek disciples and teach them the way of sacrificing, according to their knowledge.
The Hindu priests sit in various postures and pretend to meditate, but with their minds full of pride.
They worship images made of brass and stones, and pride themselves on their pilgrimages.
Priests wear particular caps and garlands, and distinctive sandalwood paste marks on their bodies and foreheads.
They sing the sākhīs and shabda but are lost, as they do not know the secret of the soul.
The Hindu says Rāma is dear to him, while the Muslim says it is Rahimān.

They both fight among themselves and die, neither of them knowing the secret of God.
They wander from house to house giving mantras (making disciples), and pride themselves on their greatness.
Along with their gurus, the disciples drown, and in the end, suffer great regrets.
Kabīr says, listen saintly people! All of them are lost in doubts. What more can I say, when they do not accept that those who follow the natural path unite with God more easily?

Commentary: In this shabda, Kabīr points out the general spiritual condition of the people of the world. The majority follow the superficialities of spiritual life, and leaving the kernel, grasp at the chaff of observing religious disciplines and ceremonies. When the real truth about spiritual life and their soul are explained to them, they only pay lip service to it.

Kabīr also points out the contradictions of such religious practices. He observed people performing religious ceremonies and then turning around to kill living animals and worship inanimate images made of brass or stone. How can they kill the living and worship the non-living? He observed priests and holy men from both Hindus and Muslims practicing similar religious activities. Although they outwardly practiced religious disciplines, they did so with vanity, ego, and pride without realizing the secret of spiritual knowledge and their own souls. Kabīr says all who follow such practices are still living in doubts. He observes that hardly anyone listens to the truth that when you simplify your spiritual life and live truthfully in sahaj samādhī, you easily unite with God.

It is important to distinguish between the teaching of the great mystic saints, and that of average religious priests, whether Hindu, Muslim, Christian, and so forth. Saints teach an easy and natural path, uncomplicated by all kinds of rites, rituals, pilgrimages and dogmas. They teach that you only need to develop knowledge of the union that exists between the soul and God. With such knowledge, you are automatically following, and even surpassing, all the religious practices. Those who do not obtain spiritual awakening and knowledge of their own soul continue to suffer in bondage to materialism and ignorance. They long for liberation, but persist in following the path prompted by their desires and passions.

Shabda 5

> O saints, a very surprising thing has happened! Who will believe me if I tell the truth?
> There is only one sentient purush (God) and one woman (Māyā). You should think about them.
> All the 8.4 million species came from the one universal egg (prākriti – undifferentiated matter). All the worldly people are lost in doubts.
> This one woman spread her trap everywhere, and the world has become afraid of her.
> People have searched and searched but cannot fathom her secrets. Even Brahmā, Vishnu, and Mahesh could not fathom her secrets.
> With the noose of the three attributes, she has entered the heart, and is plundering the whole world completely.
> People fight with her without the sword of knowledge and are not able to subdue her.
> She is the root, the flower and the garden, and the one who selects and eats everything up.
> Kabīr says only those who have obtained enlightenment from the guru will obtain liberation from the illusion of Māyā.

Commentary: In this shabda, Kabīr talks about the power of

Māyā, figuratively represented as a woman. He also speaks of God as the one sentient male (purush). The female is Māyā, or the creative energy of God that existed from the 'beginning'. It is because of Māyā that all things came into existence, and are manifesting in their respective ways, both animate and inanimate. However, Māyā is also spoken of as the deceiver or delusive power. This is a mystical concept and must be understood in the following way:

If God alone existed in the 'beginning' and everything came from the being of God, then even Māyā and all matter came from God. If we confine our knowledge to the manifested material things in the universe, and do not perceive God, then we are deluded. The reason we are deluded is that we do not grasp that the manifested forms are really the various aspects of God, since they all arose from God. God thus encompasses all manifested things in the universe. We can, perhaps, say that the sum total of all things in the universe is God, yet God is beyond all things. Everything that occurs in the world is, therefore, because of Māyā expressing the energy that God projected in order to make all the various 'things' in the universe manifest in their myriad forms.

Māyā figuratively spreads her net everywhere in the world, creating various types of races and religions, cultures, ignorance, attachments, and all manner of evil. But people are not able to rise above all of Māyā's entanglements because they have not obtained the proper spiritual instruction from a true guru. People of all types, and even gods and demigods, have tried to understand the power of Māyā, but have failed to fathom her secret. This secret is hidden in the mind of God.

We cannot fight with Māyā, except if we use the sword of knowledge. This knowledge is that God, or Satpurush, is the only existence. Māyā is a projection from God energizing the myriad manifestations in this world and in the universe. That which is within us as the Soul, is the only Reality, as it is eternal.

Unless we can grasp the knowledge of the soul's unity with God, we will continue to live in doubt, fear, and spiritual darkness, without obtaining liberation.

Shabda 6

O saints, a great surprising thing has happened! A son took his mother as wife!
The daughter became deluded by her father, but remained a virgin. But giving up her own husband, she went to her father-in-law. Who can understand this?
With her brother, she went to the home of her husband's parents, and became another wife beside her mother-in-law.
She did not come with her parents-in-law, and easily became the housewife.
Her sister-in-law and her brother's wife created a conspiracy in the world and are blaming me for it.
Kabīr says, listen saints! The male gave birth to the females!

Commentary: This shabda appears to contain various contradictory and silly statements. But they are allegorical statements using family relationships to explain spiritual truths. In this family things are not normal, as we would understand a family to be. In order to understand the meaning of this shabda, it is important to keep the following identities in mind:

The son is the mind, the mother is Māyā. The father is ego, the daughter is intellect, while the husband is the soul. The brother is knowledge and the husband's home is the world. The father-in-law is ignorance. The mother-in-law is attachment and the sister-in-law is evil thinking. The parents are saints, the male that gave birth to the females is the soul, and the females are desires.

All of the relationships mentioned in this shabda really deal with various conditions within the person. Māyā is the creative principle, or energy of God, and is the source of all creation. Thus Māyā is the mother of the man. The mind is the son. Māyā is also the illusory power of the world. The mind enjoys the worldly things as a husband enjoys his wife, and so is said to take his mother as wife. The daughter is intellect and her father is the ego. The ego causes the differentiation from which the intellect arises. But the intellect, because of ego, cannot function wisely, as it should. It is easily deluded or confounded by the father or ego. The intellect, being the daughter, gives up her own husband, which is the soul, and partakes in ignorance. Instead of pursuing knowledge of itself and reality and its connection with the soul and God, she becomes attracted to the material things of the world, and so remains ignorant. The intellect has a brother called knowledge, with whom she goes into the world. In the world, she becomes preoccupied with attachment, which is her mother-in-law. At the home of her in-laws, there is a sister-in-law that is evil thinking, with which the intellect often associates. Her brother's wife is illusion, or wrong perceptions and thinking. Together they cause a great deal of confusion and conspiracy, and blame each other in the process. The intellect did not seek out the saints in order to obtain pure knowledge, but instead remained in the world as a co-wife with attachments.

There are very few people who pay attention to these kinds of relationships within themselves. All seekers who wish to obtain true knowledge need to pay attention to the inner turmoil that is raging among all the family members that are within themselves. The lesson taught in this shabda is that we do not properly use our intellect, and as a result become entangled with passions and desires, and thereby create a host of problems. This results in the soul losing its way to its divine home.

Shabda 7

O saints! If I speak the truth, will anyone believe me unless he experiences it? In the world lies appear to become the truth.

The precious, flawless, and priceless jewel is shining, but there is no buyer and no owner.

This priceless jewel is shining in all directions, and its brilliance spreads everywhere.

When Satguru showered his grace on me, I was able to see the pure and invisible God.

In sahaj samādhī (natural union), enlightenment dawned in me and I easily found union with God.

Now, wherever I look, there I see Him, as my gem-like mind has pierced (seen) the perfect diamond.

You can obtain the Eternal Essence from the Satguru. This is the advice of Kabīr.

Commentary: The essence of spiritual teaching and practice is to realize divinity within. The soul is spoken of as a precious diamond that is flawless and beyond price. This precious diamond does not really have a buyer, nor does it have an owner. This is because nobody can sell or buy the soul. The soul has no owner because the soul is the gift from God; it accepts a physical body in order to live in a material world. Also, in a spiritual or mystical sense, God is not the owner of the soul because the soul is a part of God and a manifestation of God. This type of truth is hardly taught in the various religions of the world. So Kabīr asks who would believe him if he spoke what he knew to be the Truth.

Kabīr observed, as we continue to observe, that a great deal of falsehood is passed on as the truth in the world. People often gullibly accept the false paraphernalia of religion as the Truth and the Essence. They literally become bogged down with the practice of religion, but do not arrive at the realization of the peerless Essence of God dwelling within themselves.

Kabīr says the brilliance of the Eternal, Divine Light that is within is shining in all directions, and has spread everywhere. God is not hidden in any corner of the world, but manifests everywhere. That is why He is said to be Omnipresent. It is the lack of spiritual vision, on our part, that causes us to not see God. In one of his bhajans Kabīr said, "With open eyes, I joyously behold the beautiful form of God everywhere." He wants us to have the same experience. But as long as we accept the false teachings going around as truth, we will not have that realization. He states that it was with the grace of the Satguru that he was able to see the invisible God who is beyond all qualities and attributes.

How many of us can understand such Divinity? God truly has no qualities, but we ascribe qualities to Him. God is neither male, nor female, nor of neuter gender. God is neither good nor bad. God is beyond such dualities of the material world. God is the power that 'just is.' How can we realize such a being? Kabīr states that he gained unity with this Being (God) in an easy way and he became enlightened. And now wherever he looked, he saw this Divinity. His mind was pure as a gem, and was able to pierce the priceless diamond of God that dwells within as the soul. He says that we too can obtain this Eternal Essence if we follow the teachings given by the Satguru. We must seek the Reality through purity of the heart, and not accept falsehoods perpetrated in the name of religion.

Shabda 8

O saints! Whatever comes into existence and later ceases
to be, is Māyā.
God is the sustainer of all, and is not affected by time. He
neither goes to, nor comes from anywhere.

What purpose did God have to appear as a fish or tortoise, or to kill the demon Shankhasur?

God is merciful, and has no enmity. Tell me, then, how could He kill anyone?

The Creator never incarnated as a boar to hold up the Earth, nor did He make others hold it up.

These are not the works of God. The world accepts falsehoods as truth.

Everyone believes God tore the pillar and came out as the Narsingh form.

They believe He tore the abdomen of Harnakush with his nails, but God does not do such things.

The one who incarnated as the dwarf did not beg King Bali for a gift of land. He who begged was Māyā.

Without spiritual discrimination, the whole world is in doubt that is perpetrated by Māyā.

God did not come as Parshuram to kill the Kshatrīyas. This was also the deception of Māyā.

Without having knowledge and devotion of Satguru, you have accepted Māyā as the truth.

God, the Creator, did not marry Sita, and did not float the stones, nor build a bridge across the ocean.

People who say Ragunath and God are one are lacking in discriminative knowledge.

The Creator did not come to Gokul, nor did He live with the cowboys and cowgirls, nor did He kill Kansa.

God is merciful and is master of all. He does not participate in winning or losing actions.

The Creator did not come as Buddha, and He did not kill the demon.

Ignorant people create doubts about the Creator through the influence of Māyā.

The Creator will not come as Kalkī, nor will He destroy the demon Kalingā.

These deceptions are the creations of Māyā; she deludes the yatis and satis.
The ten incarnations are the Māyā of God. Do not worship them as the Creator.
Kabīr says, listen O saints! Those who are born and die are other than the Imperishable Lord, who is beyond Māyā.

Commentary: God is above Māyā. He is eternal, formless and omnipresent. God is beyond time and space, and every other type of limitation. God is Infinite Being. With these aspects of God, it is not conceivable that He will come to Earth in various forms as stated in mythology. Hindu mythology states that God has come in nine different forms already, and will come in a tenth form at the end of this present Iron Age. He came as fish, tortoise, boar, half-man-half-lion, dwarf, Parshuram, Rāma, Krishna, and Buddha. He is to come as Kalkī who will destroy the demon Kalingā at the end of this Iron Age. People accept these various incarnations of Vishnu, the preserver god of the Hindu trinity.

Kabīr says God is beyond all of these representations, and that these are only projections of Māyā. He states, emphatically, that any being that can be born and then die, cannot be the Eternal Creator. He also, emphatically states that God is merciful and kind towards all beings. He therefore could not perform some of the violent and deceptive actions attributed to God. Kabīr says people who accept all these stories as factual and true are not using their spiritual discriminative knowledge to arrive at the real truth. If God is formless and omnipresent, and is in the whole universe, the size of which is unimaginable, how can He come to one little speck of earth for the benefit of a few here and there, or for the destruction of a puny demon here and there. Kabīr says people who believe these stories are actually believing lies.

But a person on a spiritual path must have an open mind,

and realize that God is spirit and dwells in the hearts of all beings, including the hearts of the demons. It is a fallacy to think that God will appear in one form to destroy another form, in which He is also present. God is sarvavyapak, or omnipresent. It is illogical for God to attack and destroy God. This is what it amounts to, if you accept the mythologies. Proper discriminative knowledge will say that God is beyond these things, which are merely machinations of the human mind. This being so, it is Māyā, the illusive power, that has kept on deluding the whole world. Because of this, the world remains in doubts.

If we open our spiritual eyes and examine the truth, we will inevitably come to the conclusion that God does not partake in these petty things of the world. His purpose is much grander. He bestows mercy, love, and bounty on all beings. He has set His law of karma in motion. This law will automatically take care of all the demons in the world. People are the creators of demons. Imagine wiping your mind clean of all demons that you have ever imagined or heard about, and just realize that there is only you, as the soul, and God. Wouldn't that make life much simpler, and keep it on the true spiritual path? That is what Kabīr teaches us. We need to have open minds, and accept that God dwells in all of us, and that we create our own sufferings according to our karmas. There is no evil force anywhere in the universe, unless we have created them. We should free ourselves from doubts and delusions, and accept the beauty and love of God, and set our minds free.

Shabda 9

O saints, if I tell the truth people want to beat me.
If I remain silent, how can people obtain true knowledge?
No one gives due thought to my words.
First of all, the son (soul) was born, then the father (God)
was born.

Both the father and the son have the same wife (Māyā).
Who can understand this astonishment?
The frog (ignorant person) sits as a king on the throne,
and the snake (mind) is his attendant.
The poor dog (passions, lust) is owner of the house (body),
and the cat (attachment) is the wife in the house.
The court clerk (preacher) carries his files (scriptures), and
the bull (ignorance) acts as the accountant.
Kabīr says, give heed O saints! The buffalo (ego) acts as
the judge.

Commentary: This is one of the contrary sayings of Kabīr, yet it is full of deep, mystical meaning. First of all, Kabīr admits that when he tells the truth, people do not care to listen to it and often want to beat him. This has been the story for many saints throughout history. Yet, saints have to speak, because if they do not, people will not obtain true knowledge. Having said that, Kabīr then enters into the mystical explanation of the condition in which people find themselves.

He says that first the son was born, and then the father. It is important to understand that the son is likened to the soul, and the father to God. It appears contrary that the son or soul should be born before the father (God). But mystically speaking, it is a true statement, because if the soul were not present, the question of God would not arise. There must first be sentient beings (humans) who can think about a superior Being called God. If there were no people there would be no one to talk about God. Kabīr then says that both the father and the son have one wife. The wife is Māyā, that is the energy of God that projects into the manifold existence, all things in the universe. It is Māyā then, acting as the 'wife' of God, that creates the soul, who is the son. As the sentient son then created God as explained above, he had Māyā as the wife, to figuratively produce God. Through this interpenetration of relationship, it is thus that the son and the father have the same wife.

The frog spoken of here evokes an ignorant person who sits on his throne, and has an attendant who gives him bad advice, namely, the snake. The snake is the mind. The mind has the power to poison the intellect and consciousness of man, and reduce him to spiritual ignorance, instead of spiritual enlightenment. The poor dog (passions) takes up abode in the house that is the body, and the cat, which is attachment, is the wife in this house. Attachment to sensory objects ignites the fire of the passions in the house in which the poor person burns. This is why, in spiritual teaching, it is said attachments must be controlled. When attachments are controlled, the passions are controlled.

Kabīr also speaks about the clerk who carries files with him. This represents the preacher who carries scriptures which he can read and quote to others. But the bull, his ego, remains ignorant because he has not achieved God-realization or enlightenment. When ignorance acts as the accountant to keep track of one's spiritual bank account, then one is really in trouble. Preachers of religion need to become enlightened, and not merely be proficient at quoting scriptures. They must have an inner realization of the truth. When the buffalo, that is the ego, sits as a judge, how can any proper justice be achieved.

In this very interesting shabda, Kabīr explains how a person who thinks what is not good is really good is acting out of ignorance. His passions, senses, desires, and ego blind him to the Truth. The right path is not possible unless one is attuned to the Truth.

Shabda 10

O saints! I have examined the ways of both Hindus and Muslims.
Both do not listen to my instructions but are fond of satisfying their tastes.

Hindus observe the fast of Ekadasi, and eat sweets with milk. They give up regular food, but do not control the mind. When they break the fast, they then indulge in meat eating.

The Muslims observe the fast of Rozā, offer Namāz and shout 'bismillāh.' But how can they obtain heaven when they kill the chickens at night?

Both Hindus and Muslims have given up mercy in their hearts.

The Muslim kills the goat with halāl, and the Hindu with a sudden chop. Fire burns in both their homes.

Both Hindus and Muslims follow the same path of violence. Satguru has demonstrated this.

Kabīr says, listen O saints! Neither Rāma nor Khuda instructed them to kill.

Commentary: In this shabda, Kabīr talks about the hypocrisy he saw being practiced by both Hindus and Muslims. Although they say they are religious and are supposed to have mercy in their hearts, they were also practicing violence. Kabīr speaks about the fasting that Hindus observe on the Ekadasi, or 11th day of the lunar half-month. They may partake of milk and sweets and certain fruits or water chestnuts, but avoid grains and other regular types of food. But after breaking their fast, they often revert to killing chickens and feasting. The Muslims on the other hand, fast during the month of Ramadan. The fasting is called Rozā. In the name of their religion, they recite their prayers and hope to go to heaven. But Kabīr asks how they can go to heaven when they practice violence at night, killing animals? Kabīr concludes that both Hindus and Muslims have given up compassion and mercy in their hearts. They kill to satisfy their tastes, and sadly, do it in the name of religion.

Among Muslims, the animal must be sacrificed by halāl, which means a slow cutting of the throat to allow the blood to drain out. Jewish people call this kosher. If the animal is not killed in this way, it is said to be haram or unclean. The Hindus, on the other hand, kill by a sudden chop severing the head of the animal. Both forms of killing are violent, and are not becoming of people who are supposed to have mercy in their hearts. Kabīr says both their homes are burning with the fire of violence also referring to fire that is used to cook the meat.

Kabīr observes that both Hindus and Muslims are really practicing the same thing, as far as following certain religious observances, and then practicing violence. This is a hypocrisy for someone who is on a religious path. Religion means having compassion and mercy for all life. God is merciful and loves all creatures. It is not right or ethical for human beings to kill animals to satisfy their tastes. Humans can live a healthy and happy life while being vegetarians. Kabīr observes that God, whether you call him Rāma or Allah, or anything else, does not instruct anyone to be violent.

From this shabda, it is important for us to learn that hypocrisy and violence are not part of spiritual life. We need to have compassion and love instead, and follow a non-violent way of sustaining ourselves.

Shabda 11

O saints, the pandes (priests) are skillful butchers.
They kill the goat then rush to kill the buffalo. They feel no compassion in their hearts.
They bathe and apply tilak (sandalwood paste) to their foreheads, and systematically perform worship to the goddess. Then they kill a living being in a moment, and cause a stream of blood to flow.
They are thought to be holy and of high caste, and are honoured in congregations.
All the people seek initiation from them. O brother! I

laugh at seeing such behaviour.

They preach on how to get rid of sins, yet they make others perform sinful actions. I have seen this behaviour from both Hindus and Muslims. They are both deceived by Yama.

Those who kill cows are called butchers. Are the pandes any less than they are, in their violence?

Kabīr says, listen saints, the Brāhmin have degenerated in this Kaliyug.

Commentary: In this shabda, Kabīr strongly condemns the practice of sacrificing animals for any reason whatsoever, but most importantly, in the worship of any deity. Kabīr advocated compassion towards all living beings. He taught that God gave life to all creatures, and that they wish to live just as much as we do. It is therefore unethical and immoral for us to deprive them of their lives. Killing is a violent action and, because of the law of karma, everyone who kills must ultimately face the consequences.

It is common practice for priests and their followers who worship the goddess (Kali, Durga, Bhairavi) to slaughter animals in her worship. The question then arises: Are we to worship a loving and benevolent God, or are we to worship a goddess that needs a blood sacrifice? Which worship is noble and worthy of cultivation? God has given us intelligence and the power to discriminate between right and wrong. How can any divinity be happy when a life is destroyed? There are sufficient numbers of animals all over the world that any divine being can take if he or she wishes. But such is not the case. People make these unreligious rules and follow them, and then teach them to their disciples.

To the Muslims the pig is unclean, and to the Hindus the cow is sacred. Both animals have the same life force in them. God made the animals, but people made them holy or unholy, clean or unclean. The priests who practice and condone such behaviour are lacking compassion in their hearts. Yet these people lead disciples and are honoured. They are often thought to be of high caste, even when they perform lowly actions. Are people spiritually blind?

What constitutes true religious or spiritual life? It is love for God and all of His creation, including all the innocent animals. It is having compassion in our hearts for all creatures. It is kindness to all beings. It is the use of our spiritual discrimination to know right from wrong actions. Let us not get fooled and be dragged away from the true spiritual path into the labyrinth that makes us lost so that we cannot find our way back to our spiritual goal of unity with God.

Shabda 12

O saints, people absorbed in God's colour are intoxicated with love.
The satsangees are intoxicated with it and drink cupsful of nectarine love.
They fix the still in the midst of the sky, and there they extract the pungent drink.
They have overcome lust and evil actions, and partake of the drops of love that fall continuously.
The great personalities Gorakh, Dattatreya, Vashisth, Vyās, Hanuman, Nārad, and Sukh Muni all enjoyed it.
Sitting in such august assembly Shiva, Sanak and others passed the cup around.
Even Ambarish and Yajnavalkya, Janak and Jadbharat, and Sheshnag with its thousand mouths, enjoyed it.
How long can I count the endless numbers who enjoyed the nectar of love? Even those in palaces and those who wandered have been intoxicated with it.
Dhruv, Prahalād, Bhibhishan, and Shiva's wife Parvati,

were intoxicated with it.

The incarnation of Brahman (Krishna) got intoxicated in Vrindavan, and even today that intoxication is felt.

All the gods, men, munis, yatis, pīrs, and saints who drank it, know of its power.

Kabīr says, if a dumb person tastes sugar, how can he explain the taste?

Commentary: In this very interesting shabda, Kabīr explains the state of intoxication felt by those who have become absorbed in God. They have reached God-realization. Just as a person can become drunk with alcohol, a person can become drunk with the love of God. The difference is that the alcoholic person will do foolish things, and may be obnoxious, whereas the person absorbed in the love of God will sing of the glories of God, oblivious to his surroundings. He may not verbalize this singing, but experience that state as a state beyond description.

In this shabda Kabīr uses the symbol of the still to illustrate the making of the wine of love, but this still is in the midst of the sky. This highlights that God-intoxicated people have gone into meditation and have reached a high state of consciousness. That is where they distill their wine of love. Once they have reached this stage, they have overcome lust and evil actions and are drinking the nectar of love that is flowing continuously by God's grace.

Kabīr lists a number of great sages of India mentioned in scriptures and mythology who attained such a state. All of these personalities were great in many ways and can be read about in epics such as the Ramayana, Gita, Purānas as well as other scriptures of India. Kabīr says the people who have attained this state of consciousness are countless, considering he is relating events of many ages from the past.

Most people are familiar with Krishna, hailed as an incarnation of God. Even he was intoxicated with the divine nectar. The effect of his influence is seen in the world today. The gods, men, munis (philosophers), yatis (ascetics), pīrs and awliyā (Muslim holy people) tasted this nectar and became intoxicated. Kabīr says this state of intoxication is difficult to explain to other people. It is like a dumb person who has tasted sugar, enjoys it, but cannot explain the sweetness to others.

Shabda 13

O Rāma! Your Māyā is the cause of duality (pairs of opposites) in the world.
Māyā's condition and whereabouts are difficult to understand. She makes the gods, men, and munis dance to her tune.
O semar tree! Of what use are your huge branches and beautiful flowers?
Many birds await your ripe fruit, and as they watch, your cotton flies away.
O date palm! Of what use is your great height, when no one can reach your fruit?
When the hot weather of summer arrives, your scanty shade is not of much use to anyone.
Some people are clever in the subject of gold and women, and teach their cleverness to others.
Kabīr says, listen, O saints! Offer your love at the feet of God.

Commentary: In this shabda Kabīr speaks again about the power of Māyā. Māyā is the power of illusion that fools many people. The semar tree (silk cotton tree) produces lovely pods that are like beautiful fruits. Parrots wait for the fruit to ripen, but even while they wait, the pod ripens, bursts, and the cotton flies away. The parrot is left disappointed. Similarly, people who have hopes of satisfying their material desires, find that there is no end to them. People are left disappointed. The attractions of the world are fascinating, but in the end, prove empty.

Another example Kabīr uses is of the tall date palm that grows mostly in deserts. A traveller in the desert cannot pluck the fruits, as they are very high. The scanty branches also do not provide adequate shade. People in the world often behave like the date palm being full of pride and ego about their greatness. But their pride is of no use to other people. Kabīr also talks about the people who are very cunning in terms of obtaining wealth and favours of women. They teach their cunning to others. In the end though, this cleverness is not of much use to them, as old age and death consume them, and they have to leave everything behind.

Kabīr is teaching that it is difficult to understand the power of Māyā and how it has fascinated the world. Māyā has myriads of beings in her grip, gods, angels, ordinary human beings, sages, and philosophers. He advises everyone to give up their fascination with the transitory and illusory Māyā, and to offer love at the 'feet' of God. Spiritual life is for liberation, not bondage. Māyā creates bondage, but the 'feet' of God give liberation.

Shabda 14

O soul, since you will not give up your knot of doubts,
  Yama will repeatedly attack and rob you.
You speak of your humility and noble birth, that you are
  a yogi and sanyāsī.
You speak of your wisdom, virtue, bravery, poetry, and
  generosity, and cannot get rid of this type of thinking.
You have read the Smritis, Vedas, and Purānas, but have
  not experienced the Reality.
How can iron turn to gold when it has not been touched
  by the philosopher's stone?
If you cannot liberate yourself while alive, how can you do

it after death?
Whatever you deeply believe and are attached to, that is what you will become after death.
O wise man! Try to understand that whatever you did through knowledge or ignorance, that is what you will reap.
Kabīr says what can I say to him, who while seeing everything, still does not understand, and continues to be lost?

Commentary: There are many people in the world who feel that they are living a religious life, yet they are full of spiritual doubts. They perform all the external religious activities, but their own hearts are not enlightened with Divine knowledge. Kabīr talks about such people. These people feel themselves to be of noble birth, or to be full of wisdom. They pride themselves about virtuous deeds and their learning and charity. They read the scriptures and say their prayers. But in the depth of their hearts they have not experienced the Ultimate Reality. Kabīr asks how iron can become gold when it has not been touched by the philosopher's stone? This is an alchemical saying. Kabīr is asking how a person can become divine if he has not been touched by the grace of a spiritual master?

Many people feel that they are liberated because they say they are 'born again.' Some feel that they are liberated because they perform their religious duties regularly. But when they do not have direct perception of God, how can they obtain liberation? Many people are taught that liberation is obtained after death. Kabīr points out that it is only while a person has consciousness that he can ever hope to attain liberation. The dead cannot perform anything. Whatever the person strongly adheres to, and desires while alive, that is what he will become after death. He has to continue on an onward journey before he can obtain liberation. The law of karma assures that whatever one does in thought, word, and deed, that is what he will reap in this life, or in another life.

In spiritual life people cannot fool themselves or God, by saying they take part in the various paraphernalia of religion. They may fool other people but their actions are recorded in the 'cosmic library,' and that is what they will reap. Kabīr asks what could he say about a person who has eyes but refuses to see? Such a person is spiritually in the dark. Only when he chooses to perceive properly will he start his spiritual journey.

Shabda 15

The weaver is leaving his house, but the Māyā of Rāma goes and makes him create a new house.
One yard, nine yards, ten yards and nineteen yards, Māyā made him weave the cloth.
She wove seven different threads, nine cords and seventy-two strands, and the cloth became very valuable.
This cloth is so great that none other is equal to it, but people, not knowing its value, reduce its value to almost nothing.
They decrease its value, and cannot increase it, though they struggle very much.
When the weaver tries to make good cloth, his wife rushes on him quarrelling.
When the bundle of yarn becomes wet it is useless, and the weaver departs disappointed.
Kabīr says, listen saints! Give up all the paraphernalia and sing the glories of Him who made this creation. O foolish people, crossing the worldly ocean is difficult.

Commentary: This is a very mystical and allegorical shabda in which Kabīr talks about the soul, the body, Māyā, illusions, desires, God, and liberation. The weaver is the soul and the house is the body. One yard is the mind and nine yards is the body with its nine apertures. The ten yards are the five organs of sense and five of actions. The nineteen yards are the five organs of sense, five organs of action, five subtle elements, and the mind, intellect, consciousness, and ego. This body is made up of all of these various elements. The seven threads are components of the body, which are the skin, blood, flesh, sinews, bone, marrow, and semen/eggs. The nine 'cords' (apertures) are two eyes, two nostrils, two ears, one mouth, one anus, and one genital organ. The seventy-two strands are seventy-two different nerve currents that are thought to make up the body. Once this body is made, it is really very valuable, but people do not use the body effectively to enhance its progress towards God.

The wife Kabīr mentions is illusion that confounds the mind and makes the weaver (soul) restless and confused. The power of Māyā creates this illusion, and also fills the mind with the water of desires. This figuratively makes the body wet and therefore useless, just as wet yarn cannot be used to make cloth. Kabīr advises people to give up all the paraphernalia of Māyā and illusion. Unless we are clear-sighted about our devotion and connection with God then it is indeed very difficult to cross this worldly ocean.

From this shabda we learn that the body is wonderfully made, and that it must be used wisely to obtain knowledge and freedom. It is not to be subjected to illusion and ignorance that create bondage, resulting in karmic effects and rebirths. Unless liberation is obtained through knowledge, one is destined to keep suffering in this worldly ocean.

Shabda 16

O soul, the musical instrument plays softly and there is
dancing without hands and feet.
The music is played without hands, and is heard without

ears. The listener and the listening merge into one.

The mind is controlled, and listens to the divine melody that is always playing in the master's court. O intelligent people! Try to understand this.

In that state, there is enjoyment without the senses, tasting without the tongue, and immortality without the body.

The thief (Māyā) plunders the temple (body), though the house is empty and the master is immortal.

In that state the shoot grows without seed, tree without stem, and fruit without flowers.

In the barren womb (empty mind) a son (meditation) is born, and without feet climbs the tree (God-realization).

The inkpot is full without ink, and the paper is written without pen. Without any writing, all is known.

Without recollection there is intuitive knowledge in the soul, and it knows all without pursuing knowledge. Kabīr says it is the real devotee who understands this.

Commentary: This shabda is full of incompatibilities when seen superficially. How can there be dancing without hands and feet, and enjoyment without any sense organ? What does it mean when the listener and the listening merge into one? Who is the thief that plunders the house when the master is right there, and the house is empty? How can the shoot grow without seed, or a tree without stem, and fruit without flowers? In order to understand this shabda, it is important to realize that when the knowledge of God is obtained, all incompatibilities disappear.

The soft music is the divine melody that is heard when one is in meditation. There is no need for hands and feet to make the mind dance in ecstasy. There is no need for hands to play such music, for the divine melody resounds eternally. In that exalted state of unity, there is no listener or listening. In that state there is no need for any of the sense organs to enjoy the bliss that is obtained in God-realization. The soul is immortal, and that immortality is realized while knowing the body to be mortal.

There is a thief that is called Māyā (illusion) that plunders the temple of the body. It creates various desires and attachments, and robs the mind of the tranquility needed for meditation. The immortal soul resides there, but because of the illusive power of Māyā, the house, or the body, appears to be abandoned.

In the realized state there is only consciousness in which there is no direction such as up and down, front or back, past or present. Such a mind is simply absorbed in meditation. In meditation, divine knowledge dawns in the consciousness, and divine knowledge encompasses every other type of knowledge available to man. Kabīr says without learning and remembering anything, intuitive knowledge appears. There is no language, yet all is known. This knowledge is supreme, and supersedes all other knowledge. Kabīr says the person who can understand what he is saying is one truly devoted to God.

Shabda 17

There are some priests who sing of Rāma and explain him to others, but without knowing God they wander restlessly.

They recite the Vedas and the Gayatri, and the ignorant people think those hearing the words will obtain liberation.

The Brahmins, at whose feet the people bow down in devotion, kill living creatures as sacrificial offerings.

They think high of themselves, but are content to eat at the homes of the low caste, filling their bellies by doing evil actions.

When there is an eclipse and the night is dark, they go

house to house begging. Even with light (Vedas) in their hands they fall into the well (ignorance).

They do not know the secret of the Ekadasi fast, and their minds are filled with stories of demons and ghosts.

They give up camphor (truth) and accept a knot of poison (ignorance). Wasting knowledge, they foolishly wander from place to place.

They destroy nobility and nurture thieves. They even tease the saints.

Kabīr says these people are lustful for taste, and will become victims of hell.

Commentary: There are many false teachers of religion who are bound up with evils and passions. The Brahmins think of themselves as belonging to the high caste, and others to be of lower caste. But they do not realize the truth, that the soul in all people is the same. They do not know the secret of God, so they wander around with restless minds. They recite the Vedas and the Gayatri, and the ignorant people who follow them feel they will obtain liberation by listening to the words of these unenlightened preachers.

Because people have accepted the Brahmins as belonging to a high caste, they will often bow down at their feet and do devotion to them. But many of these Brahmins kill animals in sacrifice, having no real compassion in their hearts towards innocent creatures. When it comes to filling their bellies, they will happily eat at the home of a low caste person, yet at other times will hypocritically say they do not want to be touched by the 'untouchables.' Yet during the dark nights, some will deceptively go from house to house begging, which is considered a lowly action for a high caste person. They have the light (Vedas) in their hands, but still fall into the well of ignorance. They observe the fast of Ekadasi, the eleventh day of each lunar fortnight, but do not understand the real secret of that fasting. Instead, their minds are full of stories of spirits, ghosts, demons, and devils.

Kabīr says such people give up the camphor of true knowledge, and instead tie a knot of ignorance in their hearts, wandering foolishly from place to place. They think highly of themselves, but their actions betray their lack of nobility. Instead, they nurture the thieves of lust, anger, greed, attachments, and ego. They are even scornful of the true saints of God. Kabīr ends by saying such preachers are lustful for the tastes of the senses and are laying a path to hell.

Shabda 18

The attributes of God are different from the three qualities of satogun, rajogun, and tamogun (goodness, activity, and inertia)
How much can unthinking people understand of this, but knowledgeable people may understand it.
Many great souls like Ramchandra, who did great austerities, have confused this world.
Many like Krishna have come into this world, but they also could not fathom God's mystery.
They came in the form of fish, tortoise, and boar, and were also called the Dwarf.
Many like Buddha and Kalkī, who are said to be incarnations of Vishnu, did not fathom the mystery of God (Kalkī is yet to incarnate).
How many perfection seekers and sanyasis came, with many dwelling in the forests? How many munis and yogis like Gorakhnath came, and still did not fathom the mystery of God?
Even Brahmā could not know His attributes, and Shiva, Sanak and others were defeated in their search for Him.
Kabīr asks all the people: How can ordinary mortals know the greatness and glory of God when Brahmā, Shiva,

Sanak and others were defeated in the search?

Commentary: In this shabda Kabīr makes it clear that God is beyond all qualities and limitations. He is beyond space, time, and causation. He cannot be categorized as either good or evil, or as having form or no form. Whatever description we give of God, is of our own making, for God is beyond our thinking. We can only form our personal conceptions of who God is. Kabīr, however, states that God is the mysterious Universal Being beyond all qualities and limitations, and yet dwells intimately in the hearts of all. Those who are deep thinkers on this type of subject can form some opinion about who God is. God is not apparent to perceptive knowledge, but only to a subjective intuitive experience.

Kabīr lists many famous personalities of the past who are often worshipped as manifestations of God. These include Ramchandra of Ayodhya who did great austerities and lived in the jungle for fourteen years. He never claimed himself to be God, nor was he thought of as God, initially. Later on people made him an incarnation of God, and so Kabīr says he has confused the world. Similarly, personalities like Krishna have come with the qualities of human beings, subject to birth and death. Kabīr is saying God is beyond these limitations. The mythology of India states that God even came in the form of a fish, a tortoise, a boar, and a dwarf to save people from the various calamities that they faced. Similarly, many great personalities like Lord Buddha, and Kalkī who is to come, have not really fathomed the mystery of God. Actually, Lord Buddha avoided any discussion about God, but stressed goodness and compassion, and sought liberation from the bondage of karmas. Many holy people called munis, and many yogis, like the famous Gorakhnath, have practiced their austerities and yoga, but have not found the secret of God. Even Brahmā, who is supposed to be the creative aspect of God, and Shiva, the destructive aspect of God, and the sons of Brahmā, all accepted defeat in knowing the Eternal Being. Kabīr then asks the question: If such great personalities came and went without fathoming the secret of God, how can we who are mere mortals, understand the glory and the mystery of God?

We need to understand what Kabīr is telling us in this shabda. God is eternal, formless, and omnipresent. He is the embodiment of all knowledge and all power. He cannot be limited to a human or animal body, even when it is called an incarnation of God. God represents power, intelligence, and consciousness that are diffuse and pervasive throughout the universe. What qualities can we ascribe to such a power? In meditation, we try to have some concept of what that great power is, but we cannot, through logical reasoning, arrive at any conclusion about this 'Mysterious Being.'

Shabda 19

O soul, recite the glory of God, that glory which is beyond description and understanding.
He who is devoted to God, awakens from the night of ignorance to the dawn of knowledge.
The witch (Māyā) tries to control the dog (mind), while the lion (ego) runs rampant in the forest (world).
The five relatives (senses) engage in a fight, while battle music (desires) plays in abundance.
The deer (mind) drives all the doubts from the forest (heart), as the hunter (guru) aims and shoots the arrow of the Word.
The ocean of desires is burnt, as is the forest of passions. The fish (soul) then enjoys the game of hunting (removing doubts).
Kabīr says, listen seekers! He who can explain this verse and can sing it meaningfully, will gain liberation and will

liberate others.

Commentary: This again is one of the famous allegorical teachings of Kabīr in which he challenges people to explain the intricacies of the soul, the mind, the ego, the senses, and passions. He starts off by saying we should recite the glories of God, but that the glory is beyond description. It then necessitates an explanation of how one can recite what is indescribable. God is beyond description, and Kabīr has always taught that we cannot describe God, and that we have to realize Him. Elsewhere, he stated that if reciting the name of God could give liberation, then uttering the word sugar would make your mouth sweet, and saying water would quench your thirst. So singing the glories of God means going on an inner journey, and developing deep love for God who dwells within the heart of all beings. Kabīr states that if you are truly devoted to God, then all your ignorance, or darkness (night) will be removed, and knowledge will dawn in your consciousness.

Kabīr states that the witch (Māyā) is always trying to control the dog that is the mind. Meanwhile, ego remains in the hearts of all people. He also mentions five relatives – the five senses that keep the mind restless trying to satiate their particular tastes. These are figuratively driven by the plentiful battle music of desires. The deer is the mind that can drive out all doubts from the forest, that here represents the hearts of people, if they will submit to the arrows (words) of the Guru. The arrows are divine words and teachings imparted by a spiritual master to his disciple. Once this happens, Kabīr is saying the whole ocean of desires will be burnt, as will the forest of passions. The fish which here represents the soul, then enjoys the game of hunting – removing doubts and passions from the heart.

Kabīr, in his usual manner, challenges the audience he calls santo or saints, to explain this shabda. He says that, he who is able to explain it and understand it, will find liberation and will be able to liberate others from the bondage of Māyā.

The Bījak of Kabīr means exactly what is says, that is bījak or secret map that shows the way to hidden treasure. The hidden treasure here is God dwelling in the hearts of all people. But to realize this requires devotion and dedication. It requires understanding Māyā, the various sense objects and passions, the desires and the ego, that drive all people. These must be brought under control. Only then can the soul enjoy the liberation and bliss that are its eternal and essential nature.

Shabda 20

Only few people drink the nectar of God's love and obtain
a blissful life.
This bliss is like a wonderful juicy fruit that has no seed
and skin. The parrot enjoys the nectarine juice.
This nectar does not fall in drops, nor does it touch any
part of the body of the devotees who swarm like bees to
obtain it.
The Vedas are like a fruit tree bearing four fruits, of which
three are close and perishable. The fourth is far away, yet
desired by all, but rarely obtained with great effort.
Spring has vanished and summer has arrived, and the soul
unfortunately cannot again reach the tree of salvation.
Kabīr says the master is the ocean of bliss, and those absorbed in Him will obtain that bliss.

Commentary: In this shabda, Kabīr discusses the differences between those few fortunate devotees who will drink the bliss of God's love and obtain salvation, and those who swarm like bees to obtain nectar but cannot obtain it. The nectar here is bliss that is obtained by realizing God as the indwelling Soul. This is also salvation. Kabīr states those who drink the nectar of God's love will obtain this bliss. Figuratively, this bliss is like fruit that has no seed nor skin that need to be thrown away. Bliss is complete in itself. The parrot is the fortunate soul that drinks the nectar of bliss. The word *shuk* means parrot. It allegorically refers to Shukacharya who was a sage said to have realized God in the mother's womb. He had given up Māyā and attained bliss before birth.

Kabīr says many devotees swarm to religious and spiritual places, but not even a drop of the bliss falls on them to give them realization. He states that the scriptures have outlined four fruits – dharma, artha, kāma, and moksha (righteousness, wealth, fulfillment of desires, and liberation). The first three are really materialistic and perishable, but the fourth, liberation, is difficult to obtain even with great effort.

Kabīr states the spring season (youth) has departed and summer (old age and death) has arrived. The soul will not again have the opportunity to attain the state of bliss unless it is reborn, and struggles upward to obtain liberation. In conclusion, Kabīr states that the master (God) is really the very same ocean of bliss, and only those who are absorbed in Him will obtain the bliss.

God is said to be Existence, Consciousness, and Bliss Absolute. The soul is of the essence of God and, therefore, partakes of the same attributes. These attributes, however, are hidden from human consciousness because of ego, passions, and ignorance. Māyā deludes them. Few people, through intense devotion and longing for God-realization, will taste the bliss of that realization.

Shabda 21

What calamity has befallen you that you do not delight in God? What will you do when you are dying?

Some people go to pilgrimages and some shave their heads, while some give false mantras and doubtful instructions.

They study the Vedas but are full of ego. In the end they will bite the dust.
Through suffering and happiness you raise your family, but at the time of death you suffer alone.
Kabīr says that this is the Kaliyug, and it is full of evil. Whatever is inside the pitcher will come out from the spout.

Commentary: In this shabda, Kabīr explains that if we do not live in the love of God, we will die not having known the secret of our life. God is our source, and also our destination. If we do not know our destination, then we are truly lost in this world. He mentions that in an effort to live a religious life, many people go to places of pilgrimages, and many shave their heads. Many so-called teachers give doubtful instructions that do not give liberation to the seekers. Kabīr explains that many study the Vedas but are full of ego, and this is what accompanies them at death.

Kabīr also states that people, whether they are happy or suffering, raise their families but, in the end, die alone, for no one can help them. Kabīr says this is the Kaliyug (Iron Age) and that it is full of evils. He says that what is in the pitcher is what will come out from the spout. That is, what people are deep within themselves, that is what they will be at the time of death, and that is what will pursue them beyond death into another life. In this shabda, Kabīr explains that we must practice simplicity, sincerity, and purity in life. We must not be proud about what we are, nor should we follow practices that are of no practical value in terms of spiritual development. We must realize that God dwells in us, and go within to find Him. All external practices can be great obstacles towards reaching that spiritual goal which all religious people should seek.

Shabda 22

O ascetic, give up your imaginations!
Attain the state of perfect Self-realization (liberation), that Pārbrahm is different from other states.
In that state the Atma alone existed; there was no Mahadev nor Mohammed, nor was there Hari or Hazrat.
There was no Adam nor Brahmā, and there was neither sunlight nor shade.
Moreover, the eighty thousand prophets and eighty-eight thousand sages did not exist then. There was no existence of the moon, the sun, or the stars, nor the two manifestations of the fish and the tortoise.
There were no Vedas and Koran, no books of social laws, nor the principles of control, and there was no emperorship of the Muslims.
The Muslim prayers did not exist, nor did the turrets, the Namāz, and the Kalmā.
There was no incarnation of Rāma, nor did Khuda live in the seventh heaven.
There was no concept of beginning, end, or middle, and there was no fire, air, or water.
There was no existence of the 8.4 million forms of life, nor was there poetry, words, nor speech.
Kabīr says, listen to me, ascetics! Try to think about the state of existence that was prior to what is now called creation.
From where did the Supreme Brahm appear, and who created this artificial world?

Commentary: In this very mystical shabda, Kabīr talks about that original state before any manifestation of creation existed. This is the state in which the Soul, or God, existed in the very 'beginning,' but we must understand that there was no beginning as we ordinarily think of it. It was a state of pure consciousness. Kabīr is exhorting the ascetics to attain that state of consciousness that gives liberation, and which is different from all the other states of consciousness we see in the manifested world.

He further instructs the ascetics that they must try to realize that original unmanifested state (avyakta) in which the Soul was one with Pārbrahm, the Eternal Self-existent God of the Universe. In that state there was no Māyā – the power of projection into various forms. It was because of Māyā that God 'projected' Himself into the various manifestations Kabīr described. Kabīr is asking where that original Supreme Power called Brahm came from, and how this world created by the power of Māyā came into existence.

Kabīr was a mystic attuned to God in a state of supreme consciousness in which there was no duality, but only unity in the Divine Being. He is teaching that only realization of this original state of consciousness can free us from the illusions of Māyā and material bondage. It is this state of attainment that will give us perfect bliss.

Shabda 23

O seeker, the ways of God's Māyā are strange! They are inscrutable.
They can make a poor person into a king, but can also reduce a king to a beggar.
It is strange that a clove tree bears no fruit, and a sandalwood bears no flowers.
The fish (Māyā) hunts in the forest (world), and the lion (soul) swings to and fro in the ocean of desires.
The castor oil plant (devotee) can become a mountain of sandalwood (realized soul), and spread its fragrance all around.
One who is blind to desires can see this strange sport in

the three worlds, the universe, and the earth.
The lame person (man) climbs the Meru and Sumeru mountains and, achieving liberation, moves in the three worlds.
The self-realized person speaks of worldly and spiritual knowledge, and of the divine melody of God.
God's Māyā can tie the firmament and send it to hell, and place the hell-dwelling serpent, Sheshnag, as ruler in heaven.
Kabīr says God is the supreme ruler, and whatever he does is right.

Commentary: In this shabda, Kabīr talks about the powers of Māyā that appear strange according to human perception. All things and events that take place in the world are the products of Māyā. Māyā arises from the power of God that allows God to manifest in all forms. There are many contradictory situations in the world that can be reconciled only if we consider the power of Māyā. Kabīr gives the example of the clove tree that bears flowers but no fruit because the clove itself is the flower. Similarly, the sandalwood tree gives neither flowers nor fruit, but yields a beautiful fragrance. He figuratively explains that Māyā roams around the forest of this world and makes the soul rock back and forth according to the desires that rise up in the mind. Māyā can also transform a simple disciple into one who has attained spiritual heights, which is here compared to a mountain of sandalwood. A person who is blind to desires, that is, has control over his passions and senses, can figuratively sit back and watch this play of Māyā as it keeps the world in its clutches.

Kabīr says that a lame person can climb the mountain, which means that a mind that was previously undeveloped, can develop to reach great heights and obtain liberation. Such a person can then move about freely everywhere. But Kabīr also adds that the person who is self-realized does not speak much, but is full of spiritual wisdom, and hears the divine melody of God within.

For God nothing is impossible. That which we call heaven, can be sent to the nether world, and the mythological serpent, Sheshnag, that is said to be supporting the Earth, and thus, is figuratively in hell, can be made to dwell in heaven. Kabīr summarizes that God is the Supreme Ruler of the universe, and that everything happens because of His Māyā. It is His will that manifests in the universe.

In this shabda, Kabīr is teaching us that Māyā manifests in strange ways and can fool us. We must develop spiritual insight and realize the true knowledge of the Self that will give us liberation from the bondage of desires, cravings, materialism, and false perceptions.

Shabda 24

O seeker! The yogi who can explain the mystery of this poem will be my guru.
There is a tree standing without roots, and without producing flowers, bears fruits.
It has no branches and no leaves, yet it thunders upon reaching the eighth sky.
The tree's flower petals have no form, and the gourd is produced without a flowering.
There is a song of God's glory sung without a tongue. Its singer has no form and no outline, but if found, a Satguru can make Him visible.
There are two ways of approaching the Supreme – the path of the bird, or of the fish, and Kabīr says both are difficult.
The Supreme Being is fathomless, and I am a sacrifice to Him.

Commentary: This shabda is one of the many allegorical

teachings of Kabīr. In order to understand it, we will need to understand the references used. The tree is the tree of meditation that has no roots. This tree bears the fruit of bliss, but there is no necessity for flowers to precede the fruit. It has no branches nor leaves, but it reaches the eighth sky. The eighth sky is a symbol for the eighth chakra, being one above the seventh chakra of traditional yoga teachings. This eighth chakra is called surati chakra or unmuni chakra. The thundering heard in it is the anāhad nād, or divine melody, that the devotee hears when he reaches this highest state in meditation.

Chakras are generally represented as lotus flowers. But Kabīr says that the petals of this eighth chakra have no form, and that the fruit of it is realized without a need for flowers. When one is in the meditative state and the eighth chakra is awakened, he does not need a tongue with which to sing the glories of God. One is in an inner realization, a state of bliss that amounts to singing the glories of God. It is a state in which there is no form or outline of realization, for God has no form. But if one has a true Satguru, he can be helped to realize the formless God.

Kabīr says there are two ways one can approach God-realization. The first is the way of birds flying free in the air. This relates to the mind that can rise above all the material aspects of life, and float into the vast infinity of God Consciousness. The second is the way of the fish. Just as the fish cannot live without water, just so the true devotee cannot live without God and has an intense longing for God-realization. Kabīr says both of these paths are difficult for the average person to follow. A devotee must have dedication and perseverance, and follow the instructions of the Guru in order to reach the highest state of meditation in which he realizes the formless God that is manifesting in the whole universe. Kabīr concludes that the mystery of this most exalted Supreme Being is fathomless, and cannot be understood by any rational or intellectual exercise.

Shabda 25

O ascetic, great personalities have been absorbed in the great Truth. In that Truth musical instruments dance, while the wedding party is being played.
The bridegroom sits above his wedding crown. This union of the soul and God is difficult to explain.
The people sitting in the marriage hall attained a balanced intellect, seeing that the son had married the mother.
The bride sits in the polished square, where she becomes aware of the fearless abode.
The rice turns around and eats up the wedding guests. This is a very beneficial achievement.
The handholding ceremony was performed, birth became justified, and meditation became absorbed in sushumna.
Kabīr says, listen O saints, O pandits! Please consider this teaching.

Commentary: In this shabda, Kabīr speaks in his familiar allegorical style. This shabda can be interpreted in different ways, but the following explanation is a reasonable one, given the mystic intent of Kabīr.

People who practice meditation and are burning with the desire to realize God are great personalities, once they have realized that union. When they have achieved that union, they are blissful, and the instruments, which are their sense organs, dance for joy while the wedding guests, or souls, are being played. This means they are in a blissful state. The bridegroom is the soul, and the crown atop his head, but on which he sits, is God-realization. Kabīr says the nature of this union of the soul and God is difficult to explain, because people often think it is only fanciful thinking.

In any wedding there is a mandap, or a wedding platform on

which the wedding party sits. The wedding party are the senses, mind, ego, and intellect. They all become balanced and attain a blissful harmony. The son marries the mother which means that the son (soul) marries meditation that is, figuratively, the bride. The bride is sitting in the polished open chowk, which means meditation is not hidden, and the person realizing union is fearless and attains that abode of fearlessness which is union with God.

Kabīr also says the rice turns around and eats the wedding party. Here the rice means meditation and the wedding party again are the souls. Souls lose their identity when they merge with God, a state of being that is truly a great achievement. When the handholding ceremony takes place, indicating the soul and God are united, then the birth of such realized souls is justified. Meditation enters into that channel of God-realization called sushumna. This results in liberation of the soul from karmic bondage. Kabīr is challenging the learned pandits to consider what he is saying.

Kabīr is speaking in parables because it is difficult to understand what God-realization is, and what the union of the soul and God is. So he uses material examples, such as a bride and bridegroom getting married, or sense organs dancing in rapture. He is, as always, saying we must attain this state so we can be freed from the bondage of karmas.

Shabda 26

O brother, what is the use of much talking? There is hardly anyone who is our friend.
God is the power that creates, destroys, and beautifies, so remain as God wishes to keep you.
By the practice of asanas, pranayamas, hatha yoga, and study of the Srutis and Smritis, and astrology, people have become confused.

People have been preoccupied with the six philosophies and ninety-six hypocrisies. They have not acquired the art of surrendering to God.

They have wandered throughout the world, but have not obtained the art of Self-realization.

They give up their homes, and people consider them highly evolved, yet their minds cannot be concentrated.

Kabīr says the hope of salvation of such yogis and wandering sanyasis is weak.

If you recite the name of God with concentration, as the chatrik bird does concentrating on the moon, then definitely you will have devotion in your heart.

Commentary: It is a common occurrence in the world that people keep talking about spiritual life and religion, but not much is attained from such practice. Attainment results only when the teachings are put into practice. This is why Kabīr is asking what the point of much talking is. People do not often like to hear the truth because 'the truth hurts.' It is for this reason that people who did not understand the message, persecuted the saints. Kabīr tells people that God is responsible for their lives – for their creation, destruction, and beautification. In fact, the same applies to the whole universe. The wise instruction is therefore to be content, and to live as God wishes, surrendering to His will.

Many people believe that they will obtain God-realization by practicing various yoga asanas (postures) of Hatha yoga, and by studying the Vedas and social laws and astrology. But these cause confusion, as people do not often practice the good that is taught in them. The path to God is straightforward. One need not get into all forms of argumentative philosophies and hypocrisies often taught by religious people. The secret is to obtain the art of surrendering to God.

Sometimes people wander throughout the world for religious

purposes, yet God-realization escapes them. There are many who are held in high respect because they have abandoned their homes, and have become wandering monks, or learned people. But Kabīr says their minds are still not concentrated enough to realize Divinity. He says their hope for salvation is indeed weak. As a solution for God-realization, Kabīr says we must surrender to and concentrate on God. He uses the mythological image of the chatrik bird that longingly concentrates on the moon. If a devotee concentrates on God intently, then he will have devotion in his heart. All the other religious practices fall short of this simple goal.

Shabda 27

O brother, it is said God's form is matchless and mysterious. If I speak about it, who will believe.
Wherever I glance I see His form; He pervades every heart.
He is neither happy with wealth nor unhappy with poverty. He is sleepless but remains happy.
He has fame and beauty without light, and is a lover without form. Without this jewel, ignorant people cry sadly.
In Self-realization, my doubt disappears, and the testing occurs without jewels.
Without form God manifests all forms. Without concentration He is in meditation, and is blissful without mystic experience. He possesses a matchless nature.
Kabīr says, in this world, God is like a diamond. Think carefully and understand this.
Give up the greed of wealth and attachment to relations, and recite the name of God.

Commentary: In this shabda, Kabīr talks about the nature of God. God is not limited by time and space, so He is said to be of mysterious and matchless form. No one can truly describe God, yet He manifests in the hearts of all beings. Kabīr asks who would believe him if he talked about God because God is not part of the direct experience of the lives of most people. But not having Him as a precious jewel in their lives, people suffer a great loss, and so are said to be sadly crying. Once God is realized, there are no doubts or troubles in the mind.

Kabīr says wherever he looks, he sees God because God is Omnipresent. One needs only develop a spiritual vision in order to see God. Although God has no form, God is manifest in all forms in the universe. Kabīr goes on to say God is beyond wealth and poverty, or the need for sleep. He needs no light to show His fame or beauty, and is always blissful. God does not need to concentrate in order to go into meditation, as His very nature is one of meditation. His nature is one of bliss that is matchless and is beyond all description.

Kabīr says that God is like a precious diamond that needs to be coveted and kept securely. He advises that we must consider this carefully, and see God as this precious diamond. In order to realize this precious jewel in our own hearts, we need to give up the greed for other kinds of wealth, and even attachment to family relationships, because they create bondage and prevent the liberation of the soul. This does not mean not having love for relationships and for people, but it means cultivating a detached, spiritual love. Once we obtain this, we will indeed feel a sense of freedom.

Shabda 28

O brother, Brahmā (creator) has produced a cow. Her immense weight is unbearable.
She drinks the water of nine streams (types of worship), but still her thirst is not quenched.
She has seventy-two rooms (nerve divisions) at her dis-

posal, all with strong doors.
She is tied to a peg with a strong rope, but even then she breaks loose and runs away.
She has four trees (Vedas), six branches (philosophies), and eighteen leaves (Purānas).
She has eaten up all these, yet remains dissatisfied, and wanders about everywhere.
She has seven divisions of hell and seven of heaven, along with nine and fourteen other parts (nine body portals and fourteen body parts).
This cow has eaten up everything. Even then she remains unsatisfied.
She is pursuing fulfillment and has horns of no colour.
She is neither with caste nor is she casteless.
She eats both the inedible and the edible.
Brahmā and Vishnu searched for her, so did Shiva and the sons of Brahmā.
Countless adepts have searched for her, but none of them have found this cow.
Kabīr says listen dear ones! Who is there who can explain this poem? He who sings this song and understands its meaning will obtain Nirvānā.

Commentary: This shabda is another of Kabīr's allegorical poems in which he explains certain mystical teachings using symbolic images. Brahmā is the creator of the world, and the cow he produced is Māyā. It is the power of Māyā that has enabled all phenomena in the universe to become differentiated from the primordial undifferentiated Universal Being. Māyā thus has the power of being veiled under the guise of the apparent.

The nine streams are the nine types of worships explained in the scriptures. The seventy-two rooms are the seventy-two nerve divisions said to be in the body. The strong door is the mind. The peg is also the mind, and the strong rope is the will. But all of these prove to be useless before the power of Māyā.

Māyā is also the source of the four trees (Vedas) and the six branches or philosophies of India. The eighteen leaves are the eighteen Purānas that are scriptures of India. Through her power, Māyā has swallowed all of these yet remains unsatisfied, and still wanders about. Although people have mastered all the scriptures, because of Māyā, they remain restless because they have not found the precious gem for which they are looking.

The seven divisions spoken of are the seven 'netherworlds' and seven 'heavens' according to mythology. The nine parts represent the nine portals of the body, and the fourteen are the five organs of sense and five of action, the mind, intellect, consciousness, and ego. Māyā has, figuratively, eaten up all of these, but remains unsatisfied. All of these aspects of creation are under the control of Māyā for they are products of Māyā. However, Māyā is still engaged in the pursuit of all desires. This is the state of affairs of humanity.

Māyā is said to have horns of no colour meaning Māyā has no colour, caste, race, clan and so forth. The edible and inedible that Māyā consumes is an indication that Māyā does not discriminate between what is right and lawful, and what is wrong and unlawful. Because of this undiscriminating power of Māyā, people are engaged in all types of activities, whether negative or positive.

Kabīr says that the three gods of the trinity – Brahmā, Vishnu and Shiva – along with the sons of Brahmā, have all searched for the secret of Māyā, but they have not been able to uncover it. This is because they are themselves the products of Māyā and, therefore, cannot fathom the cause of their own being. Similarly, countless adepts have searched for the secret of Māyā, but they also have not been able to find it. Kabīr is saying one should try to understand the meaning of this shabda and, in addition, contemplate it, and sing it. If one understands this shabda and its inner meaning, then he is on his way to Nirvānā.

Shabda 29

O brother! If the lover truly awakens and opens his eyes, then his mind will become attached to Pārbrahm – the Unfathomable and Eternal Being.
How can the craving people, intoxicated with thirst for the world, find contentment?
They are intoxicated with lust and anger, and Māyā supplies them the drinks of passions in abundance. Brahmā himself is the winemaker who prepared the wine of all the desires and the senses.
They keep company with evil but speak of knowledge. Only the shrewd one will find God.
In this Kaliyug there are plenty of miseries and anxieties, and many diseases that afflict the body.
Kabīr says that place where a man has patience, depth, and steadfastness, go there and meet him.

Commentary: People in this world appear to be afflicted with 'tons' of cravings and desires for worldly things. They appear to be intoxicated with an unquenchable thirst that keeps them pursuing one thing or another, in an attempt to fulfill their desires. Once they are caught up in this type of activity, how can they find contentment in their lives? Kabīr uses the image of a person intoxicated with wine. He craves more wine until he becomes addicted or he loses consciousness. He is no longer in control of his senses. Similarly, the person who is intoxicated with lust, anger, and cravings for worldly things, does not have control over his mind. Conversely, Kabīr says if the lover of God awakens to his spiritual potential, then his mind will be absorbed in Pārbrahm, the Supreme Being. That Supreme Being dwells within one's own heart and that is where He must be realized through loving devotion, and the development of spiritual wisdom.

In this shabda Brahmā represents rajogun or the principle of passion and activity that are part of our being, and which need to be controlled. Without control this principle seeks gratification of all the senses. This makes life restless, and keeps us from realizing the divinity that resides within.

What some people do, instead, is seek out and keep evil and lowly company, indulge in undesirable activities, and yet still speak of divine knowledge. They are content to merely use words without any realization of Divinity. But one who is shrewd in spiritual matters, is one who seeks out and realizes the indwelling Divinity. Kabīr observes that in this Kaliyug (Iron Age), people are afflicted with various types of mental and physical suffering. They are not able to escape because they do not have the self-control and proper spiritual direction in their lives. He advises the people to seek out the place where there is a person with patience, spiritual depth, and steadfastness, then go there and meet that person in order to emulate their qualities.

We need to understand that all worldly pleasures are transitory and, at best, give us only momentary happiness and, at worst, keep us trapped in a merry-go-round of sense gratifications, frustrations, and anxieties. It is only when we have awakened to spiritual life that we attain everlasting contentment and happiness.

Shabda 30

O my dear brother! Where did two gods come from? Tell me who has caused this confusion?

Allah, Rāma, Karim, Keshav, Hari, and Hazrat are the names given to Him.

Gold is the same in all gold jewelry. There is no other element in it.

For the sake of speaking and hearing, they established two methods, one is namāz and the other is pujā. They both adore the same God.

The same one is called Mahadev and Mohammed or Brahmā and Adam.
Who can be said to be a Hindu and who a Turk (Muslim)? They both live on the same Earth.
These read the book of the Vedas and those read the Koran. They are called mullahs and those others are called pandits.
They variously got different names, but they are all pots of the same clay.
These kill the goat and those kill the cow and, in vain, both are wasting their lives.
Kabīr says both of them are mistaken, for neither has found God.

Commentary: Historically, it is known that there has been much dissension, intolerance, and misunderstanding in India between Hindus and the invading Muslims. This had gone on for centuries by the time Kabīr arrived on the scene. Each religion held to its own practices and beliefs, and excluded the other. Kabīr is asking them that since God is one, who caused this confusion that one calls God by the name of Rāma and the other by the name of Allah? He also points out other names that are given to God such as Krishna, Mahadev, and Vishnu by the Hindus, and Allah, Karim, and Hazrat by the Muslims. These names are given to the same Supreme Being who is without any religion, or shall we say, beyond religion.

Kabīr uses the analogy of various forms of jewelry made from the same gold. They would not have different elements in them. Just so, no matter what names we give to the Supreme Being, He remains the same everywhere, and accessible to all people. Just so, all people are made of the same matter and spirit. Kabīr goes on to say Mahadev, Mohammed, Brahmā, and Adam really refer to the same being for though the names are different, the spirit dwelling in all of them is the same. Therefore, why fight over differences in names, when in essence they are all the same being, just as the element of gold is the same in every form of jewelry.

Kabīr asks what is the use of saying one is a Hindu and the other a Muslim when both are living on, and are nurtured by the same Earth. Their needs are all the same, as they are all human beings, and should not create artificial differences and cause confusion. He observes that Hindus read the Vedas and Muslims read the Koran. The former are called pandits and the latter are called mullahs. He says though they appear to be different, both of them are mistaken and are upholding the wrong principles, and that neither of them have obtained God. In their search for God, both of them are wasting their lives by committing violent deeds killing animals. On this subject we need to bring in the law of karma. If people sacrifice the lives of innocent animals, they have to pay for it. This means they cannot obtain liberation. Similarly, if they keep on fighting among themselves in the name of religion, scriptures, doctrines and so forth, they are also wasting their lives and cannot attain liberation.

Shabda 31

The swan is cut by the knife of doubts, while the cow milks and drinks the milk of the calf.
In every house the wild animal hunts, while the hunter takes shelter hiding.
The fish is suffering in the water, and dust is creating waves.
The earth is raining and the clouds are getting wet, while the rocks are swimming.
The swan flies away as the pond dries up, yet it wishes to keep its feet in the mud.
As long as you have the use of your arms and legs, do not have hopes on any one else.

Kabīr says if you see one who is not following what he preaches, then do not take his advice.

Commentary: This shabda is one of Kabīr's famous ulta-bani or contrary style language that he uses to get people to think deeply about spiritual truths. The topic of the shabda is how the soul becomes destroyed by doubts when it gets under the influence of false gurus. The soul, in truth, is always residing in the ocean of God's love, but under the influence of false gurus, it is cut up or destroyed by doubts.

The cow Kabīr refers to is Māyā, and the calf is the soul. Māyā (illusion) is cheating the soul and figuratively drinking the milk of the calf. The wild animal (mind) without good thinking is hunting the hunter (soul) that tries to take shelter in various deities. The fish is the soul that, though living in the ocean of God's love, is still suffering because the dust (desires), rises up as waves in the ocean.

The earth that is raining is speech, the cloud is the soul, and the rocks are hypocrisies. The soul gets confused with the words of the false teachers, and this causes hypocrisies to prevail everywhere in the water, figuratively swimming. Though it tries to reach above, the soul is bound with desires and wishes to stay in the world, thus keeping the feet in the mud. But the soul must fly away from the pond of the body, and the body will dry up or becomes useless. Kabīr advises not depend on others as long as you have the use of your arms and legs. He further states you should not accept the teachings of those who do not live according to what they preach.

The essential message in this shabda is to be aware that there are false teachers and there are hypocrisies. Without obtaining true teachings, the soul can get trapped by the waves of desires, and remain trapped in this world and facing the need to be reborn over and over according to its desires. It is thus deprived of liberation. One must therefore obtain the true teachings and become free.

Shabda 32

You are a pure soul! Therefore, realize quickly that the false gurus have created many hypocrisies.
They created hypocrisies from the three gunas (qualities), and the whole world is drowning in them.
If the king who is master of the house becomes a butcher, then what can the other poor people do?
Those who do not know devotion are being called devotees. Yet they have given up the nectar and are partaking of poison. In this way their leaders (false gurus) have drowned. They did not heed my warning.
Accept my advice and tie it into a strong knot. Remain alert day and night.
In this Kaliyug (Iron Age) these gurus are quite hypocritical, and have cheated the world.
They have created a noose out of the Vedas and other scriptures, and have themselves become trapped in it.
Kabīr says the soul will not be lost once it has found a true guru as liberator.

Commentary: In this shabda, Kabīr gives a warning that there are many false gurus who have created hypocrisies, and have fooled innocent people. It is common knowledge that many people held in high esteem as leaders of religions are often betraying their teachings and followers. Although it appears that Kabīr is being very blunt in stating these hypocrisies, and criticizing these teachers, we must realize that he was a realized guru and was speaking from that vantage point of awareness and instructing people to be aware of false gurus.

Many people in the world innocently convey great honour to false gurus who say that they are great. Many of these false gurus are quite conversant with the Vedas and scriptures, but have not lived the essence of the true spiritual teachings. In fact, they make a noose out of these scriptures. They do not not realize the fundamental truth of God as the ever-present Master in the hearts of all beings. Many are still caught in the trap of passions and ego. How then can they be able to free others. They are themselves caught in the noose that they created and, unfortunately, innocent people also become their victims. Kabīr says the soul that obtains a true guru who is indeed a liberator will be liberated from the bondage of the passions and illusions of material existence.

In this shabda Kabīr is instructing us to use our own innate ability to decide right from wrong, true from false so we can be aware of false gurus and their teachings. Unless we use our intellectual ability properly, we will fall under the sway of false spiritual teachers.

Shabda 33

O dear soul! Where will you go when you leave this lake (body)?
In this lake you are plucking pearls of knowledge and, in many ways, are enjoying your life.
When you depart from this lake it will dry up, and the lotus leaves and flowers will wither.
Kabīr says if you become separated from this lake now, when will you again get such an opportunity?

Commentary: In this shabda Kabīr is comparing the body to a lake. Just as the lotus leaves and flowers are in the lake, just so the senses dwell in this body. The lotus represents the senses. While we have this body we are able to enjoy many things in life. We are also able to glean pearls of wisdom if we care to do so. However, we often neglect these pearls of wisdom to our own detriment.

When old age creeps up, and the body dies, then all the lotus leaves and flowers will dry up along with it. The senses, the mind and all pleasures vanish. If we did not obtain wisdom and liberation in this life, Kabīr asks when we will again have such an opportunity.

Life is a precious gift and is meant for spiritual evolution. Our consciousness must evolve to such a state that we can obtain realization of the divinity dwelling in all beings. We need to use this gift of life wisely and not squander it and figuratively become like a dry lake with dead lotus flowers.

Shabda 34

Godly people move about as hansas (pure, unattached).
They utter the pure name of God with great love, choosing it from many other words.
They extend the beak (mind) to pluck the pearls of wisdom. They remain silent or sing the glories of God.
They reside on the bank of the Mansarovar lake (heart). Their mind is attached to the feet of God, and remains unattached to other places.
Evil thoughts of the crow do not come near them, and day after day they have the vision of hansas (pure souls).
They can discriminate between water and milk (bad and good). Kabīr says these are the ones dear to me.

Commentary: In this shabda, Kabīr is speaking about the pure devotees who move about in the world unattached to worldly things. Their minds are attached to the name of God and purity. The hansā is the swan and is used symbolically to portray the pure soul that is on its journey to God. Mythologically, the swan is supposed to be able to pluck pearls from the Mansarovar lake. Pearls represent wisdom, primarily spiritual wisdom needed to awaken to a spiritual consciousness. The beak represents the mind of such a devotee that is eager to pluck such spiritual gems. Such devotees tend to remain silent, rather than engage in useless talk. Whenever they speak, they utter words of wisdom for the welfare of others.

According to Kabīr, such devotees live on the bank of the Mansarover lake, as the swans do. The Mansarovar lake is a symbolic reflection of the heart. This means that the mind of such a devotee is turned towards the inward contemplation of the reality of God residing within. It can thus be said their mind is attached to the feet of God and unattached to things in the world.

The crow is known to eat carrion and to make a raucous noise. A devotee of God avoids the evil thoughts of the crow (eating carrion, being noisy) and seeks the company of pure souls. By developing their minds in this way and remaining close to God, the pure souls are able to discriminate between the good and the bad so they can walk the righteous path. Kabīr affirms that these are the kind of people dear to him.

Shabda 35

God is my husband, and I am his beloved wife. God is older, and I am younger.
God is my spinning wheel, and I am His roll of cotton. Taking the name of God, I spin the cotton into yarn.
I spin the thread for six months, and make a fabric in a year, and the people say that beautiful wife spins well.
Kabīr says you have spun a fine thread (of God's name), but the spinning wheel is not the means of salvation.

Commentary: In this shabda, Kabīr is concerned about people who keep on repeating the name of God. First of all, he says that the devotee is the wife of God. This accords with mystical language because the soul is often thought of as the bride, and God as the husband. The goal is for two to be united as in a marriage. Since God precedes the soul, God is said to be the older and the soul the younger. The soul, having entered a physical body, begins to worship God in some particular religion. In the case of this shabda the worship is the repetition of God's name. This repetition is similar to the spinning of the spinning wheel that makes the yarn for weaving cloth.

One may spin a beautiful thread for six months, and make a fabric in a year, figuratively the repetition of God's name or mantras to try to obtain liberation. But this does not give liberation. Observers may say the person repeating God's name is indeed a very noble person, and worthy of adoration, but Kabīr says the mere repetition of the name of God is not the means of liberation, as many religious teachers say. If such liberation was possible, then repeating the word 'sugar' would sweeten the mouth. Life must be purified in every respect, and noble qualities must be consciously developed along with the repetition of God's name. Only in this way can liberation be made possible.

Shabda 36

The deluded mind uses the name of God to cheat the world. O brother, how can you live with this separation from God?
Who is whose husband, and who is whose wife?
The story of Yama (death) is inexplicable and it has spread its cruel vision everywhere.
Who is whose son, and who is whose father? Who dies and who suffers?
Through repetitive cheating the mind has robbed capital (knowledge of the soul) from everyone. No one could recognize that the mind was cheating them of the wealth of God.

Kabīr says, understand that the mind is the cheater. This cheating disappears when one recognizes the cheater.

Commentary: In this shabda Kabīr speaks of the network of delusion created by the mind. We all know that the mind plays tricks on all of us. When it comes to religious or spiritual practices, the mind becomes more prone to deception since it is dealing with subjects it has not experienced. It is a rare spiritually developed person who experiences God, and the nature of the soul. The majority of people practice their religious duties but do not fathom the secret of God. They use the name of God and, without knowing it, are being deprived of the real treasure that the name of God offers. They often delude other people, thus robbing them of the ultimate spiritual knowledge that they could obtain.

People spend time arguing about God and religion, about karma and its effects, about gods and goddesses, about rites and rituals, and about doctrines and dogmas. All of these diversions are machinations of the mind. The common denominator is that there is God called by different names. There is also the soul that is in intimate communion with God, if the veil of ignorance is removed. However, the veil of ignorance exists because of the cunning and lack of spiritual enlightenment of the mind. In other words, people preach their 'half-baked' philosophies to others with the result that no one becomes enlightened.

It sounds far-fetched when Kabīr asks what appear to be absurd questions about who is whose husband and who is whose wife, who is whose son and who is whose father, who dies and who suffers. These are rhetorical questions. They either deserve an answer based on spiritual insight, or they need no answer. From the spiritual angle, the answer is quite simple. The soul is the same whether it is in a husband or a wife, a son or a father, or in any other person. The relationships are only external, and only have relevance with the body, the mind, and the intellect. These have little to do with the soul that is always the spirit dwelling in the hearts of all beings. The soul neither dies nor suffers, but when the soul takes on a body and is 'born,' it is the body and mind that suffer.

Kabīr says it is necessary to introspect and understand that the mind is a cheater, unless it is controlled and made to meditate on the nature of the soul and divinity. Without this attainment, the mind cheats one of one's capital, or the divine knowledge of the soul and God. If one understands that the mind is the cheater, he is then able to control it, and direct it inwards to the spirit. Then one has the opportunity to remove one's self from the clutches of the cycle of death and rebirth awaiting all. Metaphysical teaching is concerned with the mind, the intellect, the consciousness, the soul and God. These are realized through the process of introspection, allowing for an inner realization of their nature, and of the intimate union that exists between the soul and God. Removal of the veil of ignorance perpetrated by the mind is all that is necessary.

Shabda 37

O mind, you are a cheater and you silently move around cheating the whole world! You do not even tell me of your departure (death).
You have been my friend since infancy. Giving me up, where are you rushing to in a hurry.
You are my husband and I am your wife, but your conduct is heavier than a stone.
The gross body is made of clay, and the subtle body of air.
Kabīr says the devotee is wary of the thief cheating the world.

Commentary: As in the previous shabda, Kabīr points out that the mind is the cheater that keeps on cheating the world and that it does so silently. One's ego and evil intentions lurk within one's self. Similarly, hypocrisy is hidden within one's self. In all of these it is the mind that is working silently. The cheating is that the mind works in stealthy and devious ways to distract the devotee from his proper path of purity, simplicity, love, and devotion, which is the path leading to enlightenment. Kabīr says that the mind has been a friend from birth, meaning the body and the mind go together, but the mind appears to always be in a hurry running in one direction or another. At the end of life, the mind withdraws from the body leaving a corpse; all of its cheating resulting only in negative karmas.

Kabīr says the mind is the husband and the body is the wife because the body obeys the commands of the mind. But the body says that the conduct of the mind is heavier than a stone. The helpless body, being personified, realizes that the conduct of the mind is contrary to its well being and thus, figuratively, is heavier than a stone weighing it down to the world of materialism. Kabīr says the gross body is made of clay, but the subtle or astral body is transparent like the air, and that both are subject to the cheating of the mind. The true devotee is wary of the mind. The devoted seeker practices introspection to understand his inner tendencies and the wayward wanderings of the mind, and tries to control them. It is control of the mind that allows discipline and development of positive ideals leading to spirituality.

Shabda 38

O evil man! Without God, doubts have ensnared you in many difficulties.
Wherever you go you lose your self, since doubts have you trapped in their snares.
The yogi says yoga is the best, and that there is nothing else equal to it.
Those who pluck the hair, shave the head, remain silent,

or wear matted hair, tell me, how are they going to get perfection?

The intellectual, the noble, the brave, the poets and the altruists, each of them say they are the greatest.

Wherever they came from (birth), that is where they will go (death). In a moment they will leave everything.

Give up the defects of the 'left-handed' and 'right-handed' paths, and obtain realization of God.

Kabīr asks, how can the dumb person, after eating sugar, describe its taste?

Commentary: In this shabda, Kabīr is speaking of doubts that cause difficulty for people all over the world. Unless a person is clear-sighted about his spiritual course, he faces difficulties according to the dictates of various traditions, dogmas, scriptures, rituals, and practices. Spiritual life is a simple and straightforward path, free of doubts. Kabīr says people are losing themselves going here and there, because doubts keep following them and entrapping them. Kabīr gives a few examples such as the yogi who praises yoga and says there is nothing greater than his path. Similarly, there are those who pluck their hairs, shave their heads, practice silence, or wear matted hair who claim the same thing. Kabīr asks how such practices can enable them to reach a state of perfection.

External activities, when not accompanied by purity and discipline of the mind, cannot bring perfection, even if done by people who are intellectuals, noble and brave, or by poets and altruists. Any pride in performing such external religious activities is a manifestation of the ego. Spiritual teaching is to do these things with humility. How many people who perform such religious practices are really humble?

Kabīr says we need to realize that we have been born and we will die, and leave everything here in an instant. These include all of our misguided activities, ego, possessions, and pride. He advises us to give up the two paths that are pursuing the 'left-hand' path (vām marga), or the 'right-hand' path (dakshin marga). The former is the Epicurian ideal of indulging the passions, eating, drinking, and making merry. The second is the Stoic path of self-discipline, and following a religious tradition. The true spiritual path is actually neither of these, for it is focused on inner growth and realization of the Divinity within. Kabīr illustrates this with the example of the dumb person who eats sugar and enjoys the taste, but is not able to explain it to others. Just so the person who realizes God enjoys immense bliss, but is not able to explain it to others. It is for this reason that realized saints remain silent or speak very little. Often they speak in parables because there is no language available to explain the infinite experience that is entirely subjective and indescribable.

Kabīr says we should follow the true spiritual path that is devoid of all external show and ego. Only this path can reach the abode of God.

Shabda 39

Worldly people fettered by illusion, fight furiously with God and His devotees.
How can the water snake get hold of the eagle?
What friendship can there be between the mouse and cat?
How can the jackal defeat the lion?
I see a great marvel in the world where the dog is chasing the elephant and its rider.
Kabīr says, listen brother saints! Rarely does anyone realize this state of union with God.

Commentary: In this shabda, Kabīr speaks of the spiritually ignorant people opposing those devoted to God. The meaning of the people fighting furiously with God is that they are deluded by the power of Māyā. They are deluded by false doctrines, and are under the sway of hypocritical teachers. When a true saint imparts divine teachings, such people are not willing to accept them. On the contrary, they set up obstacles for the saint and will even endeavour to destroy him. Kabīr sometimes points out that when he speaks the truth, people want to believe lies and want to beat him.

Kabīr uses a few examples of incompatible life forms just as the spiritually ignorant people (manmukh) are incompatible with the devotees (gurmukh) of God. He asks how the water snake can get hold of the garuda bird (eagle). The garuda is known to kill snakes. Similarly, how can there be friendship between a mouse and a cat? The mouse represents foolish people, and the cat the spiritually wise. Or again, he asks how the jackal can defeat the lion. The lion, representing the saintly person, can physically be destroyed, but his saintliness goes with him. Again, he speaks about the dog barking and chasing the elephant with its rider. What can the dog do to the elephant rider who is so high up? It is indeed a wonder how foolish people, like the barking dog, try to destroy saintly people.

Kabīr continually gives instruction that we must not behave like foolish people, putting blindfolds over our eyes and refusing to see the truth revealed to us. We must use our intelligence and have an open mind to recognize the truth that is taught to us by the great spiritual teachers.

Shabda 40

O pandit! All your rhetoric is false!
If by saying God the world could get liberation, then repeating 'sugar, sugar' would make the mouth sweet.
If by saying fire your feet could get burned, then saying water would quench your thirst.
If by saying food your hunger could be satisfied, then the

whole world would become free of hunger.
The parrot, in the company of man, may chant God's name, but that does not mean it understands God's glory.
If perchance it flew into the jungle, it would not have any recollection of God.
Without realizing God, what can one obtain by the empty repetition of His name?
If the repetition of wealth could make one wealthy, then no one would remain poor.
People have profound love for passions and Māyā, and quickly hang the true lovers of God.
Kabīr says that without realization of God, people are heading to the abode of death in a state of bondage.

Commentary: It is fashionable among religious people to say that the repetition (sumiran) of the name of God gives salvation. Many people actually make this their life's goal. But the truth is that people must realize God in order to obtain true liberation. Kabīr gives many examples to show that the mere repetition of a name does not give the realization of what is named. By repeating the word sugar no one tastes sugar, by repetition of fire no one gets his foot burned, and by saying water no one gets his thirst quenched. If they really did, then the mere repetition of the name of God would also give salvation.

Kabīr gives the example of the parrot that can be taught to repeat the name of God, but which still has no conception of what it is saying. If that same parrot flew into the jungle, it would soon forget to say God. It would be like every other parrot without any knowledge of God. Just so, there are people who repeat the name of God without knowing or seeking to know God. Such repetition does not give the people liberation.

Kabīr asks what you would gain by the mere repetition of God's name, if you do not realize or see Him with your spiritual eyes. He goes on to observe that people who partake of this type of practice have passions, are still full of cravings, and are deluded by Māyā. They do not understand true devotees of God, and are liable to persecute and even kill them. He further states that if one does not realize God within his own heart, then he is heading to the abode of death in a state of bondage. This means he will not obtain liberation, and will be subject to the cycle of birth and death (samsara) according to his karmas.

In very simple and logical language, Kabīr explains the importance of an intuitive realization of God before salvation can be obtained. The mere repetition of God's name without the concomitant development of spiritual awakening and destruction of ignorance does not procure salvation.

Shabda 41

O scholar! Carefully contemplate this:
From where did untouchability arise so that you have accepted it as part of your life?
Everyone comes from the ovum, the sperm and blood, and their body develops within another.
Each one is formed of eight lotuses (chakras) and comes to Earth. From where then does untouchability arise?
There are 8.4 million forms of life in different bodies, but they all decay and turn to clay.
All are seated (placed) on the same earth. Who then should call another untouchable?
Your type of thinking will make everything untouchable, including food, water and everything that is on the Earth.
Kabīr says only he who is not beguiled by Māyā (illusion), is free from the idea of untouchability.

Commentary: Untouchability has been a big problem in India, and continues to be even to this day. Because the Brahmins felt that they belonged to the high caste, and felt superior to all others, they often subjugated other people in terms of status, liberty, economic opportunities, and religious practices. The word Kabīr uses is *chhut*, meaning unclean, untouchable, filthy, and so forth. The higher classes formulated a system that allowed people to belong either to a high or a low caste according to birth. This was never intended to be so. People were supposed to be divided into castes according to their work and merit, but not by birth. Now it is common to see people who are not deserving of a high title still being looked upon with a great deal of respect even when their actions are unworthy. Simultaneously, people who are called untouchable, even though they are righteous in their behaviour, are still not accepted among the higher castes.

Kabīr emphasizes that there is no high or low caste, and that all human beings are similar. He appeals to our sense of logic, that we are all produced the same way from the ovum of the mother and the sperm of the father. We are all made of the same blood. Each one of us grows within the womb of the mother, and is born the same way. We all have a body, mind, and spirit. He mentions the eight lotuses that are the eight chakras, or vortices of spiritual energy. These lie along the spine, from its base to the brain. He further emphasizes that all of us are made, figuratively, of clay and that we return to the earth. Death is a great leveler and no respecter of high or low castes. He tells people who believe in the caste system that according to their thinking, everything should be thought of as untouchable, including food and water, and all the material manifestation that God has put on Earth. In the end, he points out that when one is free from the delusion of Māyā, then one would also be free of the idea of untouchability.

Kabīr teaches that if we have divine love in our hearts, and if we see divinity manifesting in the hearts of all beings, then we cannot, with a clear conscience, call anyone untouchable. We are all children of God and one family of humanity. All are equal before God.

Shabda 42

O scholar! Investigate carefully, and explain to me the secret by which birth and death may cease.
O brother! Tell me in which direction the four goals of life – wealth, religion, fulfillment of desires, and salvation – reside?
Do they reside in the north or south, or the east or west, or perhaps in heaven or hell?
If you say there is no place without God, then how can one go to hell?
Those who do not understand, accept that there is heaven and hell, but there is no heaven and hell for those who know God.
That fear of which the worldly people are afraid does not scare me at all.
I have no fear or doubt about sin and virtue, and I am not subject to going to heaven or hell.
Kabīr says listen O brother saints! The God-realized person resides in God.

Commentary: In this shabda, Kabīr talks about what some pandits (scholars) were teaching the people as ordained by their religion, and then contrasts it with the higher spiritual teaching that establishes a unity with God. First of all he asks the learned pandit of the secret by which birth and death may cease. Every religious person strives for salvation, but as long as they are caught in the wheel of karma, they cannot obtain release from the cycle of birth and death. Therefore, one's karmas must be pure and, with the knowledge of God, one has to submit totally to the will of God before liberation can be achieved.

The pandits teach that there are four goals in life called purusharthas, and these are the acquisition of material wealth, the practice of righteousness (religion), the satisfaction of noble desires, and the attainment of salvation. Kabīr asks in which direction one can find them? Kabīr also points that the pandits teach that God (Gopal) dwells everywhere in the universe. If this is so, then how can there be a hell, since God must therefore also dwell in hell. He asserts that it is people who do not understand true spirituality who are caught up in the idea of heaven and hell. But for those who truly know God, there is no heaven nor hell.

People are afraid of hell, or are afraid that when they are not practicing virtues, the consequences will be suffering. People are also afraid of death, or suffering that may disable them and render them dependent on others. Kabīr states that he has no fear concerning sin and virtue because he is not subject to going to either heaven or hell. It must be understood that the idea of heaven and hell dwells in the hearts of people, and is created by man. God is omnipresent and is unconcerned about what people think is a heaven or a hell because He dwells everywhere. Similarly, the God-realized person is unconcerned about this and is concerned only with being in the presence of God. Kabīr finally asserts to all seekers that the God-realized person resides in God, for God is truly the dwelling 'place' of all people.

It is essential to understand this shabda correctly in order to remove religious doubts and the teachings that cause fear in the hearts of people. Once you know and reside in God, how can you have fear? Rise above the scriptures and realize the divinity that you are already.

Shabda 43

O pandit, you are considering the wrong philosophy!
There is no difference between the creation and the Cre-

ator (in nirvikalpa samādhī).
There are no things such as gross or subtle matter, nor air or fire. There is no sun, moon, earth, or water.
There are no things such as light, form, time, speech, or body.
There are no things such as karmas and religions, and no mantra or religious worship.
There is no idea of disciplined self-control.
Can you say whether there is unity or duality?
There is no Gorakh and Rāma, and no consideration of the Vedas.
There is no Vishnu, Shiva, Brahmā, or Shiva/Shaktī.
There are no places of pilgrimage or religious observances.
There is no mother, father, or guru.
Can you say then, whether there are two or one?
Kabīr says whoever understands this, is my guru, and I am his disciple.

Commentary: In this shabda, Kabīr is talking about that state of unitary consciousness that is realized in deep meditation. This is called nirvikalpa samādhī, as opposed to savikalpa samādhī. In the former, there is no duality, such as the meditator and the object of meditation. In the latter, there is retention of a difference between the meditator, the process of meditation, and the object of meditation. In other words, there is still some preservation of an ego identity. In nirvikalpa samādhī there's absolute non-duality. The ego-consciousness ceases to exist because it merges into the cosmic consciousness. This is the basic teaching of Advaita Vedānta.

Kabīr is asserting that in this state of nirvikalpa samādhī, all differences disappear and merge into the unitary consciousness of God. He lists a number of things that cease to manifest in the way we know them in this phenomenal world. He admonishes the pandits that when they are dealing with all their religious doctrines and dogmas, they are actually considering the wrong philosophy. They cannot reach this state of unitary consciousness in that manner. In the state of meditative realization the differences between what is gross or subtle, and whether there is air, fire, sun, moon, earth, water and so forth, cease to exist. Similarly light, form, time, words, body, actions, religions, mantras, worships, self-discipline all disappear. Even Gorakh, the great yogi, and Rāma, are not present in this state of realization. Neither are the three gods Shiva, Brahmā, and Vishnu, nor the goddess Shaktī, nor even the places of pilgrimages. Similarly mother, father, guru all disappear. Kabīr says if anyone can truly understand this philosophy, that person will be his guru, and he will gladly become the disciple.

Shabda 44

O pandit, please consider carefully and tell me if Māyā is male or female.

In the house of the Brāhmin she is a Brahmini. In the house of a yogi, she is a disciple. Reading the Kalmā she becomes a Muslim woman. Yet in this Kaliyug she remains alone.

She did not have a bridegroom or a wedding, yet she gave birth to a son.

She did not spare even a single young man, yet she remains unwed even to this day.

She remains with her parents, not going to her in-laws, and does not sleep with her husband.

Kabīr says those who free themselves from the idea of race, caste, and clan live from age to age.

Commentary: In this shabda, Kabīr personifies and speaks about Māyā that, grammatically, is feminine gender. Ordinarily,

Māyā is thought of as the goddess Lakshmi, the wife of Lord Vishnu. Māyā is also thought of as wealth, or that which attracts a person. Māyā is also delusion. But since Māyā is feminine, Kabīr asks the puzzling question whether Māyā is male or female. He goes on to give a few examples of Māyā being female, such as the wife of a Brāhmin and is therefore called Brahmini. Similarly, a yogi may have a female disciple. By reciting the Kalmā, Māyā becomes a Muslim woman.

But Kabīr says despite these assertions, Māyā remains single. Māyā never had a bridegroom and never married, yet she produced a son, and this is contrary to the natural order of things. *Kāre mund* means those with black hair, therefore youths. Māyā did not spare a single youth, yet she has remained unwed, and a virgin. This means that Māyā plays a great role in the lives of all people, and young men are often enamoured by the attraction of young women. But she has no need to get married. By remaining with her parents, and not going to her in-laws, this means that Māyā remains with the world and does not have any need to go to her in-laws who represent God-realized people. She does not sleep with her husband because she is unwed and remains freely in the whole world. Kabīr says those people, who have gone beyond Māyā, or the delusion of separation into race, caste, and clans, will remain from age to age.

Kabīr is pointing out that people are under the illusion that Māyā has a material nature, such as that of a woman, or wealth or anything that is fascinating and arrests their attention. But he explains that none of these hold true because Māyā has no gender and is simply the creative energy of God. The creative principle of God cannot have a gender, and that is the answer to the rhetorical question he asks at the beginning. According to Advaita (non-dualistic) Vedānta, Māyā is responsible for all the differentiation we see in the phenomenal world arising from God, the noumenal Being.

Pandits are supposed to be knowledgeable about the scriptures and about these things and that is why Kabīr challenges them with the question about Māyā's gender. People who are enlightened spiritually do not see Māyā as worldly phenomena, the way average people, including the priests, tend to.

Shabda 45

O pandits, tell me who has not died? Carefully explain this to me.
Brahmā, Vishnu, and Mahesh died, as did Ganesh, the son of Parvati.
The moon, the sun, and Sheshnag died, as did Hanuman who bridged the ocean.
Krishna died, as did the doers of actions. Only one, the Creator, did not die.
Kabīr says only he who has risen above the duality of births and deaths will not die.

Commentary: All things in the world are transitory, and anything that has a beginning will also have an end. Scientists know that stars die, and even our sun will die. Our earth and other planets will likewise die. What then can be said about beings that inhabit the Earth? It is thus that Kabīr says that the three aspects of God – the creator Brahmā, the sustainer Vishnu, and the destroyer Shiva – all died. These three 'personalities' though being gods, are only projections of the different aspects of God. Therefore, in reality, they do not have independent existence, thus death is not beyond their experience. Similarly, Ganesh who was the son of Parvati and Shiva, also died. The moon and the sun are mythological personalities, as is the mythological serpent Sheshnag that is supposed to support the Earth on its head. These have all died, for they are only creations of the mind. Even Hanuman, who bridged the ocean to allow Shri Rāma and his army to cross to Lanka, also died. Shri Rāma drowned in the Sarju River (also called the stairway to heaven), and Krishna died after being shot by an arrow. Kabīr says only one Being is not subject to death, and that is the Creator of the whole universe – God. He observes that only that being who rises above the dualities of birth and death does not die. In human terms, this means the person has realized union with God. The soul does not die for it is co-existent with God and is part of God. One who achieves this state of realization does not die though his body will die.

In this short shabda, Kabīr is explaining that all the mythological beings of gods and goddesses, and their incarnations must die. Death does not come to that which is beyond the physical, which is the soul itself. It is the projection of God and is beyond death.

Shabda 46

O pandits, I see a very great surprising occurrence!
When one dies you abstain from food. When another dies you prepare it for food in your kitchen.
You bathe and worship the gods, and wear the nine-stranded janeo.
There is bone in your pot, in your plate, and in your mouth. What dignity is there in the six duties you perform?
You practice righteous actions and then you kill animals. O brother, you are committing evil actions!
If someone calls you a Brāhmin then what would they call a butcher?
Kabīr says listen saints! The whole world is lost in doubts. The supreme personality is unfathomable. Only a rare person can recognize Him.

Commentary: In this shabda, Kabīr talks about the hypocrisy committed by those in high religious places. In this case he speaks about the Brahmins since the setting was in India. The same thing can however be said about the priests of other religions. He observes that there is a very strange thing taking place. When there is a death, people abstain from food because of grief, or because of ritual reasons. On the other hand, they will kill an animal and carefully prepare it for food. Life is the same in both cases, thus the conduct of the pandits and their teaching to the people, are contrary to spiritual life. He observes that they then dutifully bathe and do their worship to the various gods and wear the nine-stranded janeo. The nine strands represent nine virtues or good qualities: control of the mind, control of the senses, austerity, purity, peace, uprightness, knowledge, realization, and faith.

Kabīr makes it quite picturesque by stating that there is bone in the pot, bone in the plate, and bone in the mouth. How can this be consistent with good spiritual life? The Brahmins then go on to perform their six karmas which are to perform ceremonies and make others perform them; to read the scriptures and make others read scriptures; to receive gifts and to give gifts. Kabīr is saying on the one hand they try to practice virtuous deeds, but on the other hand they are engaged in killing animals. Can this be right? He then observes that a butcher is called a butcher because he kills animals, but what can the Brāhmin who performs the same actions be called?

Kabīr says the whole world is caught up in doubts. Why doubts? Because people do not have a clear understanding of what spiritual life is. They worship gods according to their own predilections and do not use their innate wisdom to practice love and compassion towards other living creatures. Kabīr observes that the Supreme Being is unfathomable, and not many can recognize Him. One has to be pure in thoughts, words, and deeds, and must give up all harmful actions such as killing, and then meditate soulfully in order to recognize God as the Supreme Being. Only then can people remove doubts from their lives.

Shabda 47

O pandit! You ask the caste of the server before you drink water.
Do you not know that dead creatures are absorbed in the clay of which your house is made, and in which you live?
Five hundred and sixty million Yadavs (Lord Krishna's clan) were merged in it, along with eighty thousand munis.
At every step Muslim messengers are buried. They have decomposed and turned into clay.
Fish, turtle, and crocodile are born in the water, and their blood is mixed in it.
In the same water of the river 'hell' is flowing since animals and people have rotted in it.
Where does milk come from? The bones and flesh of cows are depleted to produce it.
The pandits take the milk and sit down to a meal, but point out the uncleanliness of the milk pot.
O pandit! Stop quoting the Vedas and other scriptures. Your mind is full of confusion.
Kabīr says listen pandit! All of these are your own creations.

Commentary: Caste distinctions have been a problem in India, and the high caste (Brahmins) avoid contact with the low caste, considering them to be untouchable. Kabīr is pointing out the hypocrisy of the high caste adherents when they fail to realize that the very clay from which their houses are made contains the decayed bodies of animals, low caste people, along with those of the high castes. He points out that millions of the Yadav clan (during the Mahabharat war) died and mingled with the earth. So did many sages. Even holy Muslims were buried in many places, and the high caste people do not seem to pay attention to this. Kabīr says that the water the high caste adherent is reaching for contains the blood of various animals that are born in it. He also says the water of the river might as well be considered the water of hell since it contains the rotted bodies of animals and people. Milk too, though it seems pure, also comes from the bones and flesh of the cow, yet people drink it. Kabīr is exhorting people to stop quoting scriptures to justify their actions, and to consider that the idea of caste and untouchability are creations of their own minds.

Kabīr decried caste distinctions and untouchability because he understood and realized that all people have been created by God and are equal. It is because of people's ignorance and hypocritical thinking that caste distinctions have been created.

Shabda 48

O pandit, think carefully and then tell me if the soul is male or female.
The same soul easily pervades and speaks in all bodies. Its nature is matchless.
What name will you give it when it has neither colour nor form?
O foolish man! Why are you concerned with yours and mine? What is really yours and what is mine?
Rāma, Khuda, Shaktī, and Shiva are all names of the One, but you separate them, and pray to the different ones for their blessing.
The Vedas, the Purānas, the Koran, and other scriptures, all try to explain religion and God in different ways.
Neither the Hindu nor the Turk, the Jain nor the yogi have truly understood this secret that God is one.
According to your six philosophies, you accept the names of God according to your own imagination.

Kabīr says we are the foolish ones (speakers of truth), while the rest of the world are the wise ones.

Commentary: In this shabda, Kabīr is speaking about the unity of the soul manifesting as the same 'energy force or field' in all bodies. Since it cannot be differentiated, how can one say whether it is a male or female? Similarly, God is the Absolute manifesting in all forms, and is beyond colour, form, and gender. The pronoun "He" is used only as a term of convenience. How can one then speak of God as few or many, according to the various scriptures. The Hindus name God as Rāma, the Muslims as Khuda. The Hindus also use the term Shaktī for the power of God, often considered the consort of Lord Shiva.

Kabīr says that all of these are names given to the same Supreme Being, according to the imaginations of people belonging to the different religions. He observes that the Vedas, the Purānas and other scriptures, as well as the Koran, all try to explain religion and God in various ways. However, they do not seem to penetrate the hearts of the devotees to demonstrate that God is One, because in practice people behave as if they are worshipping different gods. Even the six philosophies that try to explain the mystery of God do so according to the imagination of the propounders of such philosophies. Kabīr observes that the true saints, who see the unity of God and all of creation manifesting the same life force, are really the foolish ones in the eyes of those who create all the distinctions and consider themselves wise. Kabīr wants us to see the unity in all beings, and to not be misled by the various forms of religion, names of God, or the various ways of explaining the scriptures.

Shabda 49

O pandit, consider what the state of Nirvānā is!
Tell me, when evening appears (death) where does the sun

(soul) then reside?

In the state of God union there is no high or low, no mountain, no soil, nor bricks to block the sun, only consciousness. In it, songs spring up without singing.

There is no dew (sense gratification), nor thirst (desires) nor temple (place for deities), but thousands of cows (rays of light) providing the milk of realization.

There is always amawas and sankranti, and the nine planets are always sitting in their orbits.

O pandits! Tell me when did the soul become overshadowed by ignorance?

Kabīr says if you don't know this much, then tell me what is the use of the mantra whispered in your ear by your guru?

Commentary: In this shabda, Kabīr speaks of the state of Nirvānā or superconsciousness – a state of Self-realization or liberation. This state cannot be realized by studying the scriptures. It is a practical process of overcoming all the material desires and bondage, and rising to a state of absolute stillness in meditation. It is only in this state that one realizes the eternity of one's true Self. This pure conscious state has no material adjuncts or paraphernalia. It is a state of absolute Truth and peace. Kabīr thus challenges the pandit about the nature of this state of realization. Pandits, like priests everywhere, are well-versed in their scriptures, but many of them have not undergone this inner journey to realize the state of pure consciousness.

Kabīr says that in the state of realization there is nothing material, such as lumps of soil or bricks, or things that we consider to be high or low, or the functioning of the nine planets. (Note: Scientists now say there are eight planets, excluding Pluto which is no longer considered a planet.) There are no pleasures of the senses, no desires, no places of worship. There are no thought waves to disturb that pure state of consciousness. There is always the union of the left and right nerve currents as taught in yoga, and they merge into the sushumna or the central nerve channel through the spinal cord proceeding to the brain. This means that one is in deep meditation. The nine planets sitting in their orbits refers to the nine apertures of the body ceasing to function at the time of death. Kabīr thus asks where the soul then resides. Scripturally learned people do not have answers to most of these questions nor ideas mentioned by Kabīr. This is why he asks of what use the guru mantra given to you at the time of initiation really is if you have not realized the state of Nirvānā. All seekers who wish to obtain liberation from the passions, desires, and material bondage, must travel the inner path and realize the super conscious state which alone gives salvation.

Shabda 50

O pandit, consider this world to be a very exceptional tree. Half of it is male (Purush) and the other half is female (Prākriti).
This whole world is like that tree. Its top is in heaven and its roots are in hell.
It has twelve petals (twelve months) and twenty-four leaves (twelve dark and twelve bright fortnights), and several arterial roots (desires) surrounding it.
By its very nature it has no flower (knowledge) or fruit (salvation). Useless water (passion) drips from it night and day.
Kabīr says, in the beginning, when God nurtured the subtle world, nothing like this gross world existed.

Commentary: Prior to the manifestation of the gross material world, the world existed in a subtle form. Purush is the conscious animating principle that is often considered to be male, whereas Prākriti is considered to be nature and the female principle. Together these create or manifest the material world of form and consciousness. Just as a tree has its top pointing to the sky and the roots grounded in the earth, people in the tree of the world are aspiring to great heights but they remain firmly fixed or grounded in worldly pursuits. The world is also divided into twelve months and twenty-four fortnights subjecting all people to the ravages of time. The various arterial roots of the tress are the desires that drive people into various types of activities, whether good or bad. The unfortunate thing with this tree of the world is that it does not bear any flowers of spiritual knowledge, nor produce fruits of salvation. Instead, night and day it produces only useless water (desires) driving the world into activity.

Kabīr says when the world was in the subtle form, prior to the gross manifestation, there were none of these various desires and passions, nor divisions of time, nor any preoccupation with knowledge, salvation, or ignorance. All was in an unmanifested state in the consciousness of God. When the gross world is 'destroyed' after its cycle of manifestation, it will exist in a subtle form, just as the mind, intellect, consciousness and ego persist in order to carry the karmas into another birth when the body is destroyed.

Shabda 51

O pandit, consider this carefully and then tell me: Sometimes it flows like a flood and sometimes it dries up?

In a moment it rises and in another it sinks. In another moment it becomes fathomless. In such a condition one cannot obtain the diamond (self realization), and cannot know its depth.

This is not a river, but the mind full of doubts. The fish (passions) cannot be killed, while the fisherman (intellect) stands helplessly on the bank. The mind has no pond (knowledge), nor lotus flowers nor leaves, but only false creations.

Kabīr says these are the deceptions of the mind. It just sits there talking of proceeding quickly to salvation.

Commentary: In this shabda, Kabīr is talking about the various states of the mind. We all know that at times the mind can be full of ideas, doubts, problems, and so forth. At other times it seems to be devoid of any activity. Thoughts will sometimes rush through the mind, and at other times completely vanish. There are also times when the mind becomes so still it becomes fathomless. Kabīr explains that when the mind is going through these vicissitudes, it cannot grasp the precious gem of Self-realization. It cannot know the depth of the soul that is beyond all the activities of the mind.

Kabīr compares the mind to a flowing river, but one full of doubts. It is full of passions, lust, anger, greed, and ego. The fisherman is the intellect that becomes helpless because it cannot always control the mind driven by emotions and passions. The mind cannot have knowledge of Self-realization, unless it undertakes meditation earnestly. The mind tends to create various ghats or landing places, which are figuratively, the various levels of consciousness called lokas (places). Kabīr speaks of people being victims of the deceptions of the mind. People talk about heading towards salvation, but remain stuck in the world of materialism, with all the passions and desires. The lotus represents purity, since it grows out of the mud and remains pure. Kabīr often uses this symbolically to show that the soul is pure, even though it remains in this world. The mind is the obstacle that prevents the purity of the soul from illuminating.

Shabda 52

O Bhramhagyani, knower of the Absolute! Ponder on this

verse!

Rain clouds are billowing in the sky, yet not a drop of rain is falling.

The elephant (mind) is tied to the leg of the ant (consciousness), while the goat (Māyā) is eating up the wolf (soul).

The fish (mind) comes out of the ocean (God) and created a huge house (doubts).

The frog (unrealized guru) and the snake (ego) live together, and the cat (mind) has wedded the dog (lust).

Everyday the lion (soul) is afraid of the jackal (doubts).

This strange story is difficult to relate.

If the knowledgeable guru shoots his arrow in the forest, he will defeat the deer (of doubts).

The ocean (of realization) would then uproot the trees (Māyā), and the fish (realized soul) would hunt the wild animals (restless mind).

Kabīr says this knowledge is strange. Whoever really understands it, will fly without wings to the skies, and will not face death (obtains liberation).

Commentary: Two ideas are notable in this shabda. The first is that it is a sarcasm directed at propounders of religion who say they know God but have not realized divinity in their hearts. The second is that it is one of the ultā bānī or contrary sayings of Kabīr. The billowing clouds represent the religious practices and austerities which are external observances, and do not yield the precious raindrops of God-realization. The elephant is often thought of as the mind that is strongly attached to the desires of the world. The elephant is consciousness tied to the leg of the ant or worldly attachments, and from which it cannot escape. The goat is Māyā, or illusion, and is eating up the wolf that is the soul. The soul longs for liberation but illusion keeps it bound to the material world.

The ocean is God-consciousness and the fish is the mind that comes from God, but forsakes God and becomes attached to the material world and to doubts. Doubts are described as a huge house because the mind is full of doubts and cannot see the clear path to liberation. Similarly, the frog is the unrealized guru who lives together with the snake of ego that prevents spiritual progress. The cat is the mind married to the dog of lust. Passions assail the mind so it cannot obtain spiritual purity to realize its divine connection. The lion is the soul that is afraid of the jackal of doubts.

Kabīr says that this is a difficult and strange story to tell because, although everybody in the world is affected by the conditions he relates, people do not truly realize the sorry state in which they find themselves. He further states that if the guru is really knowledgeable, then he can certainly defeat the deer of doubts that are prevalent in the mind. If this occurs, then the ocean of realization will uproot the trees of illusion and the realized soul would hunt and destroy the wild animals that are the desires and restlessness of the mind. Kabīr states that this knowledge is strange because people do not understand it. But he who understands it will not need wings, to figuratively fly to the skies of God-realization and liberation.

Shabda 53

Whoever understands the tree (world) will be free from old age and death.
This whole world is a tree, and it has given off three branches.
The middle branch has borne four fruits, while the other branches have countless leaves (desires).
One vine has enwrapped the three worlds and, once bound, not even the wise can escape its bonds.
Kabīr says I am proclaiming this to everyone. Let him who is a scholar solve this riddle.

Commentary: Kabīr says that he who knows the secret of the tree of the world will become free of old age and death. He will obtain liberation. This world is figuratively the tree of which he speaks. The root of the tree is Māyā and the three branches are the three gunas or attributes of satva, rajas, and tamas. These are qualities of righteousness and goodness, of activity and passions, and of inertia and evil. The four fruits are dharma (religious duties), artha (acquisition of material wealth), kama (fulfillment of noble desires), and moksha (liberation). The tree also has branches full of leaves that are countless, and these are the hopes and desires that beset humanity. These are brought about by one creeping vine, Māyā, that creates bondage through the allurements of worldly things. Kabīr says even people who are wise have difficulty escaping the clutches of Māyā. He says that he is proclaiming this type of teaching so people may awaken to true knowledge. He exclaims that he who is a learned person, should ponder on what he is saying.

A person who understands the real nature of the world, and the nature of human beings that are beset with hopes, desires and passions, and entangled in countless activities, should make an effort to comprehend the reality of their situation and the goal for which they are striving. The ultimate goal is God-realization to obtain salvation.

Shabda 54

The bride went with her husband to her father-in-law's home.
She did not sleep with her husband, nor enjoy the pleasure of his company. Her youth vanished like a dream.
Four people fixed the auspicious wedding date, and five of them prepared the wedding platform.
All the friends sang the wedding songs, and placed the

yellow turmeric paste of suffering and happiness on her head.

The mind circumambulated the sacred fire in many ways, and tying the knot, she became a loving wife.

The ceremonial water was poured, and she looked beautiful, but on the very wedding seat she became widowed at her husband's side.

The wedding was performed, but she went without her bridegroom. On the way, her father-in-law tried to console her.

Kabīr says the next time she goes to her husband, she will embrace him, and will play beautiful music.

Commentary: In this allegorical shabda, Kabīr symbolizes the soul as the bride and God as the husband. He uses the imagery of a wedding to symbolize the formation of the body in which the soul dwells. But after the wedding the bride is left as a widow and is sorrowful. The father-in-law, who here represents a true guru, then consoles her.

Kabīr is speaking as the bride, which is one of the hallmarks of many mystical saints. They feel that they are the brides of God. The soul, though wedded to God, does not enjoy the pleasures of such union because of the distractions of the mind and the pursuit of worldly things in life. While engaged in these pursuits, youth vanishes just as a dream. The four people who decided the auspicious date are the mind, intellect, consciousness, and ego. They determine when the soul will take on another body that will be composed of the five elements of earth, water, fire, air, and ether. These five elements prepare the wedding place that actually is the body. The friends are the five sense organs that sing their various types of music in reference to the pleasures of the world. But they often create suffering. The mind itself circumambulates and this is symbolic of the bride and groom walking around the sacred wedding fire (havan kund).

The circumambulation is between birth and death, and all the activities of life.

The tying of the wedding knot is the union of the soul and God. The water that is poured ceremonially represents the passions that assail the mind and then cause a separation between the soul and God. This is why at the very wedding seat the bride becomes widowed, while her husband God is still present. Having thus been widowed or separated from God, the bride departs in sorrow. But the father-in-law who is the true guru then instructs the bride in the proper way of leading a spiritual life, and realizing union with God, the husband. Kabīr then concludes that when he, as the bride (soul), goes to her husband (God), he will embrace Him and play beautiful music. This means that he will be liberated from all sorrows and will live in happy union with God.

The soul is never separated from God, but due to the distractions of the world, a person loses contact with God and suffers. With proper instruction and guidance, the person can realize the soul's unity with God and live happily.

Shabda 55

O brother, look at the audacity of man! His story is beyond explanation.

He yokes the lion (intellect) and the tiger (ego) to the same plow (karmas with desires), and sows paddy (empty rituals) in the barren field of the world.

The forest fox (cunning guru) then protects the field, and the goat (mind) becomes the farmer.

The crow (evil preceptor) washes the clothes (hearts) of the ignorant people, and the crane (disciple) supports him.

The fly (foolish people) shaves its head and says it will join the wedding party.

The she-goat (Māyā) weds the tiger (soul) and the cows

(senses) sing the wedding songs.
The small forest animals (sense objects) are given as dowry, and the lizard (desire) as the maidservant, is sent with the bride.
Kabīr says listen brothers! Whoever understands this teaching is the wise scholar and genuine devotee.

Commentary: In this allegorical shabda, Kabīr talks about people who perform various types of actions in the name of religion without really perceiving what the end result may be. They behave as if a magician has hypnotized them. He states that their activities are beyond explanation. He then goes on to explain several situations which people engage in, often without realizing what they are doing or what they will gain. He uses various types of animals to represent people or their attributes. He says that people yoke the intellect and the ego to the same plow that is plowing the field of actions and desires. Then in that field which is barren, they sow the paddy of empty actions and rituals. Kabīr is pointing out that people do not obtain realization of divinity by performing various activities using their intellect and ego.

Then again, there are people who are cunning like the fox. They are the cunning preceptors who protect this field and the goat who is the farmer or the mind participating in various activities. The evil preceptors, likened to crows, pretend to wash the hearts of the people, that is, pretend to give them spiritual knowledge, and the adherents, like cranes, follow and support those teachings. There are also foolish people who are like the fly shaving their heads pretending to be renunciates and saying they will join the marriage party consisting of the she-goat or Māyā, marrying the tiger, or the soul. The cows are the senses that, figuratively, are singing and enjoying the marriage songs and party. If Māyā were not wedded to the soul, then living beings could not exist because Māyā is also the creative power of

God.

After a wedding, the bride is usually sent with a maidservant to the bridegroom's home. In this case the lizard, or desires, goes along with the bride and bridegroom. All the small animals of the forest are given as the dowry, and these represent the various sense objects in which the bride and groom, as do other people, take delight.

Kabīr says to the people that whoever can truly understand this shabda will indeed be a learned scholar. In this shabda Kabīr is really telling us that we should not become mired in delusions, false practices, and false teachings propounded by cunning teachers. We must use our discriminative knowledge and realize the Truth that resides within us.

Shabda 56

People do not believe me when I teach them the truth.
False teachers conduct business with false people and they both lose their capital.
They made a religion out of the six philosophies and made the three gods their authorities.
The king of the country is a great deceiver who keeps on destroying his subjects.
The soul thus wanders from here to there, back and forth, riding the bullock of Yama (the mind).
It is like a juggler with his leash on the monkey, making it do what he wishes.
This world is like a tree that grows and dies, all its sense objects are defective.
Just as a dog is happy with filthy food, many people behave like that in the world.
Kabīr says this is uncommon wisdom. Who will understand my teaching? Even today I can release you from Kal (death) if you do your meditation carefully.

Commentary: Kabīr observes that people do not seek the essence of spirituality but are content to observe the external aspects of religion. There are many false religious teachers and those who follow them become equally false, thus they both lose their capital, that is, the realization of divinity or the true Self. Kabīr states that people have made a religion of their philosophies and have accepted the three gods (Brahmā, Vishnu, and Shiva) as their authorities. Having done so, people still follow the external aspects of religion and do not realize the essence of their true Self. He notes that the king of the country is very deceitful, or is a tyrant, and keeps on plundering his own subjects. Thus the soul wanders from here to there, that is, from birth to death, or heaven or hell and back to Earth in a continuous cycle, because Yama perpetuates this process.

Kabīr compares the state of mankind with that of the monkey put on the leash by the juggler who makes the monkey perform according to his wishes. The mind also does the same. The world is like a tree which grows and dies because all sense objects are perishable. This means that people are born and die, even as they are pursuing the pleasures of sense objects. Eventually the sense objects let them down because they do not give eternal knowledge or salvation. People of the world often put "filth" in their minds, and are like the dog that relishes "dirty" food. Kabīr observes that what he is teaching is uncommon wisdom, and that not many people pay attention to it. But he assures people that if they purify their minds and meditate carefully, he will show them the way to obtain salvation.

It must be pointed out here that Kabīr is not critical of the religions or their teachings as such, but having observed the behaviours of people and of religious teachers, he finds that they are preoccupied only with the externalities of religion and are pursuing the material and impermanent things of the world. The result it that they are not able to obtain the true wisdom of religion that is generally not taught by the preachers of religion. Preachers often make religion a business of performing rituals while sticking to select doctrines and dogmas.

Shabda 57

People neither truly pray to God, nor give up their bad habits.
They listen to the Word but do not improve. They remain blind, and their feelings are shattered.
They are like the stone in the water that, when struck, still brings forth fire.
Even if a thousand pitchers of water are poured on it, it remains dry (still produces a spark when struck).
The whiteness of the body becomes whiter with age (whitening of the hair), and delirium increases.
A sādhu or devotee who can destroy this disease of delirium will reach perfection.
People die repeating the word anāhad (infinite), even as the Anāhad pervades all of creation.
Departure from this world is always near, but people foolishly run towards their death still uttering the same words.
Meeting a Satguru brings immense happiness and the Satguru's words will transform you.
Kabīr says those who understand this teaching will always be happy.

Commentary: People are prone to following their fixed habits, and do not make changes for their spiritual betterment. Kabīr uses the analogy of a stone in the water. Even when drenched with water over and over again it will still produce sparks when struck. Figuratively, it remains dry despite the wetness of water. Just so, people may read and recite thousands of mantras and spiritual lessons and yet not absorb them, remaining of dry character. Even as they grow old and become white haired, the delirium, or passions and bad habits keep on increasing. That is, they continue to be driven by passions, and continue to seek pleasures in sense objects. Kabīr observes that he who is able to get rid of such delirium and purify the mind, will indeed reach spiritual perfection.

Many people make a practice of repeating certain holy words, but mere repetition is not the goal. The goal is the infinite Supreme Being that pervades all of creation who can be realized only through withdrawing the senses from all external objects and meditating within. Instead of doing this, people foolishly run towards death still uttering their various words according to their scriptures. Kabīr observes that if people would follow and practice the teaching imparted by a spiritual Master, then they would always enjoy peace and happiness.

Shabda 58

O God! People are burning in the forest fire (passions) without firewood and there is no one to douse the flames.
I know that it originates from you, but the whole world is burning in it.
There is a plume of fire (lust) in the water (mind), and no other water can be found to douse it.
Not only one burns, but all nine women as well, and no one knows the secret of removing the fire.
The city (body) is burning while the watchman (soul) sleeps soundly. He says that his house is safe.
The body burns down but the essence (soul) escapes. O God, your deeds are perplexing!
The embrace of a eunuch does not satisfy the longings of the heart.

While busy engaged in discussions, this life is wasted and remains undisciplined.
There is no one so foolish as the one who is knowingly deceitful.
Kabīr says all are the wives of Rāma (God); there is no other Rāma different from me (soul) to be realized.

Commentary: In this shabda, Kabīr is speaking of the fire of passions such as hate, lust, greed, anger, and so forth, that are burning within people and require no fuel for the conflagration. There is hardly anyone who is able to douse the fires burning within. People are caught up in the law of karma and are reaping what they have sown. The sprout or the shoot of the fire is lust raging in the water of the mind deluded by false teachings. The physical water is not able to put it out. Day by day, the fire consumes those afflicted by these passions. This fire burns not only one person, but all nine women (the body with nine apertures), and no one knows the method of putting out the flames. Yet the soul remains untouched because it is divine in nature.

This is the riddle of life which we need to understand. Just as the embrace of a eunuch will not satisfy the longings of the one embraced, embracing all kinds of desires will not satisfy the longing of the soul to connect with God. In the world, people are often full of discussions and arguments, but these prove to be useless in disciplining the life and obtaining God-realization. Cunning preachers deceive the innocent people. Kabīr says all are the wives of Rāma, which in a mystical sense, means all souls are the wives of God who is the husband. When one realizes the soul, and realizes that it is liberated and universal, then there is none other than the soul. In the last line Kabīr does not mean that he is the only one. He is speaking from the divine standpoint that for the realized soul united with God, there is only unity.

Shabda 59

I know Māyā to be a great cheater.
With the noose of three gunas in her hand she roams the world speaking sweet languages.
In the home of Keshav (Vishnu) she dwells as Kamla (Lakshmi), and in the home of Shiva she dwells as Bhawani (Parvati).
In the home of the panda (priest) she is in the form of idols, and in the holy places of pilgrimage she is in the form of sacred water.
In the home of the yogi she is the yogini, and in the palace of the king she is the queen.
For some she is the wealth of diamonds, and for others she is a useless shell (cowry).
In the home of the bhakta (devotee) she is the bhaktin (female devotee), and in the home of Brahmā she is in the form of Brahmani.
Kabīr says listen brother saints! All of these manifestations of Māyā are mysterious and beyond explanation.

Commentary: In this shabda, Kabīr deals with the power of Māyā as the great illusive power that pervades the whole world. It is because of Māyā that we do not observe the reality of God as the divine spirit dwelling in us. We may speak about divinity, about God, about soul, and so forth, but gaining realization of them is difficult. This is because our sense organs tell us that the things we observe through them are real. But, mystically speaking, they vanish in time and therefore do not constitute reality.

In life, for all beings, from the gods to the priests and to ordinary human beings, Māyā takes various forms as mentioned throughout this shabda. The beings mentioned are all attached to their Māyā counterparts. Actually, the whole of creation is the play of Māyā that is the projecting power of God the absolute Being. Thus they are all unreal and illusory. It is from this standpoint that Kabīr says Māyā is a great cheater because she keeps deluding us into thinking the things we perceive are the reality, yet these are all evanescent and unreal. The only reality is God, and He dwells as spirit in all beings.

Shabda 60

Māyā and attachment have allured the world and have stolen the diamond of knowledge.
This life is like a dream that is immersed in a dream.
The Guru has imparted the shabda to you, but you have abandoned that eternal treasure.
The moth, seeing the flame, feels happy but, being a creature, does not recognize it as fire that will burn it.
Man acts foolishly, not recognizing the noose of death, running after gold and women.
Muslims of the Sheikh and Saiyad sects read the Koran and the pandits read the Smritis and Shastras.
But without the instruction of the Satguru, they continue to willfully kill living beings.
Carefully consider the instructions of Satguru, and give up all evils. You will then obtain liberation.
Kabīr says O man recite the name of God, for there is no one else to give salvation.

Commentary: This shabda deals with the illusive power of Māyā that, through attachment, has made all people attached to various things in the world. They feel that what they are seeing and living are the reality, but the more they dwell in that so called reality, the more they drift away from that eternal knowledge of the spirit that Kabīr likens to a diamond. In a mystical sense, this life is a dream because it is a passing show. All that exists now will, in time, not exist. What will continue to always exist is the spirit that is indestructible. God exists. The true reality, therefore, is the spirit dwelling in human beings and that transcends all the ephemeral things of the world. This is the instruction given by Satguru. Once we observe this instruction, we will not lose the eternal treasure that gives salvation.

Kabīr gives the example of a moth that sees the flame, is allured by it, and gets burned. Not having enough awareness, it does not realize that the fire that is attracting it will destroy it. Just so, human beings are attracted to all types of material things through desires and attachments, but they figuratively burn in them, and are kept from obtaining freedom. We must always be aware that death can strike us at any moment and, therefore, pay attention to the immortal instructions given to us to obtain freedom from the bondage of material existence. We need to realize our true state as spiritual beings.

Kabīr further gives the example of the priests of the Muslim and Hindu religions reading their scriptures but still sacrificing the lives of animals. He has said this is not correct and is due to ignorance and not learning the true teachings of Satguru. He instructs us that we must get rid of such defects in life and obtain salvation. God is the only eternal self-existent Being, and through Him we can obtain everlasting life.

Shabda 61

When you die what will become of your body? After your life departs, people will quickly place your body outside.

They will mercilessly dispose of your body in different ways. Some will cremate you, and others will bury you in the ground. The Hindus will cremate you, and the Muslims will bury you.

In these ways both Hindu and Muslim will leave their homes.

Yama has spread his trap of karmas for you, just as the

fisherman sets traps for fish.
Without God, what kind of man will you be? You will be like the dung-eating beetle on the path.
Kabīr says at the time of death you will repent, seeing yourself having to leave this house (world) to go to that house (hell).

Commentary: In this shabda, Kabīr explains that we live in this world occupied with various degrees of illusion and material and worldly bondage. If we do not live a life of spirituality, and obtain liberation from illusions and worldly bondage, then we will only repent at the time of death. The body is only a vehicle for the imperishable soul. Its future will be determined by what you have achieved in this life.

He explains that the body is useless after death, and that people dispose of the corpse in different ways. He says that the body will be shown no mercy because it will either be mercilessly burned, or buried in the ground. But Yama, the god of death, will have spread his traps of karmas in which you become trapped, just like the fish is trapped in the net of the fisherman. Without God you will not be able to escape this trap, and will become like the dung-eating beetle on the path. The soul will eventually have to leave this world and go to the other world, which may be one of suffering. The antidote for repentance at death is to live a spiritual life so you will go to a better home after death, a home in which you are liberated from bondage and suffering.

Shabda 62

O mother, I have brightened the homes of both families!
I have tied my mother-in-law (Māyā) and sister-in-law (bad intellect) on the bed, and have cursed my brother-in-law (non-discriminative intellect).
I will burn the hair of that woman (Māyā) who always

quarrels with me.
In the womb I got five coverings, and also two and four others.
I eat the neighboring women for breakfast and along with them, I eat my mother (intellect).
My noble husband has spread a bed for me on which I sleep carefree with outstretched legs.
Now I do not come or go, nor do I die or live. My master comes forward to meet me.
I have accepted one name as my own and now am free from worldly bondage.
Kabīr proclaims, I have resolutely recognized only one name (Rāma Nām).

Commentary: In this allegorical shabda, Kabīr is portraying the soul as a bride. The bride says that she has brightened, or enlightened both families. Both families are not the external ones established through marriage, but represent internal families. The mother-in-law is Māyā or illusion, the sister-in-law is bad intellect, and the brother-in-law is non-discriminative intellect. She has controlled them so that they have no power over her. Further, she says she will burn the hair of that woman who again is Māyā or illusion, who causes quarrels and confusion.

In the mysticism of India, it is recognized that as the body develops it takes on coverings or sheaths on the soul. These sheaths are the physical body, the breath or life force, the mind, the intellect, and bliss. The soul also takes on the qualities of doubt and resolve, and four others, which are, mind, intellect, consciousness, and ego.

The realized soul eats up the neighboring women which are the passions and desires, and also eats up the intellect. The realized soul knows its unity with God and thus rises above all illusions, passions, desires, and intellectual attributes. God then figuratively spreads a bed out for the soul that now sleeps carefree above the encumbrances. The soul then realizes it neither has to come nor go, that is, it reaches a state beyond birth and death. God then approaches to meet the soul. Kabīr says that he has resolutely accepted the name of God as his own, and is now freed from worldly bondage.

Kabīr explains that when the soul has obtained realization and knows its unity with God through accepting the name of God and living a spiritual life, then there are no more troubles from the families mentioned above. The soul is enlightened and free.

Shabda 63

To whom can I speak, and who will listen and believe that the bee dies when it touches the flower.
That flower blooms in perfect meditation (gagan mandal). Its branches are below and the root is above.
That flower needs no ploughing, sowing, nor watering, and blooms without branches and leaves.
The flower blossomed perfectly and the female gardener was fascinated by it, but the flower vanished leaving the bee disappointed.
Kabīr says listen to me, brother saints! The learned people remain fascinated with the flower.

Commentary: In this shabda, Kabīr speaks about meditation that he calls gagan mandal that is reached when the mind is perfectly controlled and the consciousness rises above mind functions. The bee is the mind and the flower is the one thousand-petalled lotus spoken of in yoga as the sahasrāra chakra. This lotus chakra is located in the topmost part of the brain and is represented with the petals pointing downwards. This is not an anatomical location in the brain, but is a mystical representation for the energy centre represented as the lotus. This lotus 'blooms' when it is awakened by the rising consciousness. The consciousness then becomes absorbed in cosmic consciousness. Of course, this flower needs no ploughing, sowing, nor watering, and does not have branches or leaves. The female gardener is the consciousness, and when consciousness rises to this lotus centre in meditation, it becomes absorbed in it. But if one remains absorbed in the lotus and does not attain Self-realization, then the lotus vanishes and the mind becomes disappointed. Kabīr says learned people are fascinated by the flower, that is, they are fascinated but do not strive to attain the higher state of Self-realization or unity with God.

In the yoga system there are seven chakras and the thousand-petaled chakra is the highest. Kabīr is pointing out that one has to go beyond this thousand-petaled lotus in order to reach infinite or cosmic consciousness. The learned people often remain fascinated with reaching the level of the thousand-petaled lotus, but do not seek to attain the highest Self-realization.

Shabda 64

O weaver (soul), weave the name of God on whom gods, men, and sages meditate.
To secure the warp use the post, and the four Vedas as the spinning wheels.
Rāma and Narayan serve as pegs, and fulfill all desires.
God made the worldly ocean as a wooden vessel in which he placed the starch (Māyā).
In the starch of the body he placed an inner starch (Māyā), but there is hardly anyone who understands this starch (Māyā).
He made the right and left nostrils as two pillars, and in the centre he placed the light (sushumna).
For whoever meditates on God, the name of Sham ensures perfection.

When this devotion has become perfect, he wraps this thread of meditation on the spindle of Rāma (God).
And attaining the love of God he attains the three worlds. None is left out.
God made the three worlds into a loom and spread the light of knowledge in all directions.
The eternal Lord sits on the weaver's seat, and Kabīr merges into His Light.

Commentary: Using metaphorical language, Kabīr has expressed deep mystical meaning in this shabda. He speaks of the weaver as the soul, that is the human being, who needs to meditate on God. The various gods, demigods, men, and sages also meditate on God. Kabīr is using the warp and weft of the weaving machine to express some of these mystical ideas. The post, which has secured the warp, is meditation, and the weft consisting of all the threads are the thought waves which must be controlled in meditation. The four Vedas are instructions through which people can attain the spiritual life of meditation. Rāma and Narayan are names of God, and God's name is the peg that anchors the various threads. Meditation on God fulfils one's noble desires.

Kabīr speaks about this world as the worldly ocean, likened to a wooden bowl in which there is a thickened starch. The starch is actually Māyā, the illusive power that emanated from God. The word starch is also used to represent the body, thus he states that in this body there is the starch of Māyā, but hardly does anyone understand the play of this Māyā in life. The yogis speak of the idā and pingalā as the moon and sun, or left and right energy channels that, when in balance, lead to a central channel called sushumna. Kabīr states that when you reach this stage of single-minded meditation, then you are in sushumna, and can attain immersion in God consciousness. Whoever meditates thus, using the sushumna as the light of spiritual enlightenment, then Sham, another name of God, will help the meditator reach perfection. One then becomes bound to God in consciousness. All who meditate with their hearts filled with the love of God, will reach enlightenment. Kabīr says God has spread the warp and weft of the loom everywhere, and His Light manifests in all. Kabīr also says that God, Himself, is the weaver sitting on the weaver's seat and that he, Kabīr, has merged into the Light of God.

Essentially, Kabīr is saying that we are the soul, and that Māyā is within us and is deluding us. But if we meditate with great devotion in our hearts, then God will see to it that we reach perfection and merge into His Light.

Shabda 65

The hatha yogi traveled through the city, and returned (reborn) to it. He got attached to five ladies (five elements).
Wherever it is he went in other countries (after death) no one can tell. The yogi does not again return to the same cave (body).
His body is burned, and his flag (breath) is shattered. His spine and skull are shattered to pieces.
Kabīr says this Kaliyug is bad, and whatever is in the pot will pour forth from the spout.

Commentary: In this shabda, Kabīr speaks of the hatha yogi who tries to perfect his body in a quest to gain perfection, and perhaps to avoid death. But he dies nevertheless, and returns to life in a rebirth. The five ladies are the five gross elements of earth, water, fire, air, and ether, which compose his body, and all matter. Kabīr states that no one can tell where the soul goes to after death, but the soul, being eternal, returns to another "cave" that is not the previous body, but a new one. At death the body is burned and the breath dissipates. The whole skeletal system, including the spine and the skull is destroyed. What is left are the effects of the karmas that determine a new birth. Kabīr observes that this current Kaliyug or Iron Age, has a great deal of evil and deceitfulness. When one's desires and karmas remain, they determine what will occur to the soul in a new life. This is what Kabīr means when he says what is in the pot is what will come out of the spout.

Shabda 66

> No one should dwell in the city of the yogi, for whoever dwells there will also become a yogi.
> These yogis have inverted knowledge. They wear black clothing (ignorance) and have no protection.
> The clothing is obvious, but the soul wearing it is invisible. That soul is the root of life.
> Whoever understands the methods of the ignorant yogis, and gives them up and loves God, becomes a witness of the three worlds.
> At every moment he will drink the nectar of the vine (God's love). Kabīr says such a soul will live eternally.

Commentary: Kabīr's theme in this shabda concerns the Hatha yogi who spends an inordinate amount of time cultivating physical postures to obtain physical perfection but often remains ignorant of the divine union of the soul and God. We need to contrast this with the Sahaj yoga (easy or natural union) of Kabīr. If one follows the methods of such Hatha yogis, one is liable to become like them and not progress to a spiritual union with God. This is why Kabīr says such yogis have an inverted type of knowledge. Their ignorance, likened to black clothing, is obvious, but such yogis have no real protection for the soul. Kabīr wants us to realize that within this body is the root or essence of what we should seek and that is the soul. It is the peerless diamond and greatest treasure we have that Kabīr alludes to elsewhere.

Kabīr says that if we really understand the methods of these Hatha yogis and their external practices, we will avoid them and instead, attach ourselves to the love of God. We will then be in union with the universal love of God. Kabīr calls this being a witness of the three worlds. With such a realization, the enlightened individual "drinks" the nectar of God's love, and lives in eternity, that is, he realizes the eternity of his true Self.

Shabda 67

If God is in the form of the seed, then ask the scholar who else is there.
Where are the mind, intellect, and ego, and where are the three forms of attributes – satogun, rajogun, and tamogun.
There are many fruits of poison and of nectar, but the Vedas have shown many ways of liberation.
Kabīr asks: How do you know of you and me, or of those who are liberated or in bondage?

Commentary: In this shabda, Kabīr speaks of non-duality or of the Advaita Vedānta philosophy that is also called monism. This philosophy teaches that God is one and can be likened to the seed of the universe. The whole universe proceeds from the being of God, and is contained in God, and God is in the universe. Therefore, there is only non-duality. Kabīr asks the pandit how then can there be anything else that is outside of God. In the same vein he asks where are the mind, the intellect, and ego, or the attributes of satogun, rajogun, and tamogun – the three qualities that are inherent in creation. They must also all belong to the being of God. He then asks the question how there can be differences in individuals such as you and me indicating duality, when in fact there is non-duality. How does one account for those who are liberated, or those who are in bondage? This points to the Law of Karma according to which people are either in a state of bondage or liberation.

Kabīr instructs that in the world there are many fruits of poison and nectar, that is, of evil and good, and that people are trapped in these dualities. He says that the Vedas have shown many ways by which people can liberate themselves. Non-dualism or Advaita Vedānta is the philosophy of realized saints. This philosophy teaches that in the "beginning" there was only God and, therefore, that everything proceeded from God. This accounts for the universally accepted statement that God is omnipresent. All things therefore belong to the being of God and there is no duality in the mystical sense.

Shabda 68

Even if the spinning wheel (body) burns, the carpenter (soul) does not die.
I (devotee) can spin a thousand yarns if the body does not burn (die).
Father, please find me a good bridegroom and marry me to him.
Until you find a good bridegroom, please marry me yourself.
Reaching the first city (first stage in meditation) I was beset with sorrow and distress.
I saw an astonishing event that the daughter (soul) married the father (God).
While at the home of the father-in-law (knowledge), his father (discrimination) came, and along with him came the daughter-in-law's brother (intellect).
Using tools, the pegs (the preceding relatives) made the body strong.

The devas (gods) in heaven will die, but there is one (soul) that will not die.
For the sake of bliss this body is being made strong.
Kabīr says, listen brother saints, if someone truly observes this body, and really understands it, he will not be subject to birth and death.

Commentary: In this very allegorical shabda Kabīr is explaining the relationship between the body, the soul, God, knowledge, discrimination, intellect, and bliss. He is using human relationships to denote some of these attributes. The body is subject to death but the soul does not die. The devotee can perform thousands of actions in life if the body does not burn, that is, die. People perform various actions in life as long as they have the body, but at death the body is reduced to ashes and the soul departs.

The soul being the daughter, is pleading with the father to find a good bridegroom and marry her off. The daughter is yearning to be united with God, and for God to be the bridegroom. The father in this case can be likened to the guru who teaches the soul how to become united with God. She further states that unless such a good bridegroom can be obtained for her to marry, then the guru can marry her. In Kabīr's language the guru and God are often equated. Kabīr mentions seeing an astonishing sight where the daughter has married the father, that is, where the soul has been united with God.

But this marriage brings with it the father-in-law that is knowledge, and his father, discrimination, along with the intellect. These are attributes the soul achieves when it realizes its true nature and its unity with God. The devotee makes his body strong by using these familial relationships to perform his duty in this world. Once the soul realizes its unity with God it is then co-eternal with God. It cannot be subject to death.

For the sake of bliss the devotee tries to strengthen his body in various ways through nutrition, exercise, and so forth, but this bliss is not obtained. This is because the devotee does not truly understand the function of the body as the vehicle for the soul. That is why Kabīr says that he who understands the body will not be subject to birth and death. The lesson here is that the soul must realize its unity with God and know that the body is only a temporary home. This is achieved through applying knowledge, discrimination, and intellect, and using meditation. In meditation many problems can arise when one becomes aware of the vicissitudes and passions in life. These are obstacles that must be overcome, for example, ego, anger, greed and so forth. The purpose of life is to realize the unity of the soul and God, and in this way to obtain liberation.

Shabda 69

The musician (soul) plays the instrument (body) and produces matchless music that thunders in the eighth chakra in meditation.
You, yourself, are the musician and produce this melody, and move about with the instrument in your hand.
One shabda (word) has thirty-six melodies in it, and expresses the divine melody (anāhad nād).
The mouth forms the neck and the ears form the gourd of the instrument; Satguru has made them beautifully.
The tongue forms the strings, the nose forms the screws, and Māyā is the rosin on the strings.
In the depth of meditation there appeared light, and this light spread all around.
Kabīr says those people who develop discriminative knowledge endear themselves to the musician.

Commentary: In this shabda, Kabīr compares the body to a musical instrument, such as a guitar or a sitar. Kabīr refers to the soul as the musician while the matchless music is the anāhad nād or divine melody that is heard in deep meditation. The eighth chakra is the highest chakra that becomes enlightened in meditation. The maker of the music is really the soul as it is the animating principle of the body which is the musical instrument. It is because of the soul that the body is alive and is able to move around in this world, the soul figuratively moving about with the instrument in its hand.

In the anāhad nād are the thirty-six melodies because it is the primeval or divine sound that must contain all other melodies. Enlightenment occurs in meditation, and this enlightenment allows a divine vision where the soul or the divine presence is seen everywhere. Kabīr says that whoever truly understands the soul and becomes endeared to it, will become spiritually awakened with discriminative wisdom.

The theme of this shabda is that the soul is the producer of all sounds. We must not be attached to the sounds, but must realize the source.

Shabda 70

The meat of the animal and of man is the same, and the blood of all is the same.
All eat the meat of the animal, but no one, not even the jackal, eats the meat of man.
Brahmā is the potter who made this Earth. Creatures are born and die, and no one knows where they go.
People eat the meat and fish just as if they planted them in their farm. They make gods and goddesses of clay, and cut up living things to offer to them.
If your god is true (alive and wanting meat) why does he not take the animal as it grazes in the field?
Kabīr says listen saints! Always utter the name of God. Whatever it is they do, they do for the taste of the tongue!

The others (the killed animals) will take their revenge.

Commentary: Non-violence and compassion towards all living beings are fundamental principles in a spiritual life. This is why killing is forbidden. In this shabda Kabīr talks of people who kill animals to satisfy their own tastes and appetites. They are creating more negative karmas for themselves and will eventually have to suffer the consequences.

Kabīr points out that meat is meat, whether it is of the animal or man. However people eat the meat of animals but not of other people. They kill the animals so easily, just as if reaping them like plants sown in their fields. The natural law is that animals and people are born and die according to God's plan, and no one has the right to kill that which God has given life.

Many people, including priests, make deities of clay, worship them, and offer the killed animals to them. Kabīr points out that these gods and goddesses are not really hungry, nor do they crave meat. If they had life and meat was their natural diet, and if they desired it, they could take it themselves. He says the important thing in spiritual life is to always remember God in the depth of the heart.

Shabda 71

O chatrick, why are you calling for water from afar? The water is abundantly present all around.

The secret of nād and bind (divine melody and body) is in the water that also created the six karmas and the four vedas.

The soul and God dwell in the water that manifests both on Earth and in the heavens.

Kabīr says people do not know the secret of the water that has given life to all living beings.

Commentary: In this shabda, Kabīr speaks of God, or pure consciousness, as water that is omnipresent and thus dwells in all beings. The chatrick is a mythological bird that is said to cry out for a particular rain that falls at a certain time of the lunar cycle (swāti), and will not drink any other water. Kabīr says people behave like the chatrick bird seeking God and not finding Him, even though God is omnipresent. God is realized in meditation when the mind is fixed at the third eye or spiritual eye between the eyebrows, and all thoughts are suspended. In meditation one hears the divine melody. When one reaches this state in spiritual life, one realizes that everything emanated from God, including the various prescribed duties and scriptures (four Vedas – Rig, Yajur, Sāma and Atharva).

God and all souls dwell in the same 'water.' This means that there is no separation between the soul and God, and they occupy the same 'place.' God is spoken of as the pure consciousness that pervades everywhere. This God consciousness is the water that is manifesting everywhere, whether we think of earth or heaven. Kabīr points out that people do not understand the secret of this water that has produced all living beings everywhere. This water is the consciousness of God that produced everything, and that consciousness is also embodied in all living things. It is for this reason that non-violence towards all living beings is taught.

Shabda 72

Why do you walk (live) in so many crooked ways?
Your ten doors (body) are full of filth, yet you want to be a
 shipload of perfume.
Your eyes are blinded and your heart does not perceive,
 and your intellect is ignorant.
You are plunged in lust, anger, and the thirst of passions,
 and are drowning and will die when there is no water.

If you are cremated, you will turn to ashes and dust. If buried, worms and maggots will eat you.
You are food for the jackal, dogs, and crow. Such is the greatness of your body!
O foolish man! Don't you realize that death is not far from you? Even if you take care of your body in millions of ways, the end will be dust.
You ignorantly sit in a house of sand and do not realize your fate.
Kabīr says without singing the glories of God, many wise people have drowned and died.

Commentary: In this shabda, Kabīr is addressing pride of the body and all the wrong ways of living that emanate from it. He points out that the body which has ten apertures is full of filth (feces, urine, bacteria, et cetera) but people pamper the body in many ways and think of it as the epitome of fragrance. He says people do not realize nor understand that the body is really clay and will be reduced to dust, or will be eaten by maggots and worms. Why take so much pride in the body then?

Kabīr emphasizes that people tend to remain foolish or ignorant by not realizing that the body is only a temporary home for the soul. The body is made of flesh, and is fit to be food for wild animals and crows. That is the only greatness of the body in the end, so why be proud of it? People should realize that, ultimately, it is the soul that is important. He likens the body to a house of sand that will crumble in no time. The most essential duty is to sing the glories of God and to meditate and realize the eternity of the soul. It is this knowledge that gives liberation from the bondage of the material world. As the saying goes, we should be in the world, but not of the world.

Shabda 73

Why do you go through life so full of pride?
Why do you forget those days when, for ten lunar months, you were upside down in the mother's womb?
Just as the honeybee makes honey but does not eat it, just so, with toil and care, you have gathered wealth.
At death all will say to get rid of your body. How can a ghost be allowed to remain in the house?
The wife follows the corpse to the threshold of the house, and others to the cremation ground.
The bier also goes to the cremation ground, but the soul departs alone.
The body is burnt and turns to ashes, and if buried is mingled with the earth.
The greatness of the body is like putting water in an unbaked earthen pot.
You are intoxicated with worldly attachments and have become estranged from God, but you will fall into the well of death.
Kabīr says man has bound himself just as the parrot that foolishly thinks it has been caught in the trap.

Commentary: In this shabda, Kabīr is speaking about the pride with which people live. People feel a great deal of pride in their physical being and the material things around them which they have accumulated with great care and effort. Kabīr reminds them that they were upside down for ten lunar months in the mother's womb, and were helpless. So what is so great about their status now? He says people are behaving just like the bee which makes honey but does not eat it, just so people accumulate things beyond what they need for their immediate use. Mahatma Gandhi said if you take more than you need for your immediate use, you are stealing it from someone else.

Kabīr also talks about uselessness of the body, such that at death everybody wants to get rid of it, as it is considered to be ghostly and unclean. That same body that is dear to the wife during life, is accompanied only to the threshold of the house after death. Friends and relatives will go further along with the bier to the cremation ground. The cremated body turns to ashes and is mingled with the earth. Kabīr compares the body to the unbaked clay pot holding water and which soon breaks. Just so this body is fragile and temporary. He says we are so intoxicated with material attachments that we have forsaken God, and will die without attaining liberation because we are bound in ignorance, foolishness, and doubt. It is the same state as the parrot caught in a lalani trap. Lalani is a trap that is hung over water. Upon sitting on it, the parrot rolls over, its back near the water making it fear to let go and fly away. It holds on for dear life and feels that it is trapped. Worldly attachments have the same effect on people and must be overcome.

Shabda 74

There is a yogi of bad actions. He has no place in the heavens, the skies, or the earth.
He has neither hands nor feet, nor form, nor outline.
Without a marketplace he plies his trade, and serves both as weigher and record keeper.
He has neither good actions nor religious life. Neither does he have any skill in yoga.
He has neither a musical horn nor a begging bowl. How can he beg for enjoyment?
I know you and you know me, and I am immersed in you.
There is neither creation nor dissolution. Tell me then who is there to meditate on Brahman.
Another yogi who is fully God-realized came and instructed the ignorant one.

He brought no medicinal herbs, but he had the one life-giving medicine of God.
View this world as an actor's play or as the tricks of a magician.
Kabīr says listen saints! Being realized you enter the kingdom of God.

Commentary: In this shabda, Kabīr explains the progression from ignorance to God-realization. The yogi he mentions is the mind that is often full of evil thoughts and actions. It has none of the physical attributes such as hands, feet, or form. There is no particular place where the mind resides, except as an attribute of consciousness. But in the world, the mind is engaged in all kinds of activities, outlined here as conducting business in the marketplace. The mind in itself is not engaged in any type of noble work or spiritual discipline, nor in the practice of yoga and other skills. Thus the mind does not have any musical instruments or a begging bowl. When the mind is of such a nature, how can it even ask for enjoyment? The activities of the mind are apparent when the mind becomes attached to desires and operates through the body.

Now there is a shift in emphasis coming from the soul to the mind. At the soul level there is no duality. So Kabīr says, "I know you and you know me, and I am immersed in you." This means that the mind and soul are united, and are also united with God. At this level of realization it is a state of consciousness, therefore there is no question of creation or dissolution, and no question about meditating on any Supreme Being, as God's presence is everywhere and in all of us.

Kabīr progresses to the yogi who is a realized soul and who instructs the other yogi, the mind that is unrealized. The God-realized soul has no need for any type of medicines (rituals, beliefs, traditions, et cetera) but only the medicine of God. God-realization is a state of pure awareness and realization of unity with the Universal Being.

Kabīr says this world must be observed as an actor playing a role on the stage, and as a magician performing all types of tricks. The material world has no eternal reality, because everything decays and dissolves in time. Kabīr explains that if you obtain the realization of God in your own life, then you will indeed enter the kingdom of God.

Shabda 75

People are beset by a huge circle of doubts! There are the Vedas and Koran, and religions, and hell.
Who is male and who is female? The body is beautifully made of clay, and the vital energy flows through it.
When the body dissolves what name can we give to the soul? The foolish person is lost in searching.
All have the same skin, bones, feces, and urine, and the same blood and marrow.
All are created from a drop of semen. Who then is a Brāhmin, and who is a Shudra?
Rajogun is said to be Brahmā, tamogun to be Shiva, and satogun to be Vishnu.
Kabīr says always realize God in you; there is no Hindu and no Muslim.

Commentary: This shabda delves into the religious confusion people have in this world. People have created various scriptures, religions, castes, heaven and hell, and are very conscious of gender differences. Kabīr intends for us to look behind the material and all the adjuncts of religion, and to see the soul as being the same in all. On the physical level he points out that we are all made of skin and bones, and that we all contain feces, urine, blood, and marrow. We are all the result of a drop of semen. Since all of us share in the same processes and the same materials, and contain essentially the same things within us, who then is of high caste and who is of low caste?

We give names to bodies, but once a body dies what name does it have? In other words, how can you name the soul that is your real Self, and that is beyond all the physical attributes outlined above? People attribute qualities to the triune God such as that the quality of activity (rajogun) is Brahmā, that of inertia (tamogun) is Shiva, and that of spirituality (satogun) is Vishnu. Thus Brahmā is the creator, Shiva the destroyer, and Vishnu the preserver. Kabīr points out that God is the same for all and that the soul is the same spiritual energy manifesting in all, therefore, we should remain connected with that divinity that is beyond all the divisions people have created. He summarizes that there is no Hindu and no Muslim. We can similarly add no Christian, no Buddhist, no Jew and so forth. On analysis, we understand that man created religions but that the soul and God are beyond all religions. Realizing this, we also realize the unity of all.

Shabda 76

O soul, you are deluding yourself!
You have been fooled just like a dog in a house of mirrors,
and you bark and bark at yourself and die.
You have been fooled just like a lion seeing its own reflection in a well and, thinking it is another lion, jumps in.
You have been fooled just like an elephant seeing himself
in a shiny slab of stone, thrusts his tusks at it.
The monkey, because of greed for the tasty morsel, does
not loosen its grip, and is then made to play tricks from
house to house.
Kabīr says O dear parrot! You think you are in the trap.
Who is it that has trapped you?

Commentary: In this shabda Kabīr is speaking about a person who does not recognize he is the soul, the seat of consciousness but thinks he is the physical body. He looks in a mirror and sees his body but does not see the soul. Kabīr uses a few examples of how animals are fooled. The dog in a house of mirrors sees its own reflection, and thinking it is another dog, keeps on barking at it and dies without realizing it was barking at its own reflection. Similarly, the lion seeing its own reflection in the water thinks it is another lion, and jumps in and loses its life. Again, the elephant seeing its own image in a shining stone, such as a slab of marble, will try to pierce its tusk at the 'other' elephant. Kabīr says at other times we are like the monkey with its hand in a narrow-necked jar grabbing some grain. Because the monkey does not want to give up the grain, it cannot remove its clenched fist, and is thus caught and made to perform tricks from house to house. Similarly, the parrot thinks of itself as trapped when it has landed on to the rolling trap, and is afraid to let go and fly away to freedom. (See explanation of lalani in shabda 73.)

The message in this shabda is that we must not be deceived by our outward appearances. We must see that we are a conscious soul and not merely the physical body. If we consider ourselves to be merely the body, then we are being fooled just as the various animals mentioned in the shabda. But we have a superior intelligence, and an inquiring and logical mind, and are aware of our own consciousness and will. We need to use these attributes to discover who we really are, and reach a state of perfection and realization.

Shabda 77

Many people tried in their various ways, but none found the secret of God. Where can the senses go to obtain rest? Where did those who used to recite Rāma go?

And those who had spiritual knowledge, where did they go? Being detached from the world, they went to the

eternal abode.
Kabīr says I am tired of saying again and again, 'Be absorbed in the bliss and nectar of God.'

Commentary: In this shabda Kabīr speaks about people who have tried in many ways to know God. They practiced various religious activities, rites, and rituals. They went on pilgrimages, attended churches, observed fasts, and practiced penance. These are practices that prevented them from really knowing God. They were using their sense organs to keep themselves busy practicing their religious duties and also seeking various pleasures in life. Where have they all gone, Kabīr asks.

In contrast, Kabīr speaks of people who had spiritual knowledge, or what is called Brahm Gyān. They became detached from the material world and were 'dead while alive.' They were absorbed in the consciousness of God. This does not require any effort, only a realization or intuitive understanding of the nature of the soul and its union with God. But people generally do not follow this type of mystical understanding, so Kabīr says that he is tired of repeating the teaching to people who are not allowing themselves to awaken to spiritual truth and obtain enlightenment.

Shabda 78

I now understand the play of God, the supreme magician.
He beats the drum, shows his play, and at the end, withdraws the whole game.
By his play the gods, men, and sages are deceived. Such is the magic of his Māyā.
Placing all in the house (world), he deceived all of them; none obtained spiritual wisdom.
The magic is false, but the magician is true. This is the

understanding of realized people.
Kabīr says according to what they understand, that is the condition in which people will live.

Commentary: Kabīr is talking about the illusory tricks perpetuated by the power of Māyā. Māyā derives from God, and is the creative power of God. But Māyā also has the power to conceal the true nature of reality from our senses. Our senses allow us to see objective things, but not that which is the underlying cause of all existence. God thus, figuratively, fools all people. But at the same time God has given everyone intellect, consciousness, and wisdom to understand the reality behind material phenomena. Lacking this spiritual insight, people, gods, and sages have been fooled by the magic of Māyā. God has put us in this world, and has given us the ability to know reality. But our senses deceive us, and we become absorbed in the play of life. Kabīr says the play itself is false (has no eternal existence), but the magician who is God, is real. The spiritually wise people know this. According to what people understand, that will be the condition they express in life. People who think that the play is true become victims of Māyā. But if they understand that the play is false but playmaker true, they become the knowers of God.

Shabda 79

O immortal soul, to what non-self phenomenon are you attached? You are fortunate that you can be awakened. Therefore wake up!
O immortal one, just as stars are in the sky, in the same way, light is in you. Awaken by the one who can enlighten you.
That which you seek outside, is not to be found where you search. It resides within you.

Kabīr says only he whose words and thoughts are in harmony can understand this.

Commentary: In this shabda, Kabīr is speaking of the soul that is immortal and non-material. It cannot therefore be attached to anyone or anything. The soul comes alone and departs alone. But as human beings we are fortunate that we can use our minds and intelligence, and through meditation, be in touch with the soul. The enlightened soul can enlighten others. People generally search in various places, religions, and philosophical systems trying to find the Immortal. Kabīr says it cannot be found in these places. It can be found only in the eternity of the soul itself, by going within through meditation. Furthermore, he observes that only people whose words and thoughts are in consonance will be able to realize the Eternal Being. People who say one thing and do other things, who are hypocritical, and whose outward worship is not congruent with their thought of liberation will not be able to realize the Eternal Abode and obtain liberation.

Shabda 80

O man! Decide now what is good for you!
While you are alive, secure a stable dwelling place. After death, where will your residence be?
If you do not take the opportunity to awaken while you are alive, you will find there is no one for you in the end.
Kabīr says listen, saints! The crush of death is quite difficult to endure.

Commentary: This shabda instructs us to decide on our spiritual welfare while we are still alive. It is only in life that we have the mind and intelligence that we can use to elevate ourselves, spiritually or otherwise. We all need peace and happiness, and want to have liberation, but death does not confer this. These can be attained only during life. If we wish to abide in the Eternal Abode of Self-realization, then we have to follow the path now. If we do not obtain that knowledge we will find that, in the end, there is really no one for us. Death will strike a very unkind blow unless we understand that death is only a transient occurrence in the life of the soul. Self-realization gives us the assurance that we, as eternal soul, will continue to be. It is incumbent upon us to elevate the state of our being to such an extent that we know our own soul and its eternity, existing in the Being of God.

Shabda 81

All the saints prepare the fabric of devotion by joining the letters ra and ma to form the name of Rāma.
Valmiki sowed the cottonseed of devotion to Rāma in the forest (world), and Sukhdev harvested the cotton.
Karmabai removed the seeds of the cotton, and Jaidev spun the yarn.
Brahmā, Vishnu, and Shiva, representing activity, righteousness, and inertia, spread the loom in the three worlds.
Reciting the Name, the munis became exhausted, as did Indra and all the kings.
Without tongue (silently) they repeated the praises of Him who is without a dwelling and a country.
To whom can a guest, visiting an empty house, show his love?
The devotees made the four Vedas into the foot pedal of the loom, and the formless into the comb.
They wove the fabric imperfectly despite their devotion.

Commentary: In this shabda, Kabīr is speaking about devotion to Rāma. He likens this devotion to a fabric that has been woven by joining the letters 'ra' and 'ma' to form the name Rāma. Rāma is a name given to God. The sage Valmiki wrote the Ramayana, outlining the life and activities of Lord Rāma. Karmabai, Sukhdev and Jaidev were devotees who made use of devotion as symbolized by their harvesting, cleaning the cotton, and spinning the yarn to make this fabric of devotion. Brahmā, Vishnu, and Shiva represent the creative, upholding, and progressive aspects of God, and the three worlds they created are likened to the loom used by the weaver.

Devotees recite the name of God, either loudly or silently, but without realizing God within their own hearts, they become exhausted without reaching the goal. God has no dwelling place or country. God is ever-present in the hearts of all people. But when devotees do not have knowledge, Kabīr compares this to God coming to an empty house. To whom can God express love when the heart of the devotee is devoid of realization? Devotees use various means in their devotion, such as making use of scriptures like the four Vedas, symbolically forming them into the pedal to operate the loom. They make the formless God into the comb that tightens the weave of the fabric. But Kabīr states that people do this according to the scriptures and their understanding without realizing the underlying unity of all in the Supreme.

For devotion to bear fruit, it must be accompanied by sincerity, dedication, love, and longing for God-realization. Most people do devotion superficially, doing external rituals and repeating prayers, and not realizing God in the depth of their heart. Despite all the scriptures, praying, and religious observances they do not reach the state of peace and bliss; their hearts remain full of worldly desires and materialism.

Shabda 82

O listeners, understand the actions of yogis!
A beautiful woman (Kundalinī Shaktī) plays the musical instrument with her mouth.
The qualified yogi pierces the six chakras and, without an ox, turns the wheel of the mill.
He takes hold of Brahmā (worldly activities) and burns him in the fire of yoga, and the fish (mind) rises to the sky (sahasrāra chakra) and thunders.
There is always a dark night moon (left nostril or left sympathetic nerves) and eclipse sun (right nostril, or right sympathetic nerves), as the dragon (sushumna) swallows them.
They practice turning up the tongue (surbhi or gau bhakshan), closing the nasopharynx (khechari mudra), and drink nectar-like water that flows abundantly, but their bodies becomes lean.
At the trikuti (third eye) a musical instrument sounds, and nectar flows in that unfathomable state.
The water of the earth (kundalinī shaktī) reaches the sky (sahasrāra chakra). Seldom does anyone understand this marvel.
Kabīr says, listen saints! The yogis are fond of siddhis (perfections or powers) and do not pursue liberation.
They are always happy with their practices, but the earth always remains unmarried (beyond the yogi's power).

Commentary: In this allegorical shabda, Kabīr is speaking of yogis and their practices that he represents variously as a beautiful woman, a bull turning the oil mill, Brahmā being burnt in the fire, a fish rising to the sky, the sun and moon being swallowed up by the dragon, and so forth.

The beautiful woman represents the kundalinī shaktī that is

represented as a coiled serpent at the base of the spine. Its mouth is turned upwards and releases the energy that then pierces the six chakras along the spinal cord to reach the thousand-petaled lotus (sahasrāra chakra) at the topmost part of the brain. There the yogi, figuratively turns the energy just as the bull turns the wheel of the oil mill, grinding oil seeds or sugar cane. Brahmā represents activities (rajoguna) which the yogi burns up or controls, making the energy rise to the thousand-petaled lotus. In this state of meditation, the yogi can hear the thunder of silence (anāhad nād). To reach this level the yogi practices the merging of his left and right nostril breaths (moon and sun) into the sushumna. This is what Kabīr is pointing to when he refers to the dragon swallowing up the moon and sun. This figurative swallowing up produces the dark night moon and eclipse of the sun.

One of the yogic practices Kabīr refers to is turning the tongue backwards and upwards to close off the nasopharynx when holding the breath. This is called khechari mudra. This is a difficult exercise, but the yogi figuratively drinks nectar from it. The water of the earth represents the kundalinī shaktī that rises along the spinal cord, piercing the six chakras and reaching the seventh sahasrāra chakra where nectar flows. Kabīr observes that yogis are very fond of obtaining the siddhis (eight perfections or powers) in which they have control over the size, weight, and transference of the body, and control over nature and its elements. But Kabīr observes that despite their attainment of various perfections, they are not able to control the earth, which figuratively remains a virgin. That is, despite their other achievements, the yogis fall short of attaining union with the Eternal Being.

Shabda 83

O foolish man! You go astray because of ignorance, as you

do not attune yourself to God.
You forcefully throw the cow on the ground and, cutting her neck, take away her life.
You turn a living being into a carcass, then say it is halāl (pure and holy).
That flesh that you call holy, please understand how it is formed:
It is produced from the ovum and the semen – that is the flesh you eat.
You do not see your behaviour as foolish, and rationalize it by saying your ancestors did it.
The blood of the one who gave you such instruction to kill for sacrificial purposes is on your neck.
Your black hair (youth) has gone and white (old age) has replaced it, but even now your heart is not pure.
You do rozā, bang, and namāz, and die in a small lonely room in the mosque.
The pandits read the Vedas and Purānas, and the moulvī reads the Koran.
Kabīr says both are headed for hell as they do not know God in their hearts.

Commentary: In this shabda, Kabīr is very concerned about the violence perpetrated towards other living beings. In one of his sākhīs he says, "Do not kill helpless beings, for they all have the same life force as you." Also, "Just as you feel pain, realize other living beings feel pain the same way." It is in this vein that Kabīr uttered this shabda. People kill animals, often in the name of religion. They also read various scriptures that, in the end, do not seem to produce compassion in their hearts. In other words, they perform religious rituals and ceremonies that they feel good about, doing only what their forefathers did. They do not analyze their own behaviour to see if it is consonant with the compassion, mercy, and love that God bestows on all of

His creatures. Whether the animal's neck is cut slowly or is cut suddenly, both forms of killing are violent in that they deprive God's living creature of its life. Kabīr teaches that that which involves violence cannot be considered pure or holy, in a spiritual sense. It is therefore not fit to be offered as food.

From youth to old age, people perform the same violent actions and do not realize that God dwells in their own hearts and in the hearts of all living beings. That is why Kabīr states that both (Hindus and Muslims) will go to hell, mystically meaning both will be trapped in karmic bondage.

Followers of different religions read their particular scriptures, say prayers, and perform observances and rituals according to their teachings. However, all people need to conduct their lives based on the spiritual principles of love, compassion, mercy, non-violence, and caring, and should be striving to make God immediate in their lives. If, however, they continue to do unspiritual things, they will reap their appropriate rewards or punishments. Instead of liberation, they will suffer the effects of their karmas.

Shabda 84

O Kāzi! What Koran are you talking about?
You are expounding it day and night, but you do not know true wisdom.
According to your authority, you perform circumcision but, brother, I do not approve of it.
If God ordained circumcision for you, why were you not born circumcised by Him?
If one becomes a Muslim by circumcision, what can you say of women?
A woman is said to be half of the man, therefore, you remain a Hindu.
If wearing the janeo makes you a Brāhmin, what do wom-

en wear?

From birth she remains a Shudra, then why do you eat the food she serves?

Where did Hindus and Muslims come from, and who established these paths?

Search earnestly in your own heart: where is heaven and who attained it?

Kabīr says listen, dear brothers! These people strongly adhere to their practices. But those who have not sought the shelter of God will lament as death approaches.

Commentary: People have different ways of practicing their various religions. These generally have to do with external observances, rituals, and ceremonies. Kabīr observes that people become preoccupied with these external observances and do not get to the core of religious teaching, which is spirituality. People will fight to preserve the right to practice these external forms of religion when, in fact, their inner being is the same, and God is the same for all.

Muslims practice circumcision, but Muslim women are not circumcised. If circumcision makes a person a Muslim, then the women are not Muslims. Similarly, if putting on the janeo, or sacred thread, makes a person a Brāhmin, then women, who do not wear a janeo, are therefore not Brahmins. Kabīr points out that one should rise above external observances and see that the soul is the same in all, despite external religious differences. In essence, God did not make religion. People made religions. Having made religions, people have fought to maintain them. Kabīr says since God is the same for all, why not take the shelter of God Himself, and be free of all the confusion, hatred, violence, and intolerance that are rampant in religions.

Shabda 85

The deluded person says, "This is my house."
That house in which you dwell in delusion is not your house.
You have gathered plenty of elephants, horses, bullocks, and other conveyances.
But you will be driven from your house and given a dwelling place in the jungle.
No one gave you a bundle of money to pay your return passage, so you cannot return.
You have put your wife (good thinking) out, and keep the mistress (bad thinking) in the palace (heart), where you dwell.
Nine maunds of threads have entangled you and cannot be unraveled. You remain entangled birth after birth.
Kabīr says listen saints! Try to understand the meaning of this poem.

Commentary: Why is a person deluded by saying, "This house is mine"? The house refers to the body or to the material houses in which we live. Neither really belong to us. We die and leave both houses behind. The soul departs from the body at death and we have no control over these events. Despite accumulating a great deal of material possessions, in fact, we own nothing. We leave everything, and at death we are, figuratively, taken to the jungle, which means we are cremated or buried. Kabīr says no one gives the departing soul a bag of money to purchase a return ticket. The departed soul does not return to any of its former possessions.

In the lives of many people, the wife (good thinking) is put aside, and bad thinking takes her place. Bad thinking consists of negativities, passions, greed, egotism, anger, and so forth, that are generally detrimental to a good life. During life, despite bad thinking, the soul continues to dwell in the palace of the heart. The nine maunds of thread represent the five gross elements, the three gunas, and the mind that entangle the soul birth after birth, unless the soul attains liberation through enlightenment. Kabīr is urging us to try to understand the mystery of life, and not to go through this life in a deluded manner.

Shabda 86

Kabīr says, O ignorant people! You built your house in soggy soil and the world does not seem to know it.
People do not follow the instructions of the guru, but foolishly imagine themselves going to a non-existent palace.
In the entire creation, Kabīr remains a hansā (swan) while there are many crows with open beaks.
Because of karmas, people obtained the body and are trapped by lustful desires.
People recite their scriptures, but have built their homes in water.
There is unlimited robbery going on within, so the people do not find the secret of reality.
The lustful woman (Māyā) devours all the good qualities of people, just as the deer eats up the grass.
Very great intellectuals and thinkers have become exhausted, but were unable to control Māyā.
Brahmā, Varuna, Kuvera, Purandar, Pīpā, Prahalād, and Hiranyakush whose abdomen was torn by the fingernails of the man/lion incarnation of Vishnu, could not escape death.
Gorakh, Dattatreya, Digambar, Nāmdev, and Jaidev were all devotees, but no one has news about them, or where their dwelling place is.
The mind plays a game of dice with the soul, and birth is the casting of the dice.

No one knows what will happen from one breath to the next, and no one can determine their future.
The earth extends in all four directions, and between Turkey (idā) and Siam (pingalā) there is Delhi (sushumna).
Above them there is a marvelous sight (meditation) where the power of Yama (god of death) is destroyed.
All the incarnations that came to the Earth stand with folded hands.
You are created in a strange, unfathomable, and profound way, and all beauty is yours.
Kabīr says, authoritatively, even today you should try to become wise! I always exhort you to clean the mirror of your heart with the help of the guru.

Commentary: People are prone to building their lives on false hopes, misunderstanding, and misinformation. Thus their houses are built on soggy ground that is unstable. People do not pay attention to their true state of things, that the body is transient and that the soul is like the swan figuratively plucking pearls. There are many ignorant people who are likened to crows with open beaks trying to get hold of some gem to ennoble their lives. We all know that karmas operate in our lives, and that karmas are based on our own desires, longings, cravings, and so forth. Despite reading scriptures and reciting them, people persist in making their homes in water, that is, they continue to pursue false hopes of permanency in the world.

Limitless cravings, desires, and passions rob the soul, preventing us from realizing its reality. Because of longings and lust which entrap us, all of our good and noble living is being destroyed. Kabīr says that intellectuals and thinkers along with Brahmā (the Creator), Varuna (god of the waters), Kuvera (god of wealth), Purandar or Indra (god of thunder), Pīpā and Prahalād who were devotees, Hiranyakush (Hiranyakashipu) a tyrant king, were all destroyed by death. He lists several other devotees who vanished from the Earth without a trace. Kabīr likens life to a game of dice in which birth is the casting of the dice since in both there is uncertainty. But he goes on to explain that people can rise above physical aspects and reach a higher state of consciousness in meditation, and touch the reality of their own inner being and realize that God has made people in a very mysterious way and made them beautifully. He exhorts all people to become wise, to clean the mirror of the heart and become pure, and to free themselves from illusory material bondage.

Shabda 87

Kabīr says, O soul, your body is in the soggy dirt and your mind is playing the hunting game.
Worldly pleasures are like the deer at which the mind shoots the arrow according to its own desires.
The alert king saves his kingdom (soul) and easily pierces the root (mulādhāra chakra).
Meditation is the bow while knowledge is the arrow; the yogi remains steadfast in them.
He pierces the six chakras and the lotus (sahasrāra chakra) and becomes enlightened.
He drives away the wild animals of lust, anger, greed, and attachments.
He remains steadfast in the gagan mandal (meditation), where there is neither day nor night.
The servant Kabīr reached that state that is apart from worldly relations and companions.

Commentary: This shabda explains the relationship between the body, the mind, and the soul. The body is stuck in the material world and the mind, like a hunter, hunts everywhere to enjoy worldly pleasures according to its desires. The soul, on the other hand, wants to be free from all the worldly pleasures and to attain a state of bliss that is described as gagan mandal, or the pinnacle of meditation.

Kabīr uses the example of the yogi who, in meditation, shoots the arrow of divine knowledge and achieves self-control. He thus saves his kingdom (soul). He pierces all the chakras and reaches the thousand-petaled lotus at the top of the brain, and reaching it, he becomes enlightened. He is then free from all negative qualities and becomes pure. In this state of meditation there is no question of day or night, up or down, good or bad, and so forth. It is a state of pure being, beyond all dualities. Kabīr states that he reached that state and that it is not tied to family relations or companions. This is an individual attainment in silence.

Shabda 88

It is not an animal, brother! It is not an animal at all! Yet all the people eat its flesh.
This one animal roams all over the world; it is difficult to explain its nature.
If you open its abdomen, brother, you will not find a heart or entrails.
Such is its meat brother, but it is sold everywhere, all the time!
If you throw its bones and legs like rubbish in fire, the fire and smoke will not devour it.
This animal has no head or horns, so how can it have a tail?
The priests created a business together and made all the people sing the wedding song.

Commentary: This very allegorical shabda talks about the nature of Māyā that Kabīr likens to an animal. He calls it an animal that has no meat and yet which people of the world are continually eating. This means that the people are preoccupied with the pleasures of the senses spurred on by Māyā. It is difficult to explain the nature of Māyā. Kabīr says that looking inside its abdomen one finds no heart or entrails. People are continually pursuing the pleasures of the senses and sparking various desires that they need to have fulfilled. This is all the play of Māyā but yet remains very attractive to the majority of people. Because of this continual attraction, the priests have been able to create a business out of Māyā – stoking the fire of people's desires and longings, frustrations, expectations, fears, anxieties, and so forth. All the while people continue to sing the wedding song, extolling the pleasures of Māyā.

Shabda 89

O fortunate people! For what reason have you developed greed? You are losing this gem of a life.
Why did you sow the seed of evil in your previous birth?
Your body is made from the drop (semen) and developed in the vessel of fire (womb).
For ten months (lunar months) you remained in the mother's womb and, afterwards, you again became enmeshed in Māyā.
From youth you have now grown old, and what was to happen has happened.
When Yama comes to tie you (death), you will cry with tearful eyes.
Do not have hope that this life will continue, as death has control of your breath (death can come anytime).
The people of the world are in a betting game. Be careful how you throw the dice!

Commentary: It is often said it is a great fortune to have human birth, and that it is like acquiring a precious gem. But people get caught up in greed and other passions, and figuratively lose this gem. What is happening in this life is dependent on what has occurred in previous lives according to the law of karma. This is why Kabīr asks why we did bad karmas in the past and now have to suffer the consequences. The body is derived from semen and ovum, and is nurtured in the womb that Kabīr likens to a vessel of fire. The symbology is of a kiln that bakes the bread to perfect it. Just so, the womb nurtures the body to perfect it during its development. After ten lunar months birth occurs, and the baby grows into a youth and then into old age. People generally accumulate a great deal of karma during such a life and cannot stop the consequences. Thus, as death approaches, people are filled with various regrets and unfulfilled desires and wish to hang on to life, but death is inevitable. The world is involved in gambling in the sense that life itself is a gamble. To be careful how we throw the dice of life means we must be careful in the way we live in thought, word, and deed. Our karmas will determine our future in this life and subsequent lives.

Shabda 90

O saints and mahants worship Him who is free from the noose of death.

Dattatreya did not know the secret and was entangled in illusory practices. It is like churning water to obtain butter. Such was his samādhī.

Gorakh was not able to retain his breath (died), though he boasted of the method of yoga. He attained many perfections and sensory control, but did not know the power of Brahman (Absolute Reality).

Vashisht was imbued with pure knowledge and obtained a disciple such as Rāma. That Rāma is said to be the creator, but death did not spare even him.

The Hindu says he will take my body and cremate it, and
the Muslim says, "He is my pīr and I will bury it."
Both Hindus and Muslims will quarrel over my body, and
the liberated Kabīr will be there witnessing it.

Commentary: In spiritual life the final goal is to realize the Absolute (the Supreme Reality). Throughout religious history and mythology, great personalities have practiced various types of austerities and observances in order to realize this reality. But many have failed to experience the reality that is already in them. They suffered hardships and persecutions, and died, or were killed mercilessly.

Dattatreya was supposed to be an incarnation of Vishnu, and became a hermit. He is said to have had twenty-four gurus. Gorakh Nāth was a great Hatha yogi who strenuously practiced various Hatha yoga postures and other routines. He attained many powers. Kabīr says these practices and isolationism are not really necessary to realize the Supreme Reality. The sage Vashisht was the guru of Lord Rāma, but Lord Rāma himself died at the Guptara Ghat on the river Sarju at Ayodhya. In other words, it is not the external practices that are required for the realization of the Supreme. It is the purification of the mind and character, and realizing the Divinity that already dwells within.

In the last two lines Kabīr foresees what will happen after his own death. His Hindu disciples would want to cremate him, and his Muslim disciples would want to bury him. They would quarrel amongst themselves for the disposal of his body. He states that he will be a witness to such a quarrel. He advised his disciples prior to his death that they must not quarrel about his body's disposal. However, being human, they reverted to their own practices and forgot the unity he had taught them.

Shabda 91

I see no one born in the world who is really happy. Wherever I look, I see people suffering.
I am speaking about sunrise (birth) and sunset (death). Please carefully consider them.
Everyone is suffering on the journey of life, whether he is a householder or a renunciate.
Because of suffering in the world, Shukacharya renounced the world while he was in his mother's womb.
Yogis and wandering ascetics suffer a great deal, and those who practice austerity suffer twice as much.
Hopes and longings are present in every heart, and there is none that is free of them.
If I tell the truth the world gets angry with me, but I cannot tell a lie.
Kabīr says even those who started the path of religious actions with desires also suffered.

Commentary: People in the whole world suffer in one way or another. It is difficult to find one who is happy and not complaining about some type of unhappiness, stress, or difficulties in his or her life. Kabīr talks about the suffering that afflicts all of humanity. From birth to death, people are subject to suffering through illnesses, stresses, and natural disasters. He instructs us to carefully consider what life is all about, and why there is suffering. People may pursue different types of livelihood, such as having a family or living as renunciates. Some people practice yoga, and others wander about as ascetics. Some practice difficult austerities, and what they generally get is more suffering. They do not necessarily become enlightened, nor understand the mystery of birth and death. Shukacharya was a sage who is said to have realized the sufferings of the world and, as a realized soul, gave up all attachments to the world even before he was born.

Most people suffer because they have unfulfilled hopes and desires. Because of these hopes and desires, they pursue all types of activities to attain happiness that is ever elusive. Kabīr points out that he is focused on explaining the truth about life to people, but they often become angry. Yet he has to tell the truth. He says that even the ones who started this whole path of religious actions and desires, and ordained the path of karma also suffered. He is referring to Brahmā the creator in the first place, and also to all the priestly castes that started rites and rituals of all kinds that have not given liberation to people, but have further entangled them in misunderstanding and illusion.

Shabda 92

O my dear brother! Try to understand the mind and where it goes after it leaves the body.
Sanak, Sanandan, Jaidev, and Nāmdev, though great devotees, did not understand the mind.
Ambarish, Prahalād, and Sudāmā also were true devotees, but they did not understand the mind.
Bharthari, Gorakh, and Gopichand were absorbed in the mind and felt happy.
Shukdev was absorbed in that mind, the secret of which no one knows.
Shiva, Sanak, Nārad, and Sheshnag did not realize the mind that dwelt in their bodies.
Kabīr says only one Niranjan manifests in all bodies, All the people are wandering about in doubts about the mind.

Commentary: The mind is very mysterious, and though people, even great sages, use the mind, they do not understand the secret of the mind. Kabīr asks the question: Where does the mind go once it leaves the body? Nobody really knows. He is drawing attention to the mystical fact that the mind is subject to pain and suffering as well as happiness, but in order to realize pure consciousness the mind has to be superseded. The whole yoga system is based on the fact that the mind must be subdued in order to gain enlightenment. Shri Ramana Maharshi once stated, "Give up all thoughts and then ask yourself, where is the mind?"

Kabīr mentions great personalities of the past who were great poets, devotees, grammarians, and so forth. They lived their lives practicing their various callings, and although they were pure devotees and enjoyed happiness, they still functioned at the level of the mind. It is only by superseding the mind and reaching the region of pure transcendental consciousness, that one truly understands the nature of the soul and God. Shukdev is said to have been enlightened prior to birth and did not wish to be born into the world of illusion and rebirths. Kabīr observes that one Niranjan is embodied in all beings, yet people are still in doubt. Niranjan here refers to the mind that is really one and not divisible. But the mind is a powerful force in worldly life and difficult to overcome. Transcending the mind leads to pure consciousness, resulting in the realization of the great unity of all in God.

Shabda 93

O man! Such is the illusory condition of your world and such are the dealings in this Kaliyug (Iron Age),
Who can suffer these illusions day by day? This is not my way.
Everyone loves the teachings of the Smritis (scriptures), but they do not know the reality of the heart.
They sacrifice living animals in front of lifeless idols and see nothing with their eyes.

They give up the nectar and drink the poison, and tie the counterfeit in a knot (in the waistband).
They give a throne to a thief, and turn their faces away from the noble.
Kabīr says liars keep the company of liars, and cheaters deal with cheaters.
The three worlds are full of this type of dealing, and there is no one truly trustworthy.

Commentary: Kabīr observes the condition of the world. Day by day people are occupied in activities that keep them away from knowing the Reality of their own heart. They live in illusion so far as spirituality is concerned. People read the scriptures and feel good, but do not delve into the real meaning as it applies to the heart. They thus see nothing of that reality. Along the same lines, people sometimes sacrifice animals in the hopes of propitiating gods and idols, or winning some favour. Doing this they further entangle themselves in negative karmas. They give up the nectar of spiritual teachings (the bliss of realization), and drink the poisons (illusions) of the world.

Kabīr observes that thieves mingle with thieves, and cheaters with cheaters, because the condition of the world does not improve, although good spiritual teachings are available. People do not take the spiritual teachings to heart. They do not realize the divinity that is omnipresent in every heart. From his spiritual vantage point, Kabīr is observing the condition of this Kaliyug (Iron Age) and recognizing that there is hardly anyone truly trustworthy who can show the spiritual path and free people from the effects of their karmas.

Shabda 94

Please tell me, in what language can you explain Niranjan?

He has no hands, feet, mouth, ears, or tongue. O man, how can you describe Him?
If you say one light (soul) gives light to another (mind), then tell me what is the evidence you have for that light?
If one light (mind) merges into the other light (soul), then where has that light gone?
Brahmā produced the four Vedas, but he did not understand the mystery of this light.
Kabīr says listen saints! A learned pandit may fathom this mystery.

Commentary: It is a deep mystery to try to understand the nature of the soul. The soul is eternal and is of God, and is therefore considered a Divine Light. The light of the soul gives light to the mind that, in turn, gives light to the senses. Kabīr asks the question that if this light that he calls Niranjan has no sense organs or organs of action, how then can you describe it or experience it? And when the soul merges in the mind, or vice versa, where does the other go? And what evidence is there that you can talk about it? The mystery of this light can only be solved in the depth of meditation in which all the senses are controlled and merge into the mind, and the mind merges into the soul, and the soul into the Godhead. This experience cannot be described in words. Even Lord Brahmā, who uttered the four Vedas, could not make any one experience this state of union. The erudite people of the world also fall short of this experience until they go beyond material knowledge and merge in the light of the soul and realize, intuitively, the union of this light with the light of God.

Shabda 95

Who can act as a sheriff to protect the city (body)?
In this city, meat (sense-gratification) is spread all around

and the vulture (mind) keeps watch over it.
In this city, the rat (ignorant person) is the boat, and the cat (Māyā) is the boatman. The frog (mind) is sleeping, and the snake (passion) is keeping watch.
The bull (ignorance) gives birth to a calf, and the cow (knowledge) remains barren. The calf (desires) is milked three times a day (desires are rampant).
Everyday the lion (soul) wakes up and fights with the jackal (mind).
Only a rare person understands the words of Kabīr.

Commentary: In this allegorical shabda, Kabīr observes what the generality of life is like. The body is like a city in which there is the mind, the soul, the senses, ignorance, knowledge, desires, and evil. All of these act in their various ways to influence life. The contrary sayings, such as meat being protected by the vulture, or the cat rowing the boat that is the rat, or the frog sleeping while the snake is keeping watch, or the bull giving birth and the cow remaining barren, et cetera, are all applicable to life.

Meat is appealing to the vulture just as sense-gratification is appealing to the mind, so the person becomes a captive. Similarly, the cat or Māyā (illusion), drives the ignorant person. The mind remains sleepy and dull while the passions take over. When ignorance and evil prevail, knowledge seems to disappear. Knowledge here refers to the knowledge of the Self. The soul is striving for Self-realization and has to do battle with the mind that is beset with sense-gratifications and pleasures. It is the wise person who can perceive his condition in life and try to rectify it in order to obtain peace and liberation in this life.

Shabda 96

For whom should I weep when so many have departed from the world?

Many have died, and have not returned to the world.
When I cried out to you, you did not pay attention. You did not consider the time that you spent in the womb.
What will crying now accomplish? For what reason are you creating sorrow for me?
Kabīr says, people please listen to me! Please do not become victims of death.

Commentary: The goal of spiritual life is to realize the existence, consciousness, and bliss of the soul. These are its eternal attributes. They are beyond the world of sorrows and sufferings. By becoming intimately connected with the spirit, one rises above sorrows and the fear of death. After all, death is only for the physical body and is a natural part of living. What will it benefit anyone to feel sorrow as death approaches? All people will die and they will not come back to the world to relate their experiences.

Kabīr is saying that he has been instructing the people, literally crying out to them, but they have not paid attention. Returning to the womb indicates that one has not obtained liberation, and has to be reborn to go through the vicissitudes of life all over. When people suffer, they cry out for help, but it is often too late. Kabīr has advised that we are given precious human birth in order to realize our eternal nature and not to be victims of death.

Shabda 97

O man! Just as Allah or Rāma created you, just so He created all beings. Therefore, have compassion for others.
What is the benefit of shaving your head and bowing to the ground, or even bathing to purify the body if you do not have compassion?
You slaughter animals, yet you are called humble all the

while hiding your faults.

How can you benefit by washing your hands, brushing your teeth, and then bowing in the mosque when you have deceit in your heart? What benefit do you derive from reciting the Namāz, or going to Mecca on pilgrimage?

The Hindu observes the eleventh day fast twenty-four times a year, and the Muslim observes Rozā for thirty days.

Who advised you to avoid eleven months and confine yourself to one month of the year?

If Khuda lives in the mosque, which god is then present in the rest of the world?

If Rāma dwells in pilgrimages and idols, then you both have not realized the truth.

The Hindu says God dwells in the East, and the Muslim says He dwells in the West.

Search in your hearts, deeply in your hearts, and there you will find Karim and Rāma.

The Vedas and the Koran are not false, but he who does not ponder on God is false.

All beings have a soul, and suffer the same pleasure and pain. Then why should one kill another?

God created both female and male beings, and all are manifestations of His form.

Kabīr says he is the child of Allah and Rāma and they are his guru and pīr.

Commentary: God is omnipresent, and all people are his children irrespective of religions. For God, the various religions do not really matter. What really matters to God are the hearts of people. If people are pure in their hearts, and have love for one another, then all the religious strife and hostilities will disappear. Kabīr observed that people outwardly pay respect to their religions in various ways, mostly following outward forms but not following the inner path of the spirit.

He gives a few examples to point out the hypocrisy that religious people perpetrate. He notes that many Hindu priests will shave their heads, bathe to purify themselves, bow down in their temples, but then sacrifice animals as if they have no compassion. The Hindus also observe the eleventh-day fast every two weeks, twenty-four times a year, and turn to the East to pray to God. They also go on pilgrimages and feel that God dwells in deities, in the holy places, and temples. Kabīr also observes similar practices among Muslims. They wash their hands and feet and clean their mouths, and then go to pray in the mosque. They observe the Rozā and go on pilgrimages to Mecca. They pray facing Mecca, when God is really omnipresent. The Muslims also slaughter animals in the name of Allah.

Kabīr is wondering that if people fast twenty-four times a year, or thirty days a year, then what happens the rest of the year. Are people not supposed to be truly religious throughout the year? Similarly, if people go to holy places to worship God, then what about God who dwells everywhere and can be worshipped in the heart or in the home equally? He says we should search for God in our own hearts, and we will find that both Allah and Rāma are present there. He also teaches that we are all children of God and reflect His form, whether we are male or female. He further points out that the Vedas and the Koran are not at fault, but rather the people who do not reflect upon the teachings nor live by them, who are at fault.

The religion Kabīr is pointing to is the religion of the heart, the realization of God's omnipresence and His love and compassion for all beings. It transcends all the outward religious observances performed by people of the various religions. We need to give up cunningness, hypocrisy, rationalization, ego, and passions, and realize God's omnipresent love. Only then can we have true love and compassion in our hearts for one another, and follow the true religion of the heart.

Shabda 98

May I always remember the name of God! I give up everything else as they are useless to me.
In the beginning, where was Adam and his wife Eve? Where then were the holy men and prophets?
Where were the earth and the sky, and where were the Vedas, holy books, and Koran?
Who in this world created the mosque, the Rozā and Id, and the sacrificing of animals?
The name of God alone is true, and you call Him Allah, and bow down and offer salutation at it.
Tell me where is heaven, and by whose command do you use the knife to sacrifice innocent animals? Man is the creator of this artificiality, and started the paths of the Hindu and the Muslim.
Where were the day and night, and who created all this artificiality?
Kabīr says God is beyond caste and lineage, and is beyond day and night.

Commentary: In this shabda, Kabīr speaks about the spirit of God that is beyond all externalities. It is beyond day or night, beyond religions, doctrines, and scriptures, beyond mosques and temples, and beyond prophets and sages. It is also beyond heaven and hell. From the point of view of the spirit, all external manifestations and observances are artificial, created by people according to their own understanding, beliefs, and practices. They are not the finality. Kabīr points out that those who created all the external observances or artificialities have robbed the human spirit, and bound it through the pursuit of external observances.

God never made a rule that one building must be called a mosque and another a temple, and yet a third a church. God never made a rule that we must sacrifice animals to please Him with the hopes of getting to heaven. God never made it a rule that worshipping in one way or another takes precedence over realizing His spirit that dwells in all beings. The more people get involved in the externalities of religion, the farther away they move from the spirit of God, and the farther they are from liberation.

Shabda 99

O friend, where are you going alone? Why don't you get up and attend to your house?
You nurtured the body with milk, sugar and clarified butter, but your body will be discarded.
Your precious head, which you carefully decorated with a beautiful turban will, in the end, be destroyed by the crows.
Your bones will burn like the wood in the forest, and your hair will burn like a bundle of dry grass.
Your relatives will not go with you, much less the elephant tied up in the courtyard.
You could not enjoy the pleasures of Māyā, and death, like a cat, pounced on you.
Kabīr says people do not awaken even as they get old, and not even as Yama (death) is about to hit them on the head with his club.

Commentary: In this shabda, Kabīr uses sarcasm to try to awaken people to the realization that death will one day strike them. People spend their lives nurturing the body, and taking care of their homes, and all the materialistic pursuits they have. They seek sense gratification and do not pay much attention to the gift of life God has given them. They do not think all human relationships are transitory.

Kabīr is addressing the corpse lying on a funeral pyre and is about to be cremated as the final act of its physical existence. What will become of the soul? The body, though precious, is figuratively fit for the crows. All wealth and material possessions will be left behind. People everywhere see death, but they still do not attend to their spiritual lives even in old age, not even as Kabīr puts it, death is about to club them on the head.

Shabda 100

O people, establish a good relationship with God!
In the world, the son (ignorant person) took hold of his mother (attachments) and flirted with his daughter (bad thoughts).
His mother-in-law (Māyā) and sister-in-law (bad intellect) got together and placed the soul in the turmoil of the world (the cycle of birth and death).
I (saint) am the brother-in-law of Rāma, and he is my brother-in-law (sister's husband).
I am the father and God is my son.
Kabīr says this is the power of God, therefore, O son of Māyā, dwell in the presence of God!

Commentary: This is a very allegorical shabda. It can perhaps have more than one interpretation. Looked at superficially, it seems to make no sense, but once the human relationships Kabīr mentions are given human attributes, the meaning becomes clearer. First, Kabīr exhorts people to establish a good relationship with God. He does this because Māyā deludes people through attachment, ignorance, bad intellect, and negative karmas, thus embroiling the soul in the turmoil of the world. The soul is then subject to suffering, old age, death, and then re-birth.

Kabīr says he is the brother-in-law of Rāma and that Rāma is his brother-in-law. Lord Rāma had a sister named Shanta, and Shanta means peace. The saint has accepted peace in his life, so he has become the brother-in-law of Rāma. Next he says he, the saint or man for that matter, is the father and God is the son. What may be meant here is that the son, through his good karmas and noble conduct, is supposed to liberate his ancestors from hell. This is a belief held in Hinduism. Since the power to liberate rests with God, God thus becomes the son of man. Since only God has this power to give liberation, and Māyā entraps man, Kabīr again advises the necessity of dwelling in God and being free from Māyā.

Shabda 101

Observing life, I feel surprised. Hardly anyone understands this verse.
The earth (kundalinī shaktī) turns around and pierces the sky (sahasrāra chakra), and the ant (consciousness) swallows up the elephant (mind).
Without wind, the mountain (ego) flies, and all creatures (desires) climb the tree (life).
The dry lake (meditation) is full of waves (joy), and the goose (soul) frolics without water.
The pandit sits and reads the Purāna, but without realizing this state, why does he expound it?
Kabīr says he who understands this verse is a true saint, and is always authoritative.

Commentary: In this shabda, Kabīr is speaking of meditation in which the spiritual energy called kundalinī shaktī rises from the lowest chakra (mulādhāra) through the spinal cord and reaches the highest chakra (sahasrāra) in the brain. Once this occurs, the devotee realizes God. In meditation the elephant-like mind, that can be quite unruly, enters the mouth of the ant. That is, the mind becomes absorbed in meditative consciousness. In meditation, the ego flies away even when there is no wind, and desires float away. Waves of joy arise and the soul enjoys bliss. Many scholars will read the scriptures and not realize the essence of these teachings. Nevertheless, this does not deter them from expounding on spiritual knowledge which they have not realized. Kabīr says the person who can understand this allegorical shabda is a true saint and will speak with authority, meaning such a person will have realized the eternal Truth.

Shabda 102

O son of a slave girl, should I insult you? You need to consider and understand the true path.
The master of the house is yours but you do not meet him, even in dreams.
The Brāhmin, the Kshatria, the Vaishya, (and Shudra) do not heed my advice.
There are many yogis, jangams, and others that have created many paths due to their ego.
Kabīr says that there is one yogi (soul) who wanders in doubts and enjoys worldly pleasures (delusions).

Commentary: In this shabda, Kabīr, in a loving way, rebukes us as the son of the slave girl, or of the perverse woman who is Māyā. A human being, regardless of gender, is the son of Māyā, and she keeps deluding him, and keeping him away from paying attention to the spiritual path of life. He becomes engrossed in the material pleasures of the world and forgets his soul. Kabīr instructs us that we must follow the proper way of life so we may really know our true Self, and its relationship to God. He explains that there is a master in the house, namely, the body.

The master is God, yet even in dreams we do not have this realization and our lives become unspiritual.

Kabīr goes on to state that the priestly caste, the warrior or protective caste, and the business caste, all of which are higher than the Sudhras or low caste, are not paying attention to his advice – that life is indeed a great gift of God and must be used as such. Instead, they are all quarreling according to the various dogmas, scriptures, beliefs, and traditions. They do not see the unity that manifests in them as God. The yogis, fakirs, and so called holy people have all started different ways of worship, rituals, doctrines, and sects that deviate from the simple and true spiritual path of union with God. Kabīr observes that there is one true yogi, and that is the soul. But it is trapped in this body and in the world, and wanders about as if lost, engrossed in worldly pleasures. If it could only realize its unity with God, its existence would become sublime, peaceful, and blissful.

Shabda 103

O people, you are simple-minded and do not understand!
You say just as water mixes with water, so does the soul mix with the dust.
O Vyasa! If you are a true priest of Mithila, then you should go and die in Maghar.
If a God-realized person dies in Maghar, he will not be a victim of birth and death. Dying elsewhere will bring shame on God.
Ordinary people believe if one dies in Maghar, he will become a donkey in another life. They have lost faith in God.
What is the difference between the holy city of Kāshi and the barren Maghar if God dwells in my heart?
If dying in Kāshi takes me to heaven, then what need is there for me to do devotion to God?

Commentary: Many people have superstitions and misunderstandings about the real nature of life and its goal. They become engaged in various practices and belief systems that do not awaken them to spiritual knowledge. During Kabīr's time there was a superstition that people who died in the barren, desert-like Maghar were cursed to be reborn as donkeys. Kabīr did not accept such superstitions and so planned to die in Maghar. Knowing of this plan, a priest of Mithila warned him about this belief. It is in this context that Kabīr addresses the priest of Mithila asking what was the difference between dying in the so-called holy city of Kāshi (Varanasi) or in the barren Maghar, when God dwells in the heart. God does not care where you die, because to God, all places are equal since they are all part of His creation.

The essential fact is that you know God is with you, and therefore, any place of death, is just as good as any other. Kabīr says if dying in Kāshi takes you to heaven, then why is there a need to show devotion to God? The physical place of death has no relationship to your attainment of liberation. Liberation has to do with your own spiritual realization. Kabīr advises people not to be innocently bound up with such superstitions, but instead try to obtain true knowledge.

Shabda 104

O Nāth, how will you obtain liberation? Even now, you are full of evil thinking.

What sort of service do you render, and what type of ritual and meditation do you do? Externally you are white like the crane, but inwardly you harbor evil intentions.

Your conduct is like that of a cobra, and is immoral. Your mind is like a falcon, and your intellect like a cat, ready to snatch its prey.

You appear to be very wise, but you are really very hostile to others. You are wrapped in your six philosophies and the garb of your sect.
Kabīr says O servant of God, listen to me! The witch (Māyā) is eating up all the foolish people of the world.

Commentary: In this shabda, Kabīr is speaking about people who outwardly appear to be very religious, but inwardly have evil thoughts and intentions. Māyā is deluding them. One example he gives is of the Nāth yogi. The Nāth sect derives from Gorakhnath who was a great Hatha yogi. The Nāth yogis slit their ears, wear huge earrings, and will sit near a continuously burning fire called the dhuni. They carry the trident, smear their bodies with ashes, and wear matted hair. They are supposed to be descended from Lord Shiva. They take pride in their yoga and strive to achieve various powers.

Kabīr uses the example of the crane that is white, and stands on one leg in the water as if in meditation, but its intention is to pluck the fish. Similarly, people also behave like the snake that can bite and kill with its poison, or behave like the falcon that swoops down and grabs other birds, or like the cat that pounces on the mouse. Many religious people display these types of behaviour in terms of snatching power and authority, but driven by vanity, ego, and material possessions.

Kabīr says these are not the marks of a true devotee of God, but they are the ones of those deluded by Māyā, and have impurity in their heart. They may impress others with their outward appearance and knowledge, but become hostile to those who may oppose them. They are very fond of philosophies and appearances. Kabīr advises that true devotees of God must be pure in thoughts, words, and deeds, and be free from ego, and their intellect and meditation should be pure, reflecting the pure soul that dwells within.

Shabda 105

The demon of delusion has devoured the world. All who worship it are deceived.
Its images of worship are not from the egg, nor do they have a body or life.
How strange it is that people cut living animals and offer them as sacrifice.
They sacrifice the goat and the fowl, and do not realize that in the next birth these creatures will have their turn.
Kabīr says O man, listen to what I am saying! He who worships a demon becomes a demon.

Commentary: The essential function of religion is to set people free from spiritual ignorance, doubts, and delusions. We see people in the world that partake of all types of beliefs and worship, often with great dedication, and yet do not develop peace, love, understanding, equality, and harmony in themselves, and in their relationship with others. The highest ideals of life are reached through spiritual practices that intuitively reveal the nature of the Self, and the nature of the Divine. That is why Kabīr says people are deluded when they do not awaken to the supremacy of the spirit. People worship images, totems, and spirits, but do not travel on the internal journey in the temple of the soul.

Making living sacrifices to gods, goddess, spirits or any other being does not win God's favour. God created all life, and he certainly will be happier (if we can use such terminology for God) to see his created beings sustaining their lives. God is spirit and must be worshipped in spirit. Because of the law of karma, if we inflict harm or destroy life, we will suffer negative consequences. Thus, Kabīr says if we persist in worshipping the demon of delusion, then we will remain deluded, and will not awaken to the reality of the spirit that is our divine nature.

Shabda 106

The black bee (youth) has flown away, and the white crane (age) has arrived.
The night (youth) has passed and day (old age) is also passing.
The maiden soul trembles uncontrollably from fear, not knowing what her beloved will do to her.
Water will not remain in an unbaked clay pot. Just so, the soul will fly away and the perishable body will wither.
The arms have grown tired from chasing the crows (evils). Kabīr says that this story of life has ended.

Commentary: In this shabda, Kabīr mentions the black bee to symbolize youth and black hair, and the white crane to symbolize old age and white hair. Similarly, he symbolizes night with youth, and passing daylight with old age and wisdom. The body inevitably goes through these changes. The mind and intellect similarly pass through stages of childhood to old age, gaining wisdom, experience, and freedom from material bondage. However, the soul feels trapped in the physical body and has to follow the dictates of the mind, directed by the intellect of the person. The soul figuratively trembles in fear not knowing what God has in store for it. It is common experience that not knowing what lies ahead can cause some anxiety. Crows represent evils and desires that keep us bound to the material plane of existence. We strive to drive them away until our 'arms' become tired, and life comes to an end. What then? As Kabīr keeps reminding us, it is advisable to get in touch with the true self now, and allow the flowers of peace, love, harmony and enlightenment to flow through our lives.

Shabda 107

Without the master (God) you are like the bullock of an oilman, going round and round all day.
You do not sit in the company holy people, but remain yoked with your life that is ending.
Flowing with the worldly current of life, you suffer for selfish reasons, and edge closer to death, enduring the torture of Yama.
For the sake of riches, wife, son, and affairs of the state, you have accepted a heavy burden on your head.
You have given up the master and have indulged in the pleasures of the passions. You have sown seeds of sin.
In the vain hope of liberation in this life, you eat the leavings of the departed spirits.
According to your karmas, you are drifting in the ocean of 8.4 million forms of life.
Kabīr says listen saints! Ignorant people are holding on to a dog's tail.

Commentary: Without the Master, people drift through their life being driven by their desires and passions. They follow their daily pursuits to obtain wealth, family, fame, honour and to fulfill personal ambitions, but these only entangle them more and more. These activities take on a proper meaning only when they are done with the realization that God is the Master and that all are serving him.

In India, oil used to be pressed from oil seeds using bullocks. The bullocks would go around all day long turning the oil mill. At the end of the day, the bullock has not really gone anywhere. Kabīr likens this scenario to people going through life but not achieving the consequential goal. Yet they still hope to obtain salvation. Unfortunately, if they are not following the proper path that truly leads to liberation, salvation becomes impossible.

According to people's karmas, they will be born again and again, and be presented with the opportunity to obtain salvation. It is this regard that Kabīr speaks of the importance of keeping company with noble people, and following a true spiritual path. This must be done from the depth of one's own self in order to realize the pristine state of being and liberation. Otherwise one would be figuratively holding on to the tail of a dog. This is a reference to pinning hopes on false teachings and practices. The dog drowns in the ocean of life and cannot save us just as we also eventually drown.

Shabda 108

Now I have become like a fish out of the water, because I boasted of my penances in my previous life.
I was noble and my mind was detached. For the love of God, I forsook my people.
I forsook Kāshi, and followed ignorance.
O master, tell me what will be my condition?
Am I a bad servant or are you ignorant of my devotion?
Between the two of us, who is at fault?
I have come to your refuge, but I cannot see the feet of Hari anywhere.
I have come to your refuge, but the servant Kabīr is completely disappointed.

Commentary: In this shabda, Kabīr speaks from the point of view of the soul. The fish out of the water represents the soul longing for God but has to take birth and return to the world. Because of ego, people are prone to boast about their religious life, austerities, and accomplishments. These boasts incur karmas that result in the soul returning to reap the fruits of those karmas. A person might feel great because he has renounced family ties, wealth, and other material things, while in his mind he is not truly detached, nor attached to the feet of God. Having already suffered and now suffering in worldly bondage again, he cries out to God that he cannot find him, and wonders whether he is a bad devotee or whether God is not attentive to him. Not finding refuge in God and not realizing the presence of God, the soul feels sad. Kabīr is really saying we must get rid of ego, purify ourselves, and realize God in this life. We will then not have to suffer material bondage, and think that God has forsaken us.

Shabda 109

People say Kabīr has gone far away, but only a very wise person would know the secret.
All the people know that Rāma was the son of Dasrath, but the secret of God's name is totally different.
People see things according to their own knowledge. Thus seeing a rope, they might say it is a snake.
Although people know the fruits of noble qualities, they forget God, and cannot find salvation.
God is the support for all, just as the water is the support for the fish.
Kabīr advises you to exert more effort to attain God.

Commentary: In this shabda, Kabīr is speaking about the fathomless nature of the name of God. He reminds people that Rāma was the son of King Dasrath and though people worship him, the secret of God's name is quite different. God's name is formless and is the supreme power. If people do not understand God in this infinite and formless state, it is be difficult for them to obtain liberation. People interpret things or situations according to their own experience and knowledge. Therefore, people may have wrong interpretations and reach wrong conclusions, and not realize the truth. The imagination can tell a person that he is seeing a snake, when in fact, he would see a rope on close examination. Likewise, people accept various incarnations and deities and worship them, but fail to see God. This keeps them from being able to reach the region of pure consciousness that is above the mind and where they can obtain Self-realization. Kabīr says we need to exert more effort in the proper direction in order to obtain God-realization.

Shabda 110

No one can abolish the effects of his karmas.
How can anyone remove what is written in his karmas, even if millions of ages were to pass?
Guru Vashisht decided the most auspicious time for the wedding of Rāma and Sita, and taught them the auspicious mantra. Despite the auspicious occasion, Sita, who married Rāma, did not enjoy a moment of happiness.
He who is said to be the creator of the three worlds, killed King Bali deceitfully. But such a time came when revenge was exacted on him.
He disguised the face of Nārad, making it look like that of a monkey. He tore off the arms of Sishupal, but wound up becoming Hari without arms.
Do not say that Parvati was barren, and that Shiva was a beggar.
Kabīr says he is relating the story of God's incarnations, but the law of karma operates differently.

Commentary: Kabīr emphasizes that what is written in the law of karma cannot be removed. Every action has an equal and opposite reaction. Also, as you sow, so you shall reap. These are well known laws and they cannot be broken. Guru Vashisht was a very wise sage who instructed Lord Rāma in absolute knowledge. He chose the most auspicious time for Rāma's wedding to Sita, and taught him the Surya mantra for protection. Rāma was a prince and Sita a princess and were used to palace life, but they still had to spend fourteen years in the forest.

There is a story that Rāma killed King Bali with an arrow while hiding behind a tree. Rāma was the incarnation of Lord Vishnu. Later, Vishnu incarnated as Lord Krishna, and Bali incarnated as a hunter, shot Krishna with an arrow and he died. This is an example of how the law of karma works. A similar story is of Nārad, a celestial messenger and instructor. At one time Nārad wanted to be handsome in order to attract a bride. To abolish his pride, his face was turned into that of a monkey.

Parvati was married to Lord Shiva and had children, and therefore she cannot be said to be barren. Lord Shiva, nearly always shown in meditation, should not be thought of as a beggar or renunciate according to popular lore; he was a husband and father.

These are various stories written in Indian mythology but they explain how the law of karma operates, even among incarnations of God and holy people, saints, prophets, and saviours. Kabīr is pointing out that the law of karma is not what people may think, but is universal and operates everywhere, at all times, and applies to everyone.

Shabda 111

Is there any knowledgeable guru who can understand the contrary ways of this world?
Fire (misery) burns in the water (heart), and the blind person (ignorant) says he sees clearly.
The cow (Māyā) eats the lion (soul), and the deer (craving mind) eats the cheetah (contentment).
The crow (indiscrimination) ensnares the bird of prey (discrimination), and the pheasant (ignorance) conquers the hawk (knowledge).
The rat (doubt) eats the cat (intellect), and the jackal (de-

sires) eats the dog (consciousness).
He who knows the eternal truth of the soul, is fit to wear a saint's garb.
There is one frog (meditation) that eats the five snakes (five passions).
Kabīr loudly proclaims that these two, the soul and God, are always together.

Commentary: Many people, though professing to be religious, are not aware of true religion and spirituality. They do not understand the intimate nature of the soul and God, that they are always together and are inseparable. People shun this knowledge that will give them enlightenment, and partake in all kinds of activities that keep them trapped in ignorance. It is from this point of view that Kabīr speaks about understanding the contrary ways of the world.

Kabīr makes various, seemingly absurd statements, such as the fire burning in water, the blind seeing, the cow eating the lion, the deer eating the cheetah, and so forth. All of these examples represent things that are happening within the person. Because of ignorance, Māyā the great illusion, destroys the soul. Man's heart is full of miseries and is, figuratively, being devoured by them. The ignorant person thinks he really knows, but does not realize the extent of his own ignorance. Along the same lines, indiscrimination, or poor judgement, overshadows discriminative power so that ignorance replaces knowledge. The intellect gets clouded, and desires destroy the awareness of his own reality, namely, the soul. But if one engages in meditation, he can get rid of the five passions, and using Kabīr's symbolism, becomes the frog that eats up the five snakes.

Kabīr proclaims that only the person who knows the eternal truth, that the soul and God are always together, is really the one who should be wearing the saint's outfit. Others wear it falsely, and fool the world. Kabīr is exhorting us to realize this fundamental and eternal truth of the unity of the soul and God.

Shabda 112

O Rāma! There is a great dispute going on. He who can settle it will obtain Nirvānā.
Is Brahmā great, or is it the place where he came from?
Are the Vedas great, or he who produced them?
Is this mind great, or he who understands it?
Is Rāma great, or is it the one who has realized Rāma?
People are wandering about in confusion. Is the place of pilgrimage great, or is it the one who is the servant of the pilgrimage?

Commentary: In this shabda, Kabīr shows that there is a great dispute going on in the minds of people. This dispute leads to confusion and takes one away from the realization of the eternal Truth. Is Brahmā, the god of creation great, or is it the Supreme Absolute from where he came that is great? Similarly, are the Vedas great, or is it the mind that was able to produce them? Is the mind great, or he who understands the mind and can control it that is great? Is Rāma, the incarnation of God great, or the devotee who has God in his heart? Similarly, is the place of pilgrimage really great, or the person who has God in his heart and goes to the pilgrimage site?

People do not realize the truth that the soul is eternal and God is eternal, and that they are always united. After this, all other disputes about what is great and what is not great become secondary. Kabīr tells us to go to the heart of the matter, and to understand the Reality and disregard all the secondary and confusing details that are not important in giving us realization.

Shabda 113

O wise and saintly people, do not believe the fickle mind!
The robber (mind) is totally in your own heart. Do not forget your reality.
Both the earth and the sky are but a huge stage for such a mind.
The trap of lies is in all ten directions, and is ready to ensnare the soul.
Yoga, recitations, austerity, control, pilgrimage, fasting and alms, the nine forms of devotion, the Vedas and the Koran, all serve as dresses for various modes of the mind.
If someone's words eventually prove to be true (foretelling), then he is said to be prescient.
Both Hindus and Turks accept respectability and greatness.
They speak boastfully of the heavens, even as death is getting near.
Their hearts are filled with great pride, so they drown where there is no water.
Kabīr says to whom can I speak? The whole world is blind, lacking in discriminative knowledge. They keep running away from the truth and become followers of lies.

Commentary: In this shabda, Kabīr speaks of the robber that is the mind that believes falsehood and runs away from the truth. It is the source of hypocrisies in religion. The mind, using intelligence, must be discriminative in order to understand the truth. But the majority of people in the world do not do this. They blindly follow teachings, religions, scriptures, pilgrimages, fasting, and so forth. Even when they do not obtain spiritual knowledge, they keep on doing the same kinds of activities. A time must come in life when one needs to examine whether life is becoming more spiritual through all the religious activities, scriptures, and lectures on religion. The secret lies in going within to find the source of Truth that will then set you free from all the restrictive doctrines, dogmas, and rituals that keep one involved without providing liberation. It is spiritual knowledge that gives liberation, and ignorance that fuels bondage.

Lies and falsehood are persuasive, so Kabīr says they appear in all directions. Many people accept pride and respect by playing these falsehood games but every once in a while, a truth that appear to be miraculous is revealed. It appears miraculous only when the secret knowledge is not known. Even as life is passing, people do not make a concerted effort to seek out the true knowledge. That is why Kabīr says people are spiritually blind. They run away from the truth that will set them free, and run to the falsehood that will continue to keep them in bondage.

Shabda 114

You will obtain salvation through the essence of the Word. Believe it, and trust it.
The Primal Being (God) is like a tree, and Niranjan is the trunk.
The three gods (Brahmā, Vishnu and Shiva) are the main branches, and the whole world is the leaves.
Brahmā created the Vedas, and Shiva preached yoga. Vishnu created Māyā, and in this way, the world manifested.
In the three worlds and ten directions, Yama obstructs your passage.
All living beings became like parrots and indulged in poisonous food (passions).
In this world, light (mind) is the master that has spread its power worldwide.
It casts the hook of karmas and ensnares the whole world

like fishes.

Kabīr says, I will make you fearless if you accept the true teaching of the Word. I will remove the power of Yama, and liberate you from this worldly ocean.

Commentary: In this shabda Kabīr speaks of the essence of the Word that is the Self-Existent cause of all manifestation. But in order for the Word to manifest in the universe, it is said that other beings with powers created the universe. Kabīr speaks of this Word or Supreme Being as the tree, and the other beings that took part in the process of the manifestation of the universe as parts of the tree. But there is the power of Yama that puts obstructions in the way, and prevents people from realizing the Word as the source that gives liberation. Yama has the power to ensnare people in worldly activities, passions, and desires, making them figuratively eat poisonous food. The result is they cannot have spiritual health. People are bound up with their karmas that form the fishing hook that ensnares them. But there is a way of being free of this ensnarement by developing knowledge of the Word. This means having an inner knowledge of the Divine Reality that dwells in the hearts of all. Knowledge of the Word gives liberation. Kabīr says he will make you fearless, destroy the power of Yama, and give you liberation.

Shabda 115

O saints there is a great error in the world that makes people spend their whole lives in delusion.

First of all, they forgot the eternal Brahman and accept their own reflections (bodies) as reality.

Being deluded by this reflection, they have created multiple desires that have led to vanity.

In this vanity they think of themselves as creators and have created innumerable books (scriptures).

The whole world continues to be deluded and does not fathom the secret of the delusion.
This mistake has deluded the world and the 8.4 million forms of lives are caught in it.
People have forgotten what is eternal, and this delusion is eating up everyone.
The delusion can be removed through the guidance of a realized guru. He will enlighten you by giving you realization.
Kabīr says O brothers, there is only one medicine for this delusion, and that is knowledge of the Reality.

Commentary: In this shabda, Kabīr explains how people continue to live in delusion because they do not have knowledge of the reality that is eternal. They live materially oriented, accepting their bodies as reality and forgetting that the reality is the soul that dwells within. This soul is in direct contact with the Supreme Being, and indeed, is always united with it.

People who live materially develop all kinds of desires and passions. They think of themselves as creators and have created many types of doctrines, dogmas, creeds, rituals, and various types of practices. They have forgotten that beyond all of these is the Reality that is self-existent and cannot be reduced to scriptures, dogmas, doctrines, and so forth. Of all the life forms, humans are the ones most capable of realizing their reality. But they have forgotten this reality because they continue to live in delusion and have not been enlightened by an enlightened guru. The only medicine for this delusion is awakening to the Reality that the soul is and that it is eternal. This realization gives liberation from material bondage. This is the ultimate goal of life. The sooner we pay attention to this, the sooner we will live in peace, happiness, and bliss.

PART THREE

* GYĀN CHOWNTĪSA * VIPRAMTĪSĪ *
* KAHARĀ * BASANT * CHĀCHAR * BELI *
* BIRAHULĪ * HINDOLA * SĀKHĪ *

GYĀN CHOWNTĪSA

Gyān Chowntīsa is a type of poem in which the first letter of each couplet starts with a letter of the Hindi alphabet in increasing order, until all the letters are used. Gyān means knowledge, and chowntīsa means thirty-four indicating the number of letters in the Hindi alphabet. Each letter initiates a comment on an aspect of knowledge that leads to greater understanding of Reality. Kabīr uses this method in this portion of the Bījak to give pointed spiritual instructions. He also uses alliteration that emphasizes poetic rhythm, for example, kakka kanwal kirn. Please note that the Devanāgari alphabet is difficult to correctly transliterate into roman. The spellings of the letters are close approximations. In the Chowntīsa a few spellings of the alphabet are similar. In Hindi these are written differently and spell different words with slightly different pronunciations.

1 The letter *ka* says that through the rays of the thousand-petalled lotus, God can be realized. The mystic moonlight (trikuti or third eye at the centre of the forehead) keeps this lotus open to enlightenment. He who is illuminated by the colour of that lotus will obtain the Unfathomable in the gagan mandal (highest sphere or chakra) and reside there. (*Comment*: The one thousand-petalled lotus refers to the sahasrāra chakra in the yoga system. It is the highest chakra in the brain and nervous system that opens one to God-realization.)

2 The letter *kha* says that if one wishes, he can follow the sensual path and leaving God, run in all directions. But if he wants forgiveness from God, he has to give up false masters – desires and passions. Only then will he overcome weakness and obtain the eternal abode. (*Comment*: False masters are the objects of senses, desires, passions, ego, and materialism. People indulging in these will be weak in spirituality and will be hampered from realizing God.)

3 The letter *ga* says you must definitely obey the instructions of the Guru and not listen to the words of others. Only then will the bird (mind) not wander. Being steadfast, it will grasp and remain in the unfathomable being. (*Comment*: When the mind is steady in meditation, the soul realizes its unity with God. This knowledge does not diminish.)

4 The letter *gha* says that the body perishes and is born again as another body. Let the body be absorbed in the inner body. The body that perishes returns again as a body, and the inner body is then merged into another body. (*Comment*: Because of the mind, desires, and attachments, the soul takes on one body after another. When the mind is free of desires and passions, it merges into the inner being of the soul. This ends the cycle of births of the inner body being in another body.)

5 The letter *nya* says that a person spends day and night constantly looking at the world and with prolonged looking, the eyes become red. If for a moment he looks for God, he will find Him, as God will hide himself in his eyes. (*Comment*: If a person turns his mind away from material entanglements and truly seeks God, God will come to him in a moment. God hiding himself in the eyes means that God is not visible but is realized intuitively.)

6 The letter *cha* says that God created a mighty picture. Let go of the picture and know the Creator. The person who is fascinated by the picture, plays with it in many ways. Give up the picture and ponder the Creator. (*Comment*: The picture is the universe, the macrocosm and microcosm, and the painter or creator, is God. We become engaged in a multitude of activities and forsake God, the Creator.)

7 The letter *chha* says that Yes! God is quite near to you. Why don't you give up false hope and be satisfied? I am instructing you moment after moment. Why have you given up the Master and shackled yourself to bondage? (*Comment*: God is Omnipresent and therefore very near. We have false hopes on the material world which we have to leave behind. Kabīr is advising us to realize God and be free from bondage.)

8 The letter *ja* says that do not burn this living body alive. Burn up only your youthful desires. Nurture the body with discipline. If through discipline and knowledge the body burns, then Divine Light will dawn in it. (*Comment*: What burns the body alive is the burning of passions and ego. Through instruction by the Guru and the practice of discipline, one gains knowledge that burns up the passions and ego. The soul then becomes enlightened.)

9 The letter *jha* asks, where can one go after being entangled in quarrels? Being entangled in quarrels you depart this life. Even if you search millions of mountain peaks and imagine different forts, that is the fort you will have. (*Comment*: Life is short, but we become entangled in many types of bondage. Even if you make millions of pilgrimages, the deep desires of your heart and your karmic ties will determine the type of body or birth you will have in the next life.)

10 The letter *nya* says: O people! You who advise others to practice control of passions, please also advise us to be free of doubts. The person who does not look at, or run after the senses, is considered very wise. (*Comment*: False gurus cannot give divine knowledge and therefore people remain in doubts. The person who sees the invisible God in his own heart and does not run after outward pleasures, is the wise person.)

11 The letter *ja* says where you do not see Him, there you go in search for Him. Where He is not, there you apply yourself, body and mind. And where He is not, that is where you think all is. Where He truly is, recognize Him there. (*Comment*: People diligently search for God where they do not see Him – in temples, pilgrimages, holy sites, and so forth. They feel they will obtain everything this way. We only find God where He truly dwells – in the hearts of all beings.)

12 The letter *ta* says there is a difficult path in your mind: Open the door and enter the palace of the soul to merge into your Self. You will be steadfast and not have to seek elsewhere. (*Comment*: The mind creates an obstacle to reaching Self-knowledge. It thinks the path is difficult. But it is as easy as opening the door of the heart and merging with the soul. Only then will you be steadfast and not have the desire to seek elsewhere.)

13 The letter *tha* says the goal is far away and the cheaters are near. They are always cruel and assail the mind. One who deceives the cheater is wise. He who understands the cheater will not lose the goal. (*Comment*: The goal is God and the cheater is passions that afflict the mind. The wise person overcomes the passions and realizes the goal.)

14 The letter *da* says you yourself produce fear and become fearful. You remain immersed in fear. Fear dwells in those who are afraid of fear, and fear becomes immersed in fear. (*Comment*: God is beyond fear and if you wish to know God, you also have to be beyond fear. Fear perpetuates itself. Spiritual life requires fearlessness.)

15 The letter *dha* asks: Where do you go searching? If you keep searching and searching you will lose your life! You may search millions of mountain peaks, but you will not find Him anywhere. (*Comment*: You may search for God your whole life looking everywhere and not find Him because God is the innermost part of your own Self. Your search needs to be internalized to find God.)

16 The letter *na* says: O soul! You have established two villages – one of heaven and one of the world. In the desert of the world you search for your boat. All die and leave their wealth here. Who can count how many have died and left their wealth? (*Comment*: In this world a person is involved with heaven, earth, and hell. Living on the Earth is like living in the desert sand looking for a boat. The boat is the path to realization, but it cannot be found among the material things of the world. All material things are to be left behind.)

17 The letter *ta* says: O soul! Do not be strongly attached to the lady (Māyā). Try to find the hidden Reality in your own being. He who finds the Reality in himself will always remain united with it. (*Comment*: The Reality that is eternal dwells within as the spirit. It is therefore hidden. If you find that Reality through an inner journey in meditation, then you will realize it and will remain united with it.)

18 The letter *tha* says He is fathomless and is difficult to measure. This and that (mind and Māyā) do not remain steadfast.

O brother! Slowly, slowly develop steadfastness. It will be like a temple standing without support. (*Comment*: The mystery of God is unfathomable until the mind becomes steady and overcomes Māyā and realizes God. God is the temple that needs no support, and in that temple the heart dwells.)

19 The letter *da* says to look at all the perishable things in the world and, depending on what you see, contemplate on them accordingly. If you meditate and open the "tenth door" then you will have a vision of Merciful God. (*Comment*: Material things may perish quickly or slowly according to their nature and composition. But there is something that does not perish, and that is the Spirit dwelling within as the soul. The tenth door – *brahmrandhra* – opens in deep meditation and one realizes Divinity.)

20 The letter *dha* says as long as you are only half way, you are still in darkness. Let your mind leave it behind and proceed onwards to God. When you give up the idea of being stuck midway, and proceed onwards, you will abolish ego and develop love. (*Comment*: When the mind is occupied with material things only, then it remains in darkness. The mind should rise above materialism and the body and go to the region of super consciousness. In this state there is no ego, only Divine love.)

21 The fourth *na* says go there (the heart) where Rāma resides. Many become the donkey of Rāma and eat the dry grass. (*Comment*: Many people say that they are devotees of Rāma, but do not know Him. They remain in the clutches of Māyā and like a donkey, are burdened with objects of sense gratification and are eating the grass of worldly objects.)

22 The letter *pa* says all the people are committing sins. When sins are present, there is no room for righteousness. O brothers, listen to me! By committing sinful actions, none will gain righ-

teousness". (*Comment*: Sins are committed through thoughts, words, and deeds. Righteous living means that we are pure in all these three aspects of life activities.)

23 The letter *pha* says the fruit of devotion is very far away. The Satguru has tasted it but cannot pluck it and give it to others. O brothers listen to me! You will not find this in heaven nor hell. (The fruit of devotion is obtained through effort and purity in the heart. It cannot be obtained by just talking and listening to scriptures and paying superficial homage to religion. Most people are still caught up in worldly activities and in satisfying sensual desires. True devotion seems very far away.)

24 The letter *ba* says everyone keeps talking and talking, but by talking nothing fruitful is accomplished. They keep on expounding their teachings, but brother, they still do not know the secret of the fruit of devotion. (*Comment*: There is a great deal of talk about religion and spirituality, but talking is cheap. In order to obtain the real fruit of a spiritual life one has to live the life of purity, honesty, integrity, and truthfulness.)

25 The letter *bha* says illusion is overflowing in the world, and because of it that which is near (God) has become far. O brother, listen to me! People come to the world in illusion and leave in illusion." (*Comment*: The world is full of illusion because people generally are not awake to the truth of Ultimate Reality. Lacking the realization of ultimate Truth or Self-realization, people are subject to the cycle of birth and death through their karmas.)

26 The letter *ma* says by serving Māyā (illusion) you cannot fathom the secret and will lose your capital (soul). Attachment to illusion is widespread in the world. Think carefully and give up such attachment. (*Comment*: Māyā is the false perception of what is unreal appearing as real. Everything that changes or

vanishes in time is unreal, but people give reality to such things. The only reality is the unchangeable spirit that is the Eternal. To think spiritually is to realize the transient nature of things and to give up attachment to them.)

27 The letter *ya* says the whole world is full of illusion, so the soul has to travel far from the world. Listen to me brother! He who remains unattached to the world conquers the world of illusion. (*Comment*: To travel far from the world means to be free from the entanglements of materialism and passions. It means to connect with the spirit that is the indwelling Divine Truth. Detachment from the world gives freedom.)

28 The letter *ra* says man remains trapped in the quarrels of the world. If he recites God's name his poverty and suffering will vanish. Listen to me brother! Ask Satguru how to render service to Him. (*Comment*: Quarrels in the world represent arguments, misunderstandings, and all the activities of the mind and senses that keep us away from God. The Satguru instructs you how to find freedom from the quarrels, and how to do devotion to God.)

29 The letter *la* says fraudulent people are talkative and pretend to teach others. One meets another and their fraudulence increases. One fraudulent person talks about the fraudulence of another, yet both operate in the same field. (*Comment*: Empty barrels make the most noise, or he who knows does not speak much, and he who speaks much does not know. The spiritually awake person speaks very little, but those who are engrossed in words, scriptures, and philosophies are very talkative. The latter are not the ones to impart true spiritual teaching to awaken a person to Reality.)

30 The letter *wa* says everyone speaks about Him (God), but

speaking about Him does not serve the goal. The people who only talk and listen about God cannot see the difference between heaven and hell. (*Comment*: Talking about God and listening to words about Him do not give realization of Him. Thus talking or preaching does not serve the goal. One has to go through the practice of uplifting one's worldly life to a Divine life. Not seeing the difference between heaven and hell is the same as not knowing the difference between the spiritual and material.)

31 The letter *sha* says no one sees the pond (bliss) because the pond and its soothing quality of bliss are one. Listen to me, brother! The whole world is going towards the void. (*Comment*: The pond refers to bliss that is the nature of the soul. Sages say bliss and the soul are really inseparable. People moving towards the void represent those moving away from the soul and therefore not attaining bliss.)

32 People talk about spiritual life and liberation, but talking does not achieve anything. Listen to me brothers! The letter *kha (shaha)* says: Take the name of God and obtain liberation. (*Comment*: Talking about spiritual life, quoting scriptures, and still being entangled in worldly pursuits will not give liberation from bondage. When God's name resides in the heart, and one is tuned into it, then one obtains liberation.)

33 The letter *sa* says a huge fire of desires is burning within, and the arrows of passions are destroying people. The house of all desires is the mind. No one knows how to kill the mind. (*Comment*: In spiritual life desires and passions are likened to a fire that consumes oneself. These desires and passions arise in the mind. To kill the mind is to rise above the mind into the region of consciousness. In this region the mind does not function, thus all the passions, desires, and cravings are removed.)

34 The letter *ha* says the whole world is in perplexity, engaging in happiness and sorrow. All those who considered themselves great departed without knowing the secret of overcoming this perplexity. (*Comment*: The perplexity in the world is that people perpetually go through life either in joy or in sorrow. People may sigh and say "Alas! Alas!" or "Why me? Why me?" yet life passes without an answer. People who thought themselves great due to their ego departed the world. It is difficult to rise above the perplexities of the world unless one obtains true spiritual teaching.)

35 The letter *ksha* says in a moment all will vanish. After death who will be there to teach you? After death no one can find the end. Kabīr calls out repeatedly: Realize God while you are in this life. (*Comment*: We can realize God only while we are alive and have our faculties. Death can strike at any moment and, after death, we have no means of realizing God. Kabīr thus strongly urges us, as travellers on the journey of life, to awaken from spiritual darkness to spiritual light while we're in this life.)

Note: There is a discrepancy in the numbering of the Gyān Chowntīsa. I have seen numbers 10 and 11 joined together in one book resulting in a count of 34. When they are separated there is a count of 35. The content of both numberings remains the same.

VIPRAMTĪSĪ

The word *vipra* means a Brāhmin or priest, and *tīs* means thirty. Kabīr, in thirty couplets, relates that there are priests who are priests in name only and who do not have knowledge of Brahm, the Supreme Self. Thus they make priesthood a business while they continue to take part in undesirable behaviours. Kabīr saw their hypocrisies and revealed them to the people.

1 All of you come and listen to the religion of the Brāhmin, yet without knowing God he drowns like an overcrowded boat.

2 He is a Brāhmin, yes, but does not realize Brahman. He performs rituals of the planets then brings all the gifts home.

3 He does not know the One who created this world, but he will sit and talk endlessly of karmas and righteousness.

4 On the eclipse, the dark night, and the second day of the fortnight, whatever rituals and peace prayers he performs, are mostly for his own benefit.

5 He takes the gold that is put in the mouth of the departed, and performs the fire ceremony. But his mind is on the offerings he will get for himself.

6 In the world he is said to be of a noble caste, but again and again he allows others to do mediocre work.

7 With his son and wife he eats other people's leftovers (food that people ceremonially offer to their departed ancestors), yet he says God's devotee is untouchable.

8 Since he eats the leftovers, his actions are impure. His thinking is destroyed and he is going to his death.

9 He takes a bath and feels purified, but as he goes home and sees a devotee of Vishnu, he becomes disgusted.

10 He performs deeds for his own benefit; if someone tells him the true Name, he burns like fire.

11 He gives up hope on Rāma and Krishna, though he studies and expounds them to others. He himself, has become subject to artificiality.

12 He reads about rituals and chases after them. If someone asked him about spiritual matters, he again stresses the rituals.

13 He blames those who are not attached to rituals, and shows interest in those who perform them.

14 When he sees one full of devotion in his heart, he acts like Harnakush and wants to destroy God's devotee. (Harnakush or Hiranyakashipu, a demon king who tried to kill his son Prahalād, a devotee of Lord Vishnu.)

15 See how his foolish mind is revealed. Without inner vision he becomes a slave to artificiality.

16 The ones he worships cannot remove his sins, yet he continues to recite their names while he drowns in the world.

17 Holding the two die of sin and virtue he judges people, and has done great damage to the world by this.

18 This fire of sin and virtue burns the whole clan. It has burned this house (world) and that world (heaven).

19 Sitting in the house he is thought of as honourable, but inside he harbours evil secrets. He uses his mind to plunder others.

20 The Brāhmin and his descendants behave like this. In the name of God people give him a high seat.

21 He cannot save himself and drowns. He speaks of high and low, but does not salute anyone.

22 He thinks of high and low castes, but does he not know that air and water are the same for both.

23 There is only one clay, and the potter is also one, and the Creator of all is also one.

24 The pottery wheel is one but makes many forms. The whole creation is confined in the seed.

25 One light pervades the whole creation, but he calls the Creator by many names.

26 The actions of the Brāhmin are devilish yet he is called a god (on Earth). He argues at length about names and various castes. Gopal (God) is not happy with this behaviour.

27 When the soul becomes separated from the body, who can say what its caste is?

28 Who can say whether the soul is black, white, red, or yellow, or whether it has a caste or not, or whether it is hot or cold?

29 Who can say if the soul is a Hindu or Turk, or old or young, and whether it is female or male. Think about this!

30 Kabīr says: No one pays attention to what I am saying. Whoever accepts my words will understand my teaching.

Couplet: People are being swept away in the water of ignorance. They wander in all directions. If they do not listen to true instructions, then leave them to their fate.

KAHARĀ

Kaharā is a song set to the morning rhythm. Kabīr sings this kaharā to teach the perishability of mundane existence, and to awaken people sleeping in delusion.

A

1 Always remain in sahaj (meditation). Yes! Remain in sahaj meditation. Remain absorbed in the teachings of the guru. (*Sahaj* is the state of easy or natural realization of your unity with the Divine).

2 Make peace with the world and keep your restless mind steadfast. See all with the eye of love.

3 Just as you experience suffering now (without meditation), just so you will have happiness afterwards.

4 If you are not quickly able to control the mind, then at least try to give up anger.

5 Do not pull forcefully on the string of liberation. You will then be able to control the big fish (mind). (Liberation cannot be obtained forcefully. It is a steady spiritual progress through meditation and control of the mind.)

6 Gently say to your mind: "Remain in your limits." O man of anger, do not speak harshly to your mind.

7 Do not give up the friendship of the one you have befriended (God). Do not relinquish your duty.

8 You may enjoy pleasures in the world, but do not forget to

control your body through yoga.

9 Once you become intoxicated with this type of practice, you should strongly hold on to it.

10 But if you follow the evil ways, then that master who is very cruel (Yama – god of death) will deal harshly with you.

11 He will bind you and beat you with a strong club, and you will then forget all your foolishness.

12 When the messenger of Death comes, he will break his clubs on your back.

13 All of your relatives will stand by gazing, but none of their pleadings will release you from him.

14 One of them will bow down at the feet of the messenger of Death and plead, but the messenger of Death will not pay any heed.

15 Since you did not recognize Him (God) despite the advice of others, how then can He recognize you?

16 Before these sufferings, Satguru called out to you, but you did not seek his instruction. Instead, you spoke egotistically.

17 In your pocket (heart) there is no passage money (faith, knowledge, and mental control). You are like a pauper wandering everywhere.

18 If you had secured the passage money, then you would have easily caught the crocodile (mind), and controlled it in the basket of the heart.

19 The mind has no hands and feet, thus it cannot fight. With spiritual strength you can easily control and concentrate it.

20 You have a huge net (knowledge of yoga) at your disposal. Why don't you use it to catch the fish (mind)? Why are you wandering from bank to bank? (Wandering from bank to bank means pursuing various activities and doctrines that do not allow control of the mind.)

21 Do not go into the deep water, but remain in the shallow water, so you do not lose what you already have in hand. (Deep water is the samādhī of hatha yoga in which consciousness is

'lost.' The shallow water is *sahaj samādhī* in which you remain conscious while realizing your union with the Divine.)

22 Those without Self-knowledge suffer and burn inwardly through ignorance, and are outwardly tortured by distress. They do not find any shade (peace) anywhere.

23 O ignorant people! Why are you burning yourself in the fire (passions)? Why do you not make a small hut and take shelter? (Sheltering in the small hut is to take shelter at the feet of the Satguru.)

24 Whatever games of pleasures you have played, they are finished. You will not get this opportunity again after you have lost the human life.

25 Your mother-in-law (Māyā) and sister-in-law (bad intellect) will taunt you, and then you will hide your face in shame.

26 The mast of your ship is now loose, and the ropes are weakened. You did not listen to my advice. (Mast refers to the spine and the ropes represent the nerves and blood vessels. With age the spine becomes bent and other tissues weaken with age.)

27 You did not develop the skill of riding an Arabian horse (perfect knowledge), but you settled on riding the wooden horse (materialistic life, passions and desires).

28 People are playing their cymbals in rhythm, singing their songs, and dancing to the music. (People are occupied in enjoying the materialistic pleasures.)

29 In whatever colour the bridegroom comes to the wedding, the bride must also dress in the same colour. (The bridegroom is the mind, the bride is the intellect, and both seek the same worldly pleasures.)

30 When the boat of the human body was in good condition, you were not aware of its proper use. How will you cross the worldly ocean now?

31 Kabīr says he is intoxicated with the essence of God. The weaver Kabīr is now the servant of God.

B

1 O man, you are a precious gem! Listen! Please listen to my true instruction. Give up the obstacle of ignorance that is in your heart.

2 Your mind is like the potter making pots, but works unsystematically (involved in one thing after another, both good and bad). The cobbler (consciousness) finds no proper resting place in the village (body).

3 The weaver (senses) gets up daily and fills his belly (with sense gratification). And the cloth printer (ego) dances in the courtyard (the world intoxicated with egoism).

4 Every day the barber (lust) boards the boat (body), and keeps on drowning the boat (lust assailing the body).

5 O man! You do not know anything of your true self (soul). How will you settle these disputes (between the mind and senses)?

6 There are five maidens (five senses) in one village (body) and with them are the bride's senior brother-in-law (mind) and his wife (desire).

7 The five maidens quarrel among themselves for their separate satisfactions and thus lose love for the husband (soul) not caring what happens to him.

8 The crane (mind) lives among the water buffaloes (senses), and being preoccupied by them, does not see the soul.

9 How can a person who has not lived among the cows (intellect, discriminative power) recognize his eternal abode?

10 The traveller did not inquire about the right path to the saints, and now has started to follow foolish people.

11 You have given up the proper landing place (good company) and are crawling where there is no landing (bad company). How can you reach the other shore of liberation?

12 Because of greed for wealth you search here and there, your mind running after cheap grain (material pursuits).

13 If you are not crushed between the two grindstones (du-

alities of sin and virtue, good and bad, love and hate), you will reach the proper place of liberation.

14 The Satguru has pulled the bowstring tightly and shot the arrow of love.

15 Kabīr says the devotee who sings this song will merge into the Great One (God).

C

1 O brave mind! Worship God's name. If you relinquish your desires, then you will find He is quite near.

2 Why do you foolishly worship other gods? Ruining your hopes on them is false.

3 O foolish man! Why are you clean only on the outside, yet inside you remain black?

4 What does it matter if your body is getting old? Your mind even now is still young.

5 O foolish man! What does it matter if the teeth from your mouth are gone? Inside you still have teeth of iron (being hard-hearted).

6 Again and again you chew the grains of passions. They are lust, anger, ego, and greed.

7 All the strength of the body has gone with age, but you double your efforts to satisfy your desires.

8 Kabīr says: Brothers, listen to me. All your wisdom has become valueless.

D

1 I cover myself with the name of God. My life's business is definitely with Him.

2 I will conduct my business with Him because he is my commission agent.

3 If you invest (recite) the thousand names of God daily, then day by day, the merit earned will increase by twenty-five percent.

4 All the priests who utter names of the various gods and the Vedas are also in business.

5 But their scales (minds) are crooked. They weigh three-quarters of the weight and say that is the full weight. They beat drums to impress people that their scales are correct. (Priests of religions do not impart full spiritual teachings, but boast of their value while not valuing other religions.)

6 They weigh in this crooked way; weighing five portions when in fact the weight is half of that. The difference remains with them.

7 Kabīr says: Listen to me, saints! The priests display their power but they remain deceived.

E

1 Recite God's name, O man! Recite God's name. Look deeply into your mind and be aware.

2 You have collected a great deal of wealth and have safely buried (secured) it. But you will leave the world empty-handed.

3 Your grandfather, great-grandfather, and great great- grandfather possessed land and pots (valuable articles).

4 Why then did they leave these and go? Are you not aware, or are your inner eyes (perception) blind?

5 The world is engaged in a futile business. In the end no one stands by you, and you depart alone.

6 Birth and death are transient and take no time. They are like the shadows of passing clouds.

7 What is there to boast, about relatives, lineage, clan, and family, when all are transient?

8 Kabīr says without devotion to God's name all your cleverness will drown.

F

1 Without the name of God, O man, you spend your life in delusion.

2 You're like the foolish parrot on the silk cotton tree. It is regretful when it pecks the pod and the cotton flies away.

3 You're like the drunken man who gives away the money in his pocket. He loses his sense, not caring for his household.

4 How can you fill your belly with the mere taste of food, or quench your thirst by licking dewdrops?

5 How can a pauper invest in the welfare of others? He is wrapped up in his own misery.

6 You possess a precious gem (soul) but you do not know its value. The appraiser thus snatches it from you.

7 Kabīr says if you lose this opportunity (birth) you will not get this precious gem again.

G

1 Always remember and contemplate God. I proclaim this to you loudly.

2 You shave your head and then are puffed up with pride. You wear earrings and then sit in the cave.

3 You smear your body with ashes but inwardly your house is plundered. (Kabīr is referring to Nāth yogis. Plundering refers to the passions that rob one of equanimity.)

4 The renunciate dwells in the middle of the village, but is filled with pride and lust.

5 Attachment will make you wander here and there, and you will lose your self-respect.

6 He who knows the dweller in the midst of the heart will be a steadfast person.

7 In the city of the guru, the servant Kabīr is fearless and sleeps blissfully.

H

1 Tell me, who was given bliss, peace, and wellbeing? (Bliss is needed for the soul, peace is needed for the mind, and wellbeing is needed for the whole person.)

2 People are plundered in both coming (birth) and going (death). All are robbed in this way.

3 The gods, men, ascetics, renunciates, priests, and great personalities were all born in this world.

4 There have been millions of them. For how long could I count them? All of them departed from the world.

5 Water, air, and space will all vanish. So also will the moon and the sun.

6 These things and those beings will vanish. They have not attained perfection here.

7 People are prone to saying, "All is well," "All is well," but this utterance becomes the trap of death.

8 Kabīr says the whole world will vanish, and only God will remain as the Eternal Being.

I

1 See what little value your body has. After death no one wants to even touch it.

2 Even if you leave millions in wealth, people will still cut your waistband (to take the money tied in it).

3 When your breathing becomes labored, you are sorely afraid. You will call all your family members close to you.

4 Whoever comes after your death will urge the quick removal of your body. You will not be able to remain a moment longer.

5 Your wise relatives will place the sandalwood paste on your forehead, drape you in new clothes and place a garland of ivory around your neck.

6 Regardless, your body might as well be fit to be plucked by vultures and the abdomen torn by jackals.

7 Kabīr says: O noble people! Listen to me! All are deficient in proper knowledge and wisdom.

8 One day every body will face the same condition, whether king or pauper.

J

1 I am in all, and yet I am not in all. I see myself differentiated in all forms. (State of union with God beyond all forms, and yet manifesting in all forms).

2 I am covered with a single fabric (Māyā = prākriti = undifferentiated matter) and people say I am united with it.

3 I am one and always present in all, just as the single moon reflects in many jars of water.

4 I am the same in all, but people do not understand. If they understood this unity, their delusion about old age and death would vanish.

5 There is no night nor day; the female and male are the same. (The soul, when realized, is beyond the dualities of day and night or male and female.)

6 I am not a youth and not an old man. There is no instability in me.

7 In the three stages of life (infancy, youth and old age), I am the same. My name is Nirgun Rai (beyond limiting attributes).

8 If one sends me I do not go, and if one calls me I do not come. I am Omnipresent and remain in the state of sahaj in the world.

9 The weaver who does not know the difference between the warp and the weft will weave the fabric torn in ten places. (The devotee who does not know how to worship the Divine gets lost worshipping multiple deities. This could also mean that not knowing the Absolute, he worships the physical, symbolized by ten doors of the body.)

10 Rare are the people who obtain the grace of the guru and understand his teachings.

11 The mind that is engaged in countless forms of worship causes the diamond-like soul to lose its value.

12 The gods, noble men, and sages are all in search of the Absolute. Only few have found some trace of Him.

K

1 O sister-in-law! What an evil married woman you are. You are sleeping with the whole world. (The one speaking is a bride, or good intellect, and the sister-in-law is bad intellect. Bad intellect is persuasive and is pervasive everywhere in the world.)

2 When I came I saw that you were sleeping with my husband (soul). You deceived him.

3 My father (ego) has two wives, one is me and the other is my elder brother-in-law's wife (ignorance).

4 When we lived with our husbands in the world, everybody knew about it (bad intellect, good intellect, and the soul are all together in the world).

5 My mother died along with my father, and along with them all the other companions died. All of them died on the realization of God. (The mother is Māyā or illusion and the father is ego. All the relations are the passions and desires.)

6 My mother died along with others. Even her friends and relatives died with her. (With God-realization, illusion or Māyā, passions, desires, rites, and rituals, all perish.)

7 As long as there is breath in the body, so long can there be benefit in this life; there is still a chance to obtain God-realization.

8 Kabīr says when the breath leaves, the temple (body) gets burnt in the fire.

L

1 This Māyā of Rāma is intoxicated. She roams the world playing the hunting game.

2 One by one she killed the clever and the bright ones. She did not spare even one.

3 She destroyed those who observed silence, those who were brave, and those who observed nakedness. She even destroyed the yogi who was doing his meditation.

4 She destroyed the ascetic who confined himself to the jungle. No one can enjoy solitude with Māyā.

5 She killed the scholars who read and studied the Vedas, and the swamis occupied in their worship.

6 She destroyed the pandit who expounded the Vedas. She ensnared everyone else in her reins.

7 She hunted the sage Shringi Rishi who was in the forest, and severed the head of Brahmā. (In Puranic mythology Shiva cut off one of the five heads of Brahmā that lusted after his wife Sati (Parvati). It is Brahmā's skull that Shiva wears around his neck according to the Puranic encyclopedia.)

8 Machhandar Nāth turned away from her to get away, but she eventually caught up and drowned him in Singhaldweep (now Sri Lanka).

9 She is the owner and keeper of the house of the sakat (evil people), but she becomes a servant to the friend of God.

10 Kabīr says: O saints! Please listen! As soon as she comes, send her back immediately.

BASANT

Basant is the spring season when fresh growth and flowers appear. It is a time of happiness. In the Basant poem Kabīr teaches about the state of eternal spring that one needs to realize in oneself.

A

1 There is hardly anyone who realizes the benefit of springtime for twelve months of the year. (The spring referred to here is figurative of the blissful soul likened to the green and blooming garden.)

2 When the fire (of knowledge) showers in a continuous stream, all the forests of eighteen classifications (*bhara*) become verdant. (Bhara is a system of classification so that there are four types of fruit bearing vegetation, four of creepers, six of flower bearing vegetation, and four of thorny vegetation.)

3 All people cherish the fresh water (soul) of springtime, and the blowing wind that removes all dirt. (The freshwater of springtime is the realized soul, and the blowing wind is pranayama or breathing exercises of the yogis to purify themselves of passions and negative tendencies.)

4 Without trees, the sky is full of blooms; Shiva and Brahmā dwell there. (The flowers blooming in the sky is figurative of the meditative state. Shiva and Brahmā did meditation and realized the "flowering" of consciousness.)

5 Sanak and other sages became lost there, like bees in a flower garden. People who are in the cycles of birth and death do not understand this state.

6 If the Satguru shows you the reality, then you will not give up devotion at the feet of the Lord.

7 The devotee who realizes the truth reaps the benefit of reaching the eternal abode. Kabīr says, whoever understands this state will also attain it.

B

1 O tongue! You read the lesson of the great beauty of spring but, not attaining it, you will again fall into the trap of death. (The great beauty of spring refers to perfection attained in Hatha yoga. Merely reading the lessons of yoga will not give liberation.)

2 The spine must be controlled and the eight chakras must be traversed to reach the highest consciousness. (In Hatha yoga, the spine, head, and neck must be in an upright position to allow energy to flow from the base of the spine to the thousand-petalled lotus in the brain. The eighth lotus exists beyond the sahasrāra chakra and is called the *unmani* chakra.)

3 The yogi then realizes Brahmagni (enlightenment) and his breathing becomes harmonious with the breath flowing up and down.

4 The nine ladies, once unclean, are now full of perfume (the body with nine apertures), and the five friends (five senses) rush to it. (The perfume is bliss attained by the perfect yogi. The five senses are under the control of such a yogi.)

5 The Divine melody is resounding everywhere, and the seventy-two males frolic in the dust. (The Divine melody is the Divine Word or *anāhad nād* that is realized in meditation. The seventy-two males are figurative of the parts of the body. Frolicking in the dust indicates happiness due to inner realization.)

6 O mind! Why are you deceived by the game of Māyā? You

are like the flowers of the tree that wither quickly.

7 Kabīr says this servant of God is strange. He asks for heaven just as people ask for gifts at the Holi festival. (Kabīr is referring to a person who does not follow a spiritual life but expects spiritual rewards.)

C

1 O God, I have come to meet you. Please clothe me in the beauty of springtime.

2 The body I obtained at birth is getting old and weak. The yarns (karmas) are the same old ones, and they are still tied to the three pegs. (The three pegs are the three gunas or attributes of righteousness, activity, and slothfulness. The karmas are dependent on these three attributes.)

3 This old body is pierced with 360 arrows, and 72 strings tie them into a knot. (The arrows and strings are a figurative description of the bones and ligaments of the body.)

4 There is a murmuring flow through the blood vessels, as the female weaver sits with her legs crossed. (The female weaver that is sitting refers to the kundalinī energy at the base of the spine explained in the yoga system. When this energy rises to the topmost lotus centre (Sahasrāra chakra) in the brain, then enlightenment takes place.)

5 The girls (senses) above are enjoying themselves, and the two legs (mind and intellect) are operating the weaving machine (body). (The five senses seek their own gratifications and keep one dancing to their tune. The mind and intellect move along with the senses until they are controlled.)

6 The five gross elements and the twenty-five prakritis (components of material manifestation) make up the body of ten doors. The five friends (senses) are frolicking in that body.

7 Kabīr says the lovers of God are colorfully adorned with the colours of springtime and are singing melodiously at the feet of God. (The soul that has transcended materialism attains a state

of bliss.)

D

1 The old lady (Māyā) laughs gleefully and says: I am forever young. Which other lady is as young as me?

2 My teeth (passions) are gone from chewing the betel leaf (devotional practices). My hair (bad thoughts) is gone from constantly bathing in the Ganges (saintly company).

3 My vision (knowledge) is gone from applying collyrium (ignorance) to my eyes. My youth is gone from seeking other men (deluding people).

4 I make knowledgeable people my food (delude them), and to allure foolish people I adorn myself beautifully.

5 Kabīr says, the old lady sings merrily as she sits eating her son (soul) and her husband (God).

Commentary: This is a very allegorical and mystical basant or shabda, and could perhaps have alternate explanations. But in keeping with Kabīr's teaching, the following is a reasonable explanation: Māyā is the projecting and manifesting power of God and is co-existent with Him, therefore she is old. But being eternal, she is also young. She however deludes people, preventing them from seeing Reality. She works from within the human being, observing the activities of people, and speaking as she does in this shabda. By speaking of the old lady eating the son and the husband, Kabīr means Māyā has deluded (eaten) the soul and also hidden God from the soul.

E

1 My learned pandit! Solve the riddle of the woman who never married and remains a virgin. (The woman refers to Māyā that is feminine and is the creative energy of God.)

2 All the gods gave her to Hari (Vishnu) and she remained with Hari for all the four yugas (she remained with God eter-

nally).

3 First she appeared in the form of Padmini (Lakshmi – the consort of Vishnu). In the end she proved to be a snake eating up the people of the world. (Māyā is also the power of delusion in which the whole world is caught up, and so is eating it up.)

4 A person who is fascinated by her cannot be uplifted. The lady gains strength at night. (Night refers to ignorance of Reality. The more spiritually ignorant a person is the more Māyā will delude him.)

5 Kabīr says, this lady is very dear to the world yet she kills her own sons. (People are attracted to the illusory things of the world and die without knowing the Reality of God.)

F

1 O mother! See how clever my husband (the embodied soul) is. He toils all night until daybreak. (Night represents living in spiritual ignorance and daylight represents a rebirth.)

2 He wakes up in the morning and cleans the courtyard. He uses a huge basket and cleans the cow dung. (With a rebirth the person quickly becomes preoccupied with many activities. Cow dung represents the results of useless pursuits.)

3 He eats the stale rice and then takes a huge pitcher to fetch water. (Stale rice represents unrewarding activities that create thirsts in life. The water represents efforts to quench those thirsts.)

4 I have tied my husband securely in a sackcloth, and can now sell him from market to market. (The embodied soul is bound by its karmas. The selling from market to market represents the cycle of death and rebirth because of karmas.)

5 Kabīr says, all of this is the work of the Lord. The husband living with this woman knows no shame. (The law of karma is of God. The embodied soul living with ignorance ought to be ashamed, but keeps on living in the old way not attaining liberation.)

G

1 O brother (soul)! There is the great quarrel in your house (heart or life). The wanton lady (Māyā) gets up daily and attacks you.

2 She is powerful. She has five hands (5 gross elements) and these five have twenty-five other companions (twenty-five prakritis for the material manifestation of nature).

3 These twenty-five say there are others, and these in turn say that there are many others still. (These numbers are representative of the material bonds that entangle one's life and keep one from eternal knowledge.)

4 They enter your life and test its capacity. They violently jerk your stability and make your life restless.

5 Each of the senses wants satisfaction of its own desires. Tell me, how can there ever be well-being in the people?

6 People do not care for discriminative spiritual knowledge and thinking. They are fascinated by the illusory things of the world.

7 Thus you find both the rich and poor laughing heartily, but in doing so they are not able to find the One (God).

8 That which is with them (God) they say is far off, and they keep on searching. They find instead, the traps of Māyā spread all around.

9 There are a hundred thousand hunters (desires, passions and worldly attachments) and one soul. Thus the soul cries out, "O my beloved Lord! O my beloved Lord!"

10 Kabīr says, if the quarrel in your house abates, then your die is cast for liberation." (Abating the quarrel means understanding Māyā and her illusions, and obtaining knowledge of the Eternal Self.)

H

1 The lady (Māyā) acts as a puppet in accordance to the

strings in the fingers of the puppeteer (God). Perhaps a scholar may understand this. (The strings are the three gunas or attributes – *satogun, rajogun and tamogun*. These are controlled by God, and Māyā acts in accordance with them.)

2 She remains naked, and dearly loves insentient things. (Māyā covers everyone but no one can 'cover' her unless he is God-realized. She causes attachment to material things.)

3 She frolics up and down according to the strings, destroying some and saving others. (Māyā destroys the ignorant and spares the realized people.)

4 Kabīr says, I am the servant of the servant of God, and observe that Māyā brings happiness to some and sorrow to others according to their karmas.

I

1 Your body that is difficult to obtain is slowly passing away. Take God's name and reach your divine destination.

2 The kings Venu, Bali, Kans, Duryodhan, and all their clans have drowned (died).

3 Prithu, ruler of the earth, and Trivikram also went. Not one remained.

4 All these six and other smaller kings departed with empty hands. O man! Try to understand now while you still have a chance.

5 Hanuman, Kashyap, Janak, and Bali crowded the gate of Yama, the God of Death.

6 Gopichand who properly practised yoga, and Rāvan who enjoyed splendour, were both destroyed. (The persons mentioned are from Hindu religious literature.)

7 O man! Seeing all these people passing away, you must understand the power of Māyā. Kabīr urges you to recite God's name.

J

1 Everyone is 'intoxicated' in different ways, and no one is aware of the power of their ego. The thieves (passions) are plundering them.

2 The yogi is intoxicated by his yogic meditation, and the pandit from reciting the Purānas.

3 The ascetic is intoxicated in the secrets on his asceticism, and the renunciate in his recitation of "Aham Brahm Asmi" (Brahm and I are one).

4 The mullahs are intoxicated with reading the Koran, and the Kāẓi in dispensing justice.

5 Worldly people are intoxicated with the lure of Māyā, and the king with the pride of his kingdom.

6 Shukhdeo, Udho, and Akrur were intoxicated with their knowledge, and Hanuman with his powerful tail.

7 Shiva was intoxicated with devotion to Hari, and in Kaliyug, Nāmdev and Jaidev were intoxicated with their devotion.

8 The Vedas and Smritis explain the Truth. The egotists are destroyed just as the egotistic Rāvan was destroyed when his vulnerability was known.

9 The mind is restless and performs ignoble actions (the mind causes intoxication). Kabīr advises you to recite God's name and be free of the mind's bondage.

K

1 O Shiva! What has become of your holy city of Kāshi (now Varanasi)? Even now, please pay attention to its condition.

2 People make offerings of sandalwood paste, incense, and betel leaves, and in every house there is reading of the Smritis and Purānas (scriptures).

3 In various ways people make offerings to the Lord in their homes. In this city people also create a lot of disturbance.

4 These people living in Kāshi belong to you, but they commit bad deeds and are fearless about it. I feel it is presumptuous

of me to tell you of these things.

5 I have only childish knowledge, but I have dared to come to advise you of the state of affairs.

6 With whatever mind people come to Kāshi, you gave them refuge. But at death where will their souls go? (Many Hindus feel that dying in Kāshi automatically confers liberation.)

7 If your devotee suffers misfortune, it is not his fault, but it is a shame to your good name.

8 Shiva was pleased and revealed the secret that where he dwells, no one else can. (At death people will go to where their karmas dictate.)

9 Kabīr explains what he has seen. Be patient for a while, and you will understand.

L

1 No one believes my instructions. O man, you have drowned yourself in the worldly ocean current of Māyā.

2 The blind (ignorant) person preaches, and another blind one follows. This is as foolish as arranging the marriage of a prostitute.

3 In a manner of speaking, we are so thoughtless that the Master (God) is standing beside us (in our hearts), yet we do not recognize Him.

4 Everyone wants to maintain his honour yet chooses to accept falsehood and hypocrisy as truth. (People do not logically examine the teachings.)

5 The false guru cannot serve any good purpose. O ignorant person! I warn you that such deceitful teachers cannot lead you to liberation.

6 Give up your hypocrisy and listen to my advice, otherwise you will fall into Yama's hands.

7 Kabīr says people do not truly search for God, so they wander around and die like a deer seeking water inside a mirage.

CHĀCHAR

Chāchar is a spring festival of colour, music, and fun enjoyed by both men and women in playful rivalry. Kabīr uses this to personify the colourful and beguiling Māyā that has captivated the world.

A

1 Beguiling Māyā played a fascinating game and brought the world under her influence.

2 She created colourful veils that are fit to adorn any beautiful maiden. (Material appearances hide the reality.)

3 Her beauty of form is unmatched, and her deportment is too fascinating to be told.

4 Her face is like the moon, and her eyes are like the haunting eyes of the deer. She displays a kumkuma mark on her forehead. (Kumkum is a red powder used in adornment.)

5 The yatis and satis (holy people) became enamoured by her as she walked by like a confident young elephant.

6 She made Nārad monkey-faced, and snatched his clothes of propriety.

7 She turned proudly and walked away smiling mockingly. (Nārad was infatuated with the princess of King Shilanidhi and was made to look like a monkey.)

8 She then ran towards Brahmā and Shiva and trapped both of them. (Saraswati and Parvati are both manifestations of

Māyā.)

9 She played phagua with them then discarded them. (Phagua is the colourful Holi festival.)

10 But the Divine melody eventually played, and all hearing it were delighted. (The Divine melody is heard after Māyā is conquered. Brahmā and Shiva, once freed from Māyā, heard the anāhad nād.)

11 The brave player plays the game of spirituality according to the opportunity he gets.

12 He puts the shield of knowledge before him, and no one can budge his foot from its position. (He is steadfast in knowledge.)

13 Once the player plays his game steadfastly, Māyā cannot again disturb him.

14 The heroes, men, ascetics, gods, Gorakh, Dattatreya, and Vyās came under her sway.

15 She even defeated Sanak and Sanandan, so what can one say of mere mortals?

16 She sprinkles colours with pretended love then strikes the body with the syringe. (The syringe holds the coloured liquid and striking the body is like being struck by Cupid's arrow.)

17 She captivated all, then departed, glancing back at them again and again.

18 She planted the well known club of lust and used the three gunas to help her in her game.

19 It is said she caught Shiva and Brahmā, so what can be said of any others?

20 On one side the heroes, men, and ascetics stand, while she stands alone on the other side.

21 She never lets go of those on whom her glance has fallen. With one swoop she grasps all of them.

22 As many as were there, she ensnared all in her veil of deception.

23 She is like a circling line of kajal (collyrium) the smears everyone that it has touched.

24 Indra and Krishna are standing at her door with longing glances. (Their stories are depicted in the Purānas.)

25 Kabīr says only he whose attachment to Māyā has vanished can be liberated.

B

1-2 O foolish mind! Burn your attachment to the material world. Try to understand foolish mind! It is your attachment that causes your sorrows and sufferings.

3-4 O foolish mind! What good is there in the pride of the body and wealth? Try to understand foolish mind! Their beauty will be reduced to ashes.

5-6 O foolish mind! The body is a house of God without foundation and quickly perishes. Try to understand foolish mind! The house is built with bricks but without cement to join them together.

7-8 O foolish mind! The world is like an artificial female elephant – a decoy. Try to understand foolish mind! God made the world like a picture, a creation of the mind.

9-10 O foolish mind! The male elephant, through lust for the decoy, falls into the trap. Try to understand foolish mind! He now suffers the prodding ankush (iron hook) on his head. (Metaphor for people trapped by Māyā, the illusory material world.)

11-12 O foolish mind! The greedy monkey puts his hand in the narrow-necked jar for a tasty morsel. Try to understand foolish mind! His fist now full, he cannot release to withdraw his hand, and is trapped.

13-14 O foolish mind! He cannot escape. Try to understand foolish mind! His master now makes him dance from house to house.

15-16 O foolish mind! He has no concept of good or bad about where he has to dance. Try to understand foolish mind! If he does not obey and dance, his master whips him with a stick.

17-18 O foolish mind! The parrot grasping the lalanī thinks it is trapped. Try to understand, foolish mind! Consider that this is how doubt operates. (Lalanī is a trap to catch parrots. A piece of bamboo is slung low above water with a piece of fruit attached to it. The parrot perches on it and rolls over, its back just above the water. Afraid to let go, it becomes trapped.)

19-20 O foolish mind! What good is teaching given to it? Try to understand foolish mind! In the end the cat (Māyā) will still eat it.

21-22 O foolish mind! You are a guest in an empty house. Try to understand foolish mind! Just as you entered, just so you will have to leave. (You came empty handed and will leave empty handed.)

23-24 O foolish mind! You think there are countless places of pilgrimage for bathing. Try to understand foolish mind! You think there are countless deities to be worshipped.

25-26 O foolish mind! Believing so, you will drown without water. Try to understand foolish mind! You need to take the boat of God-realization so you won't drown.

27-28 Kabīr says: O foolish mind! People have been swayed by confusion. Try to understand foolish mind! Because of confusion, people have given up worship of the Supreme Self.

BELI

Beli is a creeping plant that spreads in all directions. Kabīr, in this poem, refers to Māyā as the creeping plant because Māyā manifests in, or has crept into, the whole world. He refers to the soul that manifests in all as the hansā that needs to be freed from the creeper.

A

1-2 You are a swan in the lake of the body. You are awake yet thieves (passions, desires) are plundering your house, O soul, dweller in the heart of all beings.

3-4 One who is awake (with soul knowledge) ought to run away from the thieves, but one who is asleep (devoid of soul knowledge) is lost, O soul, dweller in the heart of all beings.

5-6 Today your residence (liberation) is near (you have human birth), but tomorrow it can be very far away (rebirth in other forms), O soul, dweller in the heart of all beings.

7-8 You will go to a foreign land (losing freedom through rebirths) and your eyes will be filled with dust (blinded by passions and desires), O soul, dweller in the heart of all beings.

9-10 The churning of fear, just as the churning of curd, afflicts you. Really, you have been churned up completely in different lands (rebirths dictated by karmas), O soul, dweller in the heart of all beings.

11-12 The swan (soul) has again become a guest (in a human body) and is struck by the realization of the need to obtain the eternal abode, O soul, dweller in the heart of all beings.

13-14 You are a swan (soul) with a mind that is like a precious gem but you did not heed my warning, O soul, dweller in the heart of all beings.

15-16 You have reaped what you have sown, so why do you blame me for your error, O soul, dweller in the heart of all beings.

17-18 You gave up the unfathomable (God) and accepted the finite (the material). You placed your belief in a life of ease, O soul, dweller in the heart of all beings.

19-20 You traded the wealth of God's name and sought to be laden with material goods, O soul, dweller in the heart of all beings.

21-22 You have loaded the five bullocks (the body of five gross elements) with sensory objects. They are accompanied by nine supporters (nine bodily apertures) who have objects loaded in ten sacks (body organs of perception and action), O soul, dweller in the heart of all beings.

23-24 The five bullocks fell into a ditch (died). Even the skull was shattered to pieces (cremation), O soul, dweller in the heart of all beings.

25-26 The swan (soul) flew away shaking its head in repentance. It bid farewell to its friend the lake of the body, O soul, dweller in the heart of all beings.

27-28 The lake (body) was set on fire (cremated) and was reduced to ashes, O soul, dweller in the heart of all beings.

29-30 Kabīr says: Listen to what I have said O saints. Realize the difference between good and bad, O soul, dweller in the heart of all beings. (Realize the reality of God's name while in the human body.)

B

1-2 You have been well deceived by the words of the Smritis.

You placed your belief in what is doubtful, O soul, dweller in the heart of all beings.

3-4 It is like being in a forest that has no directions, yet you placed your faith in going there, O soul, dweller in the heart of all beings.

5-6 You say here are the Vedas and Smritis, but the guru has established me on the true path, O soul, dweller in the heart of all beings. (The Vedas and Smritis deal with incantations, rituals, gunas or attributes, philosophy and so forth, but they cannot give the experience of the reality that Kabīr is pointing to.)

7-8 The body is like a fort of cow dung that will be abandoned in the field, O soul, dweller in the heart of all beings. (The body is not the reality; it will end up in the cremation field.)

9-10 The mind and intellect cannot reach the enclave (spirit), so how can you search for it, O soul, dweller in the heart of all beings? (Meditation is the way that goes beyond the mind and intellect.)

11-12 O mind! Hear this and be patient. Not following this path you will be utterly ashamed, O soul, dweller in the heart of all beings. (To reach the Divine requires meditation and patient practice of the control of desires for external things. Not following the path to Self-knowledge is the cause for shame.)

13-14 Do not seek a retrograde search for the materialistic life. All objects are only transient constructs, O soul, dweller in the heart of all beings.

15-16 Kabīr says: Listen to what I am telling you O saints! Apply your mind and intellect to what is close to you, O soul, dweller in the heart of all beings. (Search for God within your own heart.)

BIRAHULĪ

Birahulī is a mantra for removing the poison of a snake's bite. Here the snake's bite are the pangs of separation from God. The snake is the mind that is full of desires. Kabīr, the remover of the poison, recites this mantra to cure the patient. This poem serves as a mantra for the separated soul to realize its connection with God that is without attributes, without beginning, end, or form.

1 O separated soul! There is no beginning nor end, and no root, branch, nor leaves. (The supreme sentient Self has no beginning nor end.)

2 There is no night nor day, and no air, water, nor roots. (The supreme Self is self-luminous and has no root cause for its existence.)

3 Brahmā and other deities, as well as the sons of Brahmā, explained many forms of yoga and departed. (Yoga for the realization of the supreme sentient Self.)

4 The month of Asadh (from mid June to the coming of rain) is cool and the farmer (individual soul) plants seven seeds in the body. (The seven seeds are actions based on ignorance, attachment, love, enmity, lust, nobility and knowledge. Another explanation is the ego, intellect and five elements.)

5 The farmer tills and waters the field every day and garners new branches and leaves. (The tilling and watering represents

the works of the mind, ego, passions, and desires. The new leaves and branches are rebirths in the phenomenal world in accordance with karmas.)

6 The separated soul is pervaded by the actions of the mind, and remains stranded in the three worlds.

7 There is a beautiful flower that blossoms. It blossoms throughout the whole world.

8 Saintly people pluck the flower and even the king bows his head to it.

9 A rare devotee accepts the fruit that comes from the flower. But once he accepts devotion, the snake bites him. (The mind begins to feel the pangs of separation from God.)

10 The snake mind pays no attention to the mantra, even though the snake charmer recites it countless times. (The mind that is scattered in mundane things does not like to hear teaching about devotion to the supreme Self.)

11 O separated soul! You have planted a bed of poison. Why do you now repent while reaping it?

12 Birth after birth Yama, the god of death, stalks you. But there is a fruit on the Kanera tree that will save you. (The words of the guru may appear bitter as the Kanera fruit, if you are not receptive.)

13 Kabīr says: O separated soul! You will obtain the truth if you taste the fruit I am offering you. (Truth refers to the eternal Reality of the Self.)

HINDOLA

Hindola is a swing that swings from one side to the other. In this hindola poem, the swing consists of doubts that cause people, gods, and other celestial beings to sway one way and then the other, not finding stability or equilibrium.

A

1 The whole world is swayed back and forth on the swing of doubts and karmas.

2-3 The swing is supported by the two posts of sin and virtue, and Māyā is the cross bar on which it is hung. (Māyā is the illusion of apparent reality. It keeps us beguiled so we remain in doubt of our Divine Self. The swing is kept in motion by our karmas, passions, desires, greed, and ego.)

4-5 Good and bad deeds are the two chains that the person holds with two hands to propel the swing. Everyone sits on the plank of the swing due to good or bad karmas. Who is there in the world that does not sit on this swing?

6-7 Whole hosts of Gandharvas (celestial musicians), sages, and Indra king of the gods, swung on this swing. So did Nārad, Sharda, Vyās, and Sheshnag. (Nārad is like a celestial messenger between gods and humans. Sharda is the goddess Durga. Vyās is the sage who compiled the Vedas. Sheshnag is the mythological multi-headed serpent supporting the world and also the seat on which Lord Vishnu reclines.)

8-9 Lord Brahmā, Lord Shiva, the sage Shuka swung on this swing. The sun and the moon swing on this swing. Even the nirgun or formless Lord Vishnu took birth in form as Govind and did the same thing. (*Comment*: Māyā is the creative power of the Supreme. Without Māyā there could be no creation of Brahmā, Shiva or other celestial beings. They were the creations of Niranjan, who in turn was a creation of the Supreme, non-dual Self or Atman. As creations they were then subject to the mind. Brahmā, the creator of the universe also had a family, as did Shiva who also begged using a skull as a bowl. Vishnu as Govind had a family and was also subjected to ten incarnations. Because of Māyā, the sun and moon travel in their orbits.)

10-11 The six philosophies, four Vedas, fourteen sciences, and twenty-one elements constitute the three worlds. Search all the various types of creatures and the scriptures and you will find all of them subject to the same swing, none remaining permanently steadfast.

12-13 Search all the parts of the universe and you will see that nothing is free of this swing. Search among the company of the holy people and see where the soul is going to find liberation.

14-15 That territory has no moon, sun, night, season, elements, nor dissolution. It is where there is no time nor absence of time, no destruction. This is the region to which a rare saint goes. (The region described is union with the Supreme and liberation from material bondage.)

16-17 You have been separated from it (the eternal abode) for many kalpas (eons), and coming to Earth you have forgotten God. Search in the company of sadhus for that territory so you will not return to the world of bondage.

18-19 The saint who is wise and knowledgeable has no fear of the swing because he escapes from it. He unites with Sat Purush the Supreme, and does not get on the swing again.

B

1-2 God created many forms of life, beautiful as pictures, and created them as a play of dancing. Who has the wisdom to realize that he has no desire to swing in this dance of worldly existence?

3-4 Many ages have passed yet the soul keeps on riding the swing. It has no desire to give it up. The swing keeps on swinging, even at night and through the four yugas and four months. (Doubt is pervasive and ever-present in all the ages.)

5-6 Just as people on a swing keep on going up and down, just so, bound by karmas and doubt, people keep going up and down. The swing of doubt is very deceptive; it does not stay still for a moment. (The up and down motion refers to higher and lower regions of existence, that is, towards heaven and earth. Motivated by satogun or noble qualities one goes up, and motivated by tamogun or negative qualities one goes down.)

7-8 People are tormented by the constant swinging, and pray, "O King of the Yadavas, please protect me." Kabīr says: O Gopal (Hari)! I submit this prayer to you. Give refuge to the seekers.

C

1-2 The mind has created a swing, and its two supports are greed and delusion. Because of greed and delusion, the worldly people keep on swinging and swinging. At no time do I see this swing being still.

3-4 Clever people, entangled by their own cleverness, keep on swinging. Even the king and the people are caught up in the swinging. So are both the moon and the sun, not heeding the command to be steadfast. (In yoga, the moon and sun are the left and right nostrils. Breathing can be controlled by a steady mind.)

5-6 The 8.4 million forms of life are swinging (cycles of birth, death, rebirth). All the while the god of death is keenly plying his trade. Millions of ages have passed, yet none accepts defeat, but instead keep on swinging.

7-8 Both the earth and sky are swinging, as are the air and water. Even God swings by assuming a human form (incarnation) on Earth. The liberated soul, Kabīr, stands as a witness of this game of swinging. (Everything Kabīr mentions here is brought about by Māyā who veils the reality of the unchangeable God, superimposing all changes to sustain the swing of delusion.)

SĀKHĪ

A sākhī is a two-line aphorism bearing testimony to spiritual truth. It has similar formatting to a doha, but Kabīr's dohas are specifically called sākhīs because he bore witness to the spiritual truth that he was teaching. The term derives from the word *sakshi* meaning a witness. Many of Kabīr's sākhīs are quoted popularly because of their poignant, concise, and clear-sighted messages that are difficult to refute. All of them are aimed at removing hypocrisy in spiritual life, and towards the attainment of liberation. They are rhythmic, almost musical in the original, and easy to remember.

1 O soul! Before birth you were free, and had no worldly bondage to a body. Then your sixth sense (mind) arose. Now where are you wandering to as if lost? (*Comment*: The soul is eternally free until it comes into the bondage of the body and the world. The mind is the cause of bondage due to ego, desires, passions, materialism, and so forth.)

2 The Shabda (Word) is mine, and you are the product of it. Listen to it and do not shun it. If you wish to realize your own Reality, then realize the Shabda. (*Comment*: Shabda is the creative energy of God that manifests in us as spirit. It is the true Reality.)

3 My Word is from the beginning; the soul resides in the Word. The basket is for holding flowers, but the horse is eating the ghee. (*Comment*: The soul animates the body and gives it consciousness and makes it 'beautiful' as flowers. This beauty is realized in meditation. In India, it is common to feed ghee (clarified butter) to horses, mixing it with other grains. Ghee is a delicacy in India. The horse eats the ghee with the grains, but does not know that the ghee is a delicacy prized by humans. Similarly, the person who is not awakened to the reality of his own Self does not realize the greatness of his own soul.)

4 Meditation without the Word is blind. Tell me, where can it lead you? When meditation does not reach the door of the Word, then the meditator strays again and again. (*Comment*: The Word gives liberation; without it you are subject to rebirths and suffering.)

5 There is a great difference between word and word; reach deep to the essence of the Word. Kabīr says, where there is no essence of the Word, that life is cursed.

6 Being struck by the Word, one falls down, and being struck, one can give up the whole kingdom. Whoever deeply considers the Word will have his life's goals fulfilled. (*Comment*: To fall down means to have become humble after realizing the Word. Historically, some kings have given up their kingdoms to follow a saint.)

7 My Word is from the very beginning. Remember it at every moment and it will bear inner fruit; all other words are useless. (*Comment*: Inner fruit is enlightenment.)

8 Even in a perfect city, whoever does not take provisions for the journey will not be able to obtain provisions after darkness has fallen and the day has ended. (*Comment*: The perfect city is the body. Provisions are devotion and the realization of the Word to obtain liberation. When old age, disease, and death approach, what then can be achieved?)

9 Make provisions for your life while you are still here in the body. The next path is full of lust for worldly enjoyments. All are trying to buy heaven, but there is no trader, and no shop for obtaining it.

10 If you think your human life is your own, then take good care of it. Human life is a guest that rarely comes a second time. (*Comment*: It is only in the human life that we can elevate ourselves from spiritual darkness to spiritual enlightenment.)

11 He who understands the mystery of life in this world will understand the soul. He should digest his own water and not ask for water to drink from others. (*Comment*: The whole mystery of life is based on the Law of Karma. The soul attaches itself to intellect, mind, ego, body, and the three gunas (attributes). We need to be self-reliant because liberation comes only from individual effort.)

12 O preacher! Why do you wander from house to house offering water (teachings) to others? He who is thirsty will helplessly come to you to drink. (*Comment*: There are many so-called gurus who travel about initiating people in order to gain disciples and make a living. But whoever is thirsty for spirituality will himself seek out the teacher.)

13 The soul is sold for a golden plate full of pearls. What can one who does not know its value do with it? (*Comment*: Pearls represent spiritual wisdom imparted by a master to his disciple. Using the gift of spiritual discrimination, that disciple will be

able to make use of the teachings.)

14 O soul! You are a wondrous golden colour. How can I adequately describe you. Having climbed the tree, if you depart stainless, then I will sing your glory. (*Comment*: Climbing the tree refers to obtaining the human body while the golden colour represents the pure soul. In the body, the soul becomes stained by Māyā. Kabīr says he will praise the soul that escapes Māyā.)

15 O soul! You were strong and your conduct was graceful. Now you are stained with evil colours, and have made another your lover. (*Comment*: Evil colours are evil tendencies, and the lover is the ego with which the soul becomes associated.)

16 The swan departed from the pond leaving it lifeless. Kabīr proclaims that it has returned to the same door and same pillar. (*Comment*: The pond is the body. The same door and the same pillar means that the soul did not obtain liberation and had to return to the material world, assuming another physical body.)

17 The swan and the crane have the same colour and move about in the same pond. The crane is immediately revealed, but the swan is only known by testing it with milk. (*Comment*: The pond is the world. There are both spiritual and non-spiritual people in the world. The spiritual ones are revealed by their righteous living, whereas the non-spiritual ones are revealed by their evil desires and passions. Mythologically, the swan can separate milk from water but the crane cannot.)

18 O deer! Why are you so emaciated when the pond is full of lush green vegetation? There are a hundred thousand hunters and one doe. How can she possibly escape their arrows? (*Comment*: The hunters are passions and desires that beset the soul. These keep the soul malnourished, and separated from the lush vegetation of God's presence.)

19 The three worlds are like a cage, and sin and virtue are like a net. All the souls have become prey to the one hunter Kal. (*Comment*: Heaven, earth, and hell are the cage created by the mind, and net it also created is the trap of sin and virtue. The one hunter is death. The pure soul is existence itself, and has nothing to do with these.)

20 Greed makes you waste your life, and evil actions nullify your good actions. If you say that Sadhi (Māyā) is only one half, I would be greatly annoyed. (*Comment*: Māyā is Vishnu's wife, so she may be called one half. But Māyā is very powerful and has beguiled the whole world. Kabīr says he is annoyed when people are not aware of what Māyā is.)

21 Half a sākhī defeats death that is standing on your head. Remove this death if you can. What use are the pandit's books that day and night talk of removing it? (*Comment*: Kabīr explains that much reading and reciting of scriptures by scholars will not give liberation. But half a sākhī of Truth properly understood and applied, will give liberation.)

22 God skillfully made this body with the five elements, and the body cried 'I,' 'I.' I ask you, pandit! Is the word greater or is the soul? (*Comment*: The five elements of the body are earth, water, fire, air, and ether. God made the body, yet it becomes full of ego and cries out, 'I,' 'I,' taking credit for its existence and accomplishments. Kabīr asks the question, which is greater, the "I" or the soul that animates the body.)

23 The body is made up of five elements, and is called human. If deprived of one element, it becomes restless at every place. (*Comment*: If the body is deprived of just one element, for ex-

ample air, it becomes restless and dies. This indicates the fragility of the human body. There is no need to be engrossed in pride and ego over it.)

24 One colour arises from another colour, but basically all colours are one. What is the colour of the soul? Try to understand the difference. (*Comment*: The primary colours - red, blue and green - can be mixed to produce a number of secondary colours, and these secondary colours can be mixed to produce an endless variety of tertiary colours. All of these exist in Māyā, and all are material, but the soul is non-material, so what colour can it be?)

25 The soul's nature is wakefulness and the Word purifies it just as as white borax purifies gold. Kabīr says the body is like the wild hen produced from a pale drop. Hardly anyone understands this. (*Comment*: The drop is semen that fertilizes the ovum to produce the body. The inert body is awakened by the conscious soul.)

26 The body is made up of five elements. Having obtained the body, what have you done with it? It is said karmas control the soul, and that the soul is given to perform karmas. (*Comment*: The body is a gift from God, but for what are we using this gift? Karmas determine the type of body we get, and its place and status of birth. The soul again becomes subject to performing karmas.)

27 Inside the body of five elements is the place of a hidden treasure. Hardly does anyone know this secret. The guru's word is the only authority. (*Comment*: The soul is imperceptible, but it animates the body and maintains its life. The guru is the spiritual master whose word is authoritative.)

28 One who sits on the steadfast throne of realization has light shining from the window of his body. I and my companions dwell in the heart of such a realized one. (*Comment*: A realized devotee is steadfast, and the noble qualities of God shine forth from him. The companions Kabīr refers to are knowledge, discrimination, wisdom, and so forth.)

29 The mirror is in your heart, but you cannot see your face in it. You will see your face only when you remove duality from your heart. (*Comment*: Seeing your face refers to realizing God and the Self as one.)

30 Kabīr says one should live on a high mountain and hold on to the arm of a strong person. One should serve a master under whose refuge he can obtain liberation. (*Comment*: A high mountain offers physical protection from bad people, and a true master gives spiritual protection from evils and from Māyā.)

31 The path followed by the learned people is also followed by worldly people. But God's abode is very high, and Kabīr has climbed there. (*Comment*: Learned people serve as examples and others follow them. If the learned people do evil in the name of religion, others will imitate them. Kabīr says that he has gone way beyond these and has reached God's abode.)

32 Kabīr says come down from your high path, you have run out of supplies. When you have run out of supplies and your feet are tired, you are at the mercy of others. (*Comment*: Supplies are the means needed to reach the high path of Self-realization. They are faith, devotion, love, humility, kindness, contentment. Without them the aspirant is at the mercy of the ego, passions, desires, and Māyā.)

33 Kabīr's house is on the top of the mountain where the path

is very slippery. Where an ant's legs cannot get a foothold, that is where people wish to go with loaded bullocks. (*Comment*: The mountain top is the high spiritual attainment of Self-realization. It is beyond phenomenal existence. The slippery path is Māyā who keeps people slipping back into material life. The ant represents reasoning and intellect. Even these cannot get one to the highest Reality.)

34 Without having experienced the terrain (God-realization), whoever talks about it is foolish. They eat bitter things and wanders about selling camphor. (*Comment*: If religious teachers do not have God-realization themselves, how can they impart it to others? They are knee-deep in enjoyment of the objects of senses, yet they preach to others about the way of obtaining supreme bliss.)

35 People say 'shabda,' 'shabda,' but that Shabda (the Word) is bodiless. It does not come to the tongue; examine this and understand. (*Comment*: The Word is the ultimate Reality and cannot be uttered, but only internally realized. It is the Supreme Spirit. So people who talk about the Word without having experienced it are foolish.)

36 God consciousness flows on the mountain top and the horse (mind) climbs up to dwell in that village. The bee (soul) wishes to drink nectar but there is no flower. What is the name of that tree which produces the flower and nectar? (*Comment*: The mountain top refers to the transcendent state as described in meditation. The horse is the mind that the yogi must control so he can 'climb' to the summit where God dwells. There is no need for a tree or flower for the soul to drink the nectar of God-realization.)

37 O sandalwood! Give up your fragrance. It is because of you that the forest is cut. Do not destroy living beings. At death all will be destroyed. (*Comment*: To obtain sandalwood people cut down other trees in order to get to it. A human being similarly destroys other lives to satisfy his desires.)

38 The snake wraps itself on the sandalwood tree. What can the sandalwood do? When every hair of the body is soaked with poison, how can nectar get in? (*Comment*: The sandalwood is prized for its fragrance, but the snake cannot appreciate it. Similarly, there are people exposed to great teachings but who do not benefit from having them.)

39 A crystalline stone reflects the colour and form of every object placed near it. Kabīr says, just so, the dog sees himself reflected and barks at the reflection. (*Comment*: The crystalline stone is the mind that reflects what is inside such as fear, doubt, and passion due to the influence of Māyā. The dog represents a human reacting to the contents reflected in the mind.)

40 Once you accept a vow do not give it up, even when the tongue and beak get burned. Even though much heat is emanating from the burning charcoal, still the chakor bird pecks at it. (*Comment*: People of strong resolve do not give up their vow of whole-hearted devotion to God. Mythology says that the chakor bird is so entranced by the moon that it even pecks at burning charcoal in seeking it.)

41 The chakor bird, completely attached to the moon, will even eat burning charcoal. Kabīr says he does not get burned; this is the nature of attachment to the noble one. (*Comment*: A devoted person will not be swayed from devotion not even due to pain or hardship. The mythological chakor bird is similarly devoted to the moon.)

42 Everyone swings in the scintillating light of the world. No one can escape it. Even Gorakh was trapped in the city of Kal (this world age). Who then could be called noble? (*Comment:* In yoga, the scintillating light can be seen in meditation, and is a sign of being on the path, but yet having some distance to go. Many yogis often end up arguing about the scintillating light, and become entangled in the same problem. This type of dispute shows that one has not yet reached God-realization and is still in bondage to the material world and at risk of ending up without liberation in this life.)

43 Gorakh was very fond of Hatha yoga and when he was departing his life of Hatha yoga practice, he instructed his disciples not to burn the body. Still, despite punishing it uselessly with the practice of Hatha yoga, his flesh melted and mixed with the soil. (*Comment:* Kabīr advises that mere physical training in yoga without training the mind in the highest spiritual attainment of God-realization, is not, in the end, beneficial. Spiritual attainment is achieved through the mind and the spirit, while the body is merely the vehicle for its attainment.)

44 According to his nature, the hare runs from the jungle and falls into a dreadful trap. To whom shall the hare tell his trouble, and who would understand it. (*Comment:* This allegorical statement is used by Kabīr to explain the condition in which people find themselves according to their natures. The hare has a habit of running from one bush to another, and because of this habit it falls into a trap from which it cannot escape. Just so, people fall into traps of materialism, illusion, doubts, passions, anxieties, depression, religious and racial intolerance, pride, vanity, and so forth.)

45 Hatha yogis, even after trying for many days to obtain samādhī in the depth of silence, do not find that state of bliss.

They will repent, just as the rabbit that falls into a ditch repents, being far away from its destination. (*Comment*: Unless God is firmly established in one's heart, and is the working and motivating power in that person's life, he will not be able to obtain the bliss of union with God. There are many yogis who become adept in Hatha yoga and long for union with God in the state called samādhī. But they fail to obtain it because they are preoccupied with their yogic practices.)

46 O Kabīr! People do not escape from doubts even when they pursue many outward forms. Without realization of the Master in the heart, the stain of doubts remained. (*Comment*: People following certain religions will put on external garbs marking religion. Thus we find people wearing robes of different colours, sandalwood marks, caps, rosaries, crucifixes, turbans, sacred threads and garlands, or carrying other symbols of their religious order. Such outward symbols do not purify the heart.)

47 People of this world suffer without being punished, just as the people of Sorath suffered. Seeing the attractions of the world, they become greedy, preferring the sweeter sugar more than molasses. (*Comment*: Sorath was the ancient name of the Gujarat state. At one time the government inflicted severe punishment on its people who apparently had done nothing wrong. Kabīr uses this incident to indicate that people in this world suffer punishment with no one actually exacting punishment on them. In other words they bring punishment upon themselves according to their own actions in thought, word, and deed. They run after the alluring sugar (Māyā) than after the more nourishing molasses (God). To the extent that people are enticed by the evanescent attractions of the world, to that same extent are they depriving themselves of spiritual growth and eternal happiness.)

48 Living in the fragrance of Malyagir, all trees begin to smell like the sandalwood tree. They may be mistaken for sandalwood, but they cannot be called the real sandalwood tree. (*Comment*: Malyagir is a mountain made famous by its fragrant sandalwood trees. Other trees there often take on the fragrance of the sandalwood tree, but are not themselves sandalwood. Merely associating with holy people does not make one holy.)

49 All the common trees like dhak and palas growing on the Maliyagir mountain become impregnated with the fragrance of sandalwood. But the bamboo, though growing among the sandalwoods for ages, cannot be impregnated with the fragrance. (*Comment*: All common trees that have woody stems absorb the sandalwood fragrance and in turn become like the sandalwood because of the fragrance. The bamboo, however, having a hollow stem, cannot take on the fragrance of the sandalwood. People cannot be 'hollow' inside if they wish enlightenment.)

50 After walking and walking your feet got tired, the city still being nine koshas away. In the midst of the journey, you had to rest. Tell me then, whose fault is it? (*Comment*: The walking referred to here is wandering from place to place in pilgrimages, or from religion to religion, or from one teaching to another, or performing one ritual after another, and so forth. The result is one fails to reach the destination of God-realization, and death intervenes.)

51 It has become dark and the day finished. It is evening on the journey. Because of contact with many lovers, the prostitute remained barren. (*Comment*: A person goes through life and the end of his days arrives when he is old, with the evening of death coming soon after. Though he worshipped many deities, and pursued many sense gratifications, he fails to reach the goal of liberation.)

52 The mind asks, "When should I go?" and the consciousness also asks, "When should I go?" Six months have gone thus, though the destination is only one kosh away. (*Comment*: Kabīr is speaking about the procrastination that hinders one from reaching the goal of liberation. The goal is very close. Its actually within. But people wander everywhere to find the destination.)

53 Pretending to be unattached, a person leaves his home and goes to the forest to practice austerities. His body becomes tired and almost lifeless, and he eventually plucks and eats the wild plums. (*Comment*: Kabīr is pointing out that it is not necessary to withdraw from the world in order to devote one's self to spirituality. That is why he taught Sahaj Marg, or the easy natural path leading to God-realization. The immature aspirant, pretending to be unattached, only weakens himself and in the end does not gain liberation.)

54 Those who realize the Name of God have light bodies. Sleep does not come to their eyes, nor does flesh gather around their bodies. (*Comment*: The saint is in such love with the Divine that all pleasures and material pursuits, including the need for sleep, food, clothing, shelter, are of little consequence. Because of this longing for liberation, the body remains light.)

55 He who is soaked with the nectar of God, remains cheerful, and is not enticed by worldly pleasures. He is immune to the allurement of worldly pleasures and remains above the dualities of happiness and sorrow. (*Comment*: When a person becomes figuratively soaked with the nectar of God's love, there is no room for him to suffer doubts, mental anguish, and other passions. He enjoys Self-realization and bliss.)

56 If the mango tree is cut, it will not produce blossoms and

fruits, just as a severed ear will not reunite. O Gorakh! Without touching the touchstone, who will suffer loss? (*Comment*: Kabīr is addressing Gorakh Nāth the famous Hatha yogi, that since he is not allowing himself to touch the touchstone of God's name, how can he reunite with God? Who then will suffer loss? The cut mango tree represents desires that have been rooted out and cannot again have influence.)

57 The soul is like a philosopher's stone, and the world like iron. With the touch of the philosopher's stone, the world became gold. (*Comment*: Kabīr is using this alchemical belief to explain that the indwelling soul is like the philosopher's stone, and the world like iron. All physical bodies have no life or consciousness until they are touched by the soul. Once the soul dwells (touches) in the body then the body becomes alive and manifests consciousness and intelligence. Our goal in life is to realize the soul and truly become golden, that is, liberated.)

58 O Kabīr! Put on the clothes of love and dance! Give honour to those who, in mind and body, uphold the truth. (*Comment*: One who is awakened to God's love, that is, is Self-realized, will often sing and dance with joy. Another thing such a devotee needs to do is honour those who live and speak the truth.)

59 The foolish dog runs hastily into a house of mirrors. Seeing his own reflection, he barks incessantly and dies from it. (*Comment*: Ignorant people in the world consider many other people to be their enemies. This is due to their own selfishness and ignorance. They create enmity and try to take revenge on others and in doing so, their egos and passions create a life of turmoil, and they die from self-inflicted suffering.)

60 If one looks at his reflection in a mirror, he will see both (himself and his reflection). From the reality (body) that reality

(reflection) exists, and from this (soul), that (body) exists. (*Comment*: This sākhī deals with the inter-dependence of the body and the soul. Without the body there can be no reflection in the mirror, just so, without the soul, the body cannot reflect life and consciousness.)

61 O Kabīr! When the ocean of youth is overflowing, a person becomes attached to worldly pleasures. Now he becomes a traveller in the world, and has to come and go. (*Comment*: A youth becomes interested in members of the opposite sex, in cars, money, entertainment, and so forth, to satisfy desires. These excursions create karmas, the effects of which have to be endured, whether good or bad. Because of karmas a person has to die and be reborn (coming and going) until he or she is able to obtain freedom from rebirths.)

62 Doha (poetic couplet) has attained a new structure, and few people are able to understand its secret. He who understands it is the sovereign master. (*Comment*: Kabīr is referring to the sākhīs which he sang, and which convey Eternal Truth. Dohas are couplets, but Kabīr called them sākhīs or testimonies. One who grasps the true meaning of a sākhī is a sovereign of the kingdom of the Supreme Self.)

63 Climbing on to the sandalwood tree branch, Kabīr is shouting to everyone. If you do not choose to follow the true path, what loss is it to me? (*Comment*: The sandalwood tree branch is the body, and Kabīr, after assuming the body, is crying out to all to awaken to the true path to liberation.)

64 Truth is the best principle, if it is from the heart. Despite innumerable pursuits, there is no happiness without Truth. (*Comment*: It is only through Truth that we find God and in truthfulness that God finds us.)

65 Always deal in Truth with a resolute heart. With Truth you will obtain the diamond, but with falsehood you will lose your capital. (*Comment*: The diamond is the most precious gem. Just so, God-realization is the most valuable spiritual attribute. Losing the capital refers to the soul being lost in the pursuit of temporal pleasures.)

66 You do not follow noble instructions, and do not give proper attention to them. Kabīr says, emphatically, you will pass your life in a dream. (*Comment*: The dream is the pursuit of worldly possesions; they will all pass like a dream.)

67 The fire of desires is lit in the ocean of the heart, but no smoke is visible from it. Only he who is burnt in it knows, or he who has kindled it. (*Comment*: People are burning in their own passions, desires, and ego. But there is no outward sign of the fire. The one who kindled the fire is also the one burning in it.)

68 The fire of longing that the person kindled in his heart, scorched his wings. I sacrifice myself to one whose fire saved the roof but burnt the house. (*Comment*: The fire is the longing for God-realization. It burnt the wings of desires and passions. The soul is the roof and the body is the house. Once God is realized, the soul obtains liberation, and the material body dies.)

69 Everyone understands it when it is said that a drop has merged into the ocean. But rarely do people understand when it is said that the ocean has merged into the drop. (*Comment*: The drop represents the individual soul, and the ocean is God consciousness in which the soul consciousness merges. Both are of the same essence, and thus merge into each other.)

70 If you seed a poisonous plant and water it a hundred times a day with nectar, it will still remains poisonous. People of the world do not give up the ways they are accustomed to. (*Comment*: Worldly-minded people will not become spiritual by merely listening to sermons.)

71 The wood, being burnt to charcoal, innocently shouts, "If I go to the blacksmith's house, I will be burnt a second time." (*Comment*: The soul 'burns' in this life of desires and passions. As it departs it cries out, figuratively, that it does not want to return to the womb a second time. Being burnt again is a metaphor for returning to the womb for another material life.)

72 The state of separation is like wet wood that hisses and smokes when it is burnt. It is saved from suffering only when it has dried out and burnt to ashes. (*Comment*: Kabīr uses the image of wet wood to symbolize the suffering experienced by a soul when it feels itself separated from God. As the 'suffering' of the wet wood ends when it is reduced to ashes, just so, the suffering of a person ends when all karmas are burnt up and the person obtains liberation.)

73 No medicine helps the person who is wounded by the arrow of separation. He lives daily, sobbing, sobbing, dying, and dying. Whenever he gets up, he groans with suffering. (*Comment*: The pangs of separation a person suffers when disconnected from God is the cause of sorrow. It is like a a living death. The medicine of preachings and sermons does not help.)

74 You will find the word of Kabīr to be true, if you examine it carefully in your heart. But people who do not pay proper attention will not understand, even though I have spoken in all four ages. (*Comment*: Materialistic people tend to ignore spiritual truth even when it is staring them in the face.)

75 If you are a true businessman, then establish a genuine shop. Even more so, use the broom and clean the inside and throw the dirt far away. (*Comment*: If a person is genuinely spiritual, then he must clean the 'inside,' that is , he must get rid of all the passions and cravings to which he is subject.)

76 This world is a mansion made of wood and is on fire everywhere. Learned people are burnt to ashes, but the ignorant ones run away and are saved. (*Comment*: Learned people tend to be proud of their wisdom, and sometimes act in an egotistic manner. As a result they are burnt up by Māyā. But people who are simple or unlettered, but are full of faith and devotion in their hearts, stay away from the traps of Māyā and are saved.)

77 In the month of Sawan, incessant raindrops from the sky garland the head like a crown. The whole population of the world becomes Vaishnāva, even though a true guru has not revealed the true mantra to them. (*Comment*: Kabīr is using the metaphor of heavy rain to point out how multitudes of people are given initiation into Vaishnavism yet such initiations are often worthless. It is the true guru who initiates disciples into Self-realization.)

78 I am concerned that near the river bank the soul cannot be saved, and is drowned. Are you sleeping in this ocean current of ignorance? (*Comment*: The river is a reference to the river of ignorance, doubt, and delusion. The riverbank of salvation is close by, but the soul remains ignorant and does not seek the proper path to salvation. Kabīr regrets that worldly people are in such a condition.)

79 O man! You recite the sākhī but do not grasp its meaning, nor do you follow the path. The current of ignorance runs deep. Where can you firmly plant your feet? (*Comment*: People often recite the teachings of the saints and sages, but do not endeavour to grasp the inner meanings, nor practice the teachings. Therefore, they do not find a firm footing in spiritual knowledge. They wander through the intricacies of life like in a dream, or in a spiritually unaware state.)

80 I have met many who speak, but I have yet to meet one who accepts and practices what he preaches. Let those speakers who do not practice what they say, be washed away by the worldly current. (*Comment*: Duplicity is sometimes evidently true in religious and spiritual life. People will preach at the top of their voices, practically shouting at their audiences or congregations, yet they themselves have not set out to practice what they are preaching. It is important for people to use proper spiritual judgement and not foolishly or blindly follow teachers because of their eloquence.)

81 Establish one principle at a time, if such a principle can be established. If you say one thing now, and another thing later, you will eventually suffer many blows. (*Comment*: To establish one principle at a time means thinking deeply and understanding what the principle is. You will then be steadfast about it and not waver from day to day about what you say or do. A person who is unreliable and without firm principles is likely to be ridiculed.)

82 Hold your tongue! Refrain from speaking too much. Keep company with the wise and meditate on the words of your guru. (*Comment*: People who talk incessantly are of no real benefit to themselves or others. It indicates a mind that is scattered and that has difficulty in concentrating itself to practice spiritual discipline. In contrast, wise company improves your spiritual life.)

83 Do not keep company with one who cannot hold his tongue, and does not have truth in his heart. He will abandon you in the middle of the path. (*Comment*: People who do not speak the truth are untrustworthy. When it is convenient for them they will let you down, and even cause trouble for you.)

84 A person falls (suffers) because of his tongue that can speak evil, from one moment to another moment. Under the influence of the mind, such a person wanders in doubt, time swinging him from here to there. (*Comment*: Kal is time and also death, which in turn occurs in time. A person who does not have purity of speech, and whose mind wavers, can say hurtful things at any moment. Being swung here and there is a reference to the birth, death, and rebirth cycle.)

85 The arrowhead has penetrated the body, and has broken from its shaft. It cannot be removed without a strong magnet; millions of rocks are useless. (Comment: In former days, when soldiers were wounded in battle and arrowheads penetrated their bodies, those arrowheads being made of iron, were removed by using a magnet. The arrowheads Kabīr is referring to are the words of false teachers that penetrate the hearts of people. They can be removed only by the strong magnet (words) of a realized teacher. Just as mere rocks cannot act as magnets, the words of unrealized teachers cannot remove the arrowheads of false teachings.)

86 The path of realization that lies ahead is very narrow, but if you turn back you will be reduced to dust. The beautiful maiden, hidden behind the veil, remains free from all danger. (*Comment*: The spiritual path is likened to a very narrow stairway. At the end this means that the traveller must be free from all bondage due to karmas motivated by desires, passions, and ego. One cannot take the ego on this narrow path. Despite the difficulty, turning back from the spiritual path reduces one to a materialistic life ending in death. The beautiful maiden is Māyā, and the veil is illusion. She works secretly to turn the mind of the traveller away from Self-realization.)

87 In this world, a householder, or a yogi, must think according to his circumstances. The opportunity of your human life is passing. Therefore, be alert, O unwise people! (*Comment*: Two types of people are mentioned here, the householder who has a family to maintain, and the yogi who lives a detached life. Each of them have certain rules of living pertaining to spiritual life. It is not appropriate for the householder to live like a yogi, or for the yogi to live like a householder. If we use our opportunities unwisely, our chance of obtaining liberation in this life will slip away.)

88 The whole world is broken up into pieces by doubt, yet no one turns around to destroy the doubt. Only that person who can destroy doubt is wise in the knowledge of the Word. (*Comment*: Doubt about the soul and Ultimate Reality is detrimental to the spiritual path and is quite pervasive in the world.)

89 There are speeches of many kinds, but the eyes perceive none of them. Kabīr says, thoughtfully, listen to and understand the speech of your own heart. (*Comment*: The eyes here are used as a figurative reference to the heart. Kabīr says to listen to and understand the language of your own heart. God speaks to the heart. There are unrealized teachers who can lead you astray spiritually.)

90 You will succeed if you hold on to the root. Do not be led astray by doubts. The mind is like an ocean, full of waves of desires; do not get swept away by them. (*Comment*: In order to accomplish anything we have to get down to the basics. The root is the Ultimate Reality, the Self that is dwelling within us. Following the dictates of the mind and of the waves of desires will sweep us away from our path to liberation.)

91 The bee lingers in the flower garden where there is the fragrance of many flowers. If one similarly lingers in the garden of worldly pleasures, he will leave the world in disappointment. (*Comment*: Various types of flowers and fragrances symbolize the world with its multitude of attractions and pleasures. Lingering among these leads to disappointment, as they will never be able to yield the bliss that the soul is seeking, and none of them can go with you at death. The soul will be subject to rebirth.)

92 The world is like a whirlpool, or a heron's trap. Countless unrealized people have already drowned and died. Kabīr says only those whose minds are full of spiritual discrimination will be saved. (*Comment*: From birth to death, people are caught up in a merry-go-around of material pursuits and sense gratifications, and then die. It is like a heron's trap – the heron stands motionless, as if in meditation, and suddenly plucks the innocent fish.)

93 People of the three worlds are like locusts that fly in swarms according to the dictates of the mind. Though they are children of God, they do not know God, and thus fall into the trap of death. (*Comment*: Kabīr is referring to a type of mass delusion. People are motivated by certain common denominators that lead them astray. It is like the blind following the blind. As a result none of them realize God.)

94 The mind is like an intoxicated elephant that does not realize the impact of the various fancies it harbours. Kabīr proclaims emphatically to all to use the art of the intellect to realize this state. (*Comment*: The mind is full of fancies, but it acts like an intoxicated elephant that does not realize how to exert control over it. Being cognizant of the things occupying the mind requires deep introspection and wisdom.)

95 As a monkey is in the hands of a juggler, just so the soul is in the grip of the mind. The mind makes the soul dance in many ways, while keeping it in its clutches. (*Comment*: The mind keeps the soul trapped, and makes it dance according to its dictates. In order to truly understand this sākhī, we need to realize that the soul is really helpless once it has become the occupant of the body. The soul is only the animating or energizing force. Though it is the 'life giving power,' it does not do anything on its own. However, the clue is that it is the basis upon which the mind functions.)

96 The mind is restless and is a thief and a great deceiver. Gods, men, and sages have lost their lives over it, for it has a hundred thousand doors. (*Comment*: The mind can bring happiness or suffering, hate or love. It can run in countless directions, pulling people hither and yon according to its dictates. And through its "hundred thousand doors," it can easily escape attempts to control it.)

97 The snake of separation from God has bitten the body. The snake does not obey any charms. Those separated from God cannot continue to live. If they lived, they would become insane. (*Comment*: A poisonous snakebite renders the body restless and results in death. Kabīr is using this analogy to show how people separated from God become restless. Continuing to live this way would bring on insanity.)

98 Those who feel the pangs of separation from God are restless in mind and body. Do not inflict further suffering on them.

They will die even from a touch, and are very, very sensitive. (*Comment*: Those who feel the pangs of separation from God are in a restless stage and should not be burdened with worldly issues. Those in contact with them need to be sensitive to their condition and aspiration, and help them along in every possible way, instead of diverting them from the path.)

99 The snake of separation has entered the body, and inflicted a severe wound on the heart. The person does not try to save any part of himself, so the snake eats whatever it likes. (*Comment*: Kabīr compares the separation that causes suffering to the bite of a snake that keeps destroying the person, yet the individual, either through lack of awareness or negligence, fails to do something about it.)

100 A stinging pain caused by a splinter from the tree of speech has penetrated deep into the heart. It cannot be removed. It remains embedded and produces fresh wounds. (*Comment*: The words of false teachers such as harsh words, fallacies, and hypocrisies get into the hearts of ignorant people and remain there. They are difficult to be removed even by the words of a true teacher. There is a reflective saying that 'a person convinced against his will is still of the same opinion.')

101 The black snake is dwelling in the body, and is eating up the whole world. Only rare people who meditate on God with understanding are able to escape it. (*Comment*: Kabīr is using the symbology of the black snake to refer to the poisonous qualities of the ego that people harbour in their hearts. Only a rare person, who meditates on God intelligently, will escape.)

102 Death is standing on your head, O friend. Awake! You are friends with strangers. How can one whose house is in the street sleep carefree? (*Comment*: Death awaits us, figuratively standing on our heads. Yet we are friends with strangers that invite death. They are ego, passions, delusions, and desires. A street is for coming and going, so it refers to the world in which we come, and go through birth and death.)

103 The black woodworm is in a piece of black wood, and is systematically eating up the inside. Just so, death resides in the body but no one knows its secret. (*Comment*: The black woodworm is not seen in the black wood, just as death is not seen lurking in the body. The body systematically decays and dies. People need to wake up from ignorance and realize this situation.)

104 The mind is the residence of Māyā, and the body is a fort of doubts. The snake of death does not obey any charms and inflicts its deadly wounds. (*Comment*: The mind is full of Māyā meaning delusions, desires, passions, and ego. Unless the mind is controlled and made a servant, it quickly becomes an unruly master. Māyā deludes us into thinking the phenomenal world is real when it is not; it perishes in time. So we live in doubt about what is real. Only the Transcendent Self is real.)

105 The mind and Māyā are really one, since Māyā is immersed in the mind. The three worlds are in doubt. To whom can I explain this fact? (*Comment*: Māyā and the mind are one, since the mind is subject to Māyā's delusion when it is not trained to see the reality of God, the Ultimate Reality. People everywhere are in bondage to Māyā unless they know this Reality.)

106 A fence for the protection of the field has been erected, but the fence is eating up the field. Because of it the three worlds are in confusion. To whom can I explain this? (*Comment*: This sākhī is a riddle that Kabīr has used to get people to think of their condition in this world. The fence is, figuratively, Māyā or illusion. The field is the body, or the mind which thinks all the material attractions, wealth, and attachments are really for its benefit. But Māyā is the source of destruction. How can one get people to awaken to this knowledge and be free of confusion?)

107 The mind is like an ocean full of waves of desires, and many careless people drown in it. Kabīr says only those with discriminative spiritual knowledge are saved. (*Comment*: The reason for calling the mind an ocean is because the mind is vast, and no one is able to fathom its extent. Kabīr said in one of his other sākhīs, "the mind is the source of bondage and also the source of liberation." We need to use our discriminative intellect in order to escape the bondage of the mind.)

108 The mind is a very intelligent thief. It makes an ocean out of the intellect and assumes multiple forms. It then deceives the whole world so that no one is able to reach the goal of liberation. (Comment: The mind is like an ocean, and although it has given intellect an important place in life, it plays cunning tricks. Because of its cunning tricks, it keeps the person on a merry-go-round in the material world, and prevents him from attaining his goal of liberation.)

109 People do not die as perfect human beings, but die as animals. They do not reach their destination, but become elephants or horses. (*Comment*: The purpose of life is to become truly human, and to attain liberation through Self-knowledge. If our lives have been evil and negative, then we can be reborn as animals. On the other hand, if our lives have been noble and spiritual, we can be reborn in a state of happiness and bliss.)

110 There is no sinner greater than the person who does not obey the words of his guru. Like a wild forest hen, he is reborn again and again, and eventually repents. (*Comment*: The guru is the dispenser of divine wisdom for overcoming the cycle of birth and death, and for obtaining liberation. He should be held in the highest esteem. It is a sin to disobey your guru. A person who disobeys his guru, will metaphorically be reborn again and again, just as the wild hens in the forest. Kabīr could have used any other creature to explain the point. The soul repents its lower state.)

111 What can the poor human do when the guru's word will not open the door of his heart. The dog sits in his courtyard and again and again, leaps to lick the aipan. (*Comment*: Because of the ego the mind does not become humble to submit itself to the teachings of the guru, that is, the door of his heart does not open. He is spiritually helpless. Aipan is a mixture of ground rice and turmeric that people use on ceremonial occasions. It is, metaphorically, the objects of the senses that the dog (mind) in the courtyard (body) repeatedly leaps to lick.)

112 What can a poor man do when his body is void inside? If he cannot see his soul inside, Kabīr asks, what can one say to him? (*Comment*: When knowledge does not dawn in the heart, it is considered spiritually void. Devoid of knowledge, a person cannot realize his soul and a teacher cannot help him.)

113 If a person, on obtaining human birth, misses the present opportunity, he goes into the wheel of rebirths and endures many miseries. (*Comment*: Human birth is an opportunity for liberation. Without liberation, a soul gets entangled in rebirths and suffering.)

114 O man! Try to obtain the precious diamond instead of decorating your body of clay. The soul came and went, and your pride of body was useless. (*Comment*: Kabīr is instructing us about our misplaced emphasis on decorating and pampering the physical body while forgetting the soul (diamond) that animates it. Of what value is pride of the body when death approaches?)

115 Human life is difficult to obtain, and may not come a second time. When the ripe fruit falls, it will not again attach to the branch. (*Comment*: When you have left the body, it is difficult to get into the same body again, just as the fallen ripe fruit does not reattach to the tree.)

116 You have twisted my arm and awakened me from sleep, and now you are leaving. Kabīr proclaims emphatically that either I realize you while in this body, or I perish. (*Comment*: This sākhī indicates the firm resolve of a true seeker of the Supreme Self. Life becomes meaningless without realizing the Supreme, and death becomes better than a life of materialism, ego, and passions. Twisting the arm is a metaphor for awakening someone and, in this case, God awakening the slumbering soul. The reference to leaving is a rhetorical statement; God is in the awakened heart.)

117 It is said that Indra fell under the influence of a two-letter word, a word with power throughout the four yugas. Kabīr says it is an exercise of the tongue to boast of virtue, when no one has been able to remove the influence of this word. (*Comment*: The two-letter word is kam and consists of two letters in Hindi, *ka* and *ma*. The god Indra is superior to the other gods in the Hindu pantheon. He was overcome by lust for Ahilya, the wife of the sage Gautama, who was away from his hermitage. Indra disguised himself as Gautama and entered the hermitage and seduced her. People talk easily about virtue, goodness, devotion and religious life, even though within their hearts they are often full of lust. The talking becomes a boast, a mere exercise of the tongue.)

118 People make a raft of snakes to cross the ocean of this world. If they leave it, they drown, and if they hold on to it, they will be bitten to death. (*Comment*: The snake represents the mind. It is both the source of bondage and of liberation. It is the instrument one uses to obtain enlightenment and freedom from the bondage of the world. An impure mind however is like holding on to a raft made of serpents (the passions and entanglements of the world) that is liable to bite the person. It is the pure mind that leads to liberation.)

119 A woman in love will await her beloved all day, keeping a bowl of delicious milk for him. Kabīr says when he is out of her mind, she does not offer him even the whey. (*Comment*: Kabīr is describing partiality towards those we love, and lack of concern for those we do not love. In spiritual life we need to be impartial, and love all people, realizing that they are at different stages of spiritual growth.)

120 If I say the Supreme Being is one, it is untrue. If I say he is two, it is a curse. Let Him be as He is, says Kabīr, after deep consideration. (*Comment*: Kabīr is expressing the highest mystical realization, a state of transcendence in which there is only 'Being.' If we say God is one then it implies the opposite, that there must be a second for comparison. One represents a number which can be enumerated. It represents a word symbol of an entity that can be defined in terms of form, dimension, and location. God is beyond these limitations. If we say God is two, then it is obviously wrong, for a unitary being cannot be two. God is pure consciousness. God is simply what He is.)

121 I have a packet of nectar, and have carefully opened it from all sides. If I find someone else like me, then I will let him also drink. (*Comment*: The packet is the nectar of knowledge that Kabīr has made available to all. But only those with spiritual merit will be able to drink it. Not all people are interested in spiritual nectar, so they would not see the benefit.)

122 People have taken the chalice of nectar (divine knowledge) from their heads and laid it aside. If I tell them of the Supreme One, they give me the name of a few others. (*Comment*: Kabīr is referring to monism and monotheism. The Supreme Being is without form, and beyond the limitations of time and space. Monotheism means one God. Monism refers to a unity of all according to Advaita Vedānta, or nondualism. Essentially it means that God is not separate from His creation, and that all creation, including God, form a single Being. This is the ultimate divine knowledge. But when Kabīr taught this, people began to mention their various gods and goddesses.)

123 What the sages undertake austerities for and what the Vedas greatly praise them for, that is what I teach the people, yet they do not believe the teachings. (*Comment*: Kabīr is saying he is teaching the realization of the Supreme Self, for which sages practiced severe penances and whom the Vedas praise immensely. Yet people do not trust his type of teaching. They are more interested in the outer forms of ritual worship, without grasping the secret of the ever-present Self within the hearts of all.)

124 From one Supreme Soul, countless other souls came, and all of them again merge into that One. When that One is realized, then the countless souls are seen to be absorbed into One. (*Comment*: Countless souls originate from the one Eternal Soul. Just as one candle lights countless other candles yet retains its own light without diminishing, just so the Supreme Reality becomes many souls manifesting in countless bodies in the universe. On realization, it is seen that all souls are contained in the Supreme.)

125 The teaching given by the guru may be only one word, but to realize it, there are countless thoughts. The munis and pandits have grown tired of explaining it, and the Vedas do not fathom its depth. (*Comment*: The one word 'Truth' can be debated endlessly. Though the guru teaches you to realize Truth, or the Self, it is an experience. The Vedas which form the ancient scriptures of India cannot give this personal, intuitive experience, even if you become very well versed in them. Spiritual attainment depends on purity and self-application and discipline, not merely on debates and the study of scriptures.)

126 O God, the four Vedas are singing your glories, but only in symbols. The soul, though it has nothing to take or give, is subject to great robbery. (*Comment*: All scriptures consist of words that are only symbols, and though they sing the glories of God, they cannot give the devotee the experience of God. The Vedas say that God is 'neti', 'neti' ('not this,' 'not this'). God is beyond words and scriptures. Being caught in the snare of symbols, the soul is looted. When it awakens to the Self, it realizes that there is nothing to give or take, but just to be.)

127 Seeing the four-legged animal, the hunter runs away. O saints look at this surprise! One who is dead is eating Kal (time or death). (*Comment*: The four-legged animal are the four ways of attaining spiritual knowledge. These are the discriminative intellect, discipline, cultivation of six virtues, and an intense desire for God-realization. The hunter or the impure mind, on seeing these four means of attaining the highest spiritual knowledge, runs away from them. Being dead here means being dead to the material world but rooted in one's Eternal Nature. The latter is not subject to time or death.)

128 Robbery has occurred in the three worlds, and everything belonging to everyone was stolen. The thief is without a head so no one can recognize him. (*Comment*: In the spiritual sense, it is the mind that robs everyone of the true wealth of spiritual knowledge. Because it does not have a head, people do not recognize the mind as the thief, and continue to be ensnared by it.)

129 Seeing the millstones grinding, tears welled up in my eyes. All those who fell between the stones were crushed. (*Comment*: The millstones referred to are birth and death that we are caught between. Without awakening to the Self, we do not obtain liberation, and the cycle of death and rebirth is our final result.)

130 Four thieves took off their shoes, and went about stealing. They placed a peg at the four doors. O pandit, try to understand this! (*Comment*: The four thieves are the passions of lust, anger, greed, and delusion, which stealthily enter the mind. The shoes are wisdom and discrimination that are abandoned. The pegs are obstacles blocking the doors of knowledge.)

131 The milk from which ghee (clarified butter) is obtained is to be praised. Half of a sākhī of Kabīr's represents the life of the four Vedas. (*Comment*: Kabīr states that half of one of his sākhīs (one line of a couplet) contains the life of the four Vedas. The Vedas were written in Sanskrit. Only a small number of scholars could understand the essence of the Vedas. Kabīr's sākhīs were given in the spoken language and were therefore easy to understand, while still containing the deepest wisdom.)

132 That man who understands the mind of others is to be congratulated. The master gives instructions to buy sugar, but the foolish man thinks he must buy salt. (*Comment*: The wise person is not deluded because he uses his intellect to guide him. He will not be cheated as he knows how the mind of the cheater (false teacher) works. The foolish man, on the other hand, is led astray by fraudulent teachers who, instead of bringing spiritual nectar, bring evil.)

133 The foolish person makes a poisonous tree (the body) his home. The snake remains coiled in it. The soul is thus fearful, and stays awake night and day. (*Comment*: The snake is the mind that drives the body into a worldly life. People who are ignorant of this are not aware of what the 'snake-mind' is doing to them. They spend sleepless days and nights in fear and anxiety.)

134 A house in which a snake lives is not suitable for devotion. A devotee dwelling there loses all wealth and becomes filled with poison. (*Comment*: The snake is a metaphor for a mind full of passions. An aspirant who has such passions and cannot control them is not yet fully devoted. With his mind not controlled, passions and worldly attachments constantly sway him. He thus loses his 'wealth' of spiritual knowledge and remains a slave to the mind.)

135 When a small ghunghuchi bead is planted, it abundantly yields eight paseris. The camp of Kal gets pitched there, and the passing of evening and morning becomes useless. (*Comment*: A ghunghuchi is a small red or white bead that has a black eye. It was used as a countermeasure for weighing gold. Kabīr is using the ghunghuchi to symbolize evil actions. When evil actions are planted, they multiply, and figuratively yield eight paseris or approximately twenty kilograms. Once this happens, death is camping at the doorstep.)

136 One can sow a mound of seeds, and not reap even a small crop. Since people do not heed my teaching, in the end, they will be ruined. (*Comment*: People study scriptures and take part in all kinds of rituals yet they reap very little in terms of spirituality. All their activities are external, and do not touch the soul. In the end, they lose their opportunity to gain enlightenment.)

137 Give up the ego, and all evils from your entire being, and worship God. Give up enmity towards all living beings. This forms the essence of the knowledge of the saints.

138 People of the world are misguided because of partiality. The wise devotee worships God impartially. (*Comment*: Practically all the people of the world have partial views towards certain religions, doctrines, dogmas, or rituals. Kabīr states that the wise person, who is spiritually awakened, has no partiality because he sees God everywhere and realizes that no religion has a monopoly on God.)

139 Great ones have gone from the world with their pride. Every hair of their bodies bristled with ego. Without recognizing God, all four castes are chamars. (*Comment*: Ego is the great stumbling block in spiritual life, and prevents one from truly realizing God. In India the high castes are supposed to know God, while the low castes are barred from reading the scriptures or receiving instruction in spiritual wisdom. Kabīr says that without knowing God, none are greater than the low caste cobbler.)

140 Spiritual progress cannot be made by merely giving up Māyā. One also has to give up the ego. The subtle ego that has cheated the sages, is devouring everyone. (*Comment*: The Supreme is present in all of existence, but illusion and people's egos are afflicting the whole world and preventing them from realizing God.)

141 The world is burning in the waves of Māyā, but men are busy pursuing gold and women. Kabīr asks, how can a person be saved when he keeps fire (Māyā) wrapped inside his cotton robe? (*Comment*: The desire for wealth and the opposite sex are two powerful forces of Māyā.)

142 Māyā is like a snake in the world, lying on the road shimmering with poison. She has ensnared the whole world in her noose, but Kabīr pushed her away and proceeded on his way. (*Comment*: Spiritual people are able to rise above the power of Māyā.)

143 There is a charm for removing the poison of a snake or a scorpion, and mantras for removing other poisons. But if a man gets in the clutches of the treacherous woman, she will tear out and devour his heart.

144 There are three gunas or qualities where the bee (mind) alights and relishes their fragrance. There are three fruits on one branch – eggplant, sugarcane, and cotton. (*Comment*: The mind is preoccupied with the three gunas or qualities: tamogun, consisting of inertia, spiritual ignorance, and negativity; rajogun, consisting of activity, passion, and restlessness; and satogun, consisting of purity, spirituality, and knowledge. The eggplant, sugarcane, and cotton are symbols of the three gunas.)

145 The mind is like an intoxicated elephant killing other animals, while desires are like a falcon seizing its prey. The elephant does not obey charms nor amulets, and desires just keep flying and seizing objects. (*Comment*: The mind of people under the spell of desires does not easily come under control.)

146 The mind is like a huge elephant that does not obey instructions, but follows its own desires. What can the poor mahout do if he does not have the ankush in his hand? (*Comment*: The ankush is the iron goad the mahout uses to control the elephant. Here it represents proper judgement used to direct the mind.)

147 Māyā is like a sweeper woman of the streets who is a concubine of many sweepers. She has ensnared both the father and the son, yet she belongs to no one. (*Comment*: The sweeper woman is figurative of a woman of loose morals. The father and son refer to God and the soul. Māyā enabled the conscious soul to manifest from undifferentiated God. The conscious soul then develops an awareness of God, so God then 'exists.' In this way Māyā deludes us from knowing Reality.)

148 O soul, do not be fooled by Māyā appearing as the beauty of gold and women. Obtaining and losing both is just like the snake sloughing off its dead skin.

149 Brahmā, Vishnu, and Mahesh came under the spell of Māyā. So did Nārad, Sharad, Sanandan, and Ganesh the son of Parvati. (*Comment*: The stories of these gods and sages are written in the Purānas. Māyā projected all of them from the Supreme Brahman.)

150 There is a huge pipal tree that has spread everywhere, but no one knows her secret. She has long branches, but no one reaches her fruit. Her husband is present, but people flock to her. (*Comment*: Māyā is the feminine energy principle of God. Māyā is also the manifestation of sense gratifications, passions, and material attachments so people flock to her.)

151 You behave like a thief in front of saintly people (shy away from them), yet befriend the thieves (evil people). You will come to realize your situation when calamity strikes you, when Yama the god of death approaches.

152 How can you obtain success when the guru has not shown you the path? Your boat of life will sink, and you will face the difficulties of birth and death again and again. (*Comment*: The boat is the body, and the soul is the passenger. Life is meant to be a crossing of the ocean of rebirths. The guru is the helmsman who guides the boat across this ocean to the shore of liberation.)

153 You did not consider and learn the right path, nor follow it after understanding it. If a blind person meets another blind person, who then will show the path? (*Comment*: A disciple learns the right path from his guru. If an ignorant disciple meets an ignorant guru, then the spiritual path will not be known.)

154 What can the disciple do if the guru is blind? The blind pushes the blind and both fall into the well. (*Comment*: There are 'gurus' who take advantage of gullible disciples. Kabīr taught that the guru must be knowledgeable, compassionate, and sincere. The disciple must examine the guru's conduct and character before accepting him.)

155 There is a stage where the people meet. No one should rush to go there. The tiger, the donkey, and the cow all graze in the same field. (*Comment*: The tiger, donkey, and cow refer to people who gather for idle talk. Wise people avoid such a gathering.)

156 It rains for four months in the rainy season, and there is plenty of water. But if you wear an impenetrable armour, not a single drop will strike you. (*Comment*: Just as it rains heavily, a guru showers drops of instruction on you. However, your armour or insensitive mind can prevent even a single instruction from reaching you.)

157 A person who waters the body (someone attached to worldly pleasures), is afraid to be in the company of the guru.

The earnings of evil thinking occupy his mind, and he drools after the earnings of gambling.

158 The body is like a rabbit, the mind like a hound, while death is the hunter. All three dwell in the same forest of worldly existence. How can you ask about their welfare?

159 Someone who cannot tell the difference between an honest person and a thief is blind and devoid of a discriminative intellect. Without a discriminative intellect he will be destroyed. Consider this carefully and avoid destruction. (*Comment*: In other words, know the difference between Reality and unreality. Embrace Reality and obtain liberation.)

160 Make your guru the polisher, and let him apply the polishing lathe to your mind. He will use the Word to remove your stains, and make your mind shine like a mirror.

161 The guru wastes his knowledge trying to teach wisdom to a fool. Charcoal will never become white, even if you wash it with hundreds of kilograms of soap.

162 A person who does foolish things, is like someone covered by armour. What can the archer (guru) do if his arrows (teachings) do not penetrate him?

163 The soul is like a parrot sitting on the silk cotton tree, hoping to eat its fruit. It strikes its beak and then shakes its head. This is behaviour fit for a parrot. (*Comment*: The silk cotton pod bursts upon being struck and the cotton flies away. The parrot, lacking discriminative knowledge, thinks it is a fruit and is disappointed. Similarly, a person who lacks discriminative knowledge is fooled by unscrupulous teachers.)

164 O parrot, give up the silk cotton tree immediately, as you have spoiled your plentiful feathers getting to it. Only he who has no heart and no eyes would favour such a tree.

165 The parrot is attracted to the silk cotton tree (the world) in the hopes of eating 'two' of the fruit. The pods break with a snapping noise, and the parrot departs sadly. (*Comment*: The worldly person is attracted to sense gratification, that is, to the fruit. However materialistic life is illusory and unfulfilling, and the disappointed soul departs at death.)

166 On whom are the people depending when they sit around lazily? Death plunders such people just as the butcher slaughters the sheep. (*Comment*: One has to depend on oneself and be spiritually alert to obtain liberation.)

167 Kabīr says that the wise person who knowingly acts as if simple and gives up strength in order to appear weak is a saint. An ordinary person cannot touch the hem of his garment. (*Comment*: Saintly people are humble, and act as if foolish among worldly people. But it is hard to measure up to them.)

168 Value that diamond that can withstand the blow of a sledgehammer. People who are deceptive and corrupt will be found to be false when examined. (*Comment*: The sledgehammer represents the passions and difficulties of life. The diamond represents people of firm spiritual resolve despite difficulties.)

169 God is the diamond, and people are the jewellers who have arranged their shops. When the true appraiser enters the shop, he will determine the value of the diamond. (*Comment*: The jewellers are selling their teachings for liberation. But the genuine and the counterfeit will be revealed when the true appraiser, the discriminating person, examines them.)

170 Do not display the diamond where there is a vegetable market. Tie it secretly in a knot, and go on your way. (*Comment*: It is futile to teach the hidden truth to indiscriminating people.)

171 The diamond is in the open bazaar, covered by dust. Many foolish people kicked it as they went by, but the discriminating appraiser quickly picked it up. (*Comment*: The soul is covered by the dust of worldly life. The discriminating person washes off the dust with the water of wisdom.)

172 Diamonds are not found in large rooms, and the sandalwood trees are not found in huge rows on the Maliyagir mountain. Similarly, lions are not found in large groups, nor sadhus in large crowds. (*Comment*: Saintly people are few and far between, just as diamonds are rare, and the sandalwood trees sparse.)

173 All people accept the dictates of their own minds. The knowledge of God is separate from these, but people do not know it. (*Comment*: People accept various gods and religious sects, but do not know that God dwells in their own hearts.)

174 The bones of the dead burn like dry wood and the hair like dry grass. But people intoxicated with the essence burn from within, just as cotton burns within a storehouse. (*Comment*: The lover of God 'burns' within, from the pangs of separation from God.)

175 The bathing place was forgotten by not knowing the proper path to it. Due to attachments to outward garbs people got lost. They failed to recognize the One (God) whose fame is all-pervading in the world. (*Comment*: The destination to the Self was forgotten by people who sang the glories of their outward garbs, sects, and scriptures. They were deluded by Māyā.)

176 What benefit is there in talking to a foolish person, or in arguing with one who is deceitful? What is the point in striking a rock with an arrow, when even a sharp arrow will be destroyed?

177 Just as a marble placed on the dome of a temple will roll down to the ground, just so will the heart of a fool when wise words cannot find a resting place.

178 The two outer eyes are lost, and the two inner eyes are lost. Kabīr says when all four eyes are lost there is no hope of gaining salvation. (*Comment*: The outer eyes are to behold the beauty of God everywhere, but people still do not see God. The inner eyes of wisdom and discrimination are to lead one to the Ultimate Truth.)

179 Many days have gone in vain, just as love that is falsely shown. Seeds planted in barren soil will not grow, even if the clouds rain heavily. (*Comment*: It is fruitless to give spiritual instruction to people who have no interest in spiritual matters.)

180 I weep for the world but no one weeps for me. Only he who weeps for me knows the Word. (*Comment*: Kabīr felt profound sorrow for the world, so he kept instructing people about the Truth. Only those who understood and practiced his teachings felt for him as he felt for them.)

181 All the people repeat the name of God, but I have this doubt. They do not have knowledge of Him, so what type of destination are they going to reach? (*Comment*: Speaking God's name without realizing Him is not going to lead to salvation.)

182 A living being cannot sustain itself without another living being. A living being is the support of another living being. Therefore, be compassionate and protect life. O pandit! Consider this carefully. (*Comment*: Protecting all life is the duty of a spiritual aspirant. Those who kill in the name of religion, or offer sacrifices to gods and goddesses, are practicing violence.)

183 I have spoken of much, but no one knows of me. I have spoken of what was good, as I am doing now. In age after age I have remained the same. (*Comment*: Kabīr spoke of the Supreme Sentient Self in all the ages to awaken the people to the Reality of the Self.)

184 If I speak the truth openly, people want to beat me. And if I speak in parables, they do not understand. The guard (soul) lies hidden under the straw (Māyā). One who tells the truth becomes an enemy. (*Comment*: One has to remove the veil of Māyā to realize the soul. People love Māyā – the illusory worldly pleasures. One who teaches the removal of Māyā thus becomes an enemy.)

185 I have travelled in many countries with my mind full of God's love. But when I searched for people whose hearts were filled with God's love, I found that they were scarce. (*Comment*: Spiritually destitute people are everywhere, there are only few who are truly interested in the highest Reality.)

186 This Kaliyug is full of evil, and people are spiritually blind. They do not obey my words. When I teach them for their own good, they turn around and consider me their enemy.

187 I do not touch ink and paper nor do I hold a pen in my hand, but I have orally given the great teachings in all the four yugas for the welfare of all. (*Comment*: Kabīr stated that his name in the Sat yuga (golden age) was Sat Sukrit, in the Treta yuga or silver age it was Munindra, in the Dwapar yuga or bronze age it was Karunāmai, and in this Kali yuga or iron age it was Kabīr.)

188 It is important to have wisdom to know what lies in the future, what occurred in the past, and what the circumstances surrounding the present are. But the use of wisdom to explore all wisdom is my wisdom. (*Comment*: The wisdom Kabīr is talking about is based on knowing Reality. This wisdom transcends all wisdom.)

189 One who dwells within the limits is called human and one who dwells beyond limits is called a sādhu (ascetic). But one who has given up both the limits and the limitless is of unfathomable wisdom. (*Comment*: The limits consist of religion and its injunctions to which ordinary people adhere. Those who live beyond limits is in reference to monks and others who have renounced materialism. One who has given up both is an enlightened person with God knowledge. He is not bound by any tradition, is above the three gunas (attributes), and is full of love for all beings.)

190 Those who understand, have a consensus of knowledge that God is Omnipresent. But Kabīr says there are many half-informed religious people who excitedly proclaim otherwise, that God has a particular dwelling place.

191 What can the path do if the traveller does not walk carefully? Giving up his own way, he travels in barren lands. (*Comment*: What can religion and philosophy do if people do not understand and practice the truth? They give up the path to the Sentient Self, and engage in various kinds of worship, pilgrimages, ceremonies, rituals and so forth.)

192 People have died and will continue to die. There is the drumbeat of death hanging over their heads. The world has become a lover of dreams. All that will be left, as a sign of their lives, will the their words. (*Comment*: Worldly existence passes like a dream. It has no permanent existence.)

193 You died in the past and will die again, struck by hollow arrows. You are already lying under the tree groaning, wondering if you will die today or tomorrow. (*Comment*: The tree is the world, and the groaning is due to karmas. The hollow arrows are the hollow and false teachings of deceitful people.)

194 My language is of the East, and no one understands it. Only one who belongs to the farthest East will understand it. (Comment: East refers to the source of sunrise and the awakening of knowledge. Here Kabīr is referring to the Sentient Self that has existed before anything else. Thus only one who has realized the Sentient Self will understand what he is talking about.)

195 The mighty person whose walk made the earth tremble, is burning in the sun's heat. O pandit! Think about this. (*Comment*: The greatest of men who figuratively made the earth tremble while alive, were helpless when death came and lay as corpses in the hot sun.)

196 The one who measured the Earth by his steps (Vamana), and the one who jumped across the water (Hanuman), and the one who weighed the mountain in his hands (Rāvan), were all devoured by death. (*Comment*: In Hindu mythology, Vaman the Dwarf and fifth incarnation of Lord Vishnu, covered the Earth in two steps thus taking it away from King Bali. Hanuman jumped across the water from India to Lanka (now Sri Lanka) to find the abducted Seeta. Rāvan lifted the Kailash mountain where Shiva resided. All these powerful beings died. It is therefore futile for anyone to boast of power.)

197 You can collect nine maunds of milk (approximately *180* kilograms), and all will spoil with only one drop of vinegar. The milk will sour and curdle, and the ghee contained in it will be destroyed (*Comment*: A minimum of evil in the mind, or bad company, will spoil devotion and lead to spiritual ruin.)

198 How many people can I persuade by bowing at their feet, or even by weeping to show them the Truth? The Hindus worship their deities, and the Muslims worship none but an abstract Khuda in heaven. (*Comment*: People have forgotten that the Truth, the Sentient Self, is within their own hearts.)

199 O man! You have great qualities, but your flesh is of no use. Your bones cannot make an ornament, and your skin cannot make a musical instrument such as a drum. (*Comment*: Only the virtues of a person are useful, not his body.)

200 I acknowledge those who know and understand me with loving devotion. I do not accept the worldly and Vedic restrictions when it comes to my surrender to God. (*Comment*: Knowledge of God cannot be imparted by any scripture or tradition.)

201 The Earth is the source of all, and nurtures all. But it does not consider its own virtue. The quality of the guru is the same. (*Comment*: The Earth is very forgiving, and so is the guru.)

202 The Earth knows its own qualities, and never wavers from it. Grain by grain it has become heavy, and in many places is sold for money. (*Comment*: The Earth's matter is made up of atoms. All the atoms give weight to the Earth, and give it gravity.

Earth's resources, metals, and gems are sold and traded.)

203 There was a time when this changeable world did not exist, so there was neither earth nor water. At that time there was no creation nor dissolution. Kabīr is teaching the philosophy of that time. (*Comment*: Prior to any material manifestation there was only the Self-existent, Eternal Spirit.)

204 When there is speech, there is a need for letters. When there are no letters, the mind becomes powerful. But there is hardly anyone who can understand the state when speech and non-speech become one. (*Comment*: There are three words to be considered, *kshar* which refers to the destructible phenomenal world, *akshar* which refers to the indestructible soul, and *nirakshar* which refers to the Supreme Being beyond these two. The word akshar also means letters of the alphabet. When the mind reaches that eternal state in meditation, it is in contact with Universal Power. That state is one of pure consciousness, and is beyond the realm of speech or non-speech, letters, and words, destructible and indestructible. It is a state of pure Being.)

205 As long as the sun does not rise, the stars shine. Similarly, as long as there is not enough knowledge, the souls wander under the influence of karmas.

206 People go astray from the road when they do not know the name of the village where they are going. Tomorrow, thorns will pierce your feet. Why don't you walk carefully now? (*Comment*: It is important to know your spiritual destination, or else the thorns of evil in the world will torment you.)

207 Keep company with sadhus (holy people) because they remove the troubles of others. The company of cruel people is bad, as it is the source of misery day and night.

208 Keeping company with noble people brings happiness, while the company of evil people brings suffering. Kabīr says be in the company of your own type of noble people.

209 As your longing for good is from the beginning, you should keep it to the end. By collecting cowrie after cowrie you can gather a heap of millions.

210 Today, tomorrow, or any day, the body will cease to be steadfast. Kabīr asks, how can you keep water in an unbaked clay pot? (*Comment*: Just as the water breaks the raw clay pot and flows away, just so the soul will depart from the perishable body.)

211 The poor, helpless soul is bound by countless bonds of doubts and delusions. It can either free itself by its own power, or God can free it.

212 Do not kill helpless beings, for they all have the same life force as you. The sin of killing will not be abolished, even if you listen to the Purānas millions of times. (*Comment*: One must see oneself in all beings, and all beings in oneself. This is the essence of the transcendental experience.)

213 Do not kill any living being, because it will take revenge on you. You cannot be saved by going on a pilgrimage, even if you give millions of diamonds as alms.

214 Three people went on a pilgrimage with restless thoughts and thieving minds. The sins of none were removed, but their minds became loaded with ten more. (*Comment*: Without a pure and centered mind, there is no benefit in going on a pilgrimage. People are liable to return with more sins, being hypocritical about their religious pursuit.)

215 Those who went to the holy river and bathed in the cold water, died and floated away. Kabīr says, listen O saints, they will become demons and be full of regrets. (*Comment*: This is an indication that they were not sincere in their hearts. They took their evil with them even to the 'holy' places.)

216 Pilgrimage has become a creeping vine of poison, extending age after age. They have uprooted the poisonous vine, so how will they not eat the poison? (*Comment*: People carry their evil habits and thoughts to pilgrimages, so the place of pilgrimage also becomes tainted with poison.)

217 O creeping vine of great qualities! No one can explain your greatness. When your root is cut you become green and thrive, but when you are watered, you wither. (*Comment*: This is an allegorical sākhī. The root is the hypocrisy and confusing rituals that people take on pilgrimages, so when they are removed, the soul thrives. But by watering or nurturing rituals with hypocrisy, the soul symbolically withers.)

218 This vine is ugly and its fruit is evil. Its flowers of bad intellect have a foul smell. It brings death to the person taking it, and its leaves are withered and bitter. (*Comment*: This sākhī is similar to the one above, but here the vine is Māyā. Māyā causes ignorance of our connection with God and fosters bad intellect that causes trouble everywhere. Māyā causes spiritual death.)

219 There is a friend that is thinner than water, subtler than smoke and swifter than wind. That is the friend of the materialistic people. (*Comment*: The friend Kabīr is referring to is the mind full of desires and passions.)

220 O saints! Listen to the words of Satguru and don't take a burden on your head. I stand in your presence and advise you to be ready for battle with Māyā. (*Comment*: Overcoming Māyā leads to liberation. The burden is the troubles caused by Māyā.)

221 This vine is bitter and its fruit bitter. When you separate yourself from that vine, you will be called an adept. (*Comment*: The vine referred to is Māyā, while actions resulting from Māyā create bitter results. Those who free themselves from Māyā earn the title of adept.)

222 What does it matter if you have become an adept, and your fame has spread all around? Inside you there is still the dormant seed of Māyā, and it can sprout again. (*Comment*: An example of what Kabīr is pointing to are accomplished Hatha yogis who are called adepts, but are often still influenced by Māyā who has remained latent in them. There is a great difference between such adepts and saints.)

223 If one puts water on the cover of a vessel, the water does not get inside. O saints, consider it! For the sake of name and fame, someone puts on an outward show to avoid shame, yet Kal (death) snatches him. (*Comment*: A pretentious person is impervious to the water of spiritual knowledge. Thus he does not obtain liberation.)

224 If I say He exists no one believes me. Without knowing the Reality of the Existent, what perfection can there be? Kabīr says, O saints listen to me, only a diamond can cut a diamond! (*Comment*: God is the reality that exists as the Self within all. It takes a realized person to pierce the depth of the greater Self.)

225 Gold, and noble and saintly people, become whole again even if they break a hundred times. But the evil person is like

the pot of a potter. With one push it cracks and will not rejoin. (*Comment*: Noble people have resiliency of character and are able to remain undisturbed.)

226 The world is like a room of kajal (collyrium) and all the people are drowning in it. But it is the great glory of that person who can enter it and come out unsoiled. (*Comment*: Kajal is a symbol for Māyā that has entangled the world. A rare person becomes liberated from Māyā.)

227 The world is made of kajal and is a fort of kajal. A person entering it becomes blackened, but his navel escapes. (*Comment*: The navel is sheltered and so escapes becoming black. It represents the person sheltered by God and so escapes the influence of Māyā.)

228 Hundreds of millions, and billions in wealth, and a kingdom stretching from the East to the West, cannot be measured against the greatness of devotion that gives liberation. So of what use are they?

229 The fish is taken to be sold at the fisherman's market. A person addresses the fish, 'O fish! You have shiny red eyes, so why are you 'wearing' the net?' (*Comment*: A person who indulges in worldly pleasures gets trapped by Māyā despite having eyes.)

230 The fish answers, 'I built my house in the water and my bed in the nether world. But the die of my karmas was cast, so I got trapped in the net. (*Comment*: We reap the effects of our karmas.)

231 When you are a fish you cannot be saved. The fisherman is your death. In whatever pond you go, he will place his net there. (*Comment*: Māyā is everywhere in the world, and so is death. The soul should not be like a fish in the pond of worldly entanglements.)

232 People, in countless numbers, have bound their necks without a rope. Kabīr asks, I placed a mirror in your hand, but without eyes how can you see it? (*Comment*: God gives the mirror of knowledge but we also need eyes of discrimination to protect us from negative karmas.)

233 Although I explain things, people do not understand. They sell themselves into the hands of others (*Comment*: Māyā, ego, passions, desires, and so forth). I try to pull them towards me (liberation) but they are rushing towards death.

234 By constant polishing, the rust from iron is removed, just so, by constant noble speech, the fetters of Māyā and of attachments are broken.

235 O man, you have a boat made of iron (spiritual ignorance) loaded with heavy stones (karmas)! You place a sack of poison (evil thoughts, words, deeds) on your head, yet you want to cross the ocean of the world. (*Comment*: Crossing the ocean of the world is in reference to spiritual liberation.)

236 The Pandavas were very dear to Krishna, yet they went to the Himalayas and died. If iron touches the touchstone (philosopher's stone), how can rust spoil it? (*Comment*: The epic of the Mahabharata relates the story of the Pandavas and the great war. Krishna is said to be an incarnation of Lord Vishnu, and a dear friend, protector, and advisor to the Pandavas and charioteer of Arjuna in the war. He sent the Pandavas to the Himalayas where they all died, except Yudhishthir.)

237 The sun rises in the East and sets in the West, and eats flowers of air. Yet, the sun is eclipsed by the planet Rahu. Why then are people forgetful? (*Comment*: Eating flowers of air is figurative, meaning that the sun needs no support. In Indian mythology, Rahu swallows the sun periodically (eclipses it) despite the sun's greatness. People should remember that death is stalking them.)

238 The mind resides in front of the eyes (the eyes see according to what the mind directs) and every moment it rushes around. It is the king in the three realms, and is worshipped everywhere. (*Comment*: People become subservient to the restless mind.)

239 The mind is selfish and self-centered. It flutters with waves of desire for poison. If the body moves according to the dictates of the mind, then the whole life can be ruined. (*Comment*: Fluttering is a metaphor for a flag on the chariot of the body. The mind flutters just as the flag does. If the body is swayed by every flutter of the mind, then it is headed for ruin.)

240 How strange is the way the world follows, just like a flock of sheep. If one falls into a pit, the others follow and also fall in. (*Comment*: In spiritual life one cannot follow the crowd. The seeker must maintain integrity of spirit and live accordingly.)

241 That border is difficult and no one should go there. Those who went did not return. Who then can bring news of their welfare? (*Comment*: IThe border referred to is death. One ought to be prepared for death by gaining liberation while alive, so death has no power. No one comes back after death to tell others how the conditions were. It is important to make our paths good now.)

242 Man dies in bad company, just as the banana plant in the company of the plum tree. The banana leaves wave in the wind and are shredded by the thorns of the plum tree. (*Comment*: The mind can become corrupted by bad company.)

243 The banana plant was not observant when the plum tree was planted near it. If it realizes its position now, what can it do? It is surrounded by thorns. (*Comment*: The lesson is to choose the company you keep carefully, before it is too late. It is foolish to start digging a well when the house is on fire.)

244 People do not know the secret of the real Self. They remain ignorant about it. Their argumentative minds stand at the door, so they do not get to know Reality. They lament birth after birth.

245 He who does not find a Satguru, runs around restlessly in all directions. He is like one insane, and whose eyes do not see. His house is burning, yet he quenches a heap of rubbish. (*Comment*: Without the spiritual instructions of the Satguru, a person is preoccupied with worldly passions and desires. They are the rubbish that he is quenching, but he does not realize this, and meanwhile his house burns.)

246 The treasure is at one place, yet you search for it elsewhere. How can you obtain it? Honour the wise person who uses his discriminative intellect to find the treasure. (*Comment*: God is in the heart, so looking for Him anywhere else is useless.)

247 Listen to all, but make your own decisions. The sindur box is both a box and a lid. (*Comment*: Listening to others and making your own decisions serves the dual purpose of keeping others happy while maintaining your independence. Sindur is

vermilion.)

248 Let the drummers beat their drums. Do not touch the wild hens of this Kaliyug. What is your concern with the affairs of others? Settle your own affairs. (*Comment*: Touching the wild hens is meddling in the affairs of others. In this Iron age you can quickly get into trouble.)

249 Singing and preaching to others without consideration of the essence is like singing a song without understanding the inner meaning. Kabīr says it is like iron locked in the rock and cannot be touched by the philosopher's stone. (*Comment*: If one is not touched by the deep meaning of the singing and preaching, then one remains like iron not converted into gold.)

250 Whatever we first accepted became golden truth for us. But when tested on the philosopher's stone, it proved to be brass. (*Comment*: We cling to our first impression or experience of something as if it is the absolute thing. But when examined by the test of the Supreme Reality, it is found not to be as valuable as we first thought.)

251 Ignorant people spoil the true nature of devotion by washing pebbles and stones. They retain the poison within, and throw away the nectar. (*Comment*: Throwing away the nectar is neglecting the knowledge of the soul. Retaining the poison is holding on to superstitions based on ignorance. Pebbles and stones are the various shapes and sizes of idols people cherish.)

252 She was the wife of one but became the wife of many. This harlot had many mates. Kabīr asks, with whom will she immolate, as she was the wife of many men? (*Comment*: Māyā is the wife or feminine principle of the Supreme, so she was with Him alone. But in creation Māyā beguiled many gods, saints, sages, as well as ordinary people, so she became the wife of many. Another interpretation is of a worshipper who has given up the Supreme, and is worshipping many gods.)

253 The body is like a ship, and the mind is like a crow that flies a million miles away. Sometimes it wanders on the fathomless waters, and at other times, it wanders in the sky. (*Comment*: The mind is easily and quickly preoccupied with material things, and other times with spiritual things.)

254 The mind is like a room filled with jewels of wisdom, but is locked by a magnet. It should be opened only in the presence of the wise ones who have the key of sweet words. (*Comment*: Wisdom of the Sentient Self is locked away in the mind of all. It needs the key of the sweet teachings of the realized master to open it.)

255 Between heaven and hell people have fastened themselves with two gourds. The six philosophies are in doubt about this, and even the adepts are caught in the world of 8.4 million births. (*Comment*: The two gourds are Māyā and ignorance that affect all people, even the great and knowledgeable ones. They bind people to the cycle of rebirths.)

256 Cast away all evil thinking, and make a good life as a human being. Give up the conduct of the crow, and adopt that of the swan. (*Comment*: The crow symbolizes spiritual ignorance and evil, and the swan symbolizes purity and spiritual liberation.)

257 You must live according to what you say. Give up attachment and aversion. There should not be an iota of change, up or down, in this way of life. Conduct your life in this way.

258 Ramji is standing at your door and calls out, "O Kabīr! Come and meet me!" Kabīr replies, "You are meeting with everyone else, so I cannot meet with you." (*Comment*: Kabīr's instruction is that when devotion is scattered to many objects of worship, one cannot meet the One. Give up all, and realize the One.)

259 Confusion has increased in the three worlds, and manifests in every place. Kabīr proclaims loudly that you are dwelling in the village of confusion.

260 You have thrown away your diamond in the sand, and now you are picking up and eating pebbles. Kabīr proclaims loudly that you should realize your soul while in the body, or else the body will end uselessly. (*Comment*: The diamond refers to the soul, while pebbles are all the materialistic things. The body is meant to be an instrument for the realization of Divinity.)

261 Just as many as are the leaves in the forest, and as many as the grains of sand in the Ganges, in just so many words has Kabīr explained the Truth to the people. What can the poor scholar say?

262 I thought you were from the pedigree of swans, so I accepted your company. Had I known you were a foolish crane, I would not have allowed you to touch me. (*Comment*: The swan represents a pure soul, whereas the crane represents evil. The crane stands motionless, as if in meditation, but snatches the fish. Kabīr expresses how one would feel when duped by an apparently religious person.)

263 A virtuous person will speak of the virtue of others, but the non-virtuous person scorns the virtue of others. If you give nutmeg to a bullock, what will he think of it, and how would

he eat it? (*Comment*: A learned person who is himself virtuous, and understands the value of virtues, is rare in the world. Giving nutmeg to a bullock is like imparting wisdom to a fool.)

264 Both the cowherd and the master abandon cattle that have no teeth. Just so, liberation is lying in the streets of Vrindavan crying. (*Comment*: Cattle suffer without an owner and keep crying out. Liberation is crying out for a suppliant in, of all places, Vrindavan where Lord Krishna dwelt.)

265 There are people who speak sweetly, but have a poisonous heart. Kabīr says to such people that Rāma is clever enough to deal with them appropriately. (*Comment*: A person can fool another with sweet words, but cannot fool God.)

266 All who have gone from here went with heavy loads of karmas. No one has come back from there and can tell you of conditions there. (*Comment*: Since we do not get information of what those departed endure, we must do our best to get liberation from the weight of karmas.)

267 Devotion to God is dear to the devotee as fire is dear to all of us. Even after fire burns the village and kills everyone, still one begs for and brings fire. (*Comment*: Just as fire is necessary for livelihood, just so is devotion dear to the sincere devotee seeking God.)

268 The lady is called the wife of her beloved, yet she sleeps with someone else. Love for other friends is in her heart. How can her husband be happy? (*Comment*: Metaphorically, the soul is the wife of God who is the husband. But the soul keeps company with Māyā, so how can God be happy?)

269 A good person has become evil by listening to the advice of others. Instead of becoming valuable as gold, he has become of little value, as bronze and copper. (*Comment*: Bad counsel from so-called friends can ruin your life.)

270 O Rāma! I feel the pangs of separation from you. I am offering this arti to you, so please give me your darshan. If you give me your darshan after my death, of what value will it be? (*Comment*: This sākhī expresses the words of a sincere devotee longing to know God in this life and cries: 'Let me have the realization of the Supreme Sentient Self while I am alive.' Kabīr stressed that you cannot realize God after death.)

271 Death can come at any moment, yet people remain in delusion. They give up thought of the future, and keep calling to the past. (*Comment*: The delusion is clinging to the past instead of rectifying the present. Death can strike at any moment, yet people are not preparing themselves spiritually.)

272 The One is immersed in all, and all are immersed in that One. Kabīr is immersed in the knowledge where there is no room for a second. (*Comment*: God is manifest in all beings, and all exist in God. Kabīr is immersed in God with no duality.)

273 When you worship the One, all are worshipped. But when you worship all, then your worship is useless. Only when you water the roots, does the tree bring forth flowers and fruits in abundance. (*Comment*: Worship should be directed to the One. Kabīr says all worship is included in this. When you water the leaves and branches, the tree dies. Just so, worshipping many deities renders worship useless.)

274 The forest which the lion (soul) does not enter, and the bird (mind) does not fly in, is empty (void or unreal). The Hatha yogis enter that forest by controlling their sense organs, and going into sunya samādhī. (*Comment*: This sākhī is pointing to the yogic practice of samādhī. After coming out of the void (sunya samādhī or empty forest) the yogis are again subject to worldly desires. The soul is Reality, so it cannot go into the void of unreality.)

275 If I speak the truth people do not like it. But lies are dear to them. They put the water drawing implement on my head, yet they water the gardens of others. (*Comment*: Putting the implement on Kabīr's head and watering the gardens of others is a reference to imposters using his name to further their own religious ends.)

276 Speech is priceless if you know how to use words wisely. First weigh the words on the scale of your heart before you let them proceed from your mouth. (*Comment*: That is, be aware of the consequences of what you are about to say before you say it.)

277 Whatever you wish to do, undertake it with your own strength and ability. Give up dependence on others. When the river is flowing by your own courtyard, how can you die of thirst? (*Comment*: God given strength, will, and mind are in you to make you independent.)

278 Let that person be what he is – ignorant. You should not become ignorant in turn. He lacks virtue, but you are virtuous. Therefore, do not mix the good with the bad. (*Comment*: Kabīr is addressing a disciple.)

279 The mind of the person who is intoxicated with God remains absorbed in him. It is like the reflection of a beautiful maiden in the mirror. If you try to hold her, you cannot. (*Comment*: You can be totally absorbed in the love of God, but you cannot touch Him, just as you cannot touch the reflection.)

280 A sādhu must be true to his status, and act according to his perfect saintliness. If you grind unripe mustard seeds, you get neither oil nor oil cakes. (*Comment*: A sādhu or holy person must be 'ripe' like the mustard seed in order to express his true nature.)

281 If a ram puts on the skin of a lion, people will fear him. But when he bleats, people will recognize him to be a sheep. Speech is the revealer. (*Comment*: An 'unripe' sādhu will reveal what he is when he speaks. Putting on external garbs and symbols will not help, as he will reveal himself by what he says.)

282 The herb for which I searched for many kalpas (eons) was in my heart all the time. But because of the dominance of ego, the herb remained far away. (*Comment*: The herb refers to God, the Ultimate Self.)

283 The body is like a cage with ten doors, and the vital breath is as a bird that remains in it. It is surprising the bird remains in the cage. So what surprise can there be if it flies away? (*Comment*: The body has ten doors or apertures. The breath of life can depart from it at any time.)

284 There are people who take the name of God then fight among themselves. They travel another path. They travel around like bullocks covered in human skin. (*Comment*: Kabīr is referring to people who have a superficial devotion to God. They are garb bearers who fight to protect their identity or false sense of superiority.)

285 The land is good and the seed is good. The seed is sown by scattering by the handful. Why then are the plants dying? Is it because of the quality of the soil? (*Comment*: Metaphorically, the teacher is good, the teaching is good, so if the disciple does not prosper, then he is deficient.)

286 He who steps down from the guru's ladder turns his face away from the guru's teaching. Death will snatch him, and no one will be able to save him. (*Comment*: A disciple makes spiritual progress if he is humble and obedient to the guru. In this way, he will climb the ladder to liberation.)

287 A burning fire (passions, desires) dwells in the heart. Therefore, everybody lives under the influence of sorrow.

288 Whoever I met acted as a guru. I did not find anyone acting as a disciple. Even if I taught 696,000 ramainiyān to such a soul, it would be useless. (*Comment*: Those acting as gurus are egotistical and do not wish to learn, so Kabīr noted that teaching them spirituality was in vain.)

289 Where there is a customer, I am not there. Where I am, there is no customer. Without discriminative knowledge, people wander aimlessly, grasping only the shadow of the words. (*Comment*: Kabīr says that he dwells in spirit, not in the illusory phenomenal world. Without discriminative knowledge, people do not reach the spiritual realm.)

290 There are gems and stones everywhere in the world, but appraisers are rare. The astute appraiser is more valuable than the gems, but such an appraiser is indeed rare in the world. (*Comment*: The real appraiser can distinguish between gems or the spiritually wise, and valueless stones or spiritually ignorant people.)

291 People who are sleeping in ignorance have many imaginary dreams. They should wake up and open their eyes of wisdom. They would see that their soul is being severely looted. In the end there is nothing to take or give. (*Comment*: Materialistic life is not the Reality, but a dream, as everything will vanish. The soul is looted by a life oriented in this manner and loses spiritually. From a transcendental viewpoint, everything is perfect, so there is nothing to add or subtract.)

292 This world is the kingdom of destruction (of Māyā) and the servant (mind) rules powerfully. The essence of the Word is the Reality. Perhaps someone may take this wisdom to heart and become liberated.

293 As long as the drum (person) is intact, it will produce sound (speak). When the drum breaks (person dies), its sound disappears. No one peeps in his door then, as death is abhorrent.

294 Bow down and offer salutation to the wise saint with discriminative knowledge. There are many who put on the garb of a saint. Avoid the bondage where there is no discriminative knowledge of the Word. (*Comment*: In other words, examine the saint's wisdom and do not get fooled by the garb and pleasant words.)

295 Kabīr says gods, men, sages, deities, and the inhabitants of the seven islands and nine continents of the Earth, have all endured suffering by taking on a body.

296 Unless there is firm resolve in the heart to obtain happiness, and final beatitude, there can be no happiness and bliss. Kabīr says he proclaimed the teachings in the four yugas, but people still live with doubt in their hearts.

297 I have heard the musical instrument playing the Divine melody. Now the strings are broken. What can the poor instrument do when the musician has departed? (*Comment*: The soul hears the unstruck Divine melody (anāhad nād) while in the body. When the soul departs, what can the 'dead' instrument do? The strings refer to the idā, pingalā and sushumna nadis familiar to yogis. They 'break' at death.)

298 If you wish to realize me (the Supreme Self) then give up all desires for others (sense objects). Become desireless like me, and you will find that happiness is already within you.

299 Nothing is gained by putting on the garb of a saint, if you do not speak thoughtfully. You kill other souls and carry a sword on your tongue. (*Comment*: Having a sword on your tongue is speaking hurtful words to others.)

300 In the heart of a person there is a dirty pond full of evil. He proceeds to a village to build a fortress where there is no habitation. (*Comment*: The dirty pond is the mind full of ego and passions. Being ignorant of the Reality, a person builds a fortress (religious life) in imagination only, imagining himself to be truly spiritual.)

301 Sweet words are like a medicine that heals, but harsh words are like arrows. The harsh words enter through the ears and pierce the whole body. (*Comment*: Pleasant words are the mark of a spiritual person. Harsh words cause a great deal of suffering.)

302 Behold the courage of the diver. He dives into the depths of the ocean. He ignores the dangers from aquatic animals and comes out with the pearl. (*Comment*: In spirituality, one must dive deeply into God consciousness, and come out with the pearl of bliss.)

303 Worldly-minded people live in deception, since they do not succeed in true yoga or true pleasure. Saintly people have threshed out the sesame seeds, while the worldly thresh the seedless stalk. (*Comment*: Worldly people cannot realize union with God or achieve yoga, and enjoy only fleeting pleasures. The people of Realization have gotten the kernel of spirituality, while others are pursuing futile searches.)

304 O diver! Drink the nectar of bliss! Why risk death by diving to the depths below? By the grace of the guru and the company of sadhus, go through the door of liberation. (*Comment*: The depths below refer to the Mulādhāra chakra at the base of the spine where the kundalinī energy resides. It is part of Hatha yoga practice. Kabīr, in contrast, advocates Sahaj yoga as the door to liberation.)

305 Many drops of semen have fertilized eggs, yet many others have gone wasted. Why does a person cry for the loss of one drop? (*Comment*: In the case of humans, one sperm and egg result in a person. But many times the semen does not fertilize an egg, so it is 'wasted'. The 'wasted' semen represents the loss of many lives. Kabīr uses this analogy to compare the death of one person to the death of many, represented by the wasted semen. One drop represents one person, so why cry for the death of one, when so many have died, and nobody cried for them?

306 The fire is burning in the ocean (the world). Everyone burns in it and is reduced to ashes. But people cry bitterly saying, 'My precious diamond is burning.' (*Comment*: The fire is death that assails the whole world. All are consumed and turned to ashes. The precious diamond is a 'gem' in the family, often a son. The bitter crying is due to strong attachment to one who is dying. Kabīr said to have consolation, knowing death comes to everyone.)

307 That which was supposed to be proved in the six philosophies, was given the name Banwari. Kabīr says, the whole world is wise and in this matter I am the ignorant one. (*Comment*: Banwari is another name of Krishna, but in this context Kabīr means the Ultimate Reality. The six philosophies try to 'prove' the Ultimate Truth. Kabīr did not teach about the six philosophies, in which he says he is the ignorant one, but taught a 'direct realization' of the Ultimate Truth, that is formless and does not need to incarnate.)

308 The person who lives the Truth that he is, cannot be affected by a curse, or be destroyed by death. If the person of Truth walks the path of Truth, then nothing can destroy him. (*Comment*: Truth is the Sentient Spirit and is indestructible.)

309 Serve the Master who is perfect in all his ways. If you love and serve a mean one, you will lose even your capital. (*Comment*: A perfect master will make you perfect by making you realize your Reality. Serving many deities and shallow 'masters' makes you waste the human birth in vain.)

310 O physician, return to your home! There is no one here who would consult you for anything. The one, who has placed this burden on us, will take care of it. (*Comment*: The physician is a metaphor for one who tries to teach others to be free of the consequences of karmas. God made and controls the law of karma, and is quite capable of looking after everyone.)

311 The preachers, figuratively, get sand in their mouths, if they preach to others but do not live according to the teachings themselves. It is like protecting another farmer's grain, while the animals are eating up their own fields.

312 My mind is directed towards your welfare, but your mind is directed towards another (worldly things). Kabīr asks, how can you, the world, and me be in harmony? (*Comment*: Teaching is wasted if the disciple's mind is not concentrated on the teaching.)

313 The person who sees the target, shows it to others. They keep looking at it, but are not able to strike it. All the arrows fall uselessly, they throw down the bow and then depart. (*Comment*: The first person is the preacher who knows of the spiritual goal. He tells it to others, but none of them reach the goal of Self-realization. The bow is the body that falls at death.)

314 If a teacher's actions are in keeping with his words, then his knowledge becomes a magnet for others. Kabīr says without the magnetic weapon, how can you win the war? (*Comment*: Soldiers used to carry magnetic shields, so that the swords of the opponent tended to stick to the shields. A preacher's actions and words need to be like the magnet that helps you win the battle of life.)

315 When a person relates his philosophy, and listens to mine, on hearing each other, we ought to become united or like-minded. But even before my eyes the world is passing, yet I have not found one person with whom to share such a discussion. (*Comment*: Most people are dogmatic and hold on to their opinions, rather than seek the truth.)

316 I have travelled in country after country, and in the streets of village after village. Yet I have not found anyone who could sift out the kernel of Truth (Reality) from the untruth.

317 My mind is directed towards your welfare, but your mind is directed towards another. Cursed is a mind that is one, yet goes in two directions. (*Comment*: The uncontrolled mind is seeking both sense gratification and spirituality. It is not possible.)

318 There is an attraction between a magnet and iron. The magnet lifts up the iron. Just so do the words of Kabīr free you from the trap of death.

319 You have lost your way, birth after birth, so let bygones be bygones. Be attentive now. Use the Word as the knife, and cut out all doubt. Then by knowledge you will have liberation.

320 Day after day, according to the circumstances, Kabīr has uttered many dohas (couplets) to teach the people. Be aware that those who died have never returned, despite those calling to them repeatedly. (*Comment*: Kabīr is talking about people who keep praying to, or boasting about their ancestors. Kabīr's dohas are intended to remove people's moral and spiritual lapses.)

321 What can the helpless teacher do when the disciple has faults? He imparts knowledge, but it becomes useless, just as if he was blowing into a broken bamboo flute. (*Comment*: If the disciple is 'hollow' inside, as the bamboo is, he will not absorb instructions from the guru.)

322 The person who earns the honour that is due to a grandfather, father, and brother is worthy. I will worship at his feet. One who can liberate himself from the coil of the yarn (Māyā) will be permanently blissful.

323 Humility is the best attribute. With humility everything becomes possible. Everyone bows to such a person, just as they bow down to the moon in reverence on auspicious occasions.

324 People of the world have been dying all this time, but hardly anyone knows how to die. Those who died did not die in such a state that they did not have to die again. (*Comment*: People who have attained liberation are not subject to rebirth, so they do not have to die again.)

325 People of the world have been dying all this time, but hardly anyone gives it a second thought. Each, convinced of his wisdom, faces death helplessly. (*Comment*: Realized people give up their body in an enlightened way with understanding. Worldly people give up their body in an unenlightened way, not knowing the secret of death.)

326 The Word is available, but there are no customers. The article is there, but it is expensive. Without paying the price for them, you get no benefit. Instead you wander here and there like a rolling stone. (*Comment*: Discipline, dedication, and giving up of worldly pleasures, constitute the expense in attaining the Word. Without the Word, people have no spiritual stability.)

327 A person gives up his home and becomes a yogi. The yogi does not have a home. Without discriminative knowledge, he wanders from place to place grasping only the shadow of the Word. (*Comment*: Not having a home, the yogi wanders from place to place according to the dictates of the mind. He is still under the influence of Māyā and so is not able to grasp the reality of the Word.)

328 The lion lives in the forest alone and at a moment's notice, runs after prey. He does not think that, like his forest, there are also other forests. (*Comment*: The lion is the mind living in the forest of the body. The prey are the objects of the senses. In pursuing its prey, the mind is totally concerned with its own bodily gratification and not those of others.)

329 The Supreme resides in every heart, sitting there in full consciousness. Whenever and whatever condition the person wishes, God gives him the type of understanding to pursue it. (*Comment*: This is a sākhī on the playing out of karmas.)

330 Whether a person is a gentleman or a thief is revealed by what he says. The content of his heart is revealed by the words leaving his mouth.

331 I did not meet anyone who understood the feelings in another's heart. Whoever I met was selfish. Kabīr says when the sky is torn, how can the poor tailor mend it? (*Comment*: The torn sky represents the many selfish people everywhere. A saint cannot mend all their selfish desires.)

332 I see people in the world burning, each in his own fire (ego, desires, and passions). I have not met one with whom I could establish a meaningful relationship.

333 A man may be great by worldly standards, but lacking wisdom, he is insignificant. What is the advantage in having the beautiful red flower if it has no fragrance?

334 There is no austerity greater than Truth, and no evil greater than falsehood. The heart that is truthful is the heart where God dwells.

335 What is the advantage of being born in a great lineage, if the intellect is not also great? It is like a flower blooming in a desolate place. It is useless to anyone, and slowly withers and dies.

336 Neither Vishnu nor Brahmā created Him, the sun and moon have not glanced at Him. He is not confined to the three worlds, yet He knows all of creation. (*Comment*: Kabīr is speaking about Brahman, the Absolute)

337 There is a limitless fruit on a tall tree. The bird trying to eat the fruit dies and dries up. People also strive a great deal for it and die. The fruit is sweet, but it is far away. (This sākhī is a metaphor for people trying to reach the sweet fruit of heaven, but dying in the effort. Apparently, a bird's beak can get caught in coconut fruit and it dies.)

338 He is like a businessman who sits (like a holy person in meditation but desiring profit), and like a cowherd who stands (ostentatiously, expecting honour). And he is like a watchman who stays awake all night doing meditation, but remaining full of desires. In the end, death devours these types. (*Comment*: This type of spiritual aspirants get no spiritual benefit because their actions are motivated by desires for fame or material gain.)

339 The trees keep burning in the front, but are afterwards replaced by green growth. But the tree that bears fruit when its roots have been cut is to be praised. (*Comment*: This is a metaphor for old people dying, and young ones being born in the cycle of birth and death. The person who cuts the root of Māyā, obtains the fruit of liberation.)

340 From birth to death, one goes through youth to old age. Just like a cat keeping its gaze fixed on the rat, just so death keeps a watch on us to snuff out life.

341 Dear God! This soul has been polluted from many previous births. Please do not let this polluted soul be further polluted.

God replies, "On whom should I inflict injury? Wherever I look, I see my own life." (*Comment*: Māyā has injured the soul, so to speak, birth after birth. This is the law of karma. God does not inflict suffering on anyone, as He is in everyone. The soul is polluted by ignorance and its adjuncts due to hypocritical teachings.)

342 When the philosopher's stone touches iron, the iron becomes gold, but the gold will never become the philosopher's stone. (*Comment*: The philosopher's stone is the sentient soul that imparts consciousness to the gross body making it 'golden,' but the body by itself cannot become sentient.)

343 People searched and searched for God. Some found Him as sagun (with attributes), and others found Him to be nirgun (without attributes). Those who could not find God after searching, admitted their defeat, and said He is formless and beyond reach.

344 People have chosen God, but He is formless and difficult to be chosen. He is the Master, and His light is incomprehensible (seventh heaven). Still, at the time of death, whom do people wish to see? (*Comment*: Despite His incomprehensible nature people still expect to see God after death.)

345 Light resides in the pure heart. Recognize that light as the Supreme! When it is this light that brought the world into existence, how can you say He is beyond choosing? (*Comment*: God is the Supreme Spirit, and is not subject to human notions of having form or attributes, or being formless and without attributes. Selection and non-selection of God are limitations of the mind. God is the highest Reality, and not subject to human interpretations.)

346 Brahmā, with folded hands and bowed head, asked his

mother (Adhya Shaktī), "Mother, please explain to me the colour and form of my father." (Brahmā's father is Niranjan.)

347 Brahmā's mother replied, "He has no colour nor form. He is in the firmament and has not taken a body. Visualize Him as the bodiless Purusha in the midst of the gagan mandal. (*Comment*: Gagan mandal is the firmament. Here it refers to meditation to reach higher consciousness.)

348 On hearing their mother's words, Brahmā, Vishnu, and Shiva firmly closed the doors (doors of their sense organs), and meditated on the gagan mandal. The three of them then saw their forms there and became blissful. (*Comment*: Seeing their own forms made them realize all forms are the forms of God.)

349 The mind became soothed when Brahm gyān (knowledge of the Absolute) dawned in it. The fire (Māyā) that is burning the world, has become cooling water to the realized person. (*Comment*: The realized person has risen above the fluctuations of the thought waves. In that serenity he realizes the Absolute.)

350 The One (God) with whom you had a relationship from the very beginning, you have now forgotten. That is why you are in the trap of the world of rebirths, speaking of other things. (*Comment*: Other things refers to materialism, ego, passions, desires, and so forth, instead of spiritually elevating teachings.)

351 I see the unseeable, and I also see those who (some yogis) proclaim Alakh (invisible). I also see you, Niranjan. I am Kabīr, and I see all, but no one sees me. (*Comment*: Kabīr is referring to himself as the Supreme Sentient Self who sees all things.)

352 I have seen God in the three worlds, so how can you say He is invisible? You do not know the essence of the Word, so you have put on a garb to deceive the people. (*Comment*: Kabīr is addressing yogis who proclaim God to be 'alakh' or invisible.)

353 These sākhīs are the eyes of knowledge. Understand them well, and realize them in your heart. Without knowledge of the sākhīs, the troubles of worldly existence will not be abolished. (*Comment*: Kabīr is issuing a challenge to imbibe the essence of the sākhīs, and attain the position of a witness (sākhī, from sakshi meaning witness) to the Truth that is in the heart. This Truth is also called shabda or Word. Knowledge of the sākhīs puts one on the path of moksha or liberation.)

GLOSSARY

achint	unthinkable
adhār	support; God as our support
ādi	from the beginning; first
ādi adal	full of justice, pre-eminent
Advaita	non-dualistic or monistic school of philosophy of India
Agni	fire; also god of fire
ahankār	ego; a great stumbling block to God-realization
ahimsā	non-violence in thought, word and deed. The first prerequisite in yoga, and a cardinal teaching of Kabīr
ajapā	that which cannot be uttered
ajapā jāpa	automatic repetition of mantra or God's name
Ajar Amar	not subject to decay or death; God
akāsh	space; one of the five basic elements in creation
Alakh Purush	invisible Being. God the Absolute
Allāh	name of God in Islam
amrit	nectar; state of bliss in meditation
Anāhad	limitless; anāhad nād is the divine melody heard in meditation
Anjāwan	birthless; refers to God
antar jyoti	inner light of the soul
Antaryāmī	one knowing the thoughts of others; God
ashramas	four stages of life – brahmcharya, grihasta, vanaprashta, and sanyasa. (Also a religious place

	of living and for learning from a guru)
Avadhu	a class of ascetics
Avatār	God taking on form and attributes to come to the world; incarnation
avidyā	ignorance of Reality; one of the five kleshas in yoga philosophy
Avināshī	indestructible; eternal
āwā gawan	recurrent birth and death due to karmas
awliyā	saints, apostles in Islam
Bali	ancient king, grandson of Prahalād. Though of demonic lineage, he learned virtues from his grandfather
Bandagī Sāheb	salutation to the master within; also Saheb Bandagī (from *vandana* – to salute respectfully, and *saheb* – master)
bandhan	bondage; cause of rebirths according to karmas.
bāt	path; eg. path to God
Behad	limitless
bhajan	devotional song; hymn
bhakti	devotion full of love, especially devotion to God
bhowjāl	trap of this world of re-incarnation
bhowsāgar	ocean of re-births; this world
bhram	doubt; not knowing the real nature of oneself; religious doubt
bihisht	heaven; paradise
Bījak	map leading to hidden treasure; title of the book containing the teachings of Kabīr
Bismillāh	name of God in Islam, often invoked at the beginning of an activity
Brahm(an)	Absolute Reality; God
Brahmā	god the creator; one of a trinity
brahmand	universe
Brāhmin	priestly class in Hinduism
buddhi	intellect

chakras	seven psychic energy centres in the spinal cord from the bottom to the brain
charkhā	a spinning wheel; Kabīr used it to weave cloth; he also compares this to the chakras (energy centres) around which God wove the body
charnamrit	nectar of the guru's feet; a bit of water (second washing) from the toe of the previously washed feet of the guru sipped by a devout disciple
chelā	disciple
chit	consciousness; mind
chowkā	a religious ceremony symbolizing guru worship for the liberation of the soul (also chaukā)
chowrāsi lākh	8.4 million forms of life in Indian teachings
darshan	philosophy; sight, presence of God
Dharamrāi	same as Yama; also upholder of dharma, and dispenser of justice
dhyān	meditation; seventh step in yoga
dīdār	presence; having presence of God
dojakh	hell
dukh	suffering
ekādashi	fast fasting on the eleventh day of each lunar fortnight
fakīr	unattached, wandering devotee
gambhīr	unfathomable, e.g. mystery of God
Gandharva	a demigod, a celestial musician
Ganesha	the elephant-headed god, son of Lord Shiva and Parvati
Gāyatrī	according to Kabīr, the mother of Brahmā, Vishnu, and Shiva. In Hinduism, a sacred mantra of the Rig Veda
ghat	body; every cell of the body
gunas	inherent qualities of all manifestations - sattva, rajas, tamas
gurmukh	an initiated person living according to his

	master's instructions
guru	teacher; applied mostly to the spiritual teacher of an initiate
gyān	spiritual knowledge or wisdom
halāl	in Islam, meat that is sanctioned or permissible by Islamic law
hansā	swan; symbolic of realized soul as used by Kabīr.
Hari	name of God
idā (ingalā)	sympathetic nerves along the left side of spine; left nostril
indriyas	five organs of perception and five of action. The latter are the mouth, hands, feet, anus, and reproductive organs
Īshwar	God
jagat	this world
jāl	trap
janeo	sacred thread worn around the neck by upper caste Hindus
jangams	wandering ascetics
jāpa	repetition of a mantra
jīva	individual soul, living being, life, spirit
julahā	weaver caste; Kabīr was a weaver
jyoti	light; light of soul; light of God
Kabīr	mystic saint of India (1398-1518); one of 99 names of Allah meaning the very great; his transcendental teachings form the basis of the Kabīr Panth
Kabīr Panth	Kabīr path; the adherents of Kabīr's teachings
kāgā	crow; spiritually ignorant person
Kāl	time; also god of death
Kaliyug	the current iron age in Hinduism lasting 432,000 years. It started in 3102 BCE
Kalingā	a republic of east central India, now Odisha. Scene of the bloody Kalingā war waged by

	Ashoka the Great
Kalkī	a future incarnation of Lord Vishnu at the end of the Kaliyug
kalmā	confession of faith in Islam, "There is no God but Allah, and Mohammed is his Prophet."
kām	lust; one of five negative passions
Kansa	ancient tyrant king of Mathurā and uncle of Lord Krishna. He was killed by Krishna
karma	action in thought, words, and deeds leading to bondage or liberation
Karunāmai	full of compassion; Kabīr's name in the Dwapar yuga (bronze age)
Kāzi	muslim judge
khalak	universe
Khālik	God
khand	part or division of a whole
krodh	anger; one of five negative passions
Kshatrīya	one of the four castes of India which are Brāhmin, Kshatrīya, Vaishya and Shudra
Kudrat	God; nature
kundalinī	in yoga, the energy at the base of the spine represented as a coiled serpent (also kundalinī shaktī)
lobh	greed; one of five negative passions
mahant	priest certified to perform religious ceremonies, initiate disciples, give spiritual teachings, etc. Normally the head of an ashram or monastery
makkartār	spider's thread; mystical 'thread' by which the realized soul climbs to Sat Lok (eternal abode)
mandir	temple in Hinduism
manmukh	a person living according to the dictates of his mind
masjid	mosque
Mathurā	kingdom in Gujarat state to which Krishna and

	his clan went after the Mahabharat war. Krishna ruled this kingdom.
Māyā	in Vedānta philosophy, the creative energy of Brahman, the Absolute; commonly used to denote illusion, or entrapment by materiality.
mehar	mercy
moha	attachment to perishable things
moksha	final liberation after all karmas are 'burnt'; immersion into the being of God, and losing all identities; Self-realization
moulvī	a learned Muslim versed in arabic scripture.
mukti	liberation while alive
mulādhāra	chakra at the base of the spine; location of kundalinī energy
mullāh	a priest or holy person in Islam
muni	holy person, ascetic
Munindra	pious and holy one; Kabīr's name in the Treta Yuga (silver age)
nād	the divine melody heard in meditation
Nām	name; name of God
namāz	daily prayers of Muslims facing Mecca five times a day
Nāmdev	a medieval saint of India
Nārad	famous ancient sage in the Purānas
Narsingh	incarnation of Vishnu as half-man half-lion to destroy the tyrant king Hiranyakashipu
Nij Nām	one's true name; the reality within, the soul that is beyond name and form
Niranjan	emissary of God; father of the trinity in Hinduism according to Kabīr
nirbhai	fearless; attribute of a God-realized person
nirgun	without attributes or limiting adjuncts; God and soul beyond all attributes
Nirvānā	liberation from rebirths, final emancipation

Onkār	word symbol of the Supreme Being; Kabīr states that what can be written and erased is not Onkār; the Reality that is beyond words
owgun	evil qualities
pākhand	hypocrisy, especially in religious matters
pāndas	brahmins who perform religious duties
pandit	priest in Hinduism versed in Hindu scriptures and rituals
pāp	sin, evil
papīhā	mythological rainbird that longs for rain at a particular astrological period, refusing other kinds water
param	eternal
Parmātmā	God
phulowrī	vegetable fritters or cakes fried in clarified butter
pind	the body in contrast to the brahmand or the cosmos; microcosm contrasted to macrocosm
pingalā	sympathetic nerves along the right side of spine; right nostril
Pīpā	medieval saint, contemporary with Kabīr
Prahalād	ancient sage who worshipped Lord Vishnu instead of his demon father and king, Hiranyakashipu
prākriti	nature; original subtle, undifferentiated matter that formed the universe
pralai	dissolution of the world into original matter; *maha pralai* is the great dissolution of all matter in the universe into an unmanifested state
prāna	universal energy permeating every atom of the universe; also refers to the breath
pranāṃ	salutation with folded hands
prem	love
prithvī	earth
pujā	ceremonial worship

punya	virtue
Purānas	eighteen tales of Hindu mythology, also considered to be scriptures
purnimā vrat	fasting on the date of the full moon each month.
purshārthas	four goals of life: righteous living, earning wealth, fulfilment of noble desires, and liberation
purush	male; also used for soul and God
Raghunāth	descendant of ancient king Raghu; also refers to Lord Rāma
Rahimān	merciful, forgiving, God
Rāma	name of formless God as used by Kabīr, the Absolute; also Lord Rāma of Ayodhya, an incarnation of Lord Vishnu and hero of the Ramayana epic
ramainī	a type of poetical composition
rozā	muslim fasting in the month of Ramadan
sādhu	a holy man
sagun	with attributes; God with attributes coming into the world as an avatar; also refers to gods and deities
sahaj	easy; natural; state of continuous universal realization of God
sahasrāra	chakra; thousand-petalled lotus centre in the brain reached by a self-realized person, for example, an advanced yogi
sāheb	master, especially one who is advanced in religion
sākhī	couplet; testimony of eternal truths as used by Kabīr
samādhī	meditative absorption in God
Samrath	capable of creation; Kabīr uses it to refer to God
Sanak	son of Brahmā
Sanandan	son of Brahmā

Sankādik	usually refers to the four sons of Brahmā – Sanak, Sanandan, Sanatan, and Sanatkumar
sant	a saint or a religious person upholding spiritual values
sanyāsī	a renunciate dedicated to spiritual life
Sār Shabda	essence of the Word; inner mystic sound; divinity within
Sat	existence; the Eternal, the Self-Existent Being
Sat Chit Ānand	existence, consciousness, and bliss as the nature of the soul and God
Sat Lok	eternal abode; heaven where soul is not subject to rebirths
Sat Purush	eternal, self-existent Being; God the Absolute; Brahm(an)
Sat Sukrit	supreme virtue. Kabīr's name in the Sat Yuga (golden age)
Satguru	realized master; God
Satī	Shiva's wife as depicted in the Purānas; a widow who immolates herself on her husband's funeral pyre; this practice is outlawed
satsang	religious congregation
satya	truth
Shabda	Word; creative power of God
sharan	refuge; eg. refuge in guru or in God
Sheshnag	mythological serpent supporting the Earth on its head; the reposing bed of Lord Vishnu.
Shiva	god the destroyer; one of the Hindu trinity
Shukdev	narrator of Bhagavat and Purānas – parts of scriptures of India
siddhi	eight perfections or spiritual attainments by adepts
Sirjanhār	God the creator of the universe
Sishupāl	evil king of Cedi, killed by Lord Krishna
Smriti	'remembered' scriptures that are secondary to

	Srutis. They explain, exemplify, and uphold dharma. Examples are the Ramāyana, Mahabhārata, Laws of Manu, and Purānas
soham	mantra "I am That"; soul identity with God
Sruti	heard or revealed scriptures of India, mainly the Vedas, Brahmanas, and Upanishads
Sudāmā	close friend of Lord Krishna suffering in poverty. Lord Krishna made him wealthy.
sumati	good and noble thinking
sumiran	prayer; recitation of prayer
surat	meditation; mind fixed absolutely on God
surati & nirati	meditation and its rewards
sushumnā	central canal in the spinal cord for the flow of psychic energy
swarga	heaven; paradise
Swāti	an astrological period
tana	body
Tat	God or Brahm(an)
tattva	five gross elements – earth, water, fire, air, ether or space; they compose the body and matter; param tattva refers to soul or God
tilak	sandalwood paste marks on the foreheads of Hindu holy people
tīn tāp	three sufferings: (i) suffering arising within the body; (ii) suffering caused by other beings; (iii) suffering caused by forces of nature
trikuti	spiritual eye between the eyebrows used as a focal point in meditation
triveni	the confluence of idā, pingalā and sushumna at the spiritual eye centre; in India, the confluence of the rivers Ganges, Yamuna, and Saraswati
Vaishnāva	followers of Lord Vishnu; one of the four castes in Hinduism – Brāhmin, Kshatrīya, Vaishya, and Shudra

Vālmīki	ancient sage and composer of the Ramayana epic of Hinduism
varnas	the four castes in Hinduism – Brāhmin, Kshatrīya, Vaishya, and Shudra. The castes were originally according to profession and not according to birth
Varuna	god of waters; similar to Neptune in Roman mythology
Vashisht	guru of Lord Rāma; his teachings are in the Yog Vashisht
Vedas	holy religious scripture of Hindus – Rig, Yajur, Sāma, and Atharva
Vishnu	god the preserver; one of the Hindu trinity
vivek	spiritual discrimination of the real from the unreal
Vyās	ancient sage, compiler of the Vedas and writer of the Purānas and Mahabharata epic
Yama	god of death; assures rebirths according to karmas
yogi	one who practices yoga to realize union with God

BIBLIOGRAPHY

Bly, Robert. *The Kabir Book: Forty-four of the Ecstatic Poems of Kabir.* Boston: Beacon Press, 1997

Buch, M. T. *The Bijaka of Kabira Saheba with Commentary.* Jamnagar, Gujarat: Sri Kabir Ashram, 1987.

Dass, G.N. *Love Songs of Kabir.* New Delhi: Abhinav Publications, 1992.

Dass, Nirmal. *Songs of Kabir from the Adi Granth.* New York: State University of New York Press, 1991.

Dwyer, William J. *Bhakti in Kabir.* Patna, India: Associated Boom Agency, 1981.

Ezekiel, Izaak A. *Kabir the Great Mystic.* 2nd ed. Delhi, India: Radha Soami Satsang Beas, 1973.

Hedayetullah, Mohammed. *Kabir: The apostle of Hindu-Muslim Unity.* Delhi, India: Motilal Banarsidass, 1977.

Hess, Linda, and Shukdev Singh. *The Bījak of Kabir.* San Francisco: North Point Press, 1983.

Kumar, Sehdev. *The Vision of Kabir.* Delhi, India: Motilal Banassidass Indological Publishers, 1984.

Lorenzen, David N. *Kabir Legends and Ananta-das's Kabir Parachai.* New York: State University of New York Press, 1991.

Lorenzen, David N., ed. *Bhakti Religion in North India: Community Identity and Political Action.* New York: State University of New York Press, 1995.

Lorenzen, David N. *Praises to a Formless God: Nirguni Texts from North India.* New York: State University of New York Press, 1996.

Machwe, Prabhakar. *Kabir.* 3rd ed. New Delhi, India: Sahitya Akademi, 1984.

Mehta, Rohit and Shridevi. *Krishnamurti and Sant Kabir.* Delhi, India: Motilal Banarsidass Publishers, 1990.

Osho. *The Great Secret: Talks on the Songs of Kabir.* Poona, India: Osho Commune International, 1990.

Rajneesh, Bhagwan Shree. *The Fish in the Sea is not Thirsty: 15 Discourses Given on the Songs of Kabir.* Poona, India: Rajneesh Foundation, 1980.

Scott, David C. *Kabir's Mythology: The Religious Perceptions, Doctrines and Practices of a Medieval Indian Sant.* Delhi, India: Bharatiya Vidya Prakashan, 1985.

Sethi, V. K. *Kabir the Weaver of God's Name.* Punjab, India: Radha Soami Satsang, 1984.

Shah, Ahmad. *The Bījak of Kabir.* Delhi, India: Asian Publication Services, 1977.

Vaudeville, Charlotte. *A Weaver Named Kabir: Selected Verses with a Detailed Biographical and Historical Introduction.* Delhi, India, Oxford University Press, 1993.

Vaudeville, Charlotte. *Kabir.* London: Oxford at the Clarendon Press, 1974.

Westcot, G. H. *Kabir and the Kabir Panth.* 2nd ed. Calcutta, India: Susil Gupta (India) Ltd., 1953.

The following Hindi books were consulted:

Anon. *Kabir Bijak Mūl.* Delhi: Dehātī Pustak Bhandār, 1936.

Maharāj, Shrī Jairāmdeojī. *Mūl Bijak.* Mathurā, [India]: Hindi Pustakālay, 1971.

Prakāshmani Nām Sāheb, Shrī Hazūr. *Bijak.* Lahartārā, Varānasī: Shrī Hazūr Udit Nām Sāheb, 1982.

Shāstrī, Jagdīsh Dās, compiler. *Bijak.* Lahartārā, Varānasī: Dharmadhikārī Shrī Manohardāsjī Shāstrī Sāheb, 1987.

ABOUT THE AUTHOR

Dr. Jagessar Das was born in Guyana. He moved to Canada in 1955 to study medicine at the University of British Columbia, graduating with an M.D. in 1962. He did general practice of medicine and surgery for over forty years and retired in 2005.

Dr. Das is president of the Kabīr Association of Canada, and president of the Global Clergy Association of Canada. He has produced the Kabīr Voice for the Kabīr Association for 22 years. In 1995 he produced a 13 part television series titled, "Religious Horizons" for Rogers Multicultural Television, interviewing religious leaders from Christianity, Hinduism, Islam, Buddhism, Jainism, Sikhism, Taoism, Zoroastrianism, Kabīr Panth, Unitarianism, Baha'i Faith, and Judaism. He has also been interviewed several times on ethnic television channels.

Dr. Das has lectured on Satguru Kabīr, religions, meditation, and spiritual topics in British Columbia, Canada where he resides, as well as in California, New York, Toronto, and Trinidad. He has also travelled to India several times for Kabīr functions. He has authored the following books: *The Bījak of Guru Kabīr* in three volumes including the Hindi text; *Kabīr Bhajan Amritam*, a book of 270 bhajans; *Songs of the Divine*, a book of 180 of Kabīr's poems in English; *Sandhya Path*; and *The Brahm Ṇirupan of Kabīr*. In September 2006 he presented a paper at the *World's Religions After 9/11* in Montreal titled "Religion as the Gateway to Peace." In 2010 Dr. Das was one of 25 Canadian immigrants to be awarded the "Canadian Immigrant of the Year" award.

Website and blog: www.kabir.ca
Facebook names: jagessardas and santkabirji
Twitter name: Jagessardas